Iḥyā' 'Ulūm al-Dīn
Vol. III

IMAM AL-GHAZĀLĪ

ESSENTIAL

Iḥyā' 'Ulūm al-Dīn

THE REVIVAL OF THE RELIGIOUS SCIENCES

Completely revised edition of Fazlul Karim's translation

Volume III

Destructive Vices

وقل رب زدني علما

IBT

Islamic Book Trust

Kuala Lumpur

First published 2015
Reprint 2017
Islamic Book Trust
607 Mutiara Majestic
Jalan Othman
46000 Petaling Jaya
Selangor, Malaysia
www.ibtbooks.com

Islamic Book Trust is affiliated with The Other Press.

Perpustakaan Negara Malaysia Cataloguing-in-Publication Data

Ghazzali, 1058-1111
Essential Ihya' 'Ulum al-Din : The Revival of the Religious Sciences: Revised edition of Fazlul Karim's translation.
Volume III / Imam al-Ghazali.
ISBN 978-967-0526-17-1
1. Islam--Doctrines. 2. Religious life--Islam.
I. Fazlul Karim. II. Title.
297.2

Front calligraphy
Prayer from the Qur'an 20:114 written in Arabic calligraphy.
Translation: "Say, 'My Lord, increase me in knowledge.'"

Printed by
SS Graphic Printers (M) Sdn. Bhd.
Lot 7 & 8, Jalan TIB 3
Taman Industri Bolton
68100 Batu Caves, Selangor

Contents

Translator's preface ix

Book 1: The soul and its attributes

Introduction 3

1 "Soul," "spirit," "heart" and "intelligence" explained 4

2 The armies of the heart 7

3 Similitudes of the heart and its internal armies 9

4 Peculiarities of the human heart 11

5 The qualities of man 15

6 Kinds of knowledge 23

7 The means of acquiring spiritual powers 27

8 Inspiration and acquired knowledge 30

9 The testimony of Sharī'ah to how Sufis gain spiritual knowledge 35

10 Satan's whisperings in the heart 40

11 Satan's entry into the heart 46

12 Punishment 58

13 Constant changes of the heart 60

Book 2: Disciplining the self

Introduction 65

1 Merits of good conduct 66

2 Good conduct 70

3 The changing of one's nature 72
4 The means of acquiring good conduct 75
5 Methods to improve conduct 78
6 Symptoms of the diseases of the heart and their treatment 80
7 Ways to find one's faults 82
8 The signs of good conduct 88
9 Improving the character of children 93
Book 3: Breaking the two desires
Introduction 101
1 Merits of hunger 102
2 How to break the greed of the stomach 115
3 How to acquire moderation in eating 122
4 Sexual passion 125
5 Fornication of the eye 127
6 The rewards of opposing passions 129
Book 4: Harms of the tongue
Introduction 135
1 The merits of silence 136
2 Harms of the tongue 140
Book 5: Anger, hatred and envy
1 Anger 183
2 Hatred 201
3 Envy 207
Book 6: Attachment to the world
Introduction 219
1 Evils of the world 221
2 Similes about the world 233
3 The reality of the world 244

Book 7: Love for wealth
Introduction 249
1 Condemnation of love for wealth 250
2 The benefits of wealth 254
3 Benefits and harms of wealth 257
4 The merits of satisfaction with poverty 260
5 Medicine for greed 263
6 The merits of generosity 267
7 Condemnation of miserliness 274
8 The merits of self-sacrifice 278
9 Definition of "charity" and "miserliness" 282
10 Medicine for miserliness 285
11 Duties concerning wealth 287
12 Condemnation of wealth and praise of poverty 289
Book 8: Love for power and ostentation
Introduction 301
1 Love for power, name and fame 302
2 Ostentation 321
Book 9: Pride and self-praise
Introduction 353
1 Condemnation of pride 354
Book 10: Condemnation of delusions
Introduction 395
1 Delusions 397
2 Categories of the deluded 406
Index of Qur'anic verses 417
Index 421

Translator's preface

"Destructive Vices" is the third volume of Imam al-Ghazālī's world renowned masterpiece *Iḥyā' 'Ulūm al-Dīn* (The Revival of the Religious Sciences). The book deals with the soul and its attributes, conduct, greed and passion, the benefits and harms of the tongue, anger and envy, attachment to the world, love for wealth, the harms of miserliness, power, show, pride and erroneous beliefs.

A literal translation is avoided to omit some unnecessary matters which were prevalent in the then society, such as arguments of sects and sub-sects, and also to omit the sayings of personages and sages of less importance. But it should be noted that no verse of the Qur'an or saying of the Prophet (ṣ) has been omitted in this work.

I pray that Almighty Allah guide the people of the world in accordance with the teachings of the Holy Qur'an, Sunnah and the spirit in which the *Iḥyā'* was written by *Ḥujjah al-Islām* (the proof of Islam), a title received by Imam al-Ghazālī and about which it has been said, "If all the books of Islam were destroyed except for the *Iḥyā'* of al-Ghazālī, it would be but a slight loss."

Book 1
The soul and its attributes

Introduction

It is by means of the soul, and not any physical part of the body, that man is the master of creation. This is because by means of the soul he acquires knowledge of Allah and His attributes. It is by means of the soul that man can draw near to Allah and strive to realize Him. So the soul is the king of the body, and its parts carry out its orders and commands. It is accepted by Allah when it is free from things other than Him. When it is attached to things other than Allah, it drifts away from Him. It is the soul which will be asked and rebuked. It is fortunate if it is purified and cleansed, and it is damned if it is kept impure. It is the knowledge of the soul which is the root of the knowledge of Allah. When man does not know himself, he does not know Allah. The majority of men are ignorant of the soul and its attributes, as a screen is cast between the soul and baser self. Allah says, "Allah intervenes between man and his heart" (Qur'an, 8:24). It is between the two fingers of the Merciful. It sometimes reaches the plane of devils, and sometimes it rises as high as the Throne of the Almighty. He who does not enquire about his soul is included among those people "who forsook Allah, so He made them forsake their own souls: these it is that are the transgressors" (Qur'an, 59:19). It is therefore essential to know the soul, which is the root of religion, and its attributes.

What has been said in the earlier pages of this book relates to the limbs. Now we shall discuss the attributes and evils of the soul, which pertain to secret knowledge.

1
"Soul," "spirit," "heart" and "intelligence" explained

"Heart" (*qalb*)

"Heart" has two meanings. First, it means a hollow piece of flesh in the left breast which is filled with black blood and is the seat of the spirit. A detailed description of heart can be found in anatomy. It exists in breasts and lower animals, and appertains to the material world. This heart we shall not discuss in our book.

The second meaning of "heart," with which we are concerned with here, is a subtle, tenuous substance of an ethereal spiritual kind which has a connection with the material heart. It is the principal thing in a man. It perceives knowledge of Allah and the spiritual world, and is punished and rewarded. The connection of the soul with the heart resembles the connection of attributes with limbs, the user of a tool with the tool, or a house with its inmates. This connection is of two kinds. One is with mystical sciences, though in this book our object is to impart knowledge of proper conduct. The other connection requires knowledge of the secrets of the soul, concerning which the Prophet (ṣ) did not speak, and so everyone should refrain from doing so. We shall use "heart" in this book to mean a "subtle, tenuous thing."

"Spirit" (*rūḥ*)

This word also has two meanings. First, it means a subtle body within the heart which makes the whole body vibrate like a current of electricity and which runs through the veins of the body. It has the sense of touch, hearing, sight and smell, and has the capability of other limbs of the body. It is just like the radiation of the light of a lighted lamp pitched in a corner of the house. It is a subtle gas or steam which creates the heat of the heart. It is not our intention to explain the use of this term, as its connections are within the scope of physicians.

The second meaning of "spirit" is a subtle tenuous substance which knows and perceives. Allah says, "They ask you about the soul. Say The soul is one of the commands of my Lord" (Qur'an, 17:85).

"Soul" (*nafs*)

This word also has two meanings, which pertain to our purpose. The first meaning includes greed, anger and other evil attributes. The Prophet (ṣ) said, "Your greatest enemy is your soul lying between your two sides. The second meaning is that subtle tenuous substance we have mentioned. When the soul becomes calm and is free of passion, it is termed "the soul at rest" (*al-nafs al-muṭma'innah*). Allah says, "O soul that is at rest, return to your Lord, well-pleased (with him), well-pleasing (Him)" (Qur'an, 89:27-28). According to the first definition, the soul is with the party of Satan. When the soul is not completely at rest, it is called "the rebuking soul" (*al-nafs al-lawwāmah*), for it rebukes one for neglecting divine duties. If the soul gives up protests and surrenders itself to Satan, it is called "the soul commanding to evil" (*al-nafs al-ammārah bi al-sū'*). The Qur'an refers to this in Sūrah 12, Āyah 53.

"Intellect" (*'aql*)

It has many meanings, two of which we shall mention here. The first meaning is the force of knowledge of the true nature of things whose seat is the heart. The second meaning is the power to understand the secrets of different sciences. It is a subtle essence called "knowledge," which is an attribute. An attribute and the thing which contains it are two different things, but intellect is the name of both. This is supported by the *ḥadīth* "The first thing Allah created was the intellect." The attribute of the intellect is immaterial, but the attribute cannot exist without a material thing. So the place of the intellect should be created first, or along with it. Knowledge is the content of the intellect, so it was created first.

2
The armies of the heart

Allah says, "None knows the hosts of your Lord but Him" (Qur'an, 74:31). There are armed soldiers in the heart whose real nature is not known and whose number nobody knows except Allah. The heart has two armies. One army can be seen by the external eye, and the other army cannot be seen except by the internal eye. These two armies are necessary for the upkeep of the dominion of this king. Courtiers, servants, helpers and so on are the armies of the king seen by the external eye. Similarly, the hands, feet, eyes, ears, tongue and other external and internal body parts are the army of the heart which rules over them. They have been created to obey it and cannot go against it. When the soul orders the eyes to open, they open. When it orders the feet to walk, they walk. Their submission is like that of the angels of Allah, who have been created to obey Allah and cannot go against Him.

These armies are necessary for the heart's journey to Allah, just as conveyance and food are necessary for the body. The heart has to cross many stations to meet Him, which is what it has been created for. Allah says, "I have not created the jinn and the men except that they should serve Me" (Qur'an, 51:56). The body is the conveyance or carrier of the heart, and its provision is knowledge. The means of attaining its knowledge is good deeds. To reach Allah is impossible so long as the body is unsound.

This world is the seed ground for the next world and a station of guidance. It is called "*al-dunyā*" (the closest), as it is the closest of stations. The heart must therefore get its supply of provision from this world.

The two armies of health

To procure food which keeps the body healthy is necessary, and to avoid that which is harmful to it is to be avoided. So it is necessary to approach two armies: the hidden army of greed for food and drink, and the open army of the body parts. Appetite for food and drink has been created in the heart, as they are necessary for the upkeep of the body, and the other body parts are the armies of appetite. Two armies are also necessary to remove the outer enemies, which are destructive evils: anger and the hands and feet.

The three armies of the heart

The first army is the army of appetite, which can also be termed "will." It benefits the heart. The second army is anger, which moves body parts towards the object of greed, power and strength. The third army is the senses of sight, hearing, smell, taste and touch, which are entrusted to different body parts. These armies have fingers to seize, eyes to see and so on.

The third army is divided into two. One army lives openly—the five senses of hearing, sight, smell, taste and touch. Another army lives secretly in the brain and consists of five: the powers of idea, thought, memory, retention and consolidating them together. These five powers are in brain and they secretly stay therein.

These are the armies of the heart. A man of weak intellect will find them difficult to understand, but the wise benefit from these discussions. We shall try to make those who are weak understand by citing some similitudes.

3

Similitudes of the heart and its internal armies

Similitude one

The soul is the ruler of the body, just as a king is the ruler of a kingdom. The powers and members of the body are like craftsmen and labourers. Appetite is the collector of revenue in that town, anger its police, the intellect its minister, the soul its king. Appetite, moreover, is like the one who collects food, and anger like the police who guard it. Appetite is a downright liar and deceiver. It outwardly wishes well, but there is destructive poison in it. The reign of the soul over the body is similar and goes well if all body parts and attributes are under its rule. When the soul receives assistance from its minister, the intellect, it rules over appetite, keeping anger in check. In order to bring anger under control, it sometimes seeks the help of appetite, whereupon its character and conduct become good.

He who strays from this path becomes like him about whom Allah says, "Have you then considered him who takes his low desire for his god, and Allah has made him err having knowledge" (Qur'an, 45:23). He also says, "Followed his low desire, so his parable is as the parable of the dog; if you attack him he lolls out his tongue; and if you leave him alone he lolls out his tongue" (Qur'an, 7:176). In another verse, Allah speaks of the person who controls his passion: "As for him who fears to stand in the presence of his Lord and forbids the soul from low desires, then surely the garden—that is the abode" (Qur'an, 79:40-41).

Similitude two

Know that the body is a town, and the intellect rules over that town like a king. Its armies are its external and internal senses, and its subjects are its various parts. Sexual passion and anger are the enemies of the body, and the soul is its guard. If the soul fights against its enemies, defeats them and compels them to do what it likes, the body's actions become commendable and return to the Almighty, who says that He gives superiority to those who fight with their lives and possessions over those who worship sitting (Qur'an, 4:95). If the soul acts as a frontier guard and neglects the body parts, it is punished, and on Resurrection Day it will be asked, "O dishonest guard, you have eaten food and drunk milk, but you have neither inquired into lost animals nor arranged for the treatment of diseased animals. Today I will retaliate against you for this." In the following *ḥadīth*, such a fighter has been praised: "You have returned from the lesser jihad to the greater."

Third similitude

The intellect is like a rider, the appetite like a horse and anger like his hunting dog. When the rider is an expert and his horse and dog are trained, hunting can be successful. When the rider is inexperienced, the horse disobedient and the dog biting, then the horse does not obey the rider, and the dog does not go forth in obedience. Similarly, when the intellect is mature, and appetite and anger are submissive to the intellect, success is sure. But if the intellect is immature, and greed and anger are not under control, ruin is sure.

4

Peculiarities of the human heart

Knowledge and will

The attributes by which man's heart becomes fit to approach Allah and which are honoured are knowledge and will. "Knowledge" refers to knowledge of the material and spiritual world and the reality of the intellect. These matters lie beyond knowledge gained by the senses, and lower animals do not have them.

Regarding will, when a man can understand by his intellect the result of any action and know what will bring good, there is aroused in his heart a will to obtain that good and to do that action. It is not the will of appetite or the instinct of lower animals. It is opposed to appetite. Intellect wills what will be good for it in the future and spends for it. There is appetite for delicious food in illness, but the intellect prohibits its eating, and a wise man refrains from eating it. So the heart of man is endowed with knowledge and will, which separates him from lower animals. Even little children are void of these attributes.

A boy acquires knowledge in two stages. The first stage is his learning of all preliminary and necessary things and knowing lawful and unlawful things. He cannot gain expert knowledge at this stage but draws near it. The second stage is his acquisition of knowledge by learning and thinking, at which point he becomes like an expert writer.

Modes of gaining spiritual knowledge

The heart acquires mystical knowledge by three modes: divine inspiration (*ilhām ilāhī*), immediate knowledge (*mubāda’ah*) and unveiling (*mukāshafah*). Some hearts acquire this by learning and efforts, some quickly and some late.

There are degrees of acquiring such knowledge in the case of prophets, friends of Allah and wise and learned men. The degrees of advancement are unlimited, as the knowledge of Allah has no limit. The rank of a Prophet in this regard is the highest, and all secrets are disclosed to him without any effort on his part.

A child in its mother’s womb does not know the condition of a boy. A boy does not know the condition of a grown-up-man. A grown-up man, moreover, does not know the condition of an intelligent man and his acquired learning. Similarly, an intelligent man does not know the blessings, mercy and gifts showered by Allah on the prophets. These blessings are also cast on those souls which remain prepared and become fit to receive them.

The Prophet (ṣ) said, “Verily, your Lord has gifts in the days of your generation. Will you then not expose yourself to them?” The meaning of this exposing is to remove the impurities that have fallen on the soul as a result of sins and to purify it. This can be understood from the *ḥadīth* that says, “Allah comes down every night to the nearest heaven and says, ‘Is there any invoking man whose invocation I shall accept?” Another *ḥadīth* says, “The religious man remains eager to meet Me, but I am more eager to meet him.” In a *ḥadīth qudsī*, Allah says, “I advance one cubit towards someone who advances half a cubit towards Me.” From this it is understood that Allah does not withhold His mercy from shedding the lustre of knowledge on the heart, but the people themselves are to be blamed, for they do not cleanse their hearts from the impurities they heaped on them. As air does not enter a pot full of water, so does knowledge of Allah not enter the heart if it remains filled with things other than Allah. For this reason, the Holy Prophet said, “Had the party of the Devil not moved round the hearts of the children of Adam, they would have seen the spiritual world." Thus, knowledge is a special attribute of the human heart. Knowledge about Allah's being, attributes and actions is the most honourable. With this knowledge, man becomes complete, and within this completeness lies his fortune of approaching Allah.

Peculiarities of the human heart

The body has been framed for accommodating the soul, which is again the house of knowledge. Divine knowledge is the human goal and its speciality. An ass and a horse are the same in that they both carry loads. But a horse is superior to an ass, as a horse has additional qualities of beauty and speed, which an ass and other animals lack. Similarly, there is a difference between a man and an angel. The man who engages all his limbs, thoughts and actions to please Allah is like an angel and fit to be called an angel. Allah says about Yūsuf, "This is not a mortal; this is but a noble angel" (Qur'an, 12:31).

He who makes efforts only for his physical comforts descends to the class of an animal. He becomes envious like an ox, greedy like a pig, biting like a dog, ravenous like a camel, vengeful like a leopard, cunning like a jackal and clever like a devil—the embodiment of the above evils. There is no such limb or sense which does not help a man to reach Allah. Whoever walks that path is successful, and whoever is misguided is unsuccessful.

Man's fortune lies in making his meeting with Allah his ultimate goal, the next world his permanent abode, this world his temporary abode, his body his vehicle, and his limbs his servants. The human soul is the centre of realising them and is a king over the region of body. The power of imagination in the front of the head is like a postman with whom all news is gathered by the senses. The power of thinking behind his brain works like a treasurer, his tongue its interpreter, and his five senses its secret police. The eyes have been given the power to receive various colours, the ears to receive different voices, the nose to smell, and the other limbs to receive other news, which they send to the power of ideas, which sends them to the power of thinking, which send them to the heart, which is the king.

Ka'b al-Aḥbār said, "I went once to 'Ā'ishah and said, 'Man's eyes are his guide, his two ears his guards, his tongue his interpreter, his two hands his wings, his two feet his couriers and his soul his king. When the king is pleased, his armies are also pleased.' 'Ā'ishah replied, 'I heard the Prophet (ṣ) say thus.'"

'Alī said, "Allah has got many vessels in this world. The dearest of them to Him is that which is the softest, purest and strongest." Then he explained, saying, "The heart which is the firmest in religion, purest in faith and kindest in treatment of brethren is the dearest to Allah." This can be seen from the verse "Firm of heart against the unbelievers, compassionate among themselves" (Qur'an, 48:29), as well as the verse "His light is as a niche in which is a lamp" (Qur'an, 24:35). Explaining the latter verse, Ubayy ibn Ka'b said, "The meaning of 'light' is the light of a believer's heart." Similarly, Allah says, "Or like utter darkness in the deep sea" (Qur'an, 24:40). The soul of a hypocrite has therefore been mentioned as an illustration.

5
The qualities of man

Man has four qualities: predatory, brutish, devilish and angelic. Predatory qualities include anger, enmity, hatred, rebuke and attacking people. Brutish qualities are seen when his sexual passion becomes strong. Devilish qualities include deceit, fraud and conspiracy. And angelic qualities include divine services, worship of Allah and doing good to all. As man's soul contains something divine, he has the quality of lordship and likes to be free from servitude and meanness.

The roots of these four natures are in a man and centred in human soul. If he has got only the nature of a lower animal, he becomes like a pig or a dog. If he has only the quality of the Devil, he becomes a devil. If he has divine qualities, he becomes a truly wise man. If he follows sexual passion and greed, he acquires the evils of impurity, shamelessness, meanness, miserliness, hatred and other bad habits. If he obeys the dictates of anger, he acquires heinous qualities such as haughtiness, pride, love of power, self-praise, jest, contempt for others and oppression. If he obeys the Devil, he acquires evil conducts such as deceit, deception, treachery and fraud. When he controls the above evils, he is endowed with divine qualities such as wisdom, knowledge, sure faith and knowledge of the natures of all things. When he becomes free from sexual passion and anger, he acquires pardon, contentment, self- satisfaction, asceticism, piety, fear of Allah, contentment and shame. If he keeps anger under control, he gains heroism, kindness, patience, silence and the like.

The heart is a mirror

The heart is like a mirror in which the above evils and virtues are reflected. The virtues make the heart shining, resplendent and bright, and the evils and sins make it dark. The Prophet (ṣ) said, "When Allah wants good for a servant, He causes his heart to admonish him." He also said, "He who has an admonishing heart has a guard from Allah." The remembrance of Allah becomes lasting in such a heart. Allah says, "Now surely by Allah's remembrance are the hearts set at rest" (Qur'an, 13:28).

Sins are like smoke full of darkness which covers the heart. One sin after another comes over the heart like layers of smoke until his heart is completely enveloped with darkness. As a result, the heart becomes removed from Allah. It is the seal on the heart of which Allah speaks in verse "No, what they used to do has become like rust upon their hearts" (Qur'an, 83:14). Likewise, Allah says, "If We please We would afflict them on account of their faults and set a seal on their hearts so they would not hear" (Qur'an, 7:100).

When sins accumulate in the heart, it becomes blind to the good things of religion. Maymūn ibn Mihrān said, "When a man commits a sin, a black spot appears on his heart. When he repents, it is blotted out. When he commits another sin, the spot increases. Thus, if sins are committed one after another, the heart becomes dark, and that is the seal on the heart." The Prophet (ṣ) said, "The heart of a believer is bright, and there is a bright lamp in it. The heart of an unbeliever is black and blind." The polish of soul is obedience to Allah with opposition to passion. Sins are impurities on the heart, and whoever sins makes his heart dark.

Kinds of hearts

The Prophet (ṣ) said, "The heart is of four kinds. The first kind of heart is bright, and in it is a lit lamp; this is the heart of a believer. The second kind of heart is black; this is the heart of an unbeliever. The third kind of heart is bound in its sheath of evil; this is the soul of a hypocrite. And the fourth kind of heart is mixed with faith and hypocrisy. Faith in such a soul is like a plant which with water grows, and if there are other liquids such as blood and pus, its growth is retarded."

Allah says, "Surely those who guard (against evil), when a visitation from Satan afflicts them, they become mindful, then, lo, they see" (Qur'an, 7:201). The brightness of the heart is gained by the remembrance of Allah, which finds consolation in a person who has God-fear. So God-fear is the gate of the remembrance of Allah, which is again the gate of inner revelation (*kashf*), which is again the gate of salvation and the gate of having the fortune of meeting Allah.

An explanation of the similitudes of the heart

The heart is a container of knowledge. Just as a mirror has a connection with a figure or form, so also does a soul have a connection with objects of knowledge. In other words, pictures or figures can be seen if placed in front of a mirror. In like manner, different objects of knowledge are reflected in the heart. And just a mirror assumes the colour of a figure placed before it, so too does a heart assume the colour or nature of an unknown object of knowledge. Every object of knowledge has a nature, and every nature a figure, which is reflected in the mirror of the heart and is clearly visible. The mirror, the figure, and its reflection in the mirror are all separate things.

Similarly, a man has three different things: a heart, the real nature of a thing, and knowledge of the real nature of that thing. The heart is the name of the thing with which knowledge is gained. The shadows of everything are reflected in it. So the container of knowledge, the object of knowledge and knowledge itself are interconnected. For instance, to catch a shield is an action, and the things involved in this action are hands, a shield and catching. Interconnected, these three things produce an action. Knowledge is also a thing which is connected with the heart, the shadow of the thing therein and the appearance of that shadow therein. Knowledge does not arise unless the object of knowledge appears in the heart. Fire cannot be said to appear in the heart to produce knowledge of fire; the shadow of fire in the heart is sufficient to produce it. The real man does not remain in mirror. The shadow of his real self remains in the mirror. In a similar manner, the real shadows of all things appear in heart, and that is called "knowledge."

Obstacles to gaining divine knowledge

A mirror may not reflect a figure for five reasons: the thing with which the mirror is made is spoiled, impurities appear on the mirror, the mirror is not directed towards the picture, there is something between the mirror and the picture, and the picture is not in front of the mirror.

Such is also the case for the human heart. It is fit to receive images of everything, but five causes prevent it from performing its function.

The first cause is a natural defect of the heart, such as the heart of a child.

The second cause is the impurities of sins owing to greed, passion and low desires. If the impurities of sins are not removed, truth is not reflected in the heart. The Prophet (ṣ) therefore said, "The intellect of a man who is accustomed to committing sins leaves and never comes back to him." In other words, rust appears on his heart unless it is removed by a good deed and repentance, just as dust on a mirror is removed by a duster. The heart becomes bright if it does not follow low desires and urges of passion. Allah says, "And (as for) those who strive hard for Us, We will most certainly guide them in Our ways" (Qur'an, 29:69). The Prophet (ṣ) said, "Allah grants to one who acts on what he knows knowledge which he did not know before."

The third cause is that the real picture of a thing does not appear on the soul if it is turned away from the real object of research and enquiry, as nothing can be seen if a mirror is not directed towards a figure or picture. The brightness of truth is not reflected in the heart owing to the object of enquiry not being directed towards the heart, although it is clean and pure. The picture of an object about which a man thinks appears on his heart. He who confines his thoughts and efforts to the different modes of health gains health. So he who engages his whole attention and energy in the attainment of Divine love can acquire it. But he whose attention is diverted only to worldly pursuits surely gets them, but he is not blessed with divine love and grace. It is an obstacle to the acquisition of secret divine knowledge.

The fourth cause is the veil. If there is something between a mirror and a figure, the figure cannot be seen in the mirror. Likewise, if there is screen between the human heart and a thing desired, its true picture cannot be reflected in the heart: Truth cannot emerge from a veiled soul. Whoever follows his passions and low desires, a veil covers his heart. Beliefs which take root in early years of life from the surrounding environments paint the future of a man and create obstacles in finding out the truth of a thing. This is also true in the case of blind faith. Such a man does not accept what is opposed to his belief, although it is true and correct.

The fifth cause is ignorance. This ignorance occurs in connection with a special object. As a result, the object of enquiry becomes defective. For instance, if a student enquires about an unknown subject, it will be impossible to know it until he ponders over the thing connected with the object of enquiry. Such pondering is not the prescribed mode of the learned, as the object of enquiry is to be known on the basis of other knowledge. A mixture of two pieces of knowledge produces knowledge of a third kind, just as a baby camel is produced through the cohabitation between a male and female camel. He who wants to have a baby horse cannot do so by uniting an ass and a camel, but will get it when a horse and a she horse cohabit. This applies to all knowledge.

Knowledge has two roots, and there is a prescribed mode of uniting the roots. Knowledge cannot arise unless the mode of union is not known. If one does not stand in front of a mirror, he cannot see his face therein. If the mirror is kept in front of the face, he cannot see his back. So there are certain methods of acquiring knowledge, and there are five hurdles in the reflection of truth in hearts, which is the reason that we hardly see truths.

The heart is a celestial thing with the natural attribute of knowing truth. Allah says about this heart, "Surely We offered the trust to the heavens and the earth and the mountains, but they refused to be unfaithful to it and feared it, and man has turned unfaithful to it" (Qur'an, 33:72). It appears from this that the heart has a special attribute which the heavens and the earth and the mountains do not possess, and so they have been made subservient to man. This trust is divine knowledge and oneness.

The heart is naturally fit to bear this trust, but cannot reach its real nature owing to the obstacles we mentioned above. For this reason, the Prophet (ṣ) said, "Every child is born with a natural conformity to religious truth, but his parents make him a Jew, Christian or Magian." He also said, "If devils did not move in the heart of the son of Adam, he could have seen the divine realm." In this *ḥadīth* is a reference to the above five obstacles which prevent man from seeing the divine realm."

The Prophet (ṣ) was once asked, "Where is Allah: in the earth or heavens?" He replied, "Allah is in the heart of the believer." Another *ḥadīth* says the Prophet (ṣ) was asked, "Who is the best man?" to which he responded, "The believer whose heart is cleansed is the best." He was then asked, "What is a cleansed heart?" He answered, "A cleansed heart is that in which there is God-fearingness and no deceit, deception, treachery, contrivance or hatred."

In this connection, 'Umar said, "My heart beheld my Lord when, because of God-fearingness, He raised the screen." Whoever lifts the screen of sins from his heart, the pictures of unseen things are disclosed in his heart. Thereupon he can see Paradise, which extends across the heavens and earth. The unseen world is outside external eyes. When the world of sight and the world of the unseen are united in a single moment, it is termed "Lordly presence" (*al-ḥaḍrah al-rubūbiyyah*), which can encompass everything.

There is no existence except that of Allah, His actions and His sovereignty, and His servants are included in His actions. The object of all actions is to make the heart pure and bright. Allah says, "He will indeed be successful who purifies it" (Qur'an, 91:9). The object of the purity of the heart is to gain the light of faith therein, or to enkindle the light of divine knowledge. Regarding this, Allah says, "Therefore whomever Allah intends to guide aright, He expands his breast for Islam" (Qur'an, 6:125), and "What! Is he whose heart Allah has opened for Islam so that he is in a light from his Lord (like the hard-hearted)?" (Qur'an, 39:22).

The stages of the light of faith

This light of faith in the heart has three stages. In the first stage, the light is that of the faith of the ordinary man: It is the light of blind faith. In the second stage, it is the light of the faith of the followers of Islamic jurisprudence. This light is mixed with some sort of proof. In the third stage, it is the light of the faith of the friends of Allah, the dazzling ray of certain faith.

Take, for instance, the stay of Zayd in his house. It can be proved in three ways. The first kind of proof is belief by hearing. If you have belief in a certain man and know that he does not speak lies, you will believe his saying that Zayd is in his house. This is the belief of the ordinary man. When little boys attain maturity, they hear from their parents and relatives that there exists an almighty God who created everything and sent messengers with books, and they believe them on hearing. This belief will be the cause of salvation in the next world. But they will be in the first stage of the fortunate, not included among those drawn near to Allah, for this faith has no mystical unveiling and no expansion of the breast, and they may have made a mistake in what they heard

The second kind of proof is that Zayd's being in his house, for example, can be inferred from hearing his voice coming from his house. This belief is stronger than the former, although he may have again erred in what he heard.

The third kind of proof is to enter into the room and see, for instance, Zayd with your own eyes. This is real knowledge gained by direct sight. This knowledge is like that of the friends of Allah and the ones brought near. There is no mistake in this belief.

There are, however, degrees of this knowledge among them. If Zayd is seen in the light or sunlight, it is an instance of perfect seeing. If he is seen in the house from a great distance, or his figure is seen at night, it is less perfect. Similarly, there are different degrees of spiritual vision and knowledge.

6
Kinds of knowledge

Knowledge which appears in the heart is of two kinds: knowledge concerning the intellect and knowledge concerning religion. The former is also of two kinds: natural knowledge and acquired knowledge. Acquired knowledge is also of two kinds: worldly knowledge and other- worldly or spiritual knowledge. We understand "knowledge concerning the intellect" to be basic, natural and necessary knowledge. It is not acquired by blind faith or hearsay. It is that which is gained but not known how or from where, such as knowledge that the same person cannot stay in two different places at the same time, or that the same thing cannot be at the same time old and new. This preliminary knowledge is imprinted in a boy's mind in his earliest years. He does not know where this knowledge comes from. Acquired knowledge concerning the intellect is gained by learning. These two kinds of knowledge are called "intellect" or "wisdom."

The Prophet (ṣ) said with regard to the natural intellect from birth, "Allah created nothing more honourable to Him than the intellect." With regard to the second kind of intellect, the Prophet (ṣ) said to 'Alī, "When people draw close to Allah through good deeds, you will be able to draw close to Him through your intellect." It is not possible to draw close to Allah through the natural intellect; it has to be acquired. So the human heart has power to see like the external eyes. One of its names is intellect or wisdom.

The power of vision is a basic ingredient which in not found in a spiritually blind man. It is found only in a person having inner sight, though he closes his two eyes or remains in darkness. All things are seen by the eye of knowledge. There is a delay in the appearance of knowledge until one attains maturity, as the tablet of the heart does not become prepared then for the light of knowledge. The pen is an instrument for depicting pictures of knowledge, as Allah says, "Who taught (to write) with the pen, taught man what he knew not" (Qur'an, 96:4-5). Allah's pen is not like the pen of man, for His attributes are not like the attributes of man. Thus, his pen is not made of materials or other things. So there is a distinction between inner vision and outer sight.

The heart's vision and blindness

The vision of the heart is a subtle essence with which spiritual things are seen. This essence is like a rider and its eye is like a conveyance. The blindness of the rider is more harmful than the blindness of the conveying horse; that is, the blindness of the heart is more harmful than the blindness of the eye. These two things have no connection with each other. Still, there is some similarity between external sight and internal sight. Allah explains the sight of the heart, saying, "The heart was not untrue in (making him see) what he saw" (Qur'an, 53:11). Here He says that the heart has the power of sight.

In another verse, Allah says, "Thus did We show Ibrāhīm the kingdom of the heavens and the earth" (Qur'an, 6:75). Here Allah speaks not of external sight, as others also have been given this power, but rather of internal sight, the opposite of which is the internal blindness. Allah says, "Whoever is blind in this will (also) be blind in the hereafter" (Qur'an, 17:72). This is the blindness of the heart. This is the exposition of knowledge concerning the intellect.

Knowledge concerning religion

This knowledge is acquired by blind faith in the prophets. It can be gained after studying the Qur'an and Sunnah of the Prophet (ṣ), or by hearing them. For the salvation of the heart, blind faith alone is insufficient, even though knowledge concerning the intellect is necessary. As for the health of the body, some measures are necessary, but they are not alone sufficient without their actual application. Special methods of medicines for cures should be learnt from physicians. The intellect alone is insufficient. He who calls to blind faith alone without the application of the intellect is a fool. Conversely, he who relies on the intellect only after giving up the Qur'an and Sunnah is a proud man. The two must be kept together.

Education concerning the intellect is like food, and religious education is like medicine. A diseased man meets with harm if he eats only food after giving up medicine. Similar is the case for a diseased heart. Its cure is not possible without the profitable medicine of Sharīʿah, which is the duties prescribed by the prophets for the purity of the heart. He who does not treat his diseased heart with the medicine of divine service as ordained by Sharīʿah and thinks the knowledge of the intellect sufficient faces ruin.

Science does not contradict religion

Some think that science is opposed to religion, but this is not at all correct. They think this because they fail to harmonise the two. As a result, such people leave the pale of religion. They are like blind men who stumble on the furniture in a house, saying, "Why has this furniture been kept in the pathway?" to which the house owner says, "They are in their proper places. It is your blindness which is responsible for your stumbling." This is also the case for someone who thinks that science contradicts religion.

Kinds of sciences

There are two kinds of sciences: material and spiritual. Medicine, mathematics and other technical sciences belong to the sciences of this world. The religious sciences are the sciences concerning the heart, Allah and His attributes and actions. He who strives with regard to worldly sciences and becomes an expert is, in most cases, ignorant of religious sciences. 'Alī cited three illustrations to explain this. He said, "This world and the next world are like two scales, or like the east and the west, or like two co-wives."

Thus, you will find that he who is intelligent in worldly matters and an expert in medicine, mathematics, philosophy, geometry or the like is ignorant about religious sciences. And he who is experienced in religious sciences is inexperienced in worldly sciences. For this reason, the Prophet (ṣ) said, "Most of the inhabitants of Paradise are indifferent." In other words, they are inattentive to worldly matters. Al-Ḥasan said, "We have seen people whom, if you saw them, you would regard as mad. If they saw you, they would call you devils. So the worldly educated men deny any wonderful event of religion. Allah says, "Surely those who do not hope in Our meeting and are pleased with this world's life and are content with it, and those who are heedless of Our communications" (Qur'an, 10:7). He also says, "They know the outward of this world's life, but of the hereafter they are absolutely heedless" (Qur'an, 30:7). It is only the prophets who combined in themselves knowledge of this world and the next with the help of the Holy Spirit and were given divine powers.

7

The means of acquiring spiritual powers

Know that there are different conditions of knowledge which are not axiomatic. Some of them suddenly appear in the heart and are called "inspiration" (*ilhām*), while others are acquired by effort (*istidlāl*). Knowledge not acquired by effort is of two kinds. As for the first, it is not known from where it comes or how it comes. As for the second, it comes through an angel who throws it into the heart. The latter is called "revelation" (*waḥy*) and is revealed to the prophets. Inspiration of the first kind enters the heart of the prophets as well as other religious personalities. In short, the human heart is the place where truths of all things are disclosed, and the obstacles we mentioned earlier stand as screens between the Guarded Tablet (*al-Lawḥ al-Maḥfūẓ*) and the mirror of the heart. Pictures of everything that will occur up to Resurrection Day have been preserved in this tablet.

The real state of every affair is reflected in the mirror of the heart, like a figure in front of a mirror. If there is no screen between the two, it is seen in the mirror of the heart from the Guarded Tablet. The essence sometimes removes the screen from the mirror of the heart so as to disclose what is in the Guarded Tablet. Sometimes future events can be seen in a dream. After death, all the screens are removed. In a wakeful state the screen is also sometimes removed provided secret mercy is showered to the heart. Then gusts of knowledge spring forth in the heart from unseen things and last for a short time.

Inspiration and revelation cannot be obtained by human will. Allah says, "It is not for any mortal that Allah should speak to him except by revelation or from behind a veil, or by sending a messenger and revealing by His permission what He pleases" (Qur'an, 42:51).

The merits of knowledge by inspiration

Sufis love knowledge through inspiration. For this reason, they do not like to have an education or read books or hold arguments. They say that the primary source of acquiring knowledge is saving oneself from the condemnable evils, severing all connections and directing all efforts towards Allah. When it is gained, Allah Himself becomes the caretaker of human heart and saves it by enkindling the light of knowledge in it. When Allah takes care of his heart, mercy appears in it, light shines, the breast expands and the secrets of the spiritual world are disclosed to him. By Allah's help, the screens of darkness are lifted from the upper portion of his soul and the real nature of divine affairs comes to him. So it is the duty of Allah's servants to purify his soul and to strive with true and sincere intention. These matters are opened to the prophets and friends of Allah, over whose breasts lights flow not because they acquired knowledge through effort but because their asceticism—their full freedom from worldly connections and the concentration of their energies on Allah.

To them the first step is to cut off all worldly connections; to make the soul vacant for Allah; to give up all efforts for family, property, children, houses, name and fame; to confine themselves to performing obligatory and non-obligatory duties; and to sit in meditation, their hearts absolutely free from everything and their thoughts centred only on one being. They even become free from the interpretations of the Qur'an, Ḥadīth and other books. They sit in lonely places and humbly invoke only Allah until they reach a stage where they give up even the movements of their tongue. Then the influence of their tongue enters their hearts, which chant, "Allah, Allah." The pictures of words are then effaced from their hearts, and only their meanings remain therein.

It is your choice to reach this stage. You have no power to claim the mercy of Allah, but you may be fit to receive its blowing, at which time the sparkling ray of truth may sparkle in your heart like lightning, which may or may not last. You will then continue to purify your heart and hope to receive Allah's blessings. This mode is very troublesome and its fruit time-consuming. If you can reach a stage, it is difficult for you to stay in it, as the Devil will constantly mislead you. The Prophet (ṣ) said, "The heart of a believer is more changing than a pot (of hot water)." During this time of efforts and trials, your health may deteriorate.

8

Inspiration and acquired knowledge

Know that the wonders of the heart are outside the knowledge gained by the senses, as the heart is outside the knowledge of the senses. So to understand the actions of the heart, some illustrations of the material world are necessary. Only two of them are cited here.

First illustration

Consider, as an example, a well dug underneath the ground. There are two ways of pouring water into it: through a pipe or canal, or to dig the well very deep, so that water may gush forth from its bottom. The second way is better because water obtained in this way is more pure and lasting. Similarly, the heart is like a well, knowledge like water, and the five senses like pipes or canals. Knowledge like water comes to the heart through the help of the five senses like pipes or canals. If you wish to get pure knowledge, you have to shut off the five senses in the same way you shut off pipes or canals to get pure water into the well and dig it very deep, so that pure water may gush forth from the bottom. The filth in the bottom of well must be cleared to allow pure water to gush forth. So to get pure and unadulterated knowledge, you have to shut off knowledge gained by the five senses, since such knowledge is full of superstitions and errors.

"But how," you may ask, "can knowledge arise from the heart when it remains without knowledge? The answer is that these matters are among the wonders of the heart. It is difficult to acquire them from worldly sciences. However, that true state of everything has been recorded in the Guarded Tablet as well as the hearts of the angels who are near Allah. Just as an architect prepares a plan before building a house and then builds it according to his plan, the Creator recorded in the Guarded Tablet His plans for everything in the heavens and earth from first to last. Thereafter, He acts according to that prepared plan.

The material world has four degrees of existence: existence in the Guarded Tablet before the creation of the world, its real existence after this, its imaginative existence and its intellectual existence.

Some worlds are material and some immaterial. Among the immaterial worlds, there are those which are more spiritual than others. These are strategies of Allah. Consider the eyeball. Though it is small, the images of the heavens and the earth appear in it. Then it enters the imagination and appears in the heart. Man, however, is not cognisant of it until it reaches the heart. Praise to Allah, who created a wonderful power in the heart and eyes and made the heart and eyes of some blind.

So pictures of the world fall in soul sometimes by the help of five senses and sometimes by the help of the Guarded Tablet as picture of the sun falls in eyes. Again picture of the sun falls in water as it falls in eyes. When obstacles are removed from between soul and Guarded Tablet, soul can see many things and thus knowledge arises therefrom. Then no help of the senses is necessary for such knowledge. It is just like the gushing forth of water from the deep bottom of a well.

The doors of the heart

One door of the heart is open to the spiritual world—the world of angels and the Guarded Tablet. Another door of the heart is open to the five senses and is connected to the material world. The first door can be better understood from dreams, in which one can see some events of the future and the past without the necessity of knowledge gained from one's five senses. That door is open to whoever remains engaged in the remembrance of Allah in solitude. The Prophet (ṣ) said, "The dwellers of solitude have preceded." He was asked, "O Prophet of Allah, who are the dwellers of solitude?" He replied, "Those who have been made pure by the remembrance of Allah, those whose burdens have been lifted by the remembrance of Allah, and those who come on Resurrection Day free of burdens." Then he described their virtues and read these words of Allah: "I kept My face before them. Do you know before whom I have kept My face? Does anybody know what I will give them?" Then Allah said, "First I cast light into their hearts, as a result of which they broadcast the news they get from Me."

There is difference between the knowledge of the prophets and friends of Allah and the knowledge of the learned and scientists. The knowledge of the prophets and the friends of Allah come out of that gate of hearts which remains open to the spiritual world, and the knowledge of the learned and the scientists comes out of that gate of souls which remains open to the material world through the five senses. So it is impossible for the latter to acquire spiritual knowledge. This illustration makes one understand the difference between the two.

Second illustration

The destination between the actions of the learned and of the friends of Allah will make one understand the second illustration, as the learned learn the basic principles of sciences. The spiritual knowledge of a believer is everlasting as the heart of a believer has no death: At the time of his death, his knowledge does not go. Al-Ḥasan said, "Earth cannot eat the place of faith." Rather, it is a means to gain the nearness of Allah.

The rank of the fortunate differs according to the degree of knowledge and faith, just as there is a difference between the rich in respect to their riches. So knowledge of Allah is a light without which the believer will not be able to secure divine vision. Allah says, "Their light running before them and on their right hand" (Qur'an, 57:12).

There is, moreover, a difference in the degrees of light. The Prophet (ṣ) said, "If the faith of Abū Bakr was weighed against that of the people of the world except prophets and messengers, the first would tip the scale." This is like someone's saying, "If the lights of all lamps were weighed against the rays of the sun, the rays of the sun would tip the scale," for the light of the faith of prophets and messengers is like the rays of the sun, the light of those with great faith (*ṣiddīqūn*) like that of the moon, the light of the friends of Allah like that of the stars, and the light of the general believers like that of a lamp. The rays of the sun illumine the whole world, and the light of a lamp gives light to a room.

Likewise, there is a difference between the expansion of the breasts of prophets and that of ordinary believers. A *ḥadīth* says that it will be said on Resurrection Day that whoever has in his heart an atom's weight of faith will be taken out of Hell. Allah says, "You will have the upper hand if you are believers" (Qur'an, 3:139). In this verse, Allah speaks of the superiority of believers over Muslims. Here "believers" means believers with great spiritual knowledge and not Muslims with mere outward faith. Allah also says, "Allah will exalt those of you who believe, and those who are given knowledge, in high degrees" (Qur'an, 58:11). Here Allah speaks of those who have blind faith and then those believers who are learned. In exposition of this verse, Ibn 'Abbās said, "Allah will keep learned believers over the ordinary believers by seven hundred degrees, the distance between every two degrees being equal to the distance between the heavens and the earth.

The Prophet (ṣ) said, "The majority of the inhabitants of Paradise are simple, but the wise will live in the highest Paradise." He also said, "The superiority of a learned man over a devotee is like mine over an ordinary man among my followers." According to another version, it is "like the superiority of the full moon over the stars." It can be understood from the above that the differences in the ranks of the inhabitants of Paradise will be in accordance with the differences in their hearts in terms of divine knowledge.

9

The testimony of Sharīʿah to how Sufis gain spiritual knowledge

Inspiration and spiritual unveiling

If anything is disclosed to anybody by inspiration from an unknown source, he is considered an ascetic who has attained knowledge of Allah through sound means. Owing to constant engagement in divine services, spiritual knowledge is disclosed to the heart by way of inspiration or spiritual unveiling. The Prophet (ṣ) said, "Allah gives him, who applies his knowledge, knowledge which he did not have before and grace in his actions, so that Paradise becomes sure for him. He who does not act on his learning roams round his learning, and Allah does not give him grace in his actions so that Hell becomes sure for him."

Allah says, "Whoever is careful of (his duty to) Allah, He will make for him an outlet and give him sustenance from whence he thinks not" (Qur'an, 65:2-3). This means that Allah takes him out from doubts and various difficulties and gives him knowledge without education, and natural understanding without experience. Allah also says, "O you who believe, if you are careful of (your duty to) Allah, He will grant you a distinction" (Qur'an, 8:29). "Distinction" means a light with which truth and falsehood are distinguished and with which one can come out of doubt. The Prophet (ṣ) used to pray, "O Allah, give me light, increase my light, give me light in my heart, give me light in my grave, give me light in my hearing, give me light in my sight." He would even pray, "Give me light in my hair, my flesh, my blood and my bones." When the Prophet (ṣ) was asked about the meaning of the verse "What! Is he whose heart Allah has opened for Islam so that he is in a light from his Lord (like the hard-hearted)?" (Qur'an, 39:22), he said, "It is enlarging. When light appears in the heart, the latter expands and spreads. Moreover, the Prophet (ṣ) prayed for Ibn 'Abbās, "O Allah, give him knowledge of religion and of interpretation." 'Alī said, "I have nothing which the Prophet (ṣ) divulged to me except that Allah gives a servant understanding in His Book." This was not by instruction.

Allah says, "He grants wisdom to whom He pleases" (Qur'an, 2:269). This knowledge is said to be that of Allah's Book. Allah says, "We made Sulaymān understand it" (Qur'an, 21:79), referring to what was revealed to him as "understanding." Abū al-Dardā' said, "A believer is he who sees with the light of Allah everything from behind a screen." By Allah, it is true that Allah casts truth into the heart and makes it move to the tongue.

An ancient sage said, "Fear the sight of a believer, as he looks only by the help of divine light." This is what is referred to in the verses "Surely in this are signs for those who examine" (Qur'an, 15:75) and "Indeed We have made the communications clear for a people who are sure" (2:118). The Prophet (ṣ) said, "Knowledge is of two kinds: one kind of knowledge lies concealed in the soul, and it is the beneficial learning." One learned man was asked about this and said, "That is one of Allah's secret matters which he casts into the hearts of His dear servants and with which he has acquainted neither angels nor ordinary men.

The scholar is he who learns from his God, his knowledge coming directly from Him. Allah says, "We had taught knowledge from Ourselves" (Qur'an, 18:65). Although some knowledge comes from Allah, some is acquired through men and therefore cannot be regarded as knowledge coming directly from Allah, which arises from the depth of the heart without any cause. The Qur'an and Ḥadīth support this view.

Following are some examples of knowledge directly from Allah.

Abū Bakr al-Ṣiddīq said to 'Ā'ishah at the time of his death, "They are both your brother and sister." At that time, his wife was pregnant and she gave birth thereafter to a daughter. He came to know beforehand that he would have a daughter born to him.

'Umar said during a Friday sermon, "O army, towards the hillock! Towards the hillock.!" When he came to know by a spiritual unveiling that the enemies were about to kill the Muslim soldiers, he cautioned them and called them to assemble in the hillock. It is miraculous that the call soon reached the Muslim soldiers.

Anas ibn Mālik said, "I entered the presence of 'Uthmān, and on the way there I met a woman and began to think of her extraordinary beauty. When I reached 'Uthmān, he said, 'One of you has come to me with the marks of fornication in his eyes. Do you not know that to look at a strange woman is fornication? Repent or otherwise I shall punish you.' I said, 'Does revelation come even after the Prophet of Allah?' 'Uthmān replied, 'Revelation does not come, but by deep insight everything can be seen.'"

There are many instances in which sages and saints could read the thoughts of men. The absolute proof which nobody can deny consists of two things: true dreams and the Prophet's ability to speak accurately of future events.

True dreams

True dreams reveal the unseen events. When it is possible in a dream, it does not become impossible in a wakeful state for the following reasons. In sleep, actions of the outward senses remain closed and suspended. The heart being free from the material world, its door of knowledge is slightly open to the spiritual world. This occurs sometimes in a wakeful state. There are many men who do not hear or see even in wakeful states, thus remaining immersed in their thoughts.

The prophecies of the Prophet (ṣ)

With regard to the prophecies of the Holy Prophet concerning future events, there are proofs in the Qur'an. A prophet is he who remains busy showing people the right path and to whom the real nature of everything is disclosed. And a friend of Allah is he who does not (necessarily) remain busy showing people the right, but it is possible for him to know the real nature of things.

The heart has two gates, and he who believes in the prophets and in true dreams must believe so. One gate is open to the external senses, and another to the spiritual world from the deepest recess of the heart, also known as inspiration, the blowing of the soul and revelation. Between these two gates, the roaming of heart discloses its real nature. Just as spiritual matters are disclosed in dreams, so they are disclosed to prophets and friends of Allah in different forms. But they cannot be understood without spiritual knowledge.

Many angels are ignorant of the human heart. A man of spiritual unveiling said, "An angel came to me and said, 'Disclose to me your insight of the Allah's oneness and secret remembrance of Allah, as I do not write anything of these matters.' I asked him, 'Do you not write obligatory duties?' He said, 'Yes, we write them.'" It appears from this that the Honoured Scribes (*Kirām Kātibūn*) do not know of secret things, but they see only physical actions.

A gnostic said that he asked a *badal* about the perception of certitude. The *badal* then asked the angels on his right and left sides, who both answered that they do not know. Then he asked his breast, which was more knowledgeable than the angels, and it also said it did not know.

The Prophet (ṣ) said, "There are true news-givers among my followers, and 'Umar is one of them."

A *ḥadīth qudsī* says, "Allah says, 'Whenever I examine the heart of a man and find persistent remembrance of Me predominant therein, I take charge of him and become his friend, admonisher and companion.'"

Abū Sulaymān al-Dārānī said, "The heart is like a closed tent all of whose doors have been shut, and whatever door is opened to it influences it." One of the doors of the heart is open to the spiritual world and the Almighty Allah. What opens it is God-fearingness and abstinence from worldly lusts, greed and effort. For this reason, ʿUmar gave orders to his commanders to remember what the religious say, as true matters are disclosed to them. A sage likewise said, "Allah's hand is over the wise. They do not say except what Allah discloses to them." Another sage said, "If you are wise, I shall tell you that Allah discloses some of His secrets to the God-fearing."

10
Satan's whisperings in the heart

As I have already stated, the heart is a closed tent which has several doors, and from every door influences and their resultant effects pour into it. It is also like a building at which arrows are shot from every direction. Or it is like a preserved mirror across which different images pass, so that one image after another appears in it. Or it is like a well which is connected to pipes through which water flows. The five senses are its open pipes, and its secret pipes are a man's character and conduct, which consists of greed, anger and so on.

Whatever is gained by the five senses appears in the heart. When sexual passion rises high on account of overeating, its effect appears on the heart, which changes from one condition to another. These effects on the heart are called "involuntary suggestions" (*khawāṭir*), out of which grows will and then intention. Such suggestions are either good or bad. Good involuntary suggestions are called "inspiration," and bad ones are called "whisperings of the Devil" (*waswās*).

Devils and angels

The cause or urge which calls to the good is called an "angel," and the cause which calls to the bad is called a "devil." What helps the heart in receiving inspiration is called "divine succour." The thing which is accepted from the whisperings of Satan is called "misguidance." The action of an angel is to give rise to good actions, to disclose truth and to command to good. Thus Allah created two opposite agencies. He says, "Of everything We have created pairs" (Qur'an, 51:49).

All things are opposed to one another, except Allah, the One, the Unique, who created these pairs. So the heart lives in dispute between angels and devils. In this connection, the Prophet (ṣ) said, "There are two impulses in the heart. One is the impulse of an angel who calls to good and confirms truth. He who feels this impulse should know that it is from Allah. Another impulse comes from the enemy, leads to doubt, belies the truth and prohibits good works. He who feels this should seek refuge in Allah from the accursed Devil." Then he recited the verse "Satan threatens you with poverty and enjoins you to be niggardly" (Qur'an, 2:268).

Al-Ḥasan said, "Two thoughts roam over the heart. One is from Allah, and the other is from the Devil. Allah shows mercy to a servant who stops at the time of the latter thought. If the heart follows low desires and passions, the Devil gets the upper hand. If it follows the habits of angels, it becomes the resting place of angels." In this regard, the Prophet (ṣ) said, "There is nobody among you in whom there is no devil." The Companions asked, "O Messenger of Allah, does it reside in you, too?" He said, "There is also a devil in me, but Allah has helped me to overcome it, and it has become submissive to me, ordering me to do nothing but good."

The Devil works havoc through the medium of sexual passion. Whoever follows it finds the Devil his guide. When he returns to the remembrance of Allah, the Devil goes behind, and the angel encourages good works. In the battlefield of the heart, there is a constant clash between the soldiers of the Devil and those of the angel until the latter gets the upper hand. After its victory, the heart remains in peace, and the Devil becomes submissive.

Al-'Alā' ibn Ziyād said, "The Devil enters a heart just as a thief enters a house. If there is anything in the house, the thief takes it away. If there is nothing in the house, the thief leaves it." That is, the Devil does not enter a heart which is free from sexual passion and evil desires. Allah says to the Devil, "Surely (as for) My servants, you have no authority over them" (Qur'an, 17: 65.)

He who follows the dictates of passion is a slave of passion and not of Allah, so He gives Satan control over him. Allah says, "Have you seen him who takes his low desires for his god?" (Qur'an, 25:43). One day, 'Amr ibn al-'Āṣ asked the Prophet (ṣ), "O Messenger of Allah, a devil enters my recitation of the Qur'an in prayer." The Prophet (ṣ) replied, "He is a devil called Khinzib. When you feel his presence, seek refuge in Allah and spit thrice to your left." He said Allah relieved him from it after he did that. Another *ḥadīth* says that there is a devil in ablution called al-Walhān, so seeks refuge from him in Allah.

In exposition of the verse "Seek refuge in Allah from the accursed Satan" (Qur'an, 16:98), Mujāhid said that it is a broad sign in the heart; when one remembers Allah, the Devil flees disappointed, but when one is heedless, the Devil stretches out his authority over the heart.

The remembrance of Allah and the Devil's contrivance are like light and darkness, which cannot exist at the same time. The Prophet (ṣ) said, "The Devil places his trunk in the heart of man. When he remembers Allah, Satan goes away, and when he is heedless, Satan catches hold of his heart."

The Prophet (ṣ) said, "When a man does not repent after he reaches his fortieth year, the Devil rubs his face with his hands and says, 'I have wiped the face of whoever has no salvation.'"

The Prophet (ṣ) said, "The Devil moves in man like the circulation of blood, so make his circulation narrow by hunger." This is because hunger cures sexual passion, which is the weapon of the Devil and surrounds the heart. Allah quotes Satan as saying, "I will certainly lie in wait for them in Your straight path. Then I will certainly come to them from before them and from behind them, and from their right-hand side and from their left-hand side" (Qur'an, 7:16-17).

The Prophet (ṣ) said, "The Devil keeps sitting in different paths for man. He sits along the path of Islam and says, 'Will you accept Islam after giving up your religion and the religion of your ancestors?' When he disobeys him and accepts Islam, he sits for him along the path of emigration and says, 'Will you leave your country after leaving your native land and your possessions?' When he disobeys him and emigrates, he sits along the path of jihad and says, 'Will you fight, ruining yourself and your possessions?' He disobeys him and fights." The Prophet (ṣ) said, "If a man dies after performing the above actions, it becomes the duty of Allah to admit him to Paradise."

Some may ask, "What is the Devil? Does he have a body? If so, how can he enter the heart of man?" These are useless talks, and He who raises such arguments is like him who, instead of removing a snake from his garment, argues as to the shape, form, length and breadth of the snake. This is sheer foolishness. When you know that evil thoughts arise in your heart and that they lead you to ruin, it is clear that they are your enemies of whom you should be cautious. Allah says, "Surely Satan is your enemy" (Qur'an, 35:6) and "Did I not charge you, O children of Adam, that you should not serve Satan? Surely he is your open enemy" (Qur'an, 36: 60). So everybody should be cautious of him and not ask about his birth, death and other particulars.

Kinds of thoughts

There are three kinds of thoughts: bad thoughts which lead to evil, good thoughts which lead to good—this is known as inspiration—and thoughts mixed with good and bad and which lead to doubt—it is not known whether these come from angels or devils.

The Devil cannot call the majority of the pious to evil deeds. He presents doubt to them in the form of good, and that is a great deception which destroys many people. For instance, he advises a learned man to make sermons and to adorn his lectures with ornamental words. His objects is to throw him to a show of deeds and to generate in his heart a desire for name and fame, making him among those about whom the Prophet (ṣ) said, "Allah will help this religion through men who have no share in religion" or, according to another *ḥadīth*, "through transgressors."

The deception of Satan

It was related that the Devil once came to 'Īsā and told him, "Say, 'There is no deity but Allah.' 'Īsā replied, "This is a true statement, but I will not utter it in obedience to your dictation."

Every man should know the source of his thoughts, whether it comes from angels or devils. He should examine them by deep insight and not by the dictates of passion and low desires. Their sources will not be disclosed to him except by the light of God-fearingness and deep knowledge. Allah says, "Surely those who guard (against evil), when a visitation from Satan afflicts them they become mindful" (Qur'an, 7:201). In other words, they return to the light of knowledge.

The means of saving oneself from the machinations of the Devil is to shut the doors of thoughts, which are the five senses, sexual passion and worldly connections. The doors of the five senses are shut if one stays alone in a dark room. The secret door of the Devil is shut if he lives separate from his family members and his possessions. Thus the door of thoughts remains open in the heart and will not be closed if the heart is not kept engaged in the remembrance of Allah. Even the Devil tries to make him forgetful of it. This fight continues until his death. As long as he lives, he is not released from the Devil, and the door of passion, hatred and greed remains open to the heart.

One day, a man asked al-Ḥasan, "O Abū Sa'īd, does the Devil sleep?" Al-Ḥasan smiled and said, "If he slept, we would be able to rest." Thus, no believer is safe from him.

It is true that there are means of driving Satan away and curbing his power. The Prophet (ṣ) said, "A believer drives out his devil just as one of you drives his camel on a journey." Ibn Mas'ūd said, "The devil of a believer is lean and thin."

It is true, also, that there are many doors open to the heart for devils, but the door of angels is the only one which is mixed with the other doors. To know the path is very difficult without the rays of the heart or deep insight enveloped with God-fearingness.

'Abdullāh ibn Mas'ūd said, "The Prophet (ṣ) drew a line before us and said, 'This is Allah's path.' He then drew up several lines to the right and left sides of that line and said, 'These are different paths, in each of which is inviting to him.' He then recited, 'And (know) that this is My path, the right one, therefore follow it, and follow not (other) ways' (Qur'an, 6:153)."

The Prophet (ṣ) said, "There was a hermit among the children of Israel. Once, the Devil snared a woman and put into the hearts of her family members that her cure was in the hands of the hermit. So they took the woman to the hermit and wanted him to keep her, but he declined to keep her. Being greatly requested, he kept the woman with him for treatment. Then the Devil came to the hermit and gave him evil advice. The hermit then cohabited with the woman, who became pregnant as a result. Now the Devil came to the hermit again and said to him, 'Kill her, otherwise her family members will come and kill you. If they ask you about her, you will say that she has died.' So the hermit killed the woman and buried her. The Devil then came to the family members of the woman and told them that the hermit killed her because the woman became pregnant because of his cohabitation with her. When they came to the hermit for the woman, he said that she had died. Then the Devil came to the hermit and said to him, 'I will save you from them if you obey my command. Prostrate before me twice.' When the hermit prostrated before the Devil, the latter said, "I am now free from you."

11

Satan's entry into the heart

Know that the heart is like a fortress, and the Devil wishes to enter it and wreak havoc. In order to save it from the Devil, one must guard the doors of this fort. It is impossible for him to guard the doors unless he is familiar with them,. The doors are character and conduct.

Anger and sexual passion

A great door through which the Devil enters is anger and sexual passion. When intelligence is weak, the forces of the Devil attack it. Whenever any man gets angry, the Devil plays with him. It was related that once the Devil came to Mūsā and said, "O Mūsā, Allah has selected you for prophethood, and He talks much with you. I have committed a sin and wish to repent. Intercede with my Lord that He may forgive my sins." Mūsā replied, "Very well. I will do it."

He ascended the hill, talked with Allah and wished to get down from it. Then he said, "Fulfil the promise." Mūsā said, "O Lord, your servant Iblīs wishes that his repentance be accepted." Allah then revealed to Mūsā, "O Mūsā, your need has been fulfilled. Tell the Devil to prostrate before the grave of Adam and to repent."

When Mūsā told this to the Devil, the latter got angry and said, "I did not prostrate before him while he was alive. Shall I now do it after his death? I owe a duty to you, as you have interceded with Allah on my behalf. So remember me on three occasions and I shall not do you any harm. When you get angry, you should remember that my life is with your heart, my eyes are with your eyes, and I move within you like the circulation of blood. When you join a fight, you should remember that I come down at that time and remind a man of his wives, children and possessions, so he flees. Do not sit by a woman who is not a *maḥram* because I remain her messenger to you and your messenger to her until I tempt you by her and tempt her by you."

From the foregoing story, it appears how dangerous anger and sexual passion are.

A friend of Allah said to the Devil, "Tell me how you control man." Satan said, "I control him when he is angry." Once, the Devil went to a hermit, who asked him what characteristic of man is the most helpful to him. The Devil replied, "Haughty temper, for when a man has haughty temper, I overturn him just as a boy overturns his toy."

Hatred and greed

Another great door through which the Devil enters the heart is hatred and greed. When a man has greed for anything, it makes him deaf and blind, for the Prophet (ṣ) said, "Your love for anything makes you deaf and blind." It was also related that when the prophet Nūḥ embarked on the boat, taking a pair of everything with him by Allah's command, He found an old man in the boat and asked him, "Why have you come?" The man answered, "I have come to throw the hearts of your companions into fear, so that their hearts may remain with me and their bodies with you." Nūḥ said, "O enemy of Allah, leave, as you are cursed." Then the old man said to him, "I will destroy people with five things, and I will not disclose to you two things." Allah then revealed to Nūḥ, "You do not need these things. Tell him to disclose to you the two things." Nūḥ informed the Devil accordingly. The Devil said, "The two things are greed and hatred. I have been cursed on account of hatred, and I created greed in Adam and misguided him."

Eating to satisfaction

Another door of the Devil is eating to the heart's content, though the food is lawful and pure, as it makes sexual passion strong. The Devil once came to the prophet Yaḥyā, the son of Zakariyyā, who saw Satan's body stout and strong, so he asked him, "Iblīs, why do you have a strong body?" Satan replied, "Because of sexual passion." Yaḥyā asked, "Do I have anything of it?" The Devil said, "Sometimes you eat to satisfaction, as a result of which you feel too heavy to pray and invoke Allah." Yaḥyā said, "Do I have anything besides this?" Satan answered, "You have nothing else." Yaḥyā said, "I shall never eat to my heart's content." Satan then said, "By Allah, I shall never again give any advice to any Muslim."

The harms of eating to satisfaction

Eating to satisfaction has six harms:

1. God-fearingness leaves the heart.
2. Kindness to people leaves the heart.
3. One finds it hard to perform acts of worship.
4. One does not feel humility upon hearing words of wisdom.
5. When one gives a sermon, one's words do not enter the hearts of the audience.
6. One gets many diseases.

Love for fine things

Another door of the Devil is love for fine clothes, houses and furniture. When a man loves fine clothes, he loves to embellish his house and decorate it with fine and beautiful furniture and the like. He also loves to paint his building, including its roofs and walls, with variegated colours.

Dependence on others

Another door of the Devil is dependence on others and to cherish hope in getting favours from them. As a result, one uses craftiness and flattery, and greed becomes one's deity.

Hastiness and absence of steadiness

Hastiness and giving up firmness in actions are another door of the Devil. The Prophet (ṣ) said, "Hastiness comes from the Devil, and delay comes from Allah." Allah says, "Man is created of haste" (Qur'an, 21:37). And addressing the Prophet (ṣ), He says, "Do not make haste with the Qur'an before its revelation is made complete to you" (Qur'an, 20:114).

It was related that when 'Īsā was born, the followers of Iblīs came to him and said, "The heads of all idols have fallen down." Iblīs replied, "It seems that some event has taken place." When he later found 'Īsā surrounded by angels, he said to his followers, "A prophet was born into the world without my knowledge. No woman has ever conceived in my absence, but this is an exception." He then praised man for hastiness and fickleness.

Wealth beyond necessity

Another great door of the Devil is to have wealth and possessions beyond necessity. He who has the bare necessities lives in peace, but if one possesses surplus wealth, he cannot enjoy peace, as he wants more and more. When the Prophet (ṣ) was born, the followers of the Devil became displeased, but the Devil said, "Give them some time. Perhaps, Allah will give them wealth, and we shall gain the upper hand."

It was related that 'Īsā was once using a piece of stone as a pillow when the Devil came to him and said, "You have greed for wealth, for you are resting on a stone." 'Īsā then threw the stone at the Devil, saying, "This is your reward." Now consider a man who uses a pillow for pleasure.

Miserliness and fear of poverty

Another great door of the Devil is miserliness and fear of poverty, since they prevent charity and spending, encourage hoarding and create greed for wealth. Khaythamah ibn 'Abd al-Raḥmān said, "The Devil says, 'Man may be able to have control over me, but he will not be able to prevail over me in three matters: misappropriation of money, unjust spending and not paying the dues of others.'" Sufyān said, "Satan has no weapon like fear of poverty."

Frequenting marketplaces

Satan lives in bazaars. The Prophet (ṣ) said, "When Satan came down to earth, he said, 'Lord, give me a place for habitation,' and Allah said, 'I give you the bathroom for habitation.' Then Satan said, 'Give me a place to assemble,' and Allah said, 'For that I give you baths, marketplaces and the centres of pathways.' Then Satan said, 'Give me food,' and Allah said, 'You are given food over which Allah's name has not been mentioned.' Then, Satan said, 'Give me something to drink,' and Allah said, 'I give you drinks which produce intoxication.' Then Satan said, 'Give me an inviter,' and Allah said, 'I give you musical instruments.' Then Satan said, 'Give me a Qur'an,' and Allah said, 'I give you poetry.' Then Satan said, 'Give me a book,' and Allah said, 'I give you pictures of animals.' Then Satan said, give me *ḥadīths*,' and Allah said, 'I give you lies.' Finally, Satan said, 'Give me a game,' and Allah said, 'I give you women.'"

Sectarianism and hatred for opponents

Another door of Satan is sectarianism and hatred for those who oppose and hold him in contempt. These are faults on account of which the religious are ruined, for to disclose the faults of others is among the savage characteristics in nature. Those who follow their own sect or party think that it is the best, cherishing hatred for other sects or parties. Some of them support Abū Bakr al-Ṣiddīq, though they do not follow him, speak lies and create disturbance. If Abū Bakr saw them, he would be their first enemy.

Some of them support 'Alī, but they do not follow his character or conduct. At the time of his caliphate, he purchased a shirt for only three dirhams and cut off his trousers up to ankles. Now his supporters wear silk dresses and consume unlawful earnings. On Resurrection Day he will be their first enemy. Those who love Imams Abū Ḥanīfah, al-Shāfi'ī, Mālik and Aḥmad should remember the above principle.

Ordinary male leaders of religion

One of the great doors of Satan is that those who have no knowledge and who do not ponder over the mysteries of creation and the actions of Allah claim to be the leaders of religion. They entertain doubt about the basic principles of religion. The Prophet (ṣ) said, "Satan comes to one of you and says, 'Who created Allah?' When anyone feels that he should say, 'I believe in Allah and His Prophet,' as this utterance will remove that feeling from him."

The Prophet (ṣ) did not recommend argumentation, as it affects the common people rather than the learned.

Bad opinions about Muslims

One of the great doors of Satan is bad ideas and opinions about Muslims. Allah says, "O you who believe, avoid most of suspicion, for surely suspicion in some cases is a sin" (Qur'an, 49:12). Satan encourages backbiting about someone whom you have a bad idea about."

Moreover, the Prophet (ṣ) said, "Save yourself from places of calumny." Even the Prophet (ṣ) saved himself from them. Once, the Prophet (ṣ) was observing spiritual retreat (*i'tikāf*) in a mosque. Then his wife Ṣafiyyah bint Ḥuyay came to him and went away in the evening. Then two Madīnan Helpers (*Anṣār*) came there and greeted him. When they were about to depart, the Prophet (ṣ) said to them that his wife Ṣafiyyah had come and gone away. He said, "Satan runs through the body of a man like the circulation of blood. I fear he may enter you." So saving oneself from the calumny of others is everyone's duty.

These are Satan's twelve great doors through which he enters into the hearts of men and commit tremendous havoc and ruin.

The means to driving out Satan

The means to shut the doors and prevent the entry of Satan into the human heart is purification of the heart from evil attributes. Satan is like a hungry dog which will come to you, so drive it out repeatedly. If you cannot drive out a dog, take a piece of meat and throw it to it and it will go away.

In like manner, the heart which is free from the food of Satan can be filled with constant remembrance of Allah. However, when passion and greed are strong in the heart, the spirit of the remembrance of Allah roams round it. And when the heart is heedless of the remembrance of Allah, machinations of Satan enter it.

Abū Hurayrah related that once the devil of a believer and the devil of a polytheist met with each other. The devil of the polytheist was stout and strong and wore fine clothes, and the devil of the believer was lean and thin, had dishevelled hair and was laden with dust. The former said to the latter, "Why are you lean and thin?" The latter said, "I remain with a man who remembers Allah when he eats, so I become hungry, and who remembers Allah when he drinks, so I become thirsty. When he clothes himself and remembers Allah, I remain without clothes. When he uses oil and remembers Allah, my hair becomes dishevelled." The devil of the unbeliever said, "I remain with a person who does not remember Allah in any case, so I become his partner in eating, drinking and clothing."

'Abd al-Raḥmān ibn Abī Laylā said, "A devil with a firebrand in hand came to the Prophet (ṣ) while he was in prayer. Jibrīl went to him at once and said, 'Recite this: 'I seek refuge in the perfect words of Allah which no religious or irreligious man may cross, from the evil which enters the world and exists it, from what descends from the heavens and ascends to them, from the trials of the day and night, from what roams about during the day and night, except what brings good, O Merciful.' When the Prophet (ṣ) recited it, the firebrand fell on the body of the Devil."

Al-Ḥasan said, "I have come to know that Jibrīl once came to the Prophet (ṣ) and said, 'A party of jinn is conspiring against you. So when you enter the evening, read Āyah al-Kursī (Qur'an, 2:255).'"

The Prophet (ṣ) said, "Once, a devil came to me, quarrelled with me, and I caught hold of his neck. By Him who sent me as a true messenger, I did not let him go until the saliva of his tongue touched my hand. Had not my brother Sulaymān called me, the devil would have remained lying down in the mosque."

The Prophet (ṣ) said, "Satan does not walk a route which is used by 'Umar." This is because his heart was free from greed. So remove it by sincere remembrance of Allah. Be like him who takes medicine after purging his bowels, which were full of undigested food. So just as you first have to purge your bowels and clear it from congested stools for the medicine to take effect, you first you have to clear your heart from passion and greed if you want to get the benefit of medicine. When the remembrance of Allah enters a heart free from thoughts other than of Allah, Satan flees from it in the same way disease is repelled when medicine enters a stomach free of food.

It was related that Satan will misguide whoever he has got control over and lead him to an endless pit of fire. Piety and remembrance of Allah remove Satan. Moreover, prayer makes the pure, disclosing its virtues and faults. The prayer of a man whose heart is filled with passion and greed is not accepted. So it is beyond doubt that Satan will not leave you in that state, but his machinations in you will increase, for to use medicine before purgation causes more harm. If you want to be free from Satan, fill your heart with God-fearingness and apply the medicine of the remembrance of Allah; Satan will flee away from you as he fled from 'Umar.

Wahb ibn Munabbih said, "Fear Allah." A sage said, "Wonder is for one who does not do good deeds after knowing them, but follows Satan, knowing his transgression."

Allah says, "Your Lord says, 'Call on Me and I shall answer you'" (Qur'an, 40:60). You call Him, but He does not respond to you; you remember Him, but Satan does not flee from you. The reason is that you are not in a state of remembrance and supplication.

The reason supplications go unanswered

Ibrāhīm ibn Adham was asked, "What is the matter with us that we supplicate, but our supplication is not answered, although Allah says, 'Call on Me and I shall answer you' (Qur'an, 40:60)?" He replied, "The cause is that your hearts have died." He was asked, "What has caused their death?" He said, "Eight bad habits bring about the death of the heart: You know your duties to Allah, but you do not fulfil them; you recite the Qur'an, but you do not consider its promise of punishment; you say that you love the Prophet (ṣ), but you do not follow his actions; you say that you fear death, but you do not prepare for it; Allah says Satan is your enemy, but you seek help in sinful acts; you say you fear Hell, but you keep your body immersed in it; you say you love Paradise, but you do not do anything for it; when you get up from bed, you conceal your sins and disclose the sins of others, thereby displeasing your Lord. How can He answer your supplication?"

Is Satan one or many? Knowledge of this is unnecessary for actions. However, every sin has its own Satan who calls to it. The

Prophet (ṣ) said Khinzib is the name of the Satan of ablution. So the number of Satans is many.

The angels are great in number as well, and every one of them is entrusted with an action. The Prophet (ṣ) said, "To each believer, a hundred and sixty angels have been assigned to ward off from him what he cannot ward off alone. Seven of such angels have been engaged for the eyes only, removing injurious things from them just as flies are driven out from a pot of honey. If any man was entrusted to himself for even a moment, a party of Satan would lift him away."

It was related that when Adam was sent down to earth, he said, "O Lord, they have created enmity between me and Satan. If you do not help me against him, I will have no strength to fight against him." Allah replied, "No child will be born except that he will have an angel with him." Adam said, "O Lord, give me more." Allah said, "I shall give one punishment for each sin, but I shall give ten rewards or more for one good deed." Iblīs then said, "O Lord, I shall have no strength to fight against a man whom You have honoured." Allah said, "A child will be born to you along with the birth of a child." Satan said, "Give me more power." Allah said, "Your riding armies and infantry will gather against him, and you will be co-sharers in their children and wealth."

Kinds of jinn

The Prophet (ṣ) said, "Allah created three kinds of jinn. One kind of jinn includes serpents, scorpions and worms of earth. Another kind roams in the sky like air. For another kind there are rewards and punishments."

Kinds of men

Allah likewise created three kinds of men. One kind is beastly. Of this kind, Allah says, "They have hearts with which they do not understand, and they have eyes with which they do not see, and they have ears with which they do not hear. They are like cattle, or rather in worse errors" (Qur'an, 7:179). Another kind of men has a human body, but its heart is like that of Satan. Still another kind of men will remain within the shade of Allah on the day on which there will be no shade except His.

The figures of devils and angels

Devils and angels have figures which cannot be seen by men except with the light of prophethood. The Prophet (ṣ) saw Jibrīl twice in his form. This took place when the Prophet (ṣ) wanted to see his actual figure. Once, he saw him in the cave of Ḥirā', covering the space between east and west, and at another time near the farthest Lote tree in the night of his ascension to heaven. At other times, he saw him in the form of a man.

Evil thoughts

Machinations of Satan are very subtle. The Prophet (ṣ) said, "Allah will forgive the thoughts of man which arise in the heart until he does not disclose them in words or translate them into action." He also said, "Allah says to the recording angels, "Do not write when one of My servants intends to commit a sin; but if he does it, then write it down as an evil deed. And when he wishes to do a good deed and translates it into action, write for him ten merits."

It appears from the above that the intention to commit a sin is forgiven. On the contrary, if one intends to do good without translating it into action, merits up to seven hundred times are written for one.

Another *ḥadīth* says, "Allah says, 'I forgive whoever intends to commit a sin without translating it into action.'"

Allah says, "Whether you manifest what is in your minds or hide it, Allah will call you to account according to it; then He will forgive whom He pleases and chastise whom He pleases" (Qur'an, 2:284).

He also says, "Follow not that of which you have not the knowledge. Surely hearing, sight and the heart, all of these, will be questioned about that" (Qur'an, 17:36). It appears from this that actions of the heart will be taken into account and are ordinarily not forgiven, for Allah says, "Allah does not call you to account for what is vain in your oaths, but He will call you to account for what your hearts have earned" (Qur'an, 2:225). So there are conflicting views about whether or not a man will be punished for his thoughts. The solution to us is as follows.

Four stages of thought

There are four stages in the formation of a thought: the rise of a thought in the heart, the inclination of passion, the judgement of the heart and will and determination.

These four stages of a thought come in order. For instance, a woman walks behind a man. It occurs in the heart of the man after seeing the woman that she is walking behind him. This is the sudden rise of a thought in his heart. Next, he thinks that he should see her again by averting his glance. This is the second stage. In the third stage, the heart gives the order to translate this inclination into action and, as a result, he directs his look to the woman.

Between the second and third stages are hurdles such as shame and fear. Out of fear or shame, he may not look back. In the fourth stage, there is will and determination to see the woman. It is will with action.

12
Punishment

There is no punishment in the first stage, as man has no control in the sudden rise of thought in the heart. In the second stage, too, there is no punishment for the above reason. The Prophet (ṣ) said regarding these two stages, "A thought that naturally arises in the heart of my followers is pardonable."

'Uthmān ibn Maẓ'ūn once asked the Prophet (ṣ), "O Messenger of Allah, my heart tells me to divorce Khawlah." The Prophet (ṣ) replied, "Go slowly, for marriage is my way." 'Uthmān said, "My heart wants me to be important." The Prophet (ṣ) replied, "Fasting among my followers works like impotency." 'Uthmān said, "My heart wants me to be a hermit." The Prophet (ṣ) replied, "Stop! Jihad and pilgrimage are the asceticism of my followers." 'Uthmān said, "My heart wants me to give up meat." The Prophet (ṣ) replied, "Stop, for I love it."

There was no will or determination to do these things. For this reason, the Prophet (ṣ) advised mutual consultation before making a decision.

In the third stage, the heart considers whether the previous thought should be translated into action. This condition of the heart is situated within willingness and unwillingness. What is subject to one's willingness will meet with punishment, and what is not subject to it will receive no punishment.

In the fourth stage, there is determination to translate the evil thought into an action for which there is punishment. But if it is not acted on, then there is room for doubt as to whether it will be punished or not. If the person fears Allah and does not repeat the sin after repentance, he will get a reward, even though his evil intention is a sin; but to refrain from it for fear of Allah is a virtue.

He who intends at night that in the morning he will kill a Muslim or commit fornication with a woman and then dies that night will die with that intention and will be resurrected in that state.

The Prophet (ṣ) said, "When two men face each other with their arms, the killer and the killed will both go to Hell." He was asked, "O Messenger of Allah, we understand why in the case of the killer. But why will the one killed go to Hell?" The Prophet (ṣ) said, "The reason is that he intended to kill his companion."

So Allah will punish for will and intention. Pride, self-praise, show, hypocrisy, hatred and other evil thoughts of the heart will surely meet with punishment.

The heart is the root, so it is fit for punishment. The Prophet (ṣ) said, "God-fearingness is here, pointing to the heart. And Allah says, "There does not reach Allah their flesh nor their blood, but to Him is acceptable the guarding (against evil) on your part" (Qur'an, 22:37).

The Prophet (ṣ) said, "The thing which irritates is sin." He also said, "What gives consolation in the heart is virtue, though men may give you one legal ruling after another." So if a man finds a woman in his bed in the dark, thinks that she is his wife and then cohabits with her, he commits no sin. But if he cohabits with his wife, thinking that she is a strange woman, he commits a sin. So every action is not an action of a body part, but an action of the heart.

13

Constant changes of the heart

Effects on the heart come from different sources. The heart is a target at which arrows are shot. When anything appears in the heart, it creates some effect; the opposite thing changes that effect. If, for example, Satan calls to passion, an angel removes it from the heart. Allah says, "We will turn their hearts and their sights" (Qur'an, 6:110).

Allah has created the human heart a wonderful thing. When the Prophet (ṣ) took an oath, he would sometimes say, "By Him who overturns hearts." Similarly, he would often say, "O overturner of hearts, keep my heart firm on your religion." Hearing this, the Companions once asked, "Are you afraid, O Prophet of Allah?" He answered, "Who will give me assurance when the heart is between the two fingers of the Merciful, who changes it as He wills."

Similitudes of the heart

The Prophet (ṣ) set forth three similitudes of the heart: "The heart is like a sparrow which He changes every moment"; "The heart in its change is like water in a pot when it is made hot"; and "The heart is like a wing in an open field to be turned over and again by wind."

The heart is of three kinds with regard to virtues, vices and doubtful matters. The first kind of heart is made of God-fearingness nurtured by divine services and free from bad qualities. Therein appear good thoughts from the unseen treasure house of the spiritual kingdom, and wisdom leads the good thoughts which appear in it to know of subtle affairs and gives clues to secret matters of fortune. One can know this by the light of insight. It then commands that there is no alternative but to translate it into action. The angel looks at such a heart and sees it naturally pure, cleansed by God-fearingness, nurtured by the rays of the intellect, or polished by the sparkling light of divine knowledge. Moreover, the angel helps such a heart. Allah says, "Then as for him who gives away and guards (against evil) and accepts the best, We will facilitate for him the easy end" (Qur'an, 92:5-7). This heart is also blessed with particular virtues—gratefulness, patience, God-fearingness, poverty, asceticism, love, contentment, reliance on Allah, good thoughts—and becomes free from vices and evils. Allah speaks of such a heart: "Now surely by Allah's remembrance are the hearts set at rest" (Qur'an, 13:28). In another verse, "O soul that is at rest, return to your Lord, well-pleased (with him), well-pleasing" (Qur'an, 89:27-28).

The second kind of heart is full of passions, low desires and other evils. The doors of Satan remain open to it, and the doors of angels remain closed to it. Regarding such a heart, Allah says, "Have you seen him who takes his low desires for his god? Will you then be a protector over him? Or do you think that most of them do hear or understand? They are like cattle, or rather straying farther off from the path" (Qur'an, 15:43-44). Similarly, He says "It is alike to them whether you warn them or warn them not: they do not believe" (Qur'an, 36:10).

The third kind of heart is a mixture of good and evil. Sometimes good leads one to guidance, and sometimes evil deeds lead to misguidance and error. The heart helps him in his guidance and misguidance. The forces of devils and the forces of angels fight in one's heart until either of them becomes victorious.

Book 2
Disciplining the self

Introduction

Know that the Prophet of Allah was a possessor of good character and conduct. Good conduct is half of religion, the fruit of the efforts of God-fearing men, and an important quality of worshippers of Allah. Bad conduct is a ruinous poison, a dangerous wound in the brain and much-condemned evil.

There are many doors of bad conduct which remain open to the fire of Hell as the doors of good conduct are open towards the bliss of Paradise. Bad conduct is a disease of the heart which ruins everlasting life. If effort is required to save the temporary body from disease, how much effort is necessary to save the heart from its everlasting diseases?

In the following verse, Allah says of the treatment of heart, "He will indeed be successful who purifies it, and he will indeed fail who corrupts it" (Qur'an, 91:9-10). In this book, we shall describe the diseases of heart and their cures.

1
Merits of good conduct

Know that Allah praised His Prophet, saying, "Most surely you conform (yourself) to sublime morality" (Qur'an, 68:4). 'Ā'ishah said, "The Qur'an is the conduct of the Messenger of Allah." When a man asked the Prophet (ṣ) about good conduct, he recited the following verse: "Take to forgiveness and enjoin good and turn aside from the ignorant" (Qur'an, 7:199). Then he explained good conduct, saying, "Good conduct is to seek reconciliation with those who avoid you and pardon those who oppress you."

The Prophet (ṣ) said, "I have been sent to perfect the noble qualities of character." He also said, "Good conduct will be the heaviest of all attributes in the Balance on Resurrection Day."

A man once came to the Prophet (ṣ) and said, "O Messenger of Allah, what is religion?" He replied, "Good conduct." Then the man came from before the Prophet (ṣ) and asked, "O Messenger of Allah, what is religion?" He replied, "Good conduct." Then he came from his left side and asked, "What is religion?" He replied, "Good conduct." Then he came from behind him and asked the same question, and the Prophet (ṣ) replied as before. Then, looking at him, the Prophet (ṣ) said, "Not to be angry is good conduct."

The Prophet (ṣ) was asked, "What is misfortune?" to which he replied, "Bad conduct."

A man asked the Prophet (ṣ), "Give me some advice." The Prophet (ṣ) said, "Fear Allah wherever you are." The man said, "Give me more advice." He said, "If you commit an evil, do a good action soon after it and the evil will vanish." The man said, "Give me more advice." He said, "Treat people well."

When asked, "What is the best action?" the Prophet (ṣ) replied, "Good conduct."

The Prophet (ṣ) said, "Allah will not throw into Hell someone whom He gave a good temperament and appearance."

He was once told, "A certain woman fasts every day and prays every night, but has a bad temper and troubles her neighbours with harsh words." He said, "There is no good in her, and her place is in Hell."

Abū al-Dardā' said, "I heard the Prophet (ṣ) say, "The first to be placed in the Balance is good conduct and benevolence. When Allah created faith, it said, 'Give me strength,' so Allah gave it strength through good conduct and benevolence. When Allah created infidelity, it said, 'O Lord, give me strength,' so He gave it miserliness and bad conduct."

The Prophet (ṣ) said, "Allah preferred this religion for Himself. There will be no good in your religion except good conduct and benevolence. Adorn your religion with these two virtues."

He said, "Allah created good conduct as the best thing."

He was asked, "O Prophet of Allah, who is best among believers." He replied, "He who is best among them in good conduct."

He said, "Do not entertain the people with your wealth, but entertain them with a smiling face and good conduct."

He said, "Bad conduct destroys worship just as a condiment destroys honey. So make your conduct good."

Al-Barā' ibn 'Āzib said, "The face of the Prophet (ṣ) was the most beautiful, and his conduct was the best."

The Prophet (ṣ) would say in supplication, "O Allah, you have made good my constitution, so make good my conduct." And he would pray frequently, "O Allah, I ask You for health, peace of mind, and good conduct."

The Prophet (ṣ) said, "Honour a believer for his religion and think him superior for good conduct and wisdom."

Some Bedouins once came to the Prophet (ṣ) and asked him, "What is the best thing which has been given to men?" He replied, "Good conduct."

He said, "He who will be dearest and nearest to me on Resurrection Day will be a man of good conduct."

He said, "Take no account of the works of a man who lacks on of these: God-fearingness, which restrains him from infidelity; patience, which restrains a fool; or good conduct, with which he lives in society."

The Prophet (ṣ) used to say at the beginning of his prayer, "O Allah, guide me to good conduct. Nobody except You can guide me to it."

Anas said, "We were once with the Prophet (ṣ), who said, 'Good conduct removes all faults just as the rays of the sun melt snow.'"

The Prophet (ṣ) said, "Good conduct is part of the fortune of a man."

He said to Abū Dharr, "O Abū Dharr, there is no wisdom like effort, and there is no virtue like good conduct."

He said, "A true Muslim can attain by his good conduct and high rank the rank of someone who fasts and prays at length."

The Prophet (ṣ) said to his Companions, "I saw a wonderful dream. I saw one of my followers sitting on his knees, and between him and Allah was only a veil, which was removed by his good conduct, and so he became close to Allah."

He said, "A man will attain a high rank and an honourable place in the next world by dint of his good conduct, even if his works are few."

He said to 'Umar, "O 'Umar, by Him in whose hand is my life, Satan does not tread a path which you tread."

He said, "Bad conduct is a sin which has no pardon, and bad ideas are a fault which spreads."

He said, "A man reaches the lowest stage of Hell for his bad conduct."

Traditions from Companions and early Muslims

The son of Luqmān asked his father, "O father, which fine qualities in a man's conduct are good?" Luqmān said, "Religion, treatment, shame, good conduct and generosity." When these five qualities are united in a person, he becomes pure, God-fearing, a friend of Allah and freed from Satan."

Al-Junayd said, "Four virtues raise a man to the highest rank, even should his works and knowledge be little: patience, modesty, generosity and good conduct. Good conduct completes faith."

Yaḥyā ibn Mu'ādh said, "Bad conduct is the worst evil. Even if a person had many virtues alongside it, they would not do him any benefit. Good conduct, on the other hand, is a good attribute. Even if a person had many sins alongside it, they would not do him any harm."

Ibn 'Abbās was asked, "What is honour?" and he replied, "Allah explains it in the Qur'an: 'Surely the most honourable of you with Allah is the one among you who is most careful (of his duties)' (Qur'an, 49:13)."

It is said, "Every building has a foundation, and the foundation of Islam is good conduct."

2
Good conduct

Know that Allah said He created man out of clay and infused His spirit into him. Then the angels prostrated before him. It appears from this that there is a connection between body and earth and between the heart and the Creator. So human nature is rooted in the heart, and actions flow from it. If good actions come out of the heart, it assumes good conduct, and if evil actions come out of it, it assumes bad conduct.

Four things are therefore involved: doing good or bad actions, possessing power to do actions, having knowledge of both, and a condition of the heart by which it inclines to one side or the other and which renders the good or bad actions easy to do. Owing to his attachment to either of them, conduct arises.

Just as a man cannot be called beautiful if he has only two beautiful eyes but no beautiful face or nose, he cannot be said to possess good conduct if he has only one of the above attributes. And just as a beautiful man is someone who has proportionate and beautiful limbs, a man is said to have good conduct if he has in him all these qualities proportionately.

The nature of heart is of four kinds: the power of discerning knowledge, the power of administration or anger, the power of greed and the power of adjusting the above three natures. If knowledge manifests and becomes mature, truth can be ascertained from falsehood, good from bad. So knowledge is the root of good conduct. Allah says, "Whoever is granted wisdom, he indeed is given a great good" (Qur'an, 2:269).

When anger conducts itself under knowledge and Sharīʿah, it can be termed "beautiful." When greed becomes subject to wisdom and shame, it can also be termed "beautiful." The power of adjusting the natures or judgement is beautiful when anger and greed are guided by wisdom and Sharīʿah. The beauty of anger is called "bravery," and the beauty of greed is called "patience." If anger exceeds the limit of moderation, it is called "cowardice." If greed exceeds moderation, it is called "hope against hope." And if it descends, it is called "sluggishness."

Moderation in greed is good, while the two extremes of greed are bad. If wisdom is used immoderately, it is called "deception." If it reaches the extreme, it is called "genius." The middle course is called "wisdom."

So there are four basic qualities of good conduct: knowledge, bravery, patience and the power of adjustment or judgement. Other qualities are their branches. Nobody was blessed with all these qualities except prophets. However, these qualities differ in people other than prophets. He who is devoid of these qualities is near the accursed Devil.

The Prophet (ṣ) was sent to perfect good conduct and good manners, and the Qur'an praised the believers for possessing these qualities: "The believers are only those who believe in Allah and His Messenger then they doubt not and struggle hard with their wealth and their lives in the way of Allah; they are the truthful ones" (Qur'an, 49:15). These are also those who are truthful. Allah describes the Companions of the Prophet (ṣ) as "firm of heart against the unbelievers, compassionate among themselves" (Qur'an, 48:29).

3

The changing of one's nature

It has been argued that one's nature cannot be changed. This mistaken belief arises for two reasons. The first reason is that just as the figure of a man or his colour cannot be changed, or a man cannot be made short or long, or a black man cannot be changed to a white man, so, too, one's nature cannot be changed. Another reason cited is that in spite of our efforts, sexual passion, anger and so on cannot be uprooted, so to strive to control them is useless.

The answer to these objections is as follows. If one's nature were unchangeable, then sermons, education and learning would be useless, yet the Prophet (ṣ) said, "Make your conduct good." If this objection were true, his advice would be meaningless. Also, when the nature of lower animals can be changed by training, human nature can all the more be changed by training, education and habit.

Everything in the world is made of two elements. Man has power over one of them, but not the other. The sun, moon, stars and the external and internal forms of animals cannot be changed.

But Allah created another element which may develop into perfection according to certain rules and regulations. For instance, a paddy seed, if kept under certain conditions, can develop into paddy plants, but cannot produce a mango tree or a date tree. Such is also the case with passion, anger, pride and the like. If they are kept under control, they cannot take to the highest degree of progress or be uprooted at will. Keeping them under control is the cause of salvation.

The classes of men according to nature

The first class of men are inattentive. They do not distinguish between truth and falsehood and remain with the nature with which they are born. Through training, their conduct can become good. The second class of men can know the evil actions of others, are not habituated to good actions and are prone to evil. The men of this class are to give up the habits of evil actions, and the seeds of good actions are to be sown in their souls. The third class of men believe bad conducts to be good. The fourth class of men are bred on evil.

The first kind of men, therefore, are illiterate to the extreme; the second kind, illiterate and misguided; the third kind, illiterate, misguided and sinful; and the fourth kind, illiterate, misguided, sinful and dishonest. The second reason for the above argument is that greed, passion, anger and pride can be uprooted, but this is a mistaken belief. These attributes are to be brought under control, not uprooted, as they are necessary. If man did not have an appetite for food, he would be ruined. The object, therefore, is to use them in moderation.

The Prophet (ṣ) said, "I am only a human being and get angry as others get angry." When anything doubtful was said to him, he used to get angry, such that his two cheeks turned red. With regard to controlling anger, Allah says, "Those who restrain (their) anger and pardon men" (Qur'an, 3:134). He did not say to uproot it.

It is better to adopt a middle course in conduct and not the two extremes. Benevolence is a good quality and is the middle course between the two extremes of extravagance and miserliness. Allah praised it in the verses "They who when they spend, are neither extravagant nor parsimonious, and (keep) between these the just mean" (Qur'an, 25:67) and "Do not make your hand to be shackled to your neck nor stretch it forth to the utmost (limit) of its stretching forth" (Qur'an, 17:29). It is likewise best to adopt a middle course in desire for food. Allah says, "Eat and drink and be not extravagant; surely He does not love the extravagant" (Qur'an, 7:31). Moreover, the Prophet (ṣ) said, "The middle course is best."

Thus, just as heat is between scorching rays and snow, free from the two extremes, benevolence is the middle course between extravagance and miserliness, and bravery is an attribute between haughtiness and cowardice.

4
The means of acquiring good conduct

Know that good conduct is the name bringing appetite and anger under the control of the intellect and Sharīʿah. This middle course can be acquired in two ways. The first way is to perfect God-given powers and inborn qualities.

Some men have been created with a perfect intellect and good conduct, and their appetite and anger have been placed under the control of the intellect and Sharīʿah. As a result, these people become wise without education and receive good conduct without training. Such people include the prophets ʿĪsā and Yaḥyā. There are, however, many who can acquire these virtues by education and training through spiritual guides.

The second means is effort. For instance, if anybody wishes to acquire the virtue of benevolence, he must become habituated to giving charity in spite of his unwillingness to spend money. It will in turn become easy for him to spend. As another example, to acquire the virtue of modesty, a person is to follow the actions of the humble for a long time, after which it will become easy. The Prophet (ṣ) said, "Do divine service with contentment, if you can not do it, it is better to do it with patience in spite of unwillingness.

Attaining felicity though habituation

To attain felicity it is necessary to be persistent. It is not enough to hate sins, but rather one must find pleasure in doing good deeds. The longer one's life is, the more firm and perfect its good will be. When the Prophet (ṣ) was asked about felicity, he replied,

“To persist in acts of worship throughout life is felicity.” For this reason, the prophets and the friends of Allah disliked death, as this world is the seed ground for the hereafter. The more acts of worship one performs throughout a long life, the greater will be the reward, the purer will be the heart and the stronger and more deeply rooted will be one’s good conduct. For the object of spiritual works is its effect on the heart.

The object of good character and conduct is to sever the heart’s attachment to the world, confining it to the love of Allah. The greatest thing for the heart is its meeting with Allah. Good habits create light in the heart, a light which shows many wonderful things. Whoever finds pleasure in playing with pigeons spends the daytime under the sun without becoming tired. In like manner, he who is accustomed to theft takes pride in acts of theft, even though his hands are cut off and he is whipped. And effeminate males take pride in growing their hair long, painting their faces and mingling with females. All these are the result of habit.

The habituation of good deeds

One should likewise habituate oneself to doing good deeds. If they are done for a long time and are not given up, pleasure will come as a matter of course, just as it comes to the aforementioned people. Thus, if a man forms the habit of eating earth, he will find pleasure in eating it. So the heart will find pleasure in doing good deeds if one does them persistently over a long period of time.

Someone who wishes to be a good scribe, then, must persist in writing for a long time. Similarly, if someone wishes to acquire the qualities of patience, generosity, modesty and the like, he must stick to these habits in deed and behaviour. This is the only means of acquiring these qualities.

Acquiring knowledge is the result not of a day, but of endless days and nights in study. The natural food of the heart is knowledge, divine knowledge and love. But its taste might change because of an illness. Because of a stomach disease, for example, food may taste bland. So diseases of the heart must be removed by effort in order to acquire divine love and knowledge.

Causes of damnation

Damnation is brought on not by a one sin, but rather by sin after sin and by disobeying the commands and prohibitions of Allah. The same is true for minor sins. The repetition of a minor sin amounts to a great sin.

When one commits a sin, a black spot is put on the heart. Thus, when one sins repeatedly, the spots multiply and the heart eventually becomes enveloped in darkness. When death suddenly comes on such a man, he dies in that condition. Allah says, "No, what they used to do has become like rust on their hearts" (Qur'an, 83:14). 'Alī said, "Faith puts a white spot on the heart. The more faith increases, the more the white spot increases. When the faith of a man becomes perfect, his heart is filled with that light. And a black spot appears on the heart of a hypocrite. The more hypocrisy increases, the more the black spot increases. When hypocrisy is disclosed in full, his heart becomes completely dark."

Now you have come to know that good conduct sometimes proceeds from one's nature, sometimes is acquired by good deeds and sometimes is acquired by following the actions of good and religious people. Allah does not oppress any man, but man himself oppresses himself and becomes damned. Allah says, "So he who has done an atom's weight of good will see it and he who has done an atom's weight of evil will see it" (Qur'an, 99:7-8) and "They did not do Us any harm, but they made their own souls suffer the loss" (Qur'an, 2:57).

5
Methods to improve conduct

You now understand that, just as the middle course is the best for preserving physical health, so it is the best in the matter of conduct and the purification of the heart, and that drifting away from this middle course diseases the heart.

The treatment for the diseases of the heart is to remove from it evil qualities and habits and to adopt good qualities and habits. According to the Prophet (ṣ), every child is born in a sound innate disposition, but his parents make him a Jew, Christian or Zoroastrian. The child, therefore, acquires bad habit through his surroundings.

A change in the temperament of moderation indicates a disease in the body, the cure of which is its opposite. For instance, heat can be removed by cold, and vice versa, and fire by water. If one catches a cold, it can be treated by using hot things. Illiteracy can be removed by learning, miserliness by charity, pride by humility, and appetite by patience.

Likewise, the diseases of the heart can be removed by the bitter pills of patience and good works. The diseases of body result in the death of the body, whereas the diseases of the heart result in the death of the heart, which is everlasting.

Appropriate medicine for the heart can be prescribed by a spiritual physician or guide. He must first be acquainted with the diseases of his disciple and then cautiously treat them. If the disciple is ignorant of Sharīʿah, he must first teach him the fundamental principles of Islam. If he earns an unlawful income, he must be told to give it up. When outward sins are removed, the guide should look to the removal of the disciple's inner faults, character and conduct. If he has wealth beyond the limit of his necessity, he should tell him to spend it in charity. If he has pride and haughtiness, he must be taught to be humble by begging in marketplaces. If he finds him too clean, he should tell him to clean his own house and kitchen, for to worship the body is to worship idols.

Thus, the ordinary means of treating the diseases of the heart is to act against its low desires. Allah says, "as for him who fears to stand in the presence of his Lord and forbids the soul from low desires, then surely the garden—that is the abode" (Qur'an, 79:40-41).

6

Symptoms of the diseases of the heart and their treatment

The medicine of a diseased heart is to accustom it to an opposite attribute. If it has, for example, the disease of miserliness, its medicine is to give constant charity and spend money. But there is a limit to charity and expenditure. Whoever exceeds the limit has another disease—extravagance. He becomes like a man suffering from a cold who uses hot things which trouble him even more.

Our object is to reach a level of moderation and avoid the two extremes. The middle path is the straight path which is narrower than a hair and sharper than a sword. Whoever can remain on the straight path in this world can cross the Bridge easily in the hereafter. While crossing it, some will suddenly fall down, while others will traverse it like lightning. Allah says, "There is not one of you but will come to it; this is an unavoidable decree of your Lord" (Qur'an, 19:71). So the God-fearing are those who tread the straight path.

If a body part does not perform its function, it has a disease. If it does that function easily, it is sound. The eye has been created to see. If it does not see, it has a disease. Such is also the case for the ear and nose. The heart has been created for acquiring divine knowledge, love of Allah and finding pleasure in acts of worship. Allah says, "I have not created the jinn and the men except that they should serve Me" (Qur'an, 51:56).

Man cannot be distinguished from beasts except by his heart because, like beasts, he requires food, cohabitation, water and so on. The heart has the quality of recognising the nature of everything. He who knows Allah loves Allah. The sign that one loves Allah is that one places his love for Him above everything in this world. Allah says, "If your fathers and your sons and your brethren and your mates and your kinsfolk and property which you have acquired, and the slackness of trade which you fear and dwellings which you like, are dearer to you than Allah and His Messenger and striving in His way, then wait till Allah brings about His command" (Qur'an, 9:24).

He who loves anything more than Allah has a diseased heart. He is just like a person who loves to eat earth more than bread. Every heart is diseased, except the heart which loves Allah. There are hardly any physicians of heart at present, for the physicians themselves are diseased. A diseased physician can hardly treat himself, much less others.

Nowadays, people are addicted to the love of the world. For this reason, it is our duty to pray to Allah seventy times a day for keeping us on the straight path. Allah directed us to pray "Show us the straight path" (Qur'an, 1:6).

One day, a man dreamt of the Prophet (ṣ) and said to him, "O Messenger of Allah, you have said that the Sūrah Hūd has made you grey-haired. Why have you said that?" The Prophet (ṣ) recited the verse "Continue then in the right way as you are commanded" (Qur'an, 11:112).

To keep firm on the path is therefore very difficult. Still one should try one's utmost to remain on it or very near it. There is no salvation except for good deeds, which cannot be achieved without good conduct.

7
Ways to find one's faults

Know that Allah shows to one for whom He wishes good his faults. Whoever has deep insight has no fear. When a man can know his faults, he can try to remove them. But the majority of men remain ignorant of their faults.

There are four ways to discover one's faults. The first is to disclose one's faults and evils to one's spiritual guide, who can treat his diseases. However, spiritual guides are very rare nowadays.

The second way is to appoint a true and pious friend to detect one's faults and defects. A religious man takes to this method of finding out his own defects and shortcomings. 'Umar prayed, "May Allah show mercy to the man who points out my defects to me." When he asked Salmān about his faults, the latter told him, "I heard that you enjoy two curries when you eat and that you have two articles of clothes to put on—one for the day, and one for the night." 'Umar said, "Have you heard anything other than this?" Salmān said, "I have heard nothing except this." Salmān also once asked Ḥudhayfah whether he had found any hypocrisy in him. Thus the Companions of the Prophet (ṣ) inquired about their own faults.

When Dāwūd al-Ṭā'ī, who remained aloof from society, was asked, "Why do you not mingle with people?" he replied, "What benefit shall I derive from them when they conceal my faults and do not inform me?"

Now, however, things have changed. Whoever informs us of our faults is our great enemy.

The third way of knowing faults is to gather them from enemies. The attention of the enemies is on the faults of their adversaries. So there is some basis to their information about one's faults.

The fourth way is to mix with people and know their faults. If you see their faults, you may assume that you have those faults in you, as a believer is a mirror to another believer and sees his own defects in others. 'Īsā was once asked, "From whom have you learnt good manners?" He replied, "Nobody has told me. When I saw the faults of the ignorant, I at once gave them up."

Evidence from Sharī'ah for the diseases of the heart and their medicine

If you ponder over what has been described above, your insight will open and the diseases of heart and their treatments will be disclosed to you in the light of sure faith. If you are unable to achieve this, still you should not secede from faith and blind belief. This is a rank of faith, just as there are ranks in education, which comes after faith. Allah says, "Allah raises the rank of those of you who have faith and those having been given learning" (Qur'an, 58:11)

To go against passion is the greatest jihad. Whoever believes that the way to reach Allah is to act against low desires is among the believers. And whoever seeks the causes of these is among the educated. Allah says, "As for him who fears to stand in the presence of his Lord and forbids the soul from low desires, then surely the garden—that is the abode" (Qur'an, 79:40).

It is said that the verse "They whose hearts Allah has proved for guarding (against evil)" (Qur'an, 49:3) means that the love of greed in their hearts has been crushed.

The Prophet (ṣ) said, "A believer is beset with five afflictions. He is envied by another believer; a hypocrite harbours hatred towards him; an unbeliever fights him; Satan misguides him; and evil desires dispute with him." When evil desires become an enemy, it is obligatory to fight them.

Allah once revealed to Dāwūd, "Warn your followers of eating objects of greed, as greed stands between hearts with worldly attachment."

'Īsā said, "Blessed is he who has given up his present greed in the hope of getting a promised future reward."

When some people returned from jihad, our Prophet said, "Thanks to you! You have returned from the lesser jihad to the greater one." When asked, "O Prophet of Allah, what is the greater jihad?" he replied, "To fight passion is the greater jihad."

The Prophet (ṣ) said, "Whoever is at war with himself is a fighter."

He said, "Keep your hearts away from harmful things and do not run after your evil desires in violation of Allah's commands. If you do so, they will dispute with you on Resurrection Day. Then one of your body parts will curse another if Allah does not forgive and conceal."

Sufyān al-Thawrī said, "I have not treated a more serious disease than the disease of my heart. It is sometimes for me and sometimes against me."

Al-Ḥasan said, "As an unruly horse is to be kept by a strong rein, the disobedient heart of man should be kept by a firmer rein."

Yaḥyā ibn Mu'ādh said, "Fight your passion with the weapons of self-discipline, which are four: eating little, sleeping little, speaking only when necessary, and tolerating all the wrong people do to you. Passion dies with hunger, and sincere intention arises out of sleep deprivation. There is safety from dangers and difficulties by speaking little. If one tolerates others, one can reach one's destined goal. There is no greater difficulty than to tolerate the harsh treatment of others and their wrongs."

He also said, "The enemies of a man are three: the world, Satan and passion. So save yourself from the world by renouncing it, from Satan by disobeying him and from passion by giving up greed."

Ja'far ibn Muḥammad said, "The learned and the wise are unanimous that happiness cannot be achieved without giving up happiness."

It has been narrated that when Yūsuf was appointed treasurer of Egypt, he was travelling one day in the country with twelve thousand respectable men astride horses. At that time, Zulaykhah was seated by the side of the pathway of Yūsuf. She said on seeing him, "Glory to Allah, who made the kings slaves of sins and the slaves of Allah the worst beings." Yūsuf replied, as Allah revealed to him, "Allah does not destroy the rewards of those who do good, fear Allah and remain patient."

Yazīd al-Ruqāshī said, "O my friends, do not give me cold water in this world, as I may be deprived of it in the hereafter."

A man once asked 'Umar ibn 'Abd al-'Azīz, "When should I talk?" He replied, "When you wish to remain silent." The man asked, "When shall I remain silent?" He replied, "When you wish to talk."

'Alī said, "Whoever is eager to go to Paradise should remain free from worldly greed."

Since there is no path to felicity in the next world except to oppose passion and temptation, we should believe in the words of the learned and sages. Keep your heart and mind engaged in knowledge of Allah, the love of Allah and thoughts about Allah. Cut of all connections to achieve these things, for man has no power to achieve these without the company of Allah.

In the above matters, mankind is of four classes. The hearts of one class remain busy with the remembrance of Allah, not look at the world except for the bare necessaries of life. They are among those of great faith (*ṣiddīqūn*). This rank cannot be attained without effort for a long time and without patience with worldly pleasures and temptations for a long time.

Men of the second class remain busy with worldly affairs and remember Allah with their tongues, not with their hearts. They are among those who are ruined.

Men of the third class remain busy with religion and the world, but religion predominates in their hearts. They will enter

Hell, but will soon be rescued therefrom, for religion was strong in their hearts.

Men of the fourth class remain busy with religion and the world, but the world predominates in their hearts. They will have to reside in Hell for a long time, but will be rescued ultimately therefrom.

The lawful

Some say that to enjoy lawful things is lawful, but why should it be a cause of drifting away from Allah? The answer is that love of the world is the root of all evils. Those things which are outside the realm of necessity are part of the world and therefore become causes of being remote from Allah.

Ibrāhīm al-Khawwāṣ said, "Once, while staying on the hillock of al-Likām, I saw some pomegranates hanging from a pomegranate tree. I was inclined to eat some of them, so I took some, found them sour, threw them and went away. I then found a man lying on the ground, and many wasps were stinging him. I greeted him, and he replied and said, 'O Ibrāhīm.' I wondered how he had come to know my name and asked him, 'How do you know me?' He replied, 'Nothing is concealed from a person who knows Allah.' I said, 'I see that you are a chosen of Allah. Why, then, do you not pray to Allah to save you from the wasps?' He replied, 'You are also a chosen of Allah. Why, then, do you not pray to save yourself from the greed of eating pomegranates? The wounds of wasp stings will be disclosed in the next world in the form of greed for pomegranates and give you pain, but the sting of wasps will end in this world.' Then I left him."

Al-Sarī said, "My heart has been longing to eat walnuts dipped in honey for the last forty years, but I have not had them yet."

If the heart is not kept under control, it is not possible to tread the path of the next world by correcting and purifying it, as it will desire unlawful things. Whoever wishes to control his tongue from backbiting and useless talks must keep silent. He should engage in the remembrance of Allah and other duties of religion until the desire to hold useless talks leaves him. He should not utter except truth.

This is the condition of every passion or low desire. If it is not kept under control and within the limit of the necessary, it becomes strong. This is a danger of lawful things.

Allah says, "They rejoice in this world's life, and this world's life is nothing compared with the hereafter but a temporary enjoyment" (Qur'an, 13:26). He also says, "Know that this world's life is but play and amusement, pomp and natural boasting and multiplying among yourselves in riches and children" (Qur'an, 57:20).

Those Sufis who possessed uncommon fortitude said from experience that the possession of wealth makes the heart hard and keeps it away from the remembrance of Allah. From experience, moreover, they found that at the time of sorrows, the heart becomes soft, pure and fit for the acceptance of grace because of the remembrance of Allah. They came to know that there is salvation in long standing sorrows and ruination in long standing enjoyment.

They gave up the paths of greed with care and knew that there will be reckoning for lawful things, punishment for unlawful things and rebuke for doubtful things. So to avoid such things, restrain your eyes from the pleasures of the world and do not enquire about what will occur after death. The Prophet (ṣ) said, "Love what you wish to love, but you will have to part with it."

8
The signs of good conduct

The following are the signs of good conduct and the qualities of believers.

The Qur'an

Allah says:

Successful indeed are the believers who are humble in their prayers, and who keep aloof from what is vain, and who are givers of poor-rate, and who guard their private parts, except before their mates or those whom their right hands possess, for they surely are not blameable, but whoever seeks to go beyond that, these are they that exceed the limits; and those who are keepers of their trusts and their covenant, And those who keep a guard on their prayers; these are they who are the heirs. (Qur'an, 23:1-10)

They who turn (to Allah), who serve (Him), who praise (Him), who fast, who bow down, who prostrate themselves, who enjoin what is good and forbid what is evil and who keep the limits of Allah. (Qur'an, 9:112)

Those only are believers whose hearts become full of fear when Allah is mentioned, and when His communications are recited to them they increase them in faith, and in their Lord do they trust. Those who keep up prayer and spend

> *(benevolently) out of what We have given them.* (Qur'an, 8:2-3)

Similar conducts have been expressed in Qur'an, 25:63. These are the signs of a believer, which one should read very carefully in order to implement them in one's life, acquiring thereby the virtues of good conduct.

Ḥadīth

The Prophet (ṣ) said:

> A believer loves for others what he loves for himself.
>
> Whoever loves Allah and the hereafter, let him honour his guests.
>
> Whoever believes in Allah and the hereafter should honour his neighbour.
>
> Whoever believes in Allah and the hereafter should utter good words or remain silent.
>
> Whoever is a perfect believer is the best in conduct.
>
> When you see a believer silent and grave, draw close to him, as he is full of wisdom.
>
> Whoever is pleased with virtues and displeased with sins is a believer.
>
> No believer should look at his Muslim brother in such a way as to trouble his heart.
>
> It is unlawful for a Muslim to frighten another Muslim.
>
> If two companions consult with each other, they are under a trust established by Allah. It is thus unlawful for one of them to disclose the secrets of the other.

Good conduct comprises the following qualities: shame, to consider a calamity little, to wish everyone good, truthfulness, little talk, much worship, few shortcomings, gravity, patience, contentment, kindness, abstinence from begging, curse, rebuke, backbiting, hatred, miserliness, haughtiness and pride and to love and hate for Allah.

Yūsuf ibn Asbāṭ said, "There are ten qualities of good conduct: not to break promises, to do justice, not to take revenge, to recognise evil as sin, not to make excuses, to bear the harms of others, to restrain passion, to know one's own faults by seeing the faults of others, to smile at everyone and to talk to others with humility.

Examples of good conduct

The Holy Prophet was once walking with Anas when they met a Bedouin with a thick cloth on his body. The Bedouin threw the cloth round the neck of the Prophet (ṣ) and began to drag him with force. Anas said, "As an effect of this forced dragging, spots of the cloth appeared on his neck." The Bedouin said, "O Muḥammad, give me something of the wealth Allah has given you." The Prophet (ṣ) smilingly looked at him and ordered something to be given to him.

When Quraysh was troubling and oppressing the Prophet (ṣ) in the Battle of Uḥud, he said, "O Allah, forgive my people, for they are ignorant." Then Allah revealed this verse: "Most surely you conform (yourself) to sublime morality" (Qur'an, 68:4).

Ibrāhīm ibn Adham was once travelling through a desert when he met a soldier who asked him, "Are you a slave?" He replied, "Yes, I am a slave." The soldier asked, "Can you tell me where the inhabited country is?" He pointed to the grave. The soldier said, "I mean the inhabited country." He said, "The graveyard is the place of habitation." The soldier was enraged at this, bound him with a chain, whipped his back and took him to a town. The disciples of Ibrāhīm came to him, and the soldier told them about him. They said, "His name is Ibrāhīm ibn Adham, and he is a friend of Allah." The soldier then fell at his feet and begged his pardon. When asked why he called himself a slave, Ibrāhīm replied, "When the soldier was beating me with a stick, I prayed that he would enter Paradise. They asked, "Why did you pray that he would enter Paradise when he oppressed you?" He replied, "I know that I will be rewarded for his oppression, and I do not want anyone because of whom I will be rewarded to be a sinner."

A man once invited Abū 'Uthmān al-Ḥīrī to test him. When he went to the man's door, the man said, "Now there is nothing for food.' Hearing this, Abū 'Uthmān left. Before he had gone a distance, the man called him again. When he came again, the man said, "Return," so he returned. He called Abū 'Uthmān a third time, who went to the man again. The man said, "You have not come in time for food." Abū 'Uthmān left. When he called Abū 'Uthmān a fourth time, he went to him, and this time he also did not give him food. As Abū 'Uthmān was leaving, the man fell at Abū 'Uthmān's feet and said, "I have done this only to test you. How good is your conduct!" He said, "You have found in me the behaviour of a dog. If a dog is called for food, it comes, and it flees when driven away."

Abū 'Uthmān was once riding in the street when somebody threw some refuse on his head. He removed the refuse from his body and prostrated on the ground in gratitude and did not retaliate. He said, "If one is fit for Hell, will having refuse thrown on one not be a cause of gratitude?"

Sahl was asked about good conduct and replied, "The lowest form of good conduct is to tolerate others, not to take revenge, to show kindness to oppressors, to ask forgiveness for him, and to be kind to him."

Al-Aḥnaf ibn Qays was once asked, "From whom have you learnt patience?" and replied, "From Qays ibn 'Āṣim." He was then asked, "How did he learn patience?" He said, "He was once seated in his house when a black female slave brought him a cup of hot roasted meat. Suddenly, the cup fell from her hand and onto the head of his child, who died as a result. The female slave was greatly fearful of her master, who said to her, 'Have no fear. Go, you are free for the sake of Allah.'"

It was related that when little boys saw Uways al-Qaranī, they would throw pebbles at him, thinking he was a mad man. He would say to them, "O dear children, if you must throw pebbles, do so with little ones, so my legs will not bleed. For if I bleed, my ablution may break."

9

Improving the character of children

Know that improving a child's character and conduct is of supreme importance. Allah has entrusted to their parents. The heart of a child is as bright as a jewel and as soft as a candle, free from all impressions. Moreover, it is as soft as soft clay in which any seed can grow. If one's character and conduct is improved, one grows in such a condition and attains bliss in both this world and the next. If he commits sins and lives the life of a beast, he is doomed to failure and destruction.

Allah says, "O you who believe, save yourselves and your families from a fire" (Qur'an, 66:6). As parents save their children from the fire of the world, so, too, they should save them from the fire of Hell in the next world. This means that they should discipline them and keep them from bad company, luxurious habits, delicious dishes and beautiful clothes.

When a boy reaches the age of discretion, he should again be watched over carefully. During this period, he gives up things out of shame and takes up other things.

He should also be disciplined regarding eating and drinking. The following are some of the rules of eating and drinking:

- Food should be eaten with the right hand
- Eating should begin with the mentioning of Allah's name.
- Food should be taken from the side of the dish which is nearest.
- Food should not be taken before others begin to eat.
- Someone who is eating should not be stared at.

- Food should be chewed well and not hastily.
- Hands should not be wiped with clothes.
- Rice or bread without curry should sometimes be eaten.
- The harms of over eating should be known.
- The rewards of little food should be known.
- The education of children

Children should then learn the Holy Qur'an, then Ḥadīth, then the biographies of prophets, saints and sages. If they do not love them at the beginning of their lives, it will be disastrous for them afterwards, as soft hearts get both good and bad impressions in the early years.

They should not be given literature and love poems. They should not be allowed to sleep during the daytime because it creates idleness. They should also be forbidden to sleep on soft beds so that their limbs become strong. They should be given coarse clothes, coarse food and coarse beddings. They should not be allowed to play sports requiring hard labour. They should be encouraged to walk on foot.

They should be taught not to spit before others, not to clean their nostrils before others, not to yawn before others, to sit with others in a good manner, not to turn his back to anyone, not to sit placing one leg on another, not to talk too much, not to tell lies, to show respect to elders and seniors, not to speak indecently and not to rebuke and backbite about others.

When a boy reaches the age of discretion, he should be told to pray, fast Ramaḍān and observe religious duties. When he reaches youth, he should be educated about everything, including the reasons for observing religious duties. He should be taught that this world is short, the next world is everlasting, death is imminent, a wise man takes provisions for the next world from this world and other profitable lessons.

Sahl ibn 'Abdullāh al-Tustarī said, "When I was three years old, I watched the prayers of my maternal uncle at night. One day, he said to me, 'Why do you not remember Allah, who created you?' I said, 'How can I remember Him?' He said, 'When you go to bed at night, say three times without moving your tongue. 'Allah is with me. Allah is near me. Allah is watching me.' Then he said, 'Recite this seven times every night.' After seven days, he said, 'Recite this eleven times every night.' After one year, he said to me, 'Recite this until you go to your grave and it will be your friend in this world and the next.'

"I learnt the Qur'an by heart at the age of 7. At 12, I began to fast all the year round. I would purchase one dirham of wheat per day, prepare food with it, fast the day and break the fast with the bread alone, no condiments or salt. After one year, I began to fast three days at a time with break it the next day. Then I would fast three days at a time, then seven days. Thus I increased my fast gradually to twenty-five days at a time, without break. I spent twenty years of my life like this."

Modes of spiritual exercise

Whoever wishes to acquire bliss in the next world should observe some rules, holding firmly to the Qur'an. Obstacles in the path of religion should be removed as they may prevent one from spiritual progress. Allah says, "We have made before them a barrier and a barrier behind them, then We have covered them over so that they do not see" (Qur'an, 36:9).

There are four barriers before a religious disciple: a barrier of wealth, a barrier of honour, a barrier of sectarianism and a barrier of sins. The barrier of wealth can be removed if wealth is spend on only the bare necessities of life. The second barrier of honour and rank can be removed by shifting from a position of honour, name and fame. The third barrier is differences of opinion in religious matters. Blind faith in a sect must be removed from the heart, and one should firmly believe that there is no deity but Allah and that Muḥammad is His messenger and best guide. The fourth barrier is sins, which can be removed by repentance for past sins, restraint from acts of oppression, and compensation to the oppressed..

When these four obstacles are removed, one becomes like a person who prepares for prayer by performing ablution. One thereafter requires a spiritual guide to show him the straight path, as this path is just one, whereas the paths of Satan are many. One should be kept, as it were, within the boundaries of a fort, so that Satan cannot enter it. This fort of religion has four walls: solitude, silence, hunger and sleeplessness. These four things prevent Satan from entering the fort.

The object of a disciple is to purify the heart so as to behold his Lord therein and attain His nearness. Hunger reduces the blood of the heart, making it pure and bright. This brightness is the light of the heart. In addition, hunger melts the fat of heart, with the result that softness and humility enter. This softness is the key of spiritual insight, as the heart becomes hard. Whenever the blood of the heart reduces, Satan's path of circulation narrows.

'Īsā said, "O my disciples, keep your stomach hungry, so that you may see your Lord.

Sahl ibn 'Abdullāh al-Tustarī said, "The *Abdāl* attained their rank only through four qualities: keeping the stomach empty, sleeplessness, silence and solitude from the troubles of society."

It is a manifest truth that the heart becomes bright due to hunger. This is the fruit of experience.

Sleeplessness, too, makes the heart bright, pure and radiant. It adds to the brightness created by hunger, making the heart as bright as a bright star or a clear mirror, so that truth shines therein. Sleeplessness is the fruit of hunger and is therefore impossible with a full stomach. Too much sleep kills and hardens the heart. Sleeping only to the extent that is necessary is a means of seeing the unseen. The *Abdāl* eat when pressed by extreme hunger, sleep in cases of extreme drowsiness, and talk only when it is absolutely necessary. Ibrāhīm al-Khawwāṣ said, "It is the unanimous opinion of seventy truthful men that too much sleep is a result of drinking too much water."

Silence facilitates solitude. But a man of silence is not free from those who are ready to serve him. As a result, he spends lavishly, feeling joy in greed. Silence likewise strengthens the intellect and encourages God-fearingness.

Loneliness saves a man from work, brings the ears and eyes under control and opens the gates of the heart. However, it is only after shutting off knowledge gained through the five senses that knowledge from the depth of the heart can arise. Such knowledge is as clear and pure as water drawn from the bottom of a well. Thus, gaining knowledge through the five senses is not necessary.

Controlling evil propensities

After these obstructions are removed, a sojourner in the path of religion can advance towards the straight path. The propensities of the heart are the result of worldly attachment and obstructions, some of which are greater than others. In order to rid oneself of these, the following rules should be observed.

First, the easiest obstructions to remove should be removed first. In other words, love for wealth, name and fame, attachment for the world, inclination towards sin and so on should be removed from the heart. This requires sustained, long and continued efforts.

Another way is by silent remembrance of Allah. One will say, "Allah, Allah" until the tongue ceases to move, but the words persist in the heart. At this point, one must be cautious of questions which may arise, such as "What is the meaning of Allah?" These are the whisperings of Satan, which are of two kinds. One kind is that Satan casts doubt into the heart. One should drive this away by remaining busy with the remembrance of Allah. In this regard, Allah says, "If a false imputation from Satan afflicts you, seek refuge in Allah; surely He is Hearing, Knowing. Surely those who guard (against evil), when a visitation from Satan afflicts them, they become mindful, then lo, they see." (Qur'an, 7:200-201).

Book 3
Breaking the two desires

Introduction

Greed for food is a destructive evil. Because of it, Adam and Ḥawwā' were expelled from Paradise. They were prohibited to eat the fruits of a certain tree, but, prompted by a strong greed, ate of them anyway, with the result that their evil deeds were disclosed to them.

The stomach is the container of greed and the breeding ground for diseases and disasters. When the stomach is satisfied, sexual passion rises high and encourages companionship with women. Desire for name and fame grows from greed, as does the evil attributes of hatred, clashes of interests, pride, conceit, and so on. These can be removed by hunger.

1
Merits of hunger

Ḥadīth

The Prophet (ṣ) said, "Fight your passion with hunger and thirst, the merits of which are equal to those gained by jihad for the sake of Allah. There is no action dearer to Allah than hunger and thirst."

He said, "No angel from heaven comes to someone who fills his stomach."

He was asked, "Who is the best?" and replied, "Whoever eats little, laughs little and is satisfied with just enough clothes to cover his nakedness."

He said, "Put on old clothes and fill half of your stomachs with food and drink, as it is a portion of prophethood."

He said, "Contemplation constitutes half of worship, whereas little food is all of it."

He said, "Hunger is the chief of all actions, and wool clothes curb passion."

He said, "Whoever among you bears hunger for a long time and ponders about Allah will be best in rank among you on Resurrection Day. Whoever sleeps long, eats much and drinks much will be the greatest object of Allah's wrath."

The Prophet (ṣ) used to remain hungry without want. That is, he kept himself hungry willingly.

He said, "Allah glorifies before His angels men who eat and drink little in the world, saying, 'O angels, look at My servant. I am trying him in the world by food and drink. He gave them up with patience. Bear witness, O angels, that he forsook not a single morsel except that I shall grant him thereby a higher degree in Paradise."

He said, "Do not make your heart dead by excessive eating and drinking, as the heart is like a field of crops: When there is excessive water in a field, its crops are damaged."

He said, "The son of Adam does not fill anything worse than his stomach. A few small mouthfuls should suffice to keep his backbone erect. If he is not able to do this, then let him fill a third of his stomach with food, a third with drink and a third for breathing."

The Prophet (ṣ) said, "Those who are often hungry, thirsty and sad will be near Almighty Allah on Resurrection Day. They are God-fearing, honest men without shoes. They cannot be recognised upon sight. If they are absent, they are not missed. The provinces of the earth know them, and the angels of heaven encircle them. They are the best of the people on the earth, and the best in worship. People spread out their soft beds, but they use their heads and knees as beds. People destroy the character and conduct of prophets, but they preserve them. The world in which they roam weeps for them if they are lost. If none of them lives in a country, Allah becomes displeased with it. They are not desirous of the world as a dog is for a corpse. They live by eating leaves and vegetables, wear torn rags, have dishevelled hair, and are laden with dust. People think that they are diseased, but in fact they are not so. Some think that they have lost their intellect, but it is not so. Their attention is on the actions of Allah, who removes attachment to the world from them. They wander among the worldly men as men without interest, but there is endless honour for them in the next world.

"O Usāmah, when you see them anywhere, know the inhabitants of that place are safeguarded, as Allah will not punish the people among whom they live. The world is happy for them, and the Almighty is pleased with them. Accept them as your brethren. Perhaps you may attain salvation because of them. It is better to die with a hungry stomach and thirsty spleen, for you will have an honourable place, and the angels will be happy at the advent of your soul. Allah will also shower His blessings on you."

The Prophet (ṣ) said, "Wear wool clothes and fill half your stomach and you will enter Paradise."

'Īsā said, "O my disciples, keep your stomachs hungry and your bodies without clothes and Allah will appear in your heart."

It is written in the Torah, "Allah is displeased with a stout and strong learned man, as it is a sign of carelessness and overeating."

The Prophet (ṣ) said, "Satan runs through a man like the circulation of blood, so make his course narrow by hunger and thirst."

He said, "If anybody eats to his heart's content, he is afflicted with leprosy."

He said, "A believer eats with one gut, whereas a hypocrite eats seven." In other words, a hypocrite eats seven times more than a believer, or the passion and greed of a hypocrite are seven times greater than those of a believer. "Gut" here means "greed."

He said, "Knock on the door of Paradise and it will be opened for you." When asked how to do that, he replied, "With hunger and thirst."

Abū Juḥayfah was once belching in an assembly of the Prophet (ṣ), who said to him, "Lessen your belching, for whoever eats to his heart's content in this world will suffer hunger on Resurrection Day."

'Ā'ishah said, "The Prophet (ṣ) never ate to his heart's content. Sometimes I wept seeing the pangs of his hunger. I would pass my hand over his stomach, saying, 'My life be sacrificed for you! What is wrong with eating so much as to strengthen yourself and appease your hunger?' He would reply, 'O 'Ā'ishah, the prophets before me suffered more than this and kept patient until they went to their Lord. Their honour is unlimited and their rewards are profuse. I fear that if I enjoy the comforts of this life, my condition may be less than theirs tomorrow. It is thus better for me to bear troubles patiently today than see my lot reduced tomorrow. Nothing is dearer to me than to live together with my brethren and Companions with dignity.' After this talk, the Prophet (ṣ) did not live longer than seven days."

Anas said, "Fāṭimah brought a piece of bread to the Prophet (ṣ), who said to her, 'This is the first food to have passed the lips of your father in three days.'"

Abū Hurayrah said that the Prophet (ṣ) never ate wheat bread for three consecutive days, after which he passed away.

The Prophet (ṣ) said, "Those who remain hungry in this world will eat to their heart's content in the next world. Whoever eats until his stomach is full is the most hateful of men in the sight of Allah."

Traditions from Companions and early Muslims

'Umar said, "Beware of satiety, as it becomes a burden in life and a source of destruction after death."

Shaqīq al-Balkhī said, "Worship is a profession, its shop is solitude, and its weapon is hunger."

Luqmān once advised his son, "O dear son, when you eat until your stomach is full, good falls asleep, wisdom becomes inactive and the limbs become slothful."

Al-Fuḍayl ibn 'Iyāḍ said to himself, "What do you fear? Why do you fear hunger? The Prophet (ṣ) and his Companions used to remain hungry. Why do you neglect it?"

Kahmas used to say, "O my Lord, you keep me without food and clothes and allow me to sit close to You in the darkness. Tell me, my Lord, by what virtue have I achieved such fortune."

Mālik ibn Dīnar said, "O my Lord, I said to Muḥammad ibn Wāsi', 'O Abū 'Abdullāh, whoever has food proportionate to his wants and does not live depending on others is happy.' He said to me, 'O Abū Yaḥyā, whoever is pleased with Allah hungry in the morning and evening is happy.'"

Yaḥyā ibn Mu'ādh said, "The hunger of the hopeful is a cause of wakefulness, the hunger of the patient controls passion, and the hunger of the ascetics is wisdom."

It is written in the Torah, "Fear Allah when you eat until you are full, and remember hunger."

Abū Sulaymān said, "To forsake one morsel is more preferable to me than to spend the whole night in prayer."He also said, "Hunger is one of the treasures of Allah, which He gives it to those He loves."

Sahl al-Tustarī would not have a meal for twenty five consecutive days. One dirham would suffice him for a whole year. He would consider the rank of hunger with honour and go to extreme lengths, saying, "On Resurrection Day, no reward will be finer than giving up surplus food in following the practice of the Prophet (ṣ)."

Sahl also said, "There is nothing more profitable than hunger"; "I do not know of a more harmful thing to a man seeking the next world than repletion"; "Knowledge lies in hunger, and sin and ignorance lie in overeating"; and "No man does an act of worship better than opposing his passion after forsaking lawful things."

The Prophet (ṣ) said, "A third of the stomach is for food. Whoever eats more than that spoils his good deeds." When asked about additional merits, he said, "He will not get additional merits until hunger becomes dearer to him than overeating and until he prays at night in hunger. When he does so, he will be entitled to get additional rewards."

He said, "One cannot become one of the *Abdāl* if he does not love to remain hungry, sleepless and silent."

He said, "Of all the virtuous deeds which have descended from heaven to earth, the greatest is hunger. Of all the evils which have descended from heaven to earth, the worst is repletion."

He said, "The machinations of Satan leave whoever remains hungry."

He said, "Allah advances towards a man who is afflicted with hunger, disease, dangers and calamities, and releases some men from these things at His will."

He said, "Know that a man of the present age will not attain salvation until he destroys his passion by hunger, sleeplessness, and does hard labour."

He said, "There is no man in the world who can save himself from sin by drinking to his heart's content, even if he expresses gratitude to Allah. If such is the case for drinking water, how, then, must the case be for repletion?"

A wise man was asked, "How can I change my passion?" and replied, "Change your passion by hunger, thirst, humility, forsaking name and fame, placing them under the feet of those who seek the next world, and constantly opposing your passions."

'Abd al-Wāḥid ibn Zayd said, "The Merciful loves a hungry man. A man can walk on water by virtue of hunger, Allah giving him power to do so."

Bakr ibn 'Abdullāh al-Muzanī said, "Allah loves three men: a man who sleeps little, a man who eats little and a man who rests little."

'Īsā once fasted consecutively for two months and began to converse secretly with his Lord. When he remembered to have his meal, the secret conversation stopped, and he found his meal placed before him. He began to weep when his secret conversation suddenly ended.

It is said that Mūsā gained the power of secretly talking with Allah while he was fasting for forty consecutive days.

Benefits of hunger and harms of overeating

The Holy Prophet said, "Fight your passion with hunger and thirst." You may ask where this good of hunger comes from and what its cause is, given that it troubles the stomach. These words are like those of a man who thinks that, after benefitting from a bitter and distasteful medicine, a bitter medicine is beneficial.

Benefit arises not from the bitterness of the medicine. A physician knows the effect of such a medicine.

Similarly, sages and saints among the learned understand the benefits of hunger. Whoever believes the truth of remaining hungry gets the benefit. Allah says, "Allah will exalt those of you who believe, and those who are given knowledge, in high degrees" (Qur'an, 58:11).

The following ten benefits are obtained from hunger.

The first benefit of hunger is that it makes the heart pure, the conduct fresh and sight sharp. On the other hand, overeating makes one lazy, blinds the heart and increases heat in the brain, which produces a form of intoxication. It afflicts even one's thoughts, so that the power of thoughts are repressed. Also, when a boy eats much, his memory weakens, and he becomes a fool.

Abū Sulaymān al-Dārānī said, "Remain hungry, as it curtails passion, makes the heart soft, and yields divine knowledge."

The Prophet (ṣ) said, "Make the heart alive by laughing little and eating little, and make it pure by hunger. It will then become pure and clean."

He said, "Hunger is like lightning, overeating is like a cloud and wisdom is like the shower of rain."

He said, "Whoever eats to his heart's content and sleeps much, his heart becomes hard." He then remarked, "Everything has a *zakāh*, and the *zakāh* of the body is hunger."

He said, "If a man keeps his stomach hungry, his power to think increases and his heart becomes sharp and strong."

Al-Shiblī said, "I saw on the very day I remained hungry for the pleasure of Allah, the door of my heart opened to wisdom and knowledge in a way I had not seen before."

It is no secret that the ultimate object of worship is to acquire thinking power which leads to divine knowledge and true knowledge of everything. Repletion is an obstacle to that object, and hunger opens its door.

Divine knowledge is a door to Paradise, so it should be unlocked by hunger. In this regard, Luqmān advised his son, "O darling, when you fill the stomach with food, the power to think becomes dormant, wisdom becomes idle and limbs abstain from worship."

Abū Yazīd al-Bisṭāmī said, "Hunger is like a cloud. When a man feels hungry, his heart showers wisdom."

The Prophet (ṣ) said, "Hunger is the light of wisdom, and repletion keeps Allah at a distance. Loving the poor and being close to them bring one near Allah near. Do not, therefore, eat to your heart's content, as it will extinguish the light of wisdom from your heart. A man who spends the night with little food is surrounded by houris until morning."

The second benefit of hunger is that it makes the heart soft and pure, thus enabling one to taste the sweetness of the remembrance of Allah and of intimate discourse with Him. Many a man of the remembrance of Allah utters invocations inattentively, with the result that the heart does not find any taste therein, as it has no affect on the soul. Its taste is found in hunger.

Abū Sulaymān al-Dārānī said, "When my back becomes attached to my stomach, I can taste worship."

Al-Junayd said, "The hope of someone who wants to taste intimate discourse, yet places a dish of food between him and his breast, will not meet with success." He also said, When the stomach becomes hungry and thirsty, the heart becomes soft and clean. When it becomes satiated, it becomes blind and hard. When the heart tastes intimate discourse or invocations, it becomes easy to think about Allah, and acts of worship increase.

The third benefit of hunger is broken-heartedness which engenders modesty, as pride and rejoicing are removed by hunger. A man cannot understand the power and glory of Allah until he feels absolutely helpless and is surrounded by darkness, unable to gather food and drink. Once he realises the power and might of Allah, he becomes modest and submissive to Him.

When all the treasures of the world were presented to the Prophet (ṣ), he rejected them all and said, "I prefer, rather, to remain hungry one day and eat the next. On the day I remain hungry, I shall be humble with patience, and on the day I eat, I shall be grateful."

In short, the stomach and sexual passion are the doors of Hell, and their root is repletion. Conversely, humility and broken-heartedness are the doors of Paradise, and their root is hunger. Whoever closes the door of Hell opens then the door of Paradise as these doors are facing the east and the west. If someone comes near a door, he moves farther away from another.

The fourth benefit of hunger is that it reminds one of Allah's punishment. In the case of repletion, one forgets the pangs of hunger. Yūsuf was once asked, "Why do you suffer from hunger, though the treasures of kingdom are in your hands?" and he replied, "Satiated, I fear I may forget the sufferings of the hungry and the poor."

The fifth benefit of hunger is that the propensity of committing a sin is curbed, as hunger arrests the desire to sin and controls evil inclinations. The root of all sins is greed and physical strength, whereas the root of these two is repletion. So a small quantity of food weakens these things. To acquire power to control passion is the root of all fortunes and to submit to passion is the root of all misfortunes. Just as wild animals can be brought under control by hunger, so, too, unruly passions.

A sage was asked, "You have grown old. Why do you not take care of your body? Your body is getting black." He replied, "The body runs for enjoyment and wishes evil. I fear it may throw me into a deep ditch. I would rather trouble it than allow it to throw me into sins."

Dhū al-Nūn said, "Whenever I ate to my heart's content, thoughts of sin arose in my mind."

'Ā'ishah said, "After the demise of the Prophet (ṣ), the first innovation was repletion."

Hunger is not only useful for suppressing passion, but can also be called the touch stone of all useful things. For this reason, a great man said, "Of all the treasures of Allah, hunger is a most valuable jewel."

The least danger that can be averted by hunger is sexual passion, evil passion and the passion to talk. A hungry man does not wish to talk much and is rescued from backbiting, indecent talk and falsehood. Satiated, a man cannot control his sexual organ. And if he can control it for fear of Allah, he cannot control his eyes and mind and does not get pleasure from his invocations.

A wise man said, "If a sojourner to the next world keeps patient by observing the rules of religion and eats for one year bread only, without any curry, Allah removes from him the evil thoughts of enjoying women."

The sixth benefit of hunger is sleeplessness. Whoever eats to his heart's content drinks much, and whoever drinks much, sleeps much. As many as seventy truthful and pious men agree that excessive drinking brings on excessive sleep, which in turn spoils life, the most valuable possession of man.

The seventh benefit of hunger is that worship becomes easy. When one overeats, one becomes lazy and idle, making it hard to perform spiritual works.

Al-Sarī said, "I saw 'Alī al-Jurjānī eating wheat soaked in water and asked him, 'Why do you do this?' He replied, 'I can say 'Glory to Allah' seventy times during the time it takes to chew wheat bread. That is why I have not eaten bread for the last forty years.'"

See how concerned he was for his time. Every breath of life, then, is a valuable asset which should be utilised by collecting the wealth of the next world. This is easy for someone who has the habit of bearing hunger.

Abū Sulaymān al-Dārānī mentioned six harms of repletion: One does not get pleasure from invocation, one forgets matters of knowledge and wisdom, one loses the attribute of showing kindness to others, one finds it hard to perform acts of worship, sexual passion and greed become strong in one's heart, and when worshippers are engaged in mosques, he is confined in privies.

The eighth benefit of hunger is the preservation of health and the removal of diseases. A small quantity of food improves health and removes diseases. Excessive eating causes diseases in the stomach and veins, which prevent one from performing acts of worship, saying invocations and pondering. Hunger removes all these difficulties.

Al-Rashīd is reported to have summoned eminent physicians from India, Byzantium, Iraq and Abyssinia and said to them, "Give me a medicine which can prevent all diseases." The Indian physician said, "If you use black myrobalan, you will not be afflicted with any disease. The Iraqi physician said, "The medicine is white seeds of Helencha." The physician of Byzantium said, "Myrobalan makes the stomach narrow and creates disease. The white seeds of Helencha make the stomach soft and create disease." They asked, "What medicine, then, do you have?" He replied, "In my opinion, what will prevent all diseases is not to eat unless you feel hungry, and to stop eating while still hungry." They all said, "You haven prescribed the right medicine."

One of the People of the Book, who was a philosopher and physician, once heard the words of the Prophet (ṣ) "One third of the stomach is for food, one third for drink, and one third for breathing. He wondered at it and said, "I have never heard wiser words about moderation in food than these. They must be the words of a wise man." The Prophet (ṣ) said, "Gluttony is the root of disease, and restraint from food and drink is the root of cure. Let every body be accustomed to that to which it is used." The physician was astonished to hear this saying of the Prophet (ṣ)." The surprise of the above physician was, in my opinion, at this latter *ḥadīth* and not the former.

Ibn Sālim said, "Whoever eats only pure wheat bread with due propriety will not be afflicted by any disease except death." He was asked, "What is due propriety?" and replied, "To eat it after being hungry, and to rise before satiation."

A certain experienced physician said with condemnation of excessive eating: The most beneficial of all foods which are allowed to enter the stomach is pomegranate and the worst is salt, yet salt in small quantity is better than pomegranate in large quantity. The Prophet (ṣ) said, Fast and you will be healthy and the body will be cured of the diseases on account of sting, hunger and little eating and the heart will be free from the diseases of infidelity, self conceit and other diseases.

The ninth benefit of hunger is little expense. If you practice little eating, a little money will be sufficient. The stomach of a man who eats to his heart's content becomes heavy. Every day, he thinks about hoarding food, saying "What shall I eat today?" He roams throughout the day collecting food, then begins earning an unlawful income and committing sins, or he earns a lawful income but faces dishonour.

When asked about expensive foods, Ibrāhīm ibn Adham replied, "Give up these foods and lower their prices."

Sahl said, "A glutton is slack in worship if he is a trader, he is not safe from dangers, and he does not do himself justice when he receives something."

In a word, attachment to the world is a cause of man's destruction. The cause of this attachment is the stomach and sexual passion. And the cause of sexual passion is satisfying the stomach. Eating little removes all these evils.

The Prophet (ṣ) said, "Knocking on the door of Paradise begins with hunger." Whoever is satisfied daily with one piece of bread becomes free from want. He does not depend on people, becomes free of sorrow and suffering, and can engage himself fully in worship and the trade of the next world. He becomes one of those of whom Allah says, "Men whom neither merchandise nor selling diverts from the remembrance of Allah" (Qur'an, 24:37).

The tenth benefit of hunger is charity and forsaking self-praise. One who keeps himself hungry and thirsty, removes the hunger and thirst of another with his own meal and gives his excess food in charity to orphans and the poor. On Resurrection Day, he will take shelter under the shadow of his charity. What he eats is saved in the privy, and what he gives in charity is hoarded in his treasury. This is the gift of Allah. A man has no wealth except what he stores up in his treasury as charity, what finishes after he eats it and what gets old after he wears it. So eat little. To give excess food in charity is better than to eat to satisfaction.

Al-Ḥasan recited the verse "Surely We offered the trust to the heavens and the earth and the mountains, but they refused to be unfaithful to it and feared from it" (Qur'an, 33:72) and then he said, "Allah asked the angels to carry this burden. He asked them, 'Will you bear the responsibility of this trust?' If you make it beautiful, you will get rewards. If you make it ugly, however, you will be punished.' They replied, 'We shall not accept it.' He then presented it to man, who accepted it, as they are prone to oppress those ignorant of the Lord's commands. By Allah, they are now selling that trust in exchange for money. They make their houses beautiful, but make their graves narrow. They make their bodies tout and strong, but make their religion lean and thin."

The Prophet (ṣ) once saw a man with a big stomach and pointed at it, saying, "If you spent it on other affairs, it would be better for you.'

These are the ten benefits of hunger, each benefit having endless more benefits. Thus, hunger is the most valuable asset for the next world. In this regard, a sage said, "Hunger is a key to the next world and the door to asceticism. Eating with satisfaction is the key to this world and the door to greed."

2

How to break the greed of the stomach

Someone who wishes to tread the path of religion should observe the following rules to control his greed for food and drink.

The first duty is that he should not eat but lawful foods. If a man worships after eating unlawful food, it is as if he lives in a house built on the waves of the sea.

Besides this, there remains duties to be observed in connection with how much to eat, when to eat and what to eat.

How much to eat

Little food is good. However, a man should lessen his meal gradually and not at once.

There are four degrees of food according to the degree of piety. The first and the highest is the degree of a person with great faith (*ṣiddīq*), who eats what is absolutely necessary. Sahl said, "A man can worship by three things: life, intellect and strength. When a man fears loss of life and intellect, he should eat, and if he is fasting during those times, he should break the fast. The scholars agree that it is better to pray sitting out of weakness from hunger than to pray standing after eating with satisfaction." When asked about his quantity of food, Sahl said, "My meal for a whole year costs me nearly three dirhams. One day, I purchased wheat for a dirham, fine rice for a dirham and clarified butter for a dirham. After mixing them all, I made three hundred and sixty small pieces. Every evening, I break my fast with one piece only."

The second degree of eating consists of half a *mudd*, which is common practice. Half a *mudd* is the equivalent of ten morsels of food, and fills up nearly one-third of the stomach. The Prophet (ṣ) said, "A few morsels are sufficient for a man," recommending this quantity of food to be eaten. 'Umar used to eat no more than seven to nine morsels.

The third degree consists of one *mudd* per day, which may fill up two thirds of the stomach.

The fourth stage consists of a little more than a *mudd* per day. If a man eats in excess of this quantity, he commits the sin of extravagance, of which Allah says, "Eat and drink and be not extravagant" (Qur'an, 7:31).

The fifth degree is the general rule, which is eating when truly hungry, as people are often fooled by false hunger.

Signs of true hunger

The first sign of hunger is the will to eat only rice or bread, even though there is no curry. If there is no will to take rice or bread without curry, there is no real hunger.

The second sign of real hunger is that a one lick the plate or dish after a meal, not allowing any grease to remain therein.

How much the Companions and saints ate

It is true that the food of a Companion did not exceed a *sa'*, which is equal to 4 *mudds*. When he ate dates or grapes, it was one *sa'*. According to this calculation, the quantity of the Companions' daily meal was half a *mudd*, which filled a third of the stomach.

The Companion Abū Dharr said, "During the time of the Prophet (ṣ), my food every week would be a *sa'* of barley, whereas now you are eating fine bread. You are now enjoying two curries, whereas you would enjoy only one in the time of the Prophet (ṣ). You now have clothes for the day and clothes for the night.

The daily food of the People of the Veranda (*ahl al-ṣuffah*) was a *mudd* of food shared between two of them.

When to eat

There are four degrees regarding when to eat. The people of the highest degree eat once every three days or more. Some of them even ate no food for forty days. This was the practice Muḥammad ibn 'Umar, 'Abd al-Raḥmān ibn Ibrāhīm Duhaym, Ibrāhīm al-Taymī, al-Ḥajjāj ibn Furāfiṣah, Ḥafṣ al-'Ābid al-Maṣīṣī, al-Muslim ibn Sa'īd, Zuhayr, Sulaymān al-Khawwāṣ, Sahl ibn 'Abdullāh al-Tustarī and Ibrāhīm ibn Aḥmad al-Khawwāṣ. Abū Bakr used to eat every six days, 'Abdullāh ibn al-Zubayr and Abū al-Jawzā' every seven days and al-Thawrī and Ibrāhīm ibn Adham every three days.

Some scholars have said that some secrets of the unseen world are disclosed to a man who can remain without food for forty consecutive days. While such a man was passing by a Christian monk, he invited him to accept Islam and to forsake conceit. There were many arguments between them over this matter. The monk said to him at last, "'Īsā fasted for forty consecutive days. This was a miracle indeed. Had he not been a prophet, he could not have done so." The man said to him, "If I can fast for fifty consecutive days, will you accept Islam?" The monk replied, "Certainly." Thereafter the man fasted for fifty consecutive days. Then he said he could fast ten more days and did so. The Christian monk was astonished at this and said, "I did not think that any man could surpass 'Īsā in this matter." Then he accepted Islam.

In the second degree, some pious men fast from two to three days consecutively. This can be done by habit.

In the third degree, people eat once a day. This is the lowest stage for a sojourner in the path of the next world. If anybody eats more than once a day, it will be considered extravagance and repletion. Such a person has no hunger and is far from following the ways of the Prophet (ṣ).

The Companion Abū Sa'īd al-Khudrī said, "If the Prophet (ṣ) ate in the morning, he would not eat at night. And if he ate at night, he would not eat in the morning."

The Prophet (ṣ) once said to 'Ā'ishah, "O 'Ā'ishah, beware of squandering, and two meals a day is squandering."

One meal every two days is the practice of Sufis of the lowest rank, while the practice of one meal per day is a rank between the two. If anybody wishes to have one meal a day, he should do so after the night vigil prayer (*tahajjud*) and before the dawn prayer, as he gets the rewards of fasting during the day and remaining hungry at night.

Abū Hurayrah said, "The Prophet (ṣ) never prayed the night vigil prayer like you. He stood so long in it that his feet became swollen. And he would not eat after it like you. Instead, he used to have the pre-dawn meal." Similarly, 'Ā'ishah said that the Prophet (ṣ) used to remain hungry until the pre-dawn meal.

Meals should be divided into two. If it is said that two pieces of bread are sufficient, then a person should eat one piece of bread when breaking his fast and another for the pre-dawn meal. If he has the pre-dawn meal, hunger during the day does not become acute, and he can pray the night vigil prayer with peace of mind.

What to eat

The seeds of wheat are the best of foods. Meat and sweet things are the best, and salt and condiments are the worst. The second best kinds of food are curries cooked with oil. Yaḥyā ibn Mu'ādh said, "O company of truthful saints, keep your passion hungry for the feast of Paradise." Thus, there are abundant rewards for forsaking greed for even lawful things because of the harms which lie in partaking of them.

The Prophet (ṣ) said, "Those who eat fine flour are the worst." It is not unlawful, but the meaning of this *ḥadīth* is that if one is habituated to eating fine flour, he may become attached to the world, which leads to sin.

The Prophet (ṣ) said, "The worst of my followers are those whose goal is food of various kinds and fine clothes and who spend most of their time in useless talks." Allah revealed to Mūsā, "O Mūsā, consider yourself an inmate of the grave. My remembrance will restrain you from greed and evil desires. The earlier sages feared for those who enjoyed delicious food and remained busy in satisfying their natural propensities."

'Umar restrained himself from drinking cold water mixed with honey saying, "Save me from the responsibility of its account."

It was related that when Ibn 'Umar once fell ill and wanted to enjoy fresh fish. After searching, a fish worth a dirham was brought to him. The fish was fried and was presented to him with bread. A beggar then came, whereupon 'Umar ordered his servant to give him the fish with the bread. The servant gave him one and a half dirhams, keeping the fish and bread for himself. But he ordered his servant to give the beggar the fish and the bread in addition to the dirhams, saying, "I heard the Prophet (ṣ) say, 'Allah forgives the sins of someone who denies himself a thing for which he has greed to enjoy.'"

The Prophet (ṣ) said, "If you do not appease your rapid hunger with a piece of bread and a pot of pure water, a calamity will befall the world and its inmates."

'Umar once heard that Yazīd ibn Abī Sufyān would eat different types of food, so he said to his servant, "When Yazīd is served supper, inform me at once." The servant informed him accordingly and 'Umar went to him, sat by his side and began to eat with him. At first, meat soup was presented, followed by baked meat. As Yazīd was going to eat it, 'Umar said to him, "O Yazīd, one food after another? By Him in whose hand is 'Umar's life, if you forsake their *sunnah*, you will drift away from their path."

Yasār Ibn 'Umayr said, "I never prepared for 'Umar thin bread made of fine flour."

'Utbah al-Ghulām used to eat dough after baking it in the sun and say, "A piece of bread and salt are sufficient. Fried meat and delicious food can be eaten in the next world." His maid once said to him, "If you give me flour, I can prepare for you bread after it is baked in fire, and I can give you cold water to drink." He said to her, "O mother of so-and-so, I have driven out from me the dog of hunger.'

Shaqīq ibn Ibrāhīm said, "I met in Makkah Ibrāhīm ibn Adham, who was then weeping. Asked why, he said, "For the last thirty years, I have been desirous of eating *sikbāj* (meat cooked in vinegar), but I have restrained myself with great difficulty. Last night when I was asleep, I found a young man with a green pot in which there was *sikbāj*. He said to me, 'O Ibrāhīm, eat it.' I said, 'I shall not eat it. I have given it up for Allah.' He said, 'Allah has given it to you to eat.' Then I began to weep and ate it."

Mālik ibn Dīnar lived in Basra for fifty years, during which time he did not enjoy fresh or dried grapes. Mūsā ibn al-Ashajj said, "For the last twenty years, I had a desire to eat bread of fine wheat, but did not."

Abū Sulaymān said, "Salt is a thing of luxury." 'Alī said, "If a man eats meat continuously for forty days, his temper becomes harsh." A wise man said, "Eating meat continuously become like drinking wine."

Duties after eating

First, when a man wishes to cohabit with his wife he should do it before he eats.

Second, it is better not to sleep after repletion, as two harms arise: idleness and hard-heartedness.

Third, after a meal, it is better to converse, pray and say invocations, as these are nearer to expressing gratefulness. The Prophet (ṣ) said, "Digest your food with prayer and the remembrance of Allah, and do not sleep soon after a meal because your heart will grow hard."

Fourth, after a meal, a man should either pray four *rak'ahs*, say "Glory to Allah" a hundred times, or read a portion of the Qur'an.

Whenever Sufyān al-Thawrī ate his fill at night, he used to pray throughout the night. When he ate his fill during the day, he used to pray and read invocations. He said, "Fill the stomach of a black slave and exact from him hard work." Moreover, he would often say, "Exact from him hard work after satiating him."

Whenever you desire to eat some food or good fruits, you should eat it in lieu of a meal, so that you may gain strength. A wise man said, "Do not eat with desire. If you eat it, do not search for it. If you search for it, do not love it." To search for various kinds of food is greed. Do not allow your greed to pursue all lawful things. If a man eats any food out of greed, he will be told, "You have enjoyed your good things in this word's life."

A wise man of Basra said, "My desire disputed with me about eating bread and fish, but I restrained myself from eating them. This has continued for the last twenty years." When he died, a man of Basra said, "I saw him in a dream and asked, 'What rewards has Allah given you?' He said, 'I cannot fully describe what rewards my God has given me. He entertained me first with bread and fish, and I have been allowed to enjoy them every day without reckoning.'" Abū Sulaymān said, "To give up a desire is more beneficial than fasting and praying for a year."

3

How to acquire moderation in eating

Know that the object of good conduct is to adopt the middle path, which is good in all actions, the two extremes being bad. What has been described above about the merits of hunger shows that no extreme is good. The secret of Sharīʻah is that whatever is taken as a result of greed and low desire is an extreme in which there is harm, as Sharīʻah has prohibited it firmly. Nature encourages eating one's fill, but Sharīʻah prohibits it. When these two things stand face to face, the middle course should be adopted.

When the Prophet (ṣ) came to learn that some of the Companions prayed throughout the night and fasted throughout the day, he prohibited it. So it is good to eat with moderation, as it does not result in a heavy stomach and prevents hunger.

The object of food is to keep oneself alive and to gain strength for worship. A heavy stomach prevents worship, as does severe hunger. So it is better to eat food which prevents hunger and as well heaviness of the stomach.

Man should acquire the qualities of an angel, after which he becomes like an angel. An angel is free from heaviness of the stomach and hunger pangs. The object of man should be to acquire that station.

The middle path between hunger and overeating is the best. The Prophet (ṣ) said, "The middle path of every action is best." Allah says, "Eat and drink and be not extravagant" (Qur'an, 7:31).

When nature runs towards greed and low desires, it should be punished by hunger until it gives up passion and greed. The object of hunger is to curb all passions until they become moderate and under control. Therefore, sojourner to the next world need not remain hungry all the time, as the lash of hunger is not necessary for a person of great faith.

The Prophet's way of eating

The Prophet (ṣ) had no fixed measure of food or a fixed time at which he ate. 'Ā'ishah said, "The Prophet (ṣ) would fast in such a way that people thought he would never eat or drink, and he would not fast in such a way that the people thought that he would never fast again."

He would often go to his wives and say, "Do you have any food?" If they said yes, he would eat. Whenever any food was served to him, he would say, "I have fasted" and break his fast.

One day, the Prophet (ṣ) came out and said, "I have fasted." 'Ā'ishah then told him, "*Hays* has been presented to us," whereupon he said, "I had wished to fast, but now bring it to me."

Sahl was once asked, "What did you do at the beginning of your religious life?" and he told him about his acts of worship, such as eating only a little, eating lote-tree leaves and living for three years on only three dirhams. When asked about when he ate, he said, "I ate without fixing a time or quantity of food."

Ma'rūf al-Karkhī used to eat whatever food, ordinary or delicious, was presented to him. He was told, "Your brother Bishr does not eat such delicious foods" to which he replied, "My brother is in a state of Constriction begotten of scrupulousness, whereas I am in a state of Expansion resulting from gnosis. I am a guest of my Lord. I eat whatever He gives me, having no power to accept or reject."

'Umar once saw his son 'Abdullāh enjoying clarified butter, meat and bread together. He whipped him and said, "Eat meat and bread one day, clarified butter another day, bread and curry another day, salt another day and bare bread another day.'

This is the middle path. Constantly eating meat and greasy things is extravagance. To give up meat forever, however, incites the evil of miserliness. The middle course lies between the two extremes.

4
Sexual passion

Sexual passion has two benefits: satisfaction from intercourse and the preservation of mankind. The pleasure that is felt in sexual intercourse between a man and his wife is a small taste of the pleasure that is to come in the next world. If it were lasting, pleasure would have been strong, as physical pain inflicted by force is great. Fear of the fire of Hell and greed for pleasure and the bliss of Paradise lead man towards guidance. If man did not taste pleasure or pain, this would not be possible. The second benefit of sexual passion is the preservation of mankind. Such are its benefits.

But in sexual passion is the danger of losing control and exceeding limits, with the result that one's next world and present world are both destroyed. It is said that Allah's words "Our Lord, do not impose on us that which we have not the strength to bear" (Qur'an, 2:286) refers to sexual desire. Ibn 'Abbās understood Allah's words "From the evil of the utterly dark night when it comes" (Qur'an, 113:3) to refer to the erection of the male organ. The wise have said, "When the sexual organ of any man becomes erect, two-thirds of his intellect leave."

The Prophet (ṣ) used to pray, "I seek refuge in You from the evils of my ears, eyes, heart, enjoyment and semen."

The Prophet (ṣ) also said, "A woman is the string of Satan." Once, Satan appeared before Mūsā and warned him of three things: remaining alone with a woman in any place because Satan becomes the companion of a man and a woman until he throws the male into the snare of the female and vice versa; keeping a promise to Allah; and spending money set aside for *zakāh* and other forms of charity, as Satan becomes the owner of that money.

There are three degrees of sexual passion: excessive, little and moderate. In the case of excessive sexual passion, a man loses his sense of right and wrong and enjoys any woman, thus destroying his religion and life. Such a man often takes recourse to medicine to increase his sexual passion, which is all the more dangerous. Such a man also takes recourse to lovemaking, the object of which is the satisfaction of sexual passion. The medicine for this is to control his eyes and thoughts. The Prophet (ṣ) prescribed marriage for such people, saying, "O young men, take recourse to marriage. And whoever is unable to do so, let him fast, as fasting for him is castration."

5
Fornication of the eye

The sin of the fornication of eye is the greatest among the minor sins. Whoever cannot control his eye cannot save his sexual organ. ʿĪsā said, "Take care of your eye, as it sows the seed of sexual passion in heat, which is sufficient for creating danger. The prophet Yaḥyā was asked, "What is the source of fornication?" He replied, "A gaze and greed."

The Prophet (ṣ) said, "A gaze is one of the poisonous arrows of Satan. Whoever abstains from it for fear of Allah, He will give him faith which gives satisfaction to his heart." He also said, "There will remain no greater danger for people after my death than women." Likewise, he said, "Fear the temptation of the world and of women, for the first temptation of the children of Israel was women."

Allah says, "Say to the believing men that they cast down their looks" (Qur'an, 24:30).

The Prophet (ṣ) said, "Everyone has a share in fornication. His two eyes commit fornication by looking. His two hands commit fornication by touching. His two feet commit fornication by walking. His mouth commits fornication by kissing. His heart commits fornication by thinking. His sexual organ commits fornication by translating the thinking into action."

Umm Salamah said, "When Ibn Umm Maktūm, a blind man, sought the Prophet's permission to see him, I and Maymūnah were present, so the Prophet (ṣ) said, 'Screen yourselves.' We said, "He is blind. He will not see us." He said, "He may not see you, but you see him."

A pious man said, "There are three kinds of people: people who cohabit with boys, people who look out of passion, and people who do indecent deeds."

These, then, are the dangers of the eye.

The dangers of a rich wife

There are five dangers in marrying a rich wife: Her dower is high, she delays the wedding, she rarely serves her husband, her expenses are high, and she cannot be devout for fear of losing her property. Such is not the case for a poor woman.

A wise man said, "A wife should be beneath her husband in four things: age, height, riches and pedigree. A husband should be beneath her wife in four things: beauty, character and conduct, piety and behaviour."

Anything which makes one forget Allah is harmful. If a man can remember Allah more in an unmarried state, it is good for him. Once, a very rich man wanted to marry Rāb'iah al-'Adawiyyah, but she declined his offer, saying, "If Allah gives me wealth like yours, or more than that, I would not be happy to be distracted from Allah even for a moment."

There are medicines for controlling sexual passion. These are hunger, restraining one's sight and preoccupying oneself. If no benefit accrues from these three methods, it is better to marry. For this reason, the earlier sages hastened to marry and had their daughters married without delay.

6
The rewards of opposing passions

Know that sexual passion is stronger in human heart than other passions, curbing the intellect at the time of excitement, when one runs after some affairs which are shameful. Few people can control it, and most people refrain from it owing to inability, fear, shame or illness, in which case they are not rewarded. If one has the ability to commit fornication, and there is no obstacle, he will be rewarded for not doing so. This is the rank of the truthful.

The Prophet (ṣ) said, "Whoever is enamoured by someone, then dies in that condition, having kept it secret, has died a martyr." He also said, "Allah will give shade to seven people under His Throne on Judgement Day, on which there will be no shade except that of His Throne." One of them is a man who refrained from satisfying the sexual desire of a beautiful woman coming from a respectable family when she calls him, and said, "I fear the Lord of the universe." A brilliant example in this connection is the story of Yūsuf and Zulaykhah, in which Yūsuf refrained from satisfying her carnal desire.

Sulaymān ibn Yasār was a beautiful man. Once, a beautiful woman asked him to lie with her, but he refrained and fled from his house, leaving her therein. Sulaymān said, "That night, I saw Yūsuf in a dream and asked him, 'Are you Yūsuf?' He answered, 'Yes, I am Yūsuf, who had a sexual desire. But you had no such desire.'"

Another more astonishing story is related of Sulaymān. Once, he set out to perform the pilgrimage from Madīnah with a companion. He alighted at a place called al-Abwā'. His companion went to a market for purchasing food, leaving Sulaymān in the tent. An Arab woman, exquisitely beautiful and young, came to the tent and said to Sulaymān, "I have not come to beg. I want only sexual enjoyment with a male." He said, "Satan has brought you to me." Then he placed his head between his knees and began to weep bitterly. Seeing this pitiable condition, she put on her veil and left. He then went to Makkah and performed the pilgrimage. One night, he saw Yūsuf in a dream and said, "Your episode with the wife of the king of Egypt was wonderful." Yūsuf said, "Your episode with the young woman of al-Abwa' is more wonderful."

The Prophet (ṣ) said that three people went on a journey. At night, they took shelter in the cave of a hillock. Suddenly, a huge stone fell over the youth of the cave and shut it completely. They found darkness all around, and there was no hope of getting out. So they recalled their good deeds, seeking the mercy of Allah. One of them said, "O merciful God, you know that I had a cousin who loved me dearly, and whom I loved dearly. During a famine, I gave her a hundred and twenty dinars on condition that she would agree to what I say. One day, I found her alone and sought to enjoy her, but she refused, saying, 'Fear Allah and do not break my seal without Allah's command.' So I refrained. O Allah, if You know best that I refrained for fear of You, move the stone a little." The stone moved a little.

So eye sight is a precursor to fornication. To control it is absolutely necessary, as it is the root of all dangers.

The Prophet (ṣ) said, "The first glance is for you, but the second is against you."

Al-'Alā' ibn Ziyād said, "Do not repeatedly glance at the cloak of a female, as a glance sows the seed of sexual passion in the heart."

Once, a meat seller fell in love with a female slave of his neighbour. Her master sent her to another village for some work one day. Knowing this, the meat seller followed her and caught her on the way. She said to him, "Do not do this. I love you more than you love me. Fear Allah." Then he became repentant and went on his way. When he was thirsty, he found no water. Finding a man, he said, "Let us both pray to Allah for rain. The meat seller said, "I will pray and you say amen." So they began to pray to Allah for water, and soon a cloud appeared over their heads. When they parted, the cloud followed the meat seller. On seeing this favour of Allah for him, his companion came there and asked him the reason. The meat seller told him the story of his love for the female slave and how he controlled his passion.

Book 4
Harms of the tongue

Introduction

Know that tongue is a great asset to man and one of the wonderful creations of Allah. Though it is insignificant, its power is unlimited, its virtues are great, and thereby disbelief and belief are expressed. It is the absolute limit of sins and virtues. The tongue can express what has been related and what has not been created, the Creator and the created, the known and the unknown. The tongue explains concepts in the mind, whether truth or untruth, and therefore may be said to be the agent of the intellect. No other body part has the power to express the contents of the mind. Eyesight, for example, extends only to figures and colours and not to any other thing. Hearing has power over only sounds and nothing else. The power to tongue, however, is unlimited. It has power over good and bad. The dangers of the tongue include useless talk, quarrelling, dispute, rebuke, scolding, harsh words, cursing, lying, backbiting and self praise. We shall proceed to discuss them one by one.

1
The merits of silence

The dangers and harms of the tongue are many, and there is no safety from them except by silence, which is why Sharī'ah recommends it.

The Prophet (ṣ) said, "He who keeps silent gets salvation." Likewise, he said, "Silence is a rule few people can observe."

Sufyān asked the Prophet (ṣ), "O Prophet of Allah, tell me something about Islam which I shall ask nobody about after you." The Prophet (ṣ) replied, "Say, 'I have believed' and stand firm on it." He then asked, "What should I fear the most?" and he pointed to his tongue.

'Uqbah ibn 'Āmir said, "I asked, 'O Messenger of Allah, how can I get salvation?' He replied, 'Hold your tongue, make your house spacious and repent for your sins.'"

The Prophet (ṣ) said, "If a man can guarantee me what is between his two cheeks and his two thighs, I can guarantee him Paradise." He said, "He who is safe from the harms of his stomach, sexual organ and tongue is safe from all troubles." Because of these three organs, the majority of the people are destroyed. The Prophet (ṣ) was asked about a great virtue which admits one to Paradise and replied, "Control of the two hollow things: the mouth and sexual organ." By "mouth" he meant "tongue."

Mu'ādh ibn Jabal said, "I asked, "O Prophet of Allah, shall we be punished for what we utter?" The Prophet (ṣ) replied, "O Ibn Jabal—your mother be heavy with you—will a man be overturned in Hell on his nose except for the harms of his tongue?"

'Abdullāh al-Thaqafī said, "I asked, 'O Prophet of Allah, what matter do you fear for me?' He grabbed his tongue and said, 'This.'" In a similar vein, Mu'ādh asked, "O Prophet of Allah, what action is best?" and the Prophet (ṣ) drew out his tongue and placed his finger on it.

The Prophet (ṣ) said, "He who is pleased with Islam should remain silent." He also said, "When a man rises from bed, his limbs get up and rebuke his tongue. That is, they say to his tongue, 'Fear Allah regarding us, for when you are straight, we are upright and when you are wrong, we are wrong.'"

Once, 'Umar ibn al-Khaṭṭāb saw Abū Bakr al-Ṣiddīq drawing out his tongue and asked him, "O caliph of the people, what are you doing?" Abū Bakr replied, "It drags me to the place of destruction."

The Prophet (ṣ) said, "There is no bodily limb which will not complain to Allah about the harsh treatment of the tongue." Ibn Mas'ūd said that the Prophet (ṣ) said, "Major sins of a man accrue from his tongue." The Prophet (ṣ) said, "Allah keeps secret the secrets of a man who controls his tongue. Allah saves whoever keeps his anger under control. Allah pardons whoever asks pardon of Allah."

Once, Mu'ādh ibn Jabal told the Prophet (ṣ), "O Prophet of Allah, give me advice." The Prophet (ṣ) replied, "Worship as if you see Allah, and consider yourself one of the dead. I shall let you know a more important thing than this if you like." He then pointed to his tongue.

Ṣafwān ibn Sulaym was once asked by the Prophet (ṣ), "Shall I not inform you about the easiest divine service and the most comfortable thing for the body? Silence and good conduct." Likewise, he said, "Let whoever believes in Allah and the next world speak good or remain silent." He said, "May Allah show mercy to whoever acquires rewards by talk or remains safe by keeping silent."

It was once said to 'Īsā, "Teach us a thing by virtue of which we can enter Paradise." He answered, "Do not speak." They said, "We shall not be able to do that." He said, "Then do not speak except good."

Al-Barā' ibn 'Āzib said, "O Prophet of Allah, teach me something by which I can enter Paradise." He said, "Give food to the hungry, quench the thirsty, enjoin good and prohibit evil. If you cannot do that, do not speak except good."

The Prophet (ṣ) said, "Save your tongue from speech except what is good." He said, "Save your tongue from speech except what is good and you can defeat Satan." He said, "Allah is near every utterance of a man, so let him mind what he utters." He said, "When you see a believer silent and grave, go to him, as there is wisdom in him." He said, "Men are divided into three classes: looters of war booties, talkers of useless things and those who are safe. A looter of war booties is one who remembers Allah. A safe man is one who remains silent. A useless talker is one who talks unnecessarily." He said, "The tongue of a believer is behind his heart, whereas the tongue of a hypocrite is before his heart. When he wishes to talk, he sends it through his tongue without thought."

'Īsā said, "There are ten portions of divine service, nine of which are in silence, the remaining one being loneliness."

The Prophet (ṣ) said, "He who talks much commits blunders. He who blunders much commits many sins. And to him whose sins are great, hellfire has a better right."

'Umar ibn 'Abd al-'Azīz said, "He who remembers death much, remains satisfied with little. He who considers his words to be of his deeds talks little." A wise man said, "Silence has two benefits for a man: religious safety and an understanding of friends." Al-Ḥasan said, "Once, many people were talking in the assembly of Mu'āwiyah, but al-Aḥnaf ibn Qays remained silent. Mālik said to him, 'O Abū Baḥr, what is the matter with you? Why are you not talking?' He replied, "If I speak a lie, I fear Allah. If I tell the truth, I fear you." Al-Manṣūr ibn al-Mu'tazz would not talk after the nightfall prayer (*'ishā'*) for forty years.

Four kinds of talk

1. That which is always beneficial
2. That which is always harmful
3. That which is mixed with harm and benefit
4. That which has no harm or benefit

Talk which is always harmful is essentially necessary to avoid it. Talk which is mixed with harm and benefit is likewise necessary to avoid. Talk which has no benefit or harm is useless. Three-fourths of the fourth kind of talk are useless. But the remaining one-fourth is not without harm, for one is unable to distinguish whether it has subtle ostentation, has backbiting or is considered excessive talk. The Prophet (ṣ) said, "He who remains silent gets salvation."

2
Harms of the tongue

Unnecessary talk

It is best to save the tongue from backbiting, falsehood, show, quarrelling, dispute and the like, for in them are words which are not beneficial and which do harm to others. If you engage in useless talk, you lose time and will be held accountable for useless talk. If you are engaged in thoughts about Allah by giving up useless talk, Allah's inspiration may suddenly enter your heart. If you say 'There is no deity but Allah' and other invocations in lieu of useless talks, it is better for you. If a man remains busy in lawful things after giving up the remembrance of Allah, it does not do him any benefit because, even though he does not commit any sin, he is in loss as a result of losing the merits of Allah's remembrance.

The silence of a believer is good thoughts, the sight of a believer is a sermon and the talks of a believer are nothing but the remembrance of Allah. This is the basis of a man's wealth. When he spends his words without necessity and does not acquire virtues for the next world, he spoils the basis of wealth.

The Prophet (ṣ) said, "The excellence of a person's Islam includes leaving what has no benefit for him." Another *ḥadīth* of a harsher nature has come in this connection. Anas reported, "A young man was martyred at the Battle of Uḥud. We later found on his stomach stones tied up. It seemed that he had tied up the stones for preventing hunger. His mother was saying, 'O darling, you have entered Paradise with a cheerful mind.' Then the Prophet (ṣ) said, 'How do you know whether he engaged in useless talk or was miserly regarding a matter which did not do him any harm." This implies that accounts of such small matters will also be taken in the next world.

According to another *ḥadīth*, the Prophet (ṣ) went once to see Ka'b, who was sick. His mother said when he expired, "O Ka'b, Paradise is yours." The Prophet (ṣ) said, "How do you know whether Ka'b uttered words of which he had no necessity, or whether he was miserly with something he did not need."

The Prophet (ṣ) once said, "The man who will come now by the door is an inmate of Paradise." It was discovered that the man was 'Abdullāh ibn Salām. The Companions gave him the good news and asked him, "What good works have you done which have gained you this rank?" He answered, "I am very weak. I pray to Allah for a sound heart and for giving up of what I do not need."

Abū Dharr said, "The Prophet (ṣ) once asked me, 'Shall I not teach you an act which is light on the body but heavy in the Balance?' I replied, 'Yes, O Prophet of Allah.' He said, 'Silence, good conduct and giving up unnecessary things.'"

Ibn 'Abbās said, "To me five things are dearer than saving money: Do not speak about things of no concern to you, as it is unnecessary, and you are not safe from the fear of its sin. Do not utter a word useless to you until you find a suitable place for it, as there is harm in many useful talks if they occur in improper places. Do not argue with a patient man or a fool, for if you argue with a patient man, it angers him, and if you argue with a fool, he will trouble you. In your brother's absence, say of him what you would like him to say of you, and pardon him for what you like him to pardon you for. And let your deeds be as those of a man who knows that he will be rewarded for good deeds and punished for sins."

Luqmān was once asked, "What is your wisdom?" He replied, "I do not ask what I know, nor do I utter what has no benefit for me."

'Umar said, "Do not dispute over what is unnecessary. Keep your enemy distant from you and be careful of all people except faithful friends. Without God-fearingness, nobody can become a faithful friend. Do not keep the company of sinners, as there is fear that you may commit sins. Do not let them ask about your secrets. Consult with the God-fearing people in all your affairs."

Useless speech is words which, if uttered, neither benefit nor harm in this world or the next. There are three reasons for not engaging in useless speech: to be eager to know what is unnecessary, to enjoy talking to someone with the object of loving him and to pass time with useless talk.

The remedies for these are based on knowledge and action. It must be understood that death is standing in front and that every word uttered will be accounted for. Every breath is a valuable asset. This is the medicine based on knowledge. The remedy based on action is to adopt silence.

Excessive talk

The second harm is excessive talk. This means to utter useless words. Necessary talk can be engaged in for a short period. If one sentence is sufficient, a second sentence is unnecessary, though it has no sin.

'Aṭā' ibn Abī Rabāḥ said, "Your predecessors used to hate' excessive talk, considering it superfluous, except for talk about the Qur'an, the Sunnah of the Prophet (ṣ), enjoying good and forbidding evils and for necessary talks for earning livelihood. The Qur'an says, 'He utters not a word but there is by him a watcher at hand' (Qur'an, 50:18). Superfluous talk is limitless, but 'there is no good in most of their secret counsels except (in his) who enjoins charity or goodness or reconciliation between people' (Qur'an, 4:114).

The Prophet (ṣ) said, "He is blessed who restrains his tongue from superfluous talk and spends out of his excess wealth." Al-Ḥasan said, "He who talks much, talks much falsehood. The sins of one who has enormous wealth are great. And he whose conduct is bad punishes his soul." Once, a man came to the Prophet (ṣ) and praised him much. The Prophet (ṣ) told him, "There is nothing between them which can prevent your words." He also said, "Nothing worse has been given to man than prolonged talk." Ibrāhīm said, "Two things destroy a man: enormous wealth and too much talk."

Useless talk

This is useless talk in untrue matters and talk of sins, such as describing the beauty of a woman, talking about an assembly of wining, praising sinners, discussing some forts of the rich and talking about the oppressions of kings and rulers. These are all unlawful. To engage in unnecessary talk and to talk much about necessary things should be avoided even if they are not unlawful. Thus, do not talk except of the good of this world and the next.

The Prophet (ṣ) said, "A man may say something pleasing to Allah, the result of which may not be known to him, but Allah writes His pleasure with it up to Resurrection Day. A man can also say something displeasing to Allah, the result of which may not be known to him, but Allah writes His displeasure with it up to Resurrection Day." He said, "A man utters a word which excites the laughter of the people of an assembly, but throws himself thereby as far as the polestar." He said, "The man who engages in useless talk about sins most of the time will be a great sinner on Resurrection Day." This is supported by the verse "Do not sit with them until they enter into some other discourse; surely then you would be like them" (Qur'an, 4:140).

Quarrelling and disputation

These are unlawful. The Prophet (ṣ) said, "Do not quarrel with your brother, do not joke with him and do not break promises with him." He said, "Give up disputation, for you will not understand its contrivance or be safe from its dangers. He who keeps away from disputing a false thing will have a place built for him in the middle of Paradise." He said, "The first thing my Lord promised me, and the first thing He prohibited me from after idol worship and wining was disputation." He said, "Allah does not misguide a people after they are guided except through quarrels and disputes." He said, "A servant does not attain the reality of faith until he abandons disputation, even if he thinks he is right." He said, "The faith of a man is known by six qualities: fasting in the summer, striking the enemies of Allah with a sword, praying in haste on hot days, patience in dangers and difficulties, completing ablution even against one's will and giving up quarrelling, knowing something to be true."

Al-Zubayr once said to his son, "Do not dispute with the people about the Qur'an, as you will not be able to make them understand. Hold fast to the ways of the Prophet (ṣ)." 'Umar ibn 'Abd al-'Azīz said, "He who presents his religion with the object of starting quarrels changes his opinion most." A wise man said, "Allah does not misguide a people after guidance except through quarrels and disputes." Mālik ibn Anas said, "Disputation about religious mattes has nothing to do with religion." He also said, "Disputation makes the heart hard and engenders hatred." Luqmān said to his son, "Do not dispute with the learned. If there is a dispute with anybody, it is expiated with two *rak'ahs* of prayer." 'Umar said, "Do not acquire knowledge for three: to dispute with it, to take pride in it and to show it off. And do not give up acquiring knowledge for three: to feel ashamed of it, to get leisure for renunciation of the world and to remain satisfied with ignorance."

'Īsā said, "The beauty of one who speaks much falsehood goes away, and the gentle manners of one who disputes with others goes away. He whose thoughts are many is afflicted with illness and he whose conduct is bad punishes his soul."

Disputation about wealth

Another harm of the tongue is disputation about wealth. The Prophet (ṣ) said, "The greatest object of hatred to Allah is he who engages in the greatest disputes about wealth." He said, "Whoever ignorantly disputes with others about wealth always remains in the displeasure of Allah until he becomes silent." A wise man said, "Do not dispute about wealth, as it destroys religion."

It is true that it is lawful to give proof of one's right to wealth and to give up their exaggeration. It is also pardonable to adopt a middle course in disputation about wealth. Disputation straightens the breast and arouses anger. It is better to use pleasing words in disputation and not to use harsh words. The Prophet (ṣ) said, "Good words and feeding will give you peace in Paradise." Allah says, "You will speak to men good words" (Qur'an, 2:83). The Prophet (ṣ) said, "There are rooms in Paradise whose inner sides are seen from their outer sides and their outer sides are seen from their inner sides. Allah has prepared them for those people who give food and are humble in speech." Similarly, he said, "Good words are charity" and "Keep Hell at a distance by giving charity, even if only a seed of grape. If you are unable, then keep it distant by good words."

Ornamentation in talk

Another harm of tongue is to ornament one's speech, to disclose oratory and to give lectures with ornamental words. The Prophet (ṣ) said, "I and the God-fearing men among my followers are free from artificiality." He said, "Of all the people among you, the object of the greatest wrath to me and the most distant from my assembly is he who engages in useless talk, ornaments his words and adopts artificiality." The Prophet (ṣ) said, "Those who grow eating various delicious foods, putting on various clothes, eating various delicious dishes and speaking in ornamental words are the worst among my followers." He said, "Beware. Those who exaggerate in speech are ruined," repeating it thrice. 'Umar said, "Eloquence in speech is attended by the eloquence of Satan."

Obscene and bad talk

These talks are prohibited, and some of them are impurities. The Prophet (ṣ) said, "Give up obscene talk, as Allah does not love obscene and excessive talk." The Prophet (ṣ) prohibited rebuking the unbelievers killed in the Battle of Badr, saying, "Do not rebuke those dead unbelievers, as these do not reach them but rather trouble those who are alive. Beware! Bad talk is an object of hatred." He said, "Those prone to backbiting, inordinate cursing and obscene and excessive talk are not true believers." He said, "Four people will trouble the inmates of Hell. They will run between hot water and fire and proclaim their sorrows. One of them will be such that his mouth will expel pus and blood. He will be asked, 'Why is this your state?' and reply, 'I used to engage in obscene and evil talk and take therein pleasure like that of cohabitation, and for that I am receiving this punishment.'"

The Prophet (ṣ) said to 'Ā'ishah, "O 'Ā'ishah, if obscene talk could have taken the figure of a man, its figure would have been ugly." He said, "To engage in obscene talk and to narrate are two branches of hypocrisy." Narration means to disclose secrets which are unlawful and to exaggerate when narrating a story, adding lies to it. The Prophet (ṣ) said, "Obscene talk or unnecessary talk has nothing to do with Islam. The best of you in character and conduct is the best of all in Islam."

Ibrāhīm ibn Maysarah said, "On Resurrection Day, the figure of a man who speaks obscenities openly will be that of a dog." Al-Aḥnaf ibn-Qays said, "Shall I not inform you of a dangerous disease: bad conduct and an obscene tongue."

The limit of obscene talk

Ibn 'Abbās said, "Allah is modest and speaks about sexual intercourse using the word 'touch.' There are many obscene words which should not be explicitly used." 'Iyāḍ ibn Ḥimār said, "I said, 'O Messenger of Allah, a man of my people rebukes me, yet he is lower than me. Is there any harm in taking revenge on him?' The Prophet (ṣ) answered, "Two rebukers are devils. They call each other liars and ascribe guilt to each other." The Prophet (ṣ) said, "There is sin in rebuking a believer, and there is infidelity in murdering him." He said, "Two rebukers remain in their rebuke. Out of the two, sin falls on the one who rebukes first. It even falls on the rebukers if the rebuked person has transgressed." He said, "He who rebukes his parents is cursed." In another narration, he said, "To rebuke parents is one of the greatest sins." The Companions asked, "O Messenger of Allah, is there any man who rebukes his parents?" He said, "He rebukes the parents of another and in turn the latter also rebukes his parents and this amounts to rebuking his own parents."

Cursing

Another evil of tongue is to curse anything, be it an animal or a man or a lifeless thing. It is condemned. The Prophet (ṣ) said, "A believer does not curse another." He said, "Do not curse another with the curse of Allah, with His anger or Hell." Ḥudhayfah said, "The curse of one on another among a people falls on the people." Once, one of the women of the Madīnan Helpers (*Anṣār*) was riding a camel by the side of the Prophet (ṣ) when she cursed the camel. The Prophet (ṣ) told her, "Take down the load from the camel and drive it out of the party, as it is cursed." Ḥudhayfah added, "It is as though I am looking at the camel which was walking to the end from among the people, and nobody approached it."

Abū al-Dardā' said, "If anybody curses a land, it says, 'The curse of Allah be on the person who is the greatest sinner among us.'" Abū Bakr was cursing one of his maidservants when the Prophet (ṣ) heard it and said, "O Abū Bakr, a man of truth and a curser are together? It can never occur, by the Lord of the Ka'bah," repeating this twice or thrice. Abū Bakr set free the slave, then went to the Prophet (ṣ) and said, "I will do it no more." The

Prophet (ṣ) said, "The cursers will not be intercessors or witnesses on Resurrection Day."

Lawful cursing

"Cursing" (*la'n*) means "to drive away a thing from Allah." This applies to the things already distant from Allah, such as infidelity, oppression and the like. It is lawful, therefore, to curse the unbelievers and oppressors with words permitted by Sharī'ah.

Three things are necessary for a curse: infidelity, innovation and great sin. Each of these three has three stages. The first stage is that the curse is allowed in general; that is, it is a curse on innovators or transgressors, for example. The second stage is that the curse is on a specific group of people, such as Jews, Christians, bribe takers, fornicators or oppressors. The third stage is that the curse is on a particular person. This is unlawful unless the person is cursed by the Qur'an or a *ḥadīth*, such as Fir'awn and Abū Jahl, as they died unbelievers.

However, it is not allowed to curse an individual unbeliever at present, as he may turn out to be Muslim before his death. The Prophet (ṣ) once said to Abū Bakr, "O Abū Bakr, when you mention unbelievers, do so in a general way, for when you mention an individual unbeliever, his children will surely be enraged for their parents. So prevent the people from that." Once, Nu'aymān, a Muslim, drank wine, for which he was whipped several times in the presence of the Prophet (ṣ). One of the Companions then said, "The curse of Allah on him." Hearing this, the Prophet (ṣ) said, "Do not help Satan against your brother." In another version, the Prophet (ṣ) said, "Do not say that, as he loves Allah and His Messenger." It appears, then, that to curse a man individually is unlawful.

The Prophet (ṣ) said, "No man should call another an unbeliever or a great transgressor if he is not so." He said, "If a man bears witness that another is an unbeliever, he reverts to one of them. If he is really an unbeliever, he becomes so. If he is really not an unbeliever, the man who calls him an unbeliever becomes himself an unbeliever." He said, "I prohibit you from rebuking a Muslim, and being disobedient to a just ruler; and to rebuke a dead man is heinous." He said, "Do not abuse the dead, as what they sent in advance has reached them." Likewise, he said, "Do not abuse the dead. It troubles those who are alive." He said, "O people, save men concerning my Companions, my brethren and my parents. Do not abuse them. O people, when a man dies, tell of his good deeds."

Songs and poems

Another harm of tongue is songs and poems. Good poetry is good, and bad poetry is bad. The Prophet (ṣ) said, "It is better to fill the stomach of a man with puss than to fill it with poetry." In short, poetry is not unlawful if it does not contain evil or indecent words, as the Prophet (ṣ) said, "There is wisdom in some poetry." Moreover, the Prophet (ṣ) appointed the poet Ḥassān ibn Thābit to attack the polytheists and to praise Islam. 'Ā'ishah related, "One day, the Prophet (ṣ) was sewing his shoes, and I was sitting by his side eating bread. I noticed that sweat was coming out of his forehead, and it was sparkling like jewels. He got tired and said to me, 'You have become tired.' I said, 'O Prophet of Allah, I looked at you and saw that sweat was coming out of your forehead and was sparkling like jewels. Had the poet Abū Kabīr al-Hudhalī seen you in this condition, he would have taken you as fit for his poetry.' The Prophet (ṣ) said, 'O 'Ā'ishah, what does he say?' I said, 'He composed these two verses:

> Free from menses, suckling and other diseases.
> It seems that her face sheds lustre of lightning.

"The Prophet (ṣ) kept what he had in his hand and kissed my forehead, saying, 'Allah bless you. You have not been pleased as much as I have been pleased with you.'"

When the Prophet (ṣ) divided the booties of Ḥunayn after the battle, he gave four camels to the poet al-'Abbās ibn Mirdās, who left in protest and demanded more through poetry:

Mirdās's mind was not troubled at Badr and Siege.
He was satisfied with what he got at both.
But he returns today with a painful heart.

The Prophet (ṣ) ordered that he receive a hundred camels and asked him, "Do you talk in poetry?" He replied, "I roam in poetry like ants, and poetry bites me as ants bite: I cannot avoid poetry." The Prophet (ṣ) smiled at his words and said, "This Bedouin will not give up poetry until he gives up the camels of Ḥunayn."

Jest

Another harm of the tongue is jest. Generally, it is not commendable, though unharmful within limits. The' Prophet said, "Do not dispute with your brother and joke with him." Excessive or continuous joking is unlawful. If done continuously, it constitutes play and jest, which, although lawful in themselves, are blameworthy if they become a habit. This is because joking gives rise to excessive laughter, and excessive laughter makes the heart dead and sometimes creates hatred and destroys seriousness and fear.

When jest is necessary, however, it is not blameworthy. The Prophet (ṣ) said, "I joke, but I speak only the truth." He said, "A man says something to make friends laugh, but takes himself down to Hell from heaven." 'Umar said, "The fear of one who laughs much is reduced. One who jokes is belittled by people. One who jokes much becomes well known. One who talks much commits much faults. One who has little shame has many faults and less piety. One whose piety is less, his heart dies. Jokes keep one away from the next world." The Prophet (ṣ) said, "If you knew what I knew, you would weep much and laugh little."

Yūsuf ibn Asbāṭ said al-Ḥasan did not laugh for thirty years. Similarly, it was said ʿAṭā' al-Sulamī did not laugh for forty years. ʿAbdullāh ibn Abī Yaʿla said, "You are laughing while your coffin is coming out of the building." Ibn ʿAbbās said, "He who commits a sin laughing will enter Hell weeping."

It is therefore blameworthy to engage in jest, smiling alone being recommended. The Prophet (ṣ) used to smile only. Saʿīd ibn al-ʿĀṣ told his son, "O dear son, do not joke with any honourable man, lest he hate you. Nor joke with any dishonourable man, lest he become daring against you."

The Prophet (ṣ) and his Companions had their jokes under control, joking only truthfully, troubling nobody thereby and not doing it to excess. Minor sins turn into major sins if one becomes accustomed to them. In like manner, if one is accustomed to lawful things, they turn into minor sins. Anas said, "The Prophet (ṣ) used to joke with his wives. Once, an old woman came to the Prophet (ṣ), who said to her, 'No old woman will enter Paradise.' The old woman began to weep at this. Then he said to her, 'On that day, you will not remain old, as Allah says, 'Then We have made them virgins' (Qur'an, 56:36)." Zayd ibn Aslam said, "Once, Umm Ayman came to the Prophet (ṣ) and said, 'My husband is calling you.' The Prophet (ṣ) asked, 'Who is your husband? Is your husband not he who has whiteness in his eyes?' The woman replied, 'By Allah, the eye of my husband is not white.' The Prophet (ṣ) said, 'Is there any man who does not have whiteness in his eyes?'"

Ridicule

Ridicule is unlawful so long as it is hurtful. Allah says, "O you who believe, let not (one) people laugh at (another) people, perhaps they may be better than they, nor let women (laugh) at (other) women, perhaps they may be better than they" (Qur'an, 49:11). "Ridicule" means "to neglect or hold another in contempt and to reveal his defects." It may be expressed by words and actions or by winks and gestures. If it is done in one's absence, it amounts to backbiting.

'Ā'ishah said, "I ridiculed one man, whereupon the Prophet (ṣ) said to me, 'By Allah, I do not want to ridicule another and commit such sins. Allah says, 'Ah! Woe to us! What a book is this! It does not omit a small one nor a great one, but numbers them (all)?' (Qur'an, 18:49)." Commenting on "a small one," Ibn 'Abbās said it is "something said by way of ridicule." This indicates that loud laughter is a great sin."

The Prophet (ṣ) said, "The door of Paradise will be opened before one of those who ridicule men, and it will be said to him, 'Come, come.' Then he will come to be relieved of his troubles. But when he comes, the door will be closed on him." The Prophet (ṣ) said, "Do not ridicule someone who passes gas. Why should you ridicule one who is led to do so as a call of nature?" He said, "'If a man accuses his brother of a sin from which he has repented, he will not die until he commits that sin." It is therefore unlawful to ridicule another with regard to his figure, conduct, writing, action and so on.

Revealing secrets

It is unlawful to reveal secrets, as it gives pain to the mind of another. The Prophet (ṣ) said, "When any man tells you something and asks you to keep it secret, it is a trust." Al-Ḥasan said, "It is a breach of trust if you disclose the secrets of your brother." It is said that Mu'āwiyah told a secret to al-Walīd ibn 'Utbah, who said to his father, "O father, the Commander of the Faithful told me a secret, and I think there is no fault in disclosing it to you." His father said, "Do not tell it to me, as he who keeps secrets secret keeps it under his control. When he discloses it, it goes under the control of another. I do not want you to humiliate your tongue by disclosing it." Then al-Walīd told this to the caliph, who said, "O al-Walīd, your father freed you from the slavery of error."

False promise

This is another harm of tongue, as one makes a promise in haste, but it does not become possible to always fulfil it and, as a result, it is broken. Allah says, "O you who believe, fulfil the obligations" (Qur'an, 5:1). The Prophet (ṣ) said, "Promises are like gifts." He said, "Promises are a kind of debt, or greater than that." Allah praised Ismā'īl for fulfilling his promise, saying, "Surely he was truthful in (his) promise" (Qur'an, 19:54). One day, Ismā'īl promised to meet a man in a certain place, but the man did not fulfil his promise, as he forgot. Ismā'īl then waited there for him for twenty-two days.

When 'Abdullāh ibn 'Umar was about to die, he said, "A Qurayshite wanted to marry my daughter, and I made him a promise. And, by Allah, I shall not meet Allah with three acts of hypocrisy. I bear witness to you that I shall marry my daughter to him." 'Abdullāh ibn Abī al-Khansā' reported, "I made a contract with the Prophet (ṣ), before his prophethood, to bring something to him. I promised that I would take that thing to him at a fixed place, but afterwards forgot it. On the third day, I remembered and, after going there, found the Prophet (ṣ) waiting. He said, 'O young man, you have given me much trouble. I have been here for the past three days for you.'" When making a promise, the Prophet (ṣ) would use such words as "perhaps" and "possibly." Similarly, Ibn Mas'ūd did not make any promise without saying 'Allah willing' (*in shā' Allah*).

The Prophet (ṣ) said, "He in whom there are three matters is a hypocrite, even if he prays, fasts and thinks that he is a Muslim: When he speaks, he speaks falsehood; when he promises, he breaks it; and when he is entrusted, he betrays." He said, "Whoever does one of four things is a hypocrite until he stops: When he speaks, he speaks falsehood; when he makes a promise, he breaks it; when he is entrusted, he betrays; and when he disputes over possessions, he rebukes." Once, the Prophet (ṣ) promised Abū al-Haytham ibn al-Tayhān three slaves. The Prophet (ṣ) got three war prisoners and gave two of them to him and kept one for himself. Then his daughter Fāṭimah came to him and said, "Do you not find on my hands signs of crushing mill?" The Prophet (ṣ) replied, "What about my promise to Abū al-Haytham?" and gave the prisoner to Abū al-Haytham and not Fāṭimah.

One day, the Prophet (ṣ) was distributing the war booty gained in the Battle of Ḥunayn when a man came and said, "O Prophet of Allah, you owe me something because of a promise you made." The Prophet (ṣ) replied, "That is true. Want what you wish." The man wanted eighty goats and one goat herder. The Prophet (ṣ) gave them to him and said, "You have wanted little."

Mūsā said to the woman whose enquiry led to the finding of Yūsuf's backbone, "You will get what you want." The woman said, "I want my youth to be restored to me, and to live in Paradise in the next world with you." She was made an example in Arabia. The Prophet (ṣ) said, "If one has the intention of fulfilling a promise, it will not be broken if one proves another." According to another narration, "when a man makes a promise to his brother and has the intention to fulfil it, but afterwards breaks it, he commits no sin thereby."

Lying

Another danger of the tongue is lying and making a false oath, both of which are great sins and heinous faults. In the first year of emigration, the Prophet (ṣ) said, "Be careful of falsehood, as it is the companion of sinners, and both will be in Hell." He also said, "Falsehood is a door of hypocrisy."

Al-Ḥasan said, "People say that there is a difference between open and secret words and actions and entering and leaving hypocrisy. But the sin on which hypocrisy is built is falsehood."

The Prophet (ṣ) said, "If you tell your brother something and he believes you, but you are lying to him about it, it is a breach of trust." He said, "A man is written as liar with Allah if he is accustomed to false words and false discussions." The Prophet (ṣ) once was passing by two men talking about the sale of two goats, and both were swearing. One of them said, "By Allah, I will not sell them for less than this price. The other said, "By Allah, I will not give more than this price." One of them purchased the goats, whereupon the Prophet (ṣ) said, "The sin of one of you has become compulsory." The Prophet (ṣ) said, "Falsehood reduces provision." He said, "Merchants are sinners." When asked, "O Prophet of Allah, has not Allah made trade lawful?" he replied, "Yes, but merchants commit sin by false oaths and lies."

The Prophet (ṣ) said, "On Resurrection Day, Allah will neither speak nor look at three people: a person who seeks benefit from charity, a person who sells things by lies and a person who loosens his trouser with pride." He said, "If any man takes an oath in the name of Allah and admits into it falsehood the like of a fly's wing, a spot will remain in his soul up to Resurrection Day." He said, "Allah loves three people: a person who fights standing in a rank in jihad until he or his companions become victorious, a person who tolerates the harms of his neighbour until death or journey separates them and a person who prays in a corner when he stays with a party of soldiers travelling and looking for a good place to rest or sleep. Allah hates three people: a tradesman who takes false oaths, a proud and poor man, and a miser who reminds others of his favours."

The Prophet (ṣ) said, "Woe to him who falsely speaks to arouse laughter of men." He said, "I dreamt that a man came to me and said, 'Rise.' I rose with him and saw myself between two men, one standing and the other seated. The man standing held a spear, the crooked iron of which pierced through the cheek of the man sitting, and the former was pulling it with force. When his face came down on his shoulder, it pierced his other cheek, and he pulled it until it also came down on his shoulder. I asked him, 'What is this?' and he replied, 'This man is a great liar. Punishment in the grave will continue in this manner until Resurrection Day.'"

'Abdullāh ibn Jarād said, "I asked the Prophet (ṣ), 'O Messenger of Allah, can a believer commit fornication?' He replied, 'Yes, he can.' I asked, 'O Prophet of Allah, can a believer be a liar?' He replied, 'No.' Then he recited the verse 'Only they forge the lie who do not believe in Allah's communications' (Qur'an, 16:105)."

The Prophet (ṣ) used to pray, "O Allah, purify my heart from hypocrisy, my private parts from fornication and my tongue from falsehood." He said, "Allah will neither speak to three people nor purify them, and there is grievous punishment for them: an elderly fornicator, a lying king and a proud beggar." He said, "If Allah gave me wealth as abundant as these heaps of stones, I would distribute them all among you. You would have found me neither a miser, liar nor coward." He said, leaning against a pillar, "Shall I not inform you of a great sin? Beware! It is to speak falsehood." He said, "If a man speaks falsehood, his companion angel goes a mile away from him."

The Prophet (ṣ) said, "I guarantee you Paradise if you do six things." The Companions asked, "What are they?" He replied, "Let nobody among you tell a lie when he speaks; let him not break a promise; let him not break a trust when he is entrusted; let him control his eye sight; let him save his private part; and let him prevent his hand." He said, "Satan has antimony, scent and taste. His scent is falsehood, his taste is anger and his antimony is sleep."

'Umar said in a sermon, "The Prophet (ṣ) said, standing among us in this place like my standing, 'Treat well my Companions, then those who come after them. Thereafter, falsehood will spread, so much so that a man will take an oath, yet say he has not taken one, and he will bear witness, yet say he has not born witness.'" The Prophet (ṣ) said, "He who attributes to me a saying, knowing it to be false, is a liar." He said, "He who appropriates the property of another Muslim unjustly by taking a false oath will meet Allah Almighty while He is displeased with him." The Prophet (ṣ) rejected the evidence of a liar. He said, "A Muslim may commit any wrong, but there cannot be in him cheating and falsehood."

Mūsā asked, "O Lord, who is the best to You in worship?" Allah answered, "One whose tongue does not speak falsehood, whose heart does not commit sin and whose private part does not commit fornication." Luqmān said to his son, "O dear son, be careful of falsehood, for it is tasteful as the meat of a sparrow, but the evil of a liar will soon be disclosed."

The Prophet (ṣ) praised truth, saying, "If you have four things, nothing will harm you, even if you do not acquire worldly things: speaking the truth, keeping trusts, good conduct and lawful food." He said, "Stick to truth, as is it connected with religion, and both are in Paradise. The Prophet (ṣ) said, "I advise you to fear Allah, speak the truth, fulfil trusts, fulfil promises, give *salām* and be humble."

Permissible lying

Know that lying is not unlawful for its own sake, but rather for the harm caused to the person lied to or other people. Sometimes lying becomes even obligatory. Maymūn ibn Mihrān said, "In some cases, lying is better than speaking the truth. If a man runs with a sword to kill another person who enters a house, you should say, on being asked about his whereabouts, 'I have not seen him.'" It is obligatory for you to tell this lie, for to save a person from unjust oppression is obligatory. If the truth is spoken, a life will perish in the hand of an oppressor. It is also permissible to lie in a battle, to compromise between two parties and to preserve goodwill between two co-wives. But one should be careful of lying even in these cases.

Umm Kulthūm said, "The Prophet (ṣ) did not allow to lie except in three cases: to bring a compromise between two parties, at the time of war, and a husband's lying to his wife and a wife's lying to her husband." The Prophet (ṣ) said, "He who settles disputes between two parties is not a liar. He speaks good or tries to do good." The Prophet (ṣ) said, "Every lie of a man is written, but the lie to bring a compromise between two Muslims is not written." A man asked the Prophet (ṣ), "Should I lie to my wife?" He replied, "There is no good in a lie." He said, "Repeat it. Should I lie to her?" The Prophet (ṣ) said, "It will not be held against you."

'Umar said, "If any women dislikes her husband, she should not express it to others, as habitation in a house is based on love. Man should live in love and amity in Islam." The Prophet (ṣ) said, "Every lie of a man is recorded. But the lie he speaks in war is not recorded, as war is strategy; the lie spoken to settle matters between two contending parties is not recorded; and the lie spoken to please a wife is not recorded." Thawbān said, "There is sin in every lie, but not in that which benefits a Muslim or removes a harm from him." The Prophet (ṣ) said, "He who commits fornication should keep it secret with the secrecy of Allah, for to disclose an obscene act is also an obscene act."

So every man should sometimes save his life, possessions and honour, taking recourse to even lies. If you are asked about a secret of your Muslim brother, you can deny it to preserve his honour. If a man has more than one wife, he can tell a wife, "I love you more." In short, two things should be weighed: truth and falsehood. If the harm in speaking the truth outweighs the benefit in it, it may be avoided.

Giving a misleading impression

Words carrying dual meanings may be spoken in crises. 'Umar said, "In giving a misleading impression, a man saves himself from falsehood." The following are some examples.

Muṭarrif was summoned once by the tyrant ruler Ziyād, who asked him, "Why have you come so late?" He replied, giving a misleading impression, "After leaving your court, I could not raise my side from bed. Allah has now raised it for me." The ruler was given to understand that he was ill.

Mu'ādh ibn Jabal was an administrative officer for 'Umar. On his return from his station of office, his wife asked him, "Have you brought anything as others bring many things?" He replied,

"I could not bring anything as there was a guard with me." By "guard" he meant "Allah."

If any man came to enquire about Ibrāhīm in his house, and he did not wish to see him, he sent his maidservant to say, "Seek him in the masjid."

The Prophet (ṣ) said, "The greatest calumny is to claim falsely that someone is one's father, to say that one has seen what he has not seen or to say I said what I did not say. He also said, " He who narrates his dream in a false manner will be asked to bind two seeds of wheat on the Resurrection Day, but he will never be able to do it.

Backbiting

Know that there has come numerous warnings in Sharī'ah regarding backbiting. Many people are accustomed to backbiting, and very few are free from it. Allah says, "Nor let some of you backbite about others. Does one of you like to eat the flesh of his dead brother? You abhor it" (Qur'an, 49:12).

The Prophet (ṣ) said, "The wealth, life and honour of every Muslim are unlawful for another Muslim. Allah joins honour with wealth and life." The Prophet (ṣ) said, "Beware of backbiting, as it is a more heinous sin than fornication. If a man commits fornication and makes repentance, Allah may accept his repentance, but his repentance for backbiting is not accepted until the one he backbit about pardons him." He said, "Do not hate one another, envy one another, sell over the sale to another, dispute with one another or backbite about one another. The servants of Allah are brethren to one another." He said, "The night in which I was taken to heaven, I passed by a group of men who where scratching the flesh of their faces with the ends of their nails. I asked, 'O Jibrīl, who are they?' He replied, "They are those who used to go about slandering people and ruining their honour."

Salīm ibn Jābir said, "I went to the Prophet (ṣ) and said, 'Teach me something which will benefit me." He said, "Do not neglect a good deed, be it pouring water from your bucket into the bucket of another or meeting your brother with good news, and when he leaves, do not backbite about him." Al-Barā' said, "One day, the Prophet (ṣ) gave us a sermon which even the freed male and female slaves heard from their houses. He said, 'O you who have become believers with their tongues and not their hearts, do not backbite about Muslims or enquire into their secrets, for Allah will enquire into the secrets of a Muslim who enquires into the secrets of his Muslim brother, and Allah dishonours in his own house him whose secrets he enquires into."

It was revealed to 'Īsā, "He who dies after repenting for his backbiting will be the last to enter Paradise. He who dies without such a repentance will be the first to enter Hell." Anas said, "The Prophet (ṣ) once ordered all his Companions to fast, saying, 'Do not break your fast before I order you.' All the Companions fasted. When night fell, a man came there and said, 'O Messenger of Allah, I have fasted. Now order me to break it.' Thus one by one they came to the Prophet (ṣ), who ordered them to break their fast. Then a man came and said, 'O Messenger of Allah, two women in my family fasted, but are not coming to you out of shame. Order them to break their fast.' The Prophet (ṣ) averted his glance from him and asked him again. Then he said, 'How have they fasted when they ate the flesh of men in the daytime? Tell them that if they fasted, they should vomit.' They vomited, and suddenly a condensed clot of blood came out from their bellies. With that, the Prophet (ṣ) said, 'By Him in whose hand is my life, if a drop of blood had remained in their bellies, hellfire would have devoured them.'"

Anas reported that the Prophet (ṣ) once mentioned interest, describing it as a great sin, saying, "One dirham of interest is more heinous to Allah than thirty-six acts of fornication. But the greatest interest is to destroy the honour of a Muslim." Jābir said, "I was on a journey with the Prophet (ṣ), who said while passing by two graves, 'These two people are punished not for any great sin. One is punished for backbiting, the other for not being accustomed to cleanse after answering the calls of nature.' Then he took a fresh palm branch, divided it into two and fixed one to each grave, saying, 'So long as this branch does not become dry and remains fresh, the punishment will be light for them.'"

The Prophet (ṣ) once ordered Mā'iz to be killed by stoning for the crime of fornication. A man present said to another, "Look, Mā'iz is dying like a dog." The Prophet (ṣ) then passed by a dead body with the two men and said to them, "Eat the meat of this dead animal." They asked, "O Messenger of Allah, how can we eat the meat of a dead animal?" He replied, "The rotten meat of your brother who you have eaten is more rotten and evil smelling than this flesh." Abū Hurayrah said, "He who eats the flesh of his brother in this world will eat that flesh in the next world. It will be said to him, 'Eat his dead flesh when dead as you have eaten his flesh when alive.' Then he will eat it, chew it and swallow it."

Qatādah said, "There are three kinds of punishments in the grave: one for backbiting, a second for taking the words of one to the ears of another and a third for breaking the rules of the calls of nature." Al-Ḥasan said, "By Allah, the effect of backbiting in the religion of Islam is the spreading of the boils of smallpox on the body." A wise man said, "We saw former sages, and they did not think that fasting and prayer alone are acts of worship. Rather, they considered not backbiting also an act of worship."

Ibn 'Abbās said, "When you wish to tell people about the fault of your companion, you first tell them of your own fault." Mālik ibn Dīnar said, "One day 'Īsā was passing with his companions by a dead dog. The disciples said, 'What a stench this dead dog has!' Then 'Īsā said, 'How white its teeth are!' deprecating the placing of blame on the dog and making them understand that there is nothing ugly in the creation of Allah.

Definition of "backbiting"

"Backbiting" means "to say anything about your brother in his absence which he would dislike, be it about his physique, pedigree, dress, house, religion, behaviours, conduct or character." If you say that someone is short or tall, and it offends him, then it is backbiting. If you say, in his absence, that he is a sinner, is of low birth or is a weaver, it is backbiting. If you say his conduct is not good, he is a miser, he is proud, he is a hypocrite, he is prone to anger or he is a coward, it is backbiting. The Prophet (ṣ) was told that a woman fasts and prays, but verbally abuses her neighbours. He said, "This woman will go to Hell." At another time, he was told that a woman is a miser and said, "This is not good talk."

Once, the Prophet (ṣ) asked, "Do you know what backbiting is?" The Companions replied, "Allah and His messenger know best." He said, "To say what your Muslim brother does not like is backbiting." Thereupon, he was asked, "And if what I say is true about my brother?" He answered, "If it is true, it is considered backbiting. If it is not, it is slander." Some Companions once said to the Prophet (ṣ), "He is an unfit person." Hearing this, the Prophet (ṣ) said, "You have backbitten about your brother." The Companions said, "O Messenger of Allah, we have said what is true of him." He said, "If what you say is not true, it is slander."

Al-Ḥasan said, "There are three kinds of bad discussions about another: backbiting, slander and gossip. These sins are mentioned in the Qur'an. Backbiting is to say what is true of another. Slander is to say what is not true of another. Gossip is to say what you have heard about another."

Backbiting by means other than the tongue

Know that backbiting can be done not only by tongue but also by signs, gestures, hints, movements of the body and writings. Every kind of backbiting is unlawful, however. 'Ā'ishah said, "A woman came to me, and when she left, I hinted to the Prophet (ṣ) with my hand that she is a dwarf. The Prophet (ṣ) said, 'You have backbitten about her.'"

The pen is like the tongue, and backbiting can be done thereby. If a writer criticises a particular man by writing, it is backbiting. It can be committed with reference to a dead man also.

When any action of a man was disliked by the Prophet (ṣ), he did not particularise that person, but said in a general way, "What will be the condition of people who do such and such acts?" The hearer of backbiting also sins. If, however, he protests with his tongue, he is exempt from its sin. If he cannot, he should protest with his mind. If he leaves that place or changes the topic, he is also exempted.

The Prophet (ṣ) said, "If a believer is dishonoured before any person who does not help him in spite of his ability to do so, Allah will dishonour him on Resurrection Day before all creatures." He said, "He who protects the honour of a Muslim in his absence, it becomes the duty of Allah to perfect his honour on Judgement Day." He said, "If a man saves the honour of his Muslim brother in his absence, it becomes the duty of Allah to save him from hellfire."

Causes of backbiting

The causes of backbiting are many. We shall discuss eleven of them here. Eight causes are applicable to all, while three are applicable to religious and special people.

The first cause is anger. If man is angry with anybody, he speaks of his faults and there arises in his mind hatred for him. This is natural if he has no religious connection with him. Sometimes he entertains hatred in his mind without mentioning it explicitly. So anger is a cause of backbiting. The second cause is to please the hearts of friends and companions. The third cause is to shake off one's own guilt by backbiting about others. The fourth cause is to free oneself of guilt by attributing it to others, saying, "I would not have done it but for others." The fifth cause is to express glory and praise of oneself, thereby belittle another, saying, "He is a fool and powerless." The sixth cause is hatred towards another.

The seventh cause is jest and ridicule. The eighth cause is to hold another in contempt.

Causes applicable to the religious

The three causes of backbiting applicable to religious men are very subtle and difficult, and the Devil paints them in good works. The first cause is that when the people see some fault in the religious, they say that a particular religious man has all qualities when he has but one. If they express that fault, it constitutes be backbiting. The second cause is sympathy for the person backbitten by saying, "The affair of that unfortunate man has caused my anxiety." If he mentions his name, he is backbiting about him. The third cause is to express anger for Allah's sake at anybody mentioning his name. If his name is not mentioned, it is not backbiting.

The cure for backbiting

Know that the medicine for backbiting is knowledge and action or a mixture of knowledge and action: The medicine for a disease is its opposite. There are two kinds of medicines for backbiting: general medicine and special medicine. The general medicine is that the backbiter should know that, in the case of backbiting, he will incite the wrath of Allah and his rewards will be lost on Resurrection Day, as his rewards will go to the person he backbit about.

Backbiting has been likened to eating a dead animal. The Prophet (ṣ) said, "Backbiting consumes the virtues of a man sooner than the fire consumes a dry wood." One day, a man said to al-Ḥasan, "I heard that you have backbitten about me." He replied, "You have not acquired such a rank that I would give you the rewards of all my good deeds." The Prophet (ṣ) said, "He is blessed who cannot see the faults of others because he remains busy with his own faults." A man said to a wise man, "O man of ugly face," to which he replied, "I would have made it unlawful if it were in my head."

The special medicines for backbiting are as follows. In order to apply these medicines, the root cause of backbiting is to be sought. There are eight causes, as described above, and those causes will have to be rooted out.

1. Anger: Anger should be brought under complete control. If you are determined to take revenge on a person out of anger, know that Allah will take revenge on you out of anger for your backbiting, as He has prohibited you from that. The Prophet (ṣ) said, "Hell has a door. He who incites the anger of Allah by committing sins will enter Hell through that door and nobody else." He said, "The tongue of one who fears Allah is under control, and his anger is also under control." He also said, "If a man appeases anger while having the right to express it, Allah will call him on Resurrection Day before all the creatures and say, "Take whichever houri you like." Allah said in one of the earlier scriptures, "O son of Adam, remember Me at the time of your wrath and I will remember you at the time of My wrath." In other words, "I will not destroy you along with others who will be destroyed."
2. Supporting the opinion of friends: Its medicine is to oppose the opinion of friends in the matter of backbiting about a man. You should know that if you incur the displeasure of Allah by pleasing your friends, Allah will be enraged with you. So how can you give up Allah for pleasing your friends?
3. Showing one's piety by backbiting about another: The medicine is as described above. You should know that Allah will be wroth with you and that you are courting destruction in the next world by absolving yourself from guilt in this world. You should also know that you are losing all your rewards by backbiting.
4. Considering oneself pure and disclose one's prestige and pride: The medicine for this is to know that your glory and dignity may vanish and people may look down on you.

5. Envy: Its medicine is as follows. You should know that if you envy anybody for his riches and honour in the world, you will be burnt by the fire of envy in this world in addition to your being burnt in Hell. You have entitled yourself thereby to the punishment of Hell and are bereft of riches and honour in this world. You should know, too, that his sins will fall on you and your rewards will go to him.
6. Ridicule and jest: You should know that you have ridiculed a man in the presence of only some people, but you will be ridiculed before all creatures in the next world.
7. Expressing sympathy for the sin of another.
8. Expressing astonishment at the conduct of another: This is mockery, which is an act of sin.

Backbiting of the mind

Know that to backbite about another in the mind is unlawful as backbiting by tongue. This means having an evil thought about a person. However, what suddenly arises in mind is pardonable. Allah says, "O you who believe, if an evildoer comes to you with a report, look carefully into it, lest you harm a people in ignorance, then be sorry for what you have done" (Qur'an, 49:6). So to support Satan is unlawful. Moreover, the Prophet (ṣ) said, "Allah has made unlawful the life and property of a Muslim and to entertain evil thoughts about him." Evil thoughts, then, are unlawful, for they lead to entry into his secrets, which is also unlawful. Allah says, "Do not spy" (Qur'an, 49:12).

Permissible backbiting

The following six causes make backbiting lawful.

1. To mention the faults of another in a trial. If a man complains against another before a judge regarding the latter's oppression, breach of trust, backbiting or any other fault, it is lawful for him to speak of it before the judge. If he is really

not oppressed or tortured, he is considered a backbiter and consequently a sinner. The Prophet (ṣ) said, "He who has a right has a right to speak." He said, "For a rich man to delay the payment of dues is oppression." He said, "If a debt is not paid, it is lawful to punish a rich man and taint his honour."

2. To help to change evil deeds. It is lawful to speak of the works of a sinner to guide him to the right path and to change his evil deed. This is lawful, however, only for a person who is able to prevent that evil act by exercising power over him. When 'Umar heard that Abū Jandal began drinking wine in Syria, he wrote to him the following: "In the name of Allah, the Most Compassionate, the Most Merciful. Ḥā' Mīm. The revelation of the Book is from Allah, the Mighty, the Knowing, the Forgiver of the faults and the Acceptor of repentance, Severe to punish, Lord of bounty. There is no god but Him. To Him is the eventual coming" (Qur'an, 40:1). When he read this letter, he repented of his evil act. 'Umar did not attribute the fault of backbiting to the one who gave him this news.
3. To seek a legal ruling (*fatwā*). It is lawful to speak of the deeds of another to seek a legal ruling for a remedy. For instance, one can say, "My father, wife or son treats me like this. What is the remedy for this?" Hind bint 'Utbah complained to the Prophet (ṣ), "Abū Sufyān is a miser. He does not bear the necessary expenses for myself and my children. May I spend anything in his absence?" The Prophet (ṣ) replied, "Take what is necessary for you and your children." Hind spoke of the miserliness and oppression of Abū Sufyān, but the Prophet (ṣ) did not scold her for backbiting, as she had the intention of seeking a legal ruling.
4. To warn a Muslim about someone's harm. It is lawful to speak of the faults of another to save a Muslim from injury and harm. If you see a learned man frequent an innovator and fear his influence on him, it is lawful to disclose his innovation and sin, but not anything else. Similarly, if a man wants to engage a

servant or to buy a slave, it is lawful to disclose his innovations, sins, bad habits, thefts and crimes, but not anything else. If a man is cited as a witness by an innocent man, he may disclose the fault of his adversary. The Prophet (ṣ) said, "Do you consider it bad to disclose the faults of a sinner? Disclose his faults so that people may know them. Disclose his faults so that people may take precaution." The ancient sages said, "There is no sin in disclosing the faults of three people: a tyrannical ruler, a learned innovator and a shameless evildoer."

5. To call by a well-known nickname. It is not backbiting if a man is called by a well-known nickname, such as "the Lame" or "the Blind," as this is for identification and not for any evil motive.
6. To disclose the bad deed of an evildoer. There is no sin in disclosing the sins of those accustomed to doing evil deeds openly, such as a male who wears female clothes, a drunkard, a fornicator or an oppressor. The Prophet (ṣ) said, "There is no sin in backbiting about a person who has shaken off the screen of shame from his face." 'Umar said, "He who commits major sins openly has no honour. He who commits sins secretly should have the honour of his fault kept secret." Al-Ḥasan said, "There is no fault in backbiting about three people: a slave of passion, an open and well-known transgressor and a tyrannical ruler."

Expiation for backbiting

There are two modes of expiation for the sin of backbiting. The first is to repent sincerely in one's heart and to be sorry for it. The second is to seek pardon of the one backbitten about very humbly. Al-Ḥasan said, "It is sufficient to seek forgiveness for the one backbitten about. There is no need to seek his pardon." He cites the following *ḥadīth*: "To seek forgiveness for the one backbitten about is the expiation for the backbiting." Mujāhid said, "The expiation for eating the rotten flesh of your brother is to praise him and to pray for his good." To me it seems that it is not sufficient. One is to seek pardon of the person he backbit about in order to get himself absolved from the sin. The Prophet (ṣ) said, "He who damages the honour or possession of his Muslim brother should seek pardon of him before Judgement Day comes. On that day, his rewards will be taken. If he has none, the sins of the one he backbit about will be mixed with his, and they will be increased."

'Ā'ishah said to another about a woman, "The border of her garment is long." It was considered backbiting, and for that she sought pardon of that woman. There is no alternative but to seek pardon if the person is alive. If he is absent or dead, he should seek forgiveness for him. Allah says, "Take to forgiveness and enjoin good and turn aside from the ignorant" (Qur'an, 7:199). The Prophet (ṣ) asked, "What is the meaning of this pardon, O Jibrīl?" The latter replied, "Allah enjoins you pardon him who wrongs you, maintain blood ties with one who severs it and give him who deprives you." Al-Ḥasan said that a man said to him, "So-and-so backbit about you." He sent him a bunch of dried grapes saying, "I heard that you gifted your rewards to me. I send you in exchange this small gift of dried grapes. I seek your pardon, for I could not repay you in full."

Cheating and slander

Allah says, "Defamer, going about with slander" (Qur'an, 68:11), Then He says, "Ignoble, besides all that, base-born" (Qur'an, 68:13). 'Abdullāh ibn al-Mubārak said, "'Base born' means an illegitimate issue who does not keep words secret." This shows that he who does not keep words secret and goes about giving news to ears is like an illegitimate son.

Allah says, "Woe to every slanderer, defamer" (Qur'an, 104:1). The meaning of "slanderer" is one who goes about with slander. He says, "The bearer of fuel" (Qur'an, 111:4). It was said this person was a tale-bearer. He says, "They acted treacherously towards them so they availed them naught against Allah" (Qur'an,

66:10). This verse was revealed in connection with the wives of prophets Lūṭ and Nūḥ. When any guest came to the prophet Lūṭ, his wife told the people. Having received this news, they satisfied their lust with the guest. The wife of Nūḥ said to the people, "Nūḥ is insane."

The Prophet (ṣ) said, "A slanderer will not enter Paradise." Another *ḥadīth* says, "A scandal monger will not enter Paradise." The Prophet (ṣ) said, "The dearest of you to Allah are those who are the best in conduct, whose minds are soft and who love and receive love. The worst of you to Allah are those who go about with slander, who create disturbance among friends and who go about picking out the faults of religious men." He said, "Shall I not inform you of the worst of you?" The Companions replied, "O Prophet of Allah, tell us." The Prophet (ṣ) said, "They are those who walk with slander, create disturbance among friends and mix falsehood with the faults of the pious."

The Prophet (ṣ) said, "If a man gives a hint to disgrace a Muslim unjustly, Allah will disgrace him in Hell on Resurrection Day." He said, "If a man uses a word in order to disgrace an innocent man in the world, it becomes the duty of Allah to burn him in hellfire on Resurrection Day." He said, "He who bears witness against a Muslim untruthfully should enquire into his place in Hell." Some pious men said, "For this slander, one third of the punishment will be meted out in the grave."

The Prophet (ṣ) said, "When Allah created Paradise, He said to it, 'Talk with me.' Paradise replied, "He who will enter me is fortunate." Allah Almighty then said, 'By My glory and honour, eight types of men will not find a place in you: a habitual drunkard, a lifelong fornicator, a slanderer, one who encourages his own wife and daughter to fornicate, an oppressor, one who severs blood ties and one who makes an oath in the name of Allah, saying, 'If I do not do such-and-such,' but then breaks the oath.'"

Once, there was severe famine among the children of Israel. Mūsā then prayed many times for rain, but there was none. Allah then revealed to him, "There is a slanderer among you. He always tells others of people's faults. Because of that I will not accept your invocation." Mūsā said, "O Lord, show me that person and I will now eject him from our party." He said, "O Mūsā, I prohibited you from slandering a person." They then all repented and it rained."

It was reported that a man crossed a path of fourteen hundred miles in search of a wise, pious man and asked him seven questions: What is heavier than the sky? What is more spacious than the earth? What is harder than stone? What is hotter than fire? What is colder than ice? What is richer than the sea? And who is more humiliated that an orphan? The wise man replied, "Slandering an innocent man is heavier than the sky. The truth is wider than the earth. The heart of an unbeliever is harder than that of a stone. Greed and hatred are hotter than fire. The heart of a man who does not remove the wants of relatives is colder than ice. A contended heart is richer than the sea. And a slanderer becomes more humiliated than an orphan when his action is disclosed."

Definition of "slander"

Know that slander means to convey to a person what another has said about him, such as by saying, "So-and-so says such and such about you." The man to whom it is communicated and the man whose fault is communicated both dislike it. A third person also does not like it, though it is expressed by hints, gestures, writing or other means.

But if a Muslim is benefited by disclosing it, there is no fault in it. For instance, if a man sees the possession of another stolen, he should bear witness. The hearer of this slander or defamation has six duties to perform.

1. He should not believe the slanderer, as he is a transgressor and sinner and his evidence is to be rejected. Allah says, "O you who believe, if an evildoer comes to you with a report, look carefully into it, lest you harm a people in ignorance" (Qur'an, 49:6).

2. He should prevent him from defamation, advise him and say to him that it is a great sin. Allah says, “Enjoin the good and forbid the evil” (Qur’an, 31:17).
3. He should hate the person in his heart for Allah’s sake, as he is hated by Allah. To hate one whom Allah hates is compulsory.
4. He should not entertain bad thoughts about his Muslim brother, as Allah says, “Avoid most suspicion, for surely suspicion in some cases is a sin” (Qur’an, 49:12).
5. He should not be busy in seeking the truth of that news, as Allah says, “Do not spy” (Qur’an, 49:12).
6. He should not disclose his defamation, saying, “So-and-so told me such and such. It was related that a person came to ‘Umar ibn ‘Abd al-‘Azīz and said something to him about a person. The caliph then said to him, “If you desire, I will verify your statement. If you are telling a lie, you are a great sinner according to the verse of Allah ‘If an evildoer comes to you with a report, look carefully into it’ (Qur’an, 49:6). And if you are telling the truth, you are a slanderer according to this verse: ‘Defamer, going about with slander’ (Qur’an, 68:11). And if you wish, I will pardon you.” He said, “O Commander of the Faithful, I want pardon. I will never do it.”

Al-Ḥasan said, “Whoever bears tales to you, bears tales about you.” It appears from this that wrath should be shown to the defamer, and he should not be believed. The Prophet (ṣ) said, “He whose harms the people fear is the worst.” He said, “A severer will not enter Paradise.” When asked, “Who is a severer?” he replied, “He who severs ties between others and who defames.”

A man one day defamed another before ‘Alī. ‘Alī said to him, “O brother, I shall enquire about what you have said. We shall hate you if you are telling the truth, punish you if you are lying and pardon you if you like.” The man said, “O Commander of the Faithful, pardon me.” Muḥammad ibn Ka‘b al-Quraẓī was once asked, “What conduct of a believer is harmful to him?” He replied, “Excessive talk, the disclosing of secrets and belief in everybody’s words." Muṣ'ab ibn al-Zubayr said, "To believe in defamation is worse than defamation, as defamation shows the way, whereas belief in defamation gives permission. He who shows the path to a thing is not equal to him who admits it and gives permission. So beware of slanderers and defamers."

Once, a man sought permission of Sulaymān ibn 'Abd al-Malik to speak. Permission was granted and the man said, "O Commander of the Faithful, some men have defamed you. They purchased your world in exchange for their religion and gained your pleasure in earning the displeasure of Allah. They fear you in matters related to Allah and do not fear Allah in matters related to you. So do not trust them with the trust Allah has given you, and do not hand over to them what Allah has given you to protect, as they will spread harm among people and will destroy you with the help of their relatives. Their aims are rebellion and slander; their means are backbiting and defamation. You are responsible for their sins; and they are not responsible for yours. Their world will not be good if they destroy your next world because the worst deception is that of a man who sells his next world in exchange of the world of another."

Luqmān advised his son, "O dear son, I am giving you admonitions which, if you stick to them, will not deprive you of influence: Treat the near and the distant well. Do not express your ignorance to people of honour or dishonour to save your friends. Maintain ties with relatives, save them from the deception of a slanderer and save yourself from one who wishes you harm and deceit. When you part with your friends and they part with you, do not speak of their evil, and they also should not speak of yours." A pious man said, "The root of slander is falsehood, envy and hypocrisy. These three things are the root of disgrace."

Ḥammād ibn Salamah said, "A man purchased a slave. The seller said to the buyer, 'He has no defects other than one which is double-dealing." The buyer said, 'I am satisfied." Then he purchased him. After some days' stay with his master, the slave said to his wife, 'Your husband does not love you and he wants to purchase a slave girl. I shall tell you of a spell. When he falls asleep, take some hair from his beard with a razor. I shall prepare with them a spell to make him love you.' He then went to the husband and said to him, 'Your wife does not love you and fell in love with another person. She may kill you if the opportunity arises.' One day, the master fell asleep, and his wife went with a razor to take some hair from his beard. When she was about to take it, he suddenly awoke and caught her with the razor and killed her. This news reached her relatives, who came at once and killed him. Thus quarrels ensued between the tribe of the husband and the tribe of the wife."

Hypocrisy

Hypocrisy is another evil of the tongue. It is to go to two enemies and introduce yourself as a friend to each of them and hold one opinion with each of them. 'Ammār ibn Yāsir said that the Prophet (ṣ) said, "He who has two tongues in the world will have two tongues in the next world." He said, "On Resurrection Day, you will see the worst man to Allah with two faces. He will come to one party with one thing and to another party with another thing." In another narration, "He will come with one face to one party and with another face to another party." Abū Hurayrah said, "A man having two faces will not be considered a faithful man to Allah." Mālik ibn Dīnar said, "I have read in the Torah, "He who talks with his friend with two tongues and yet claims to be a trustee, Allah will destroy those tongues."

The Prophet (ṣ) said, "On Resurrection Day, the worst men to Allah will be liars, the proud and those men who harboured much hatred for their brothers. When they met with them, they hated them. When they were called to Allah and His Prophet, they came late. And when they were called to Satan, they came hurriedly."

It was related that when a Companion of the Prophet (ṣ) died, Ḥudhayfah did not pray the funeral prayer for him. 'Umar then said, "He is one of the Companions of the Prophet (ṣ), but you have not prayed his funeral prayer." He replied, "O Commander of the Faithful, he is one of the hypocrites." 'Umar said, "I ask you, am I included in them?" He said, "You are not a hypocrite. Nobody after you can be trusted."

Praise

Another evil of the tongue is praise. In some cases, praise is unlawful. There are six harms of praise, out of which four harms affect the praiser and two affect the hearer of the praise.

1. Falsehood. In the case of too much praise, recourse must be had to falsehood. Khālid ibn Ma'dān said, "If a man praises a ruler or a man that does not have the quality he is being praised for, Allah will raise him in such a way that it will be difficult for him to talk to people with his tongue."
2. Ostentation. This is a harm because love is expressed by praise, but it may not be in the heart and he may not believe all he says. Thus, he becomes ostentatious and hypocritical.
3. Making statements which have not or cannot be confirmed. It is reported that a man praised another before the Prophet (ṣ), who said to them, "You have severed the neck of your brother. If he hears this, he will not get salvation." Then he said, "If you are to praise a man, say, 'I believe he is such and such, but Allah knows whether he is pure or impure. I cannot say more than what Allah knows of anybody.'" So it is danger to say that someone is a pious, God-fearing, charitable and so on. Once, 'Umar saw a man praising another and asked the praiser, "Have you travelled with him?" He replied, "No." He asked, "Have you done business with him?" He replied, "No." He asked, "Are you his neighbour morning and evening?" He replied, "No." He said, "By Allah, I think you do not know him."

4. The one praised may be an oppressor or a great sinner. To praise him in such circumstances is unlawful. The Prophet (ṣ) said, "When a great sinner is praised, Allah becomes displeased." Al-Ḥasan said, "He who prays that an oppressor live a long life disobeys Allah in His world."

The praised man suffers two harms from praise: pride and self-praise. These two things are ruinous. Al-Ḥasan said, "One day, 'Umar was seated with a stick among the people when al-Jārūd ibn al-Mundhir came. One of those present said, 'This man is the chief of the Rabī'ah tribe,' which 'Umar and those around him heard. When he approached 'Umar, the latter was brandishing his stick over his head. At this, al-Jārūd asked, 'O Commander of the Faithful, what sort of treatment is this?' 'Umar replied, 'Have you not heard what that man said about you?' He said, 'Yes, I heard it.' 'Umar said, "I feared that praise may grow in you a sense of pride, so I destroyed it by brandishing this stick."

The second harm is that when a man praises another, the latter becomes pleased and finds solace and, as such, gives up self-improvement, as he thinks that he has reached the limit of progress. He who understands that he has faults tries to improve his character. For this reason, the Prophet (ṣ) said, "You have severed his neck. If he possesses it, he will not get salvation"; "If you praise a man in his face, think that you are passing a sharp knife round his neck"; and "It is better to attack a man with sharp sword than to praise a man before his face. 'Umar said, "Praise is like murder, as a murdered person is saved from the responsibility of actions. Praise grows idleness or self-praise and pride, both of which are destructive as murder."

If the praiser and the one praised are saved from these harms, then there is no fault in praise. For this reason, the Prophet (ṣ) praised his Companions. He said about Abū Bakr, "If the faith of Abū Bakr was weighed against the faith of the people of the world, his faith will be heavier." He said regarding 'Umar, "If I was not sent as a Prophet, 'Umar would have been sent as a Prophet." They did not become proud because of these praises.

Moreover, the Prophet (ṣ) said, "I am the leader of the children of Adam and there is no boast in it." In other words, "I am not saying this out of pride." When people were praising a dead man, the Prophet (ṣ) said, "He is fit to receive praise." Mujāhid said, "The children of Adam have friends among the angels. When any Muslim mentions the good works of another Muslim, the angels says, 'O son of Adam, keep your mysteries of secrets secret, be pleased with your affairs and praise Allah, who has kept your secrets secret.'"

The duties of the praised

The praised man must save himself from pride, self-praise and idleness. He will not be able to save himself from these evils unless he thinks about his ultimate end and the result of his actions. The praiser does not know what the praised man knows about him. The former would surely not praise him if he knew of him what he knows of himself. The Prophet (ṣ) said, "Throw dust at the face of the praisers." Sufyān ibn 'Uyaynah said, "He who knows himself cannot be injured by praise." When a religious man was praised, he said, "O Allah, this servant of yours has come to me with your hatred. I cite you as a witness to his hatred." Another religious man was praised and said, "O Allah, these people do not know me." Once, 'Alī was praised and said, "O Allah, forgive me for what they say and make me better than what they think about me." A man once praised 'Umar, who in turn said, "You are ruining me."

Carelessness

Another harm of the tongue is carelessness or inattention in speech, especially when it is in connection with religious affairs. The Prophet (ṣ) said, "Let none among you say, 'Whatever Allah wishes, and what you wish.' Rather, say, "Whatever Allah wishes and then what you wish." Ibn 'Abbās said, "One man came to the Prophet (ṣ) and said in the midst of his talk, 'Whatever Allah wishes and you wish.' Thereupon, the Prophet (ṣ) said to him, "Have you made me equal to Allah? Rather, say, 'Whatever Allah Almighty wishes.'"

The Prophet (ṣ) said, "Allah has prohibited us from taking an oath in the name of your father. Let him take an oath in the name of Allah or else remain silent." 'Umar said, "I have not made an oath in the name of father since I heard that." The Prophet (ṣ) said, "Let nobody among you say 'my servant' or 'my maidservant,' as you are all the servants of Allah, and all your women are the maidservants of Allah. Rather, say 'My boy,' 'my girl,' 'my son' or 'my daughter.' Likewise, servants and maidservants should not say 'My lord.' Rather, they should say 'my chief.' All are the servants of Allah, and Allah is your Lord."

The Prophet (ṣ) said, "Never call a great sinner 'my chief' because if he becomes your chief, you will incur the displeasure of your Lord." He said, "He who says 'I am free from Islam' becomes as he has said. If he is lying, he will not be able to return to Islam safely." For this reason, the Prophet (ṣ) said, "He who remains silent has salvation."

Questions of laypeople about Allah

Another evil of tongue is the questions laypeople have about Allah, His attributes, His words and His tongue. These attributes of Allah are of two kinds: uncreated and created. It is the duty of ordinary men to follow what is in the Qur'an about commands and prohibitions. To understand the Qur'an is difficult to many. The Prophet (ṣ) said, "Leave to me what I left for you, as your predecessors were destroyed because of their excessive questions to and differences with their prophets. Give up what I have prohibited you and do, to the best of your ability, what I have ordered you."

Anas said, "The people once asked the Prophet (ṣ) many questions, at which he became enraged. He then mounted the pulpit and said, 'You are questioning me, but do not ask except what I have informed you about.' A man came to him and asked, 'Who is my father?' He replied, "Your father is Ḥudhāfah. Then two young men came and asked, 'O Prophet of Allah, who is our father?' He replied, 'Your father is he by whose name you are called.' Another man got up and said, 'Shall I enter Paradise or Hell?' He said, 'You will enter Hell and not Paradise.' When the people saw that the Prophet (ṣ) was enraged, they did not ask him further questions. 'Umar then came to his side and said, 'We are pleased with Allah as Lord, Islam as a religion and Muḥammad as a prophet.' The Prophet (ṣ) said, 'O 'Umar, sit down. May Allah shower blessings on you.'"

What you have come to know is sufficient. The Prophet (ṣ) prohibited arguments and excessive questions, saying, "Soon people will ask many questions. They will even ask, 'Allah created the creatures, but who created Allah?' When they ask this, reply, 'Say, 'He, Allah, is One. Allah is He on whom all depend" until the Sūrah is completed (Qur'an, 112). Then spit to your left thrice and seek refuge from Satan."

Excessive questions were prohibited in the story of Mūsā and al-Khaḍir. So the questions of ordinary men about the subtle matters of religion are great objects of danger. Their discussions about the language of the Qur'an are akin to the condition of one to whom the king wrote a letter, informing him of many necessary things, but instead of paying attention to these things, he wasted time thinking about whether the paper of the letter was new or old, for which he would surely be punished. Similarly, ordinary men give up many necessary things, but ask questions about many unnecessary and subtle things about Allah and His attributes.

Book 5
Anger, hatred and envy

1
Anger

Anger is a blaze of fire which arises from the fire of Allah in the heart. It burns like fire in the lowest part of the heart, like fire under husk. The hidden pride in the mind of every oppressor and disobedient man is disclosed by anger, like the fire that comes out by the rubbing of iron against stone. It appears to those who see with the light of sure faith. The conduct of Satan finds a place in the man in whom anger has found a place. Allah says, "He said, 'I am better than he. You have created me of fire, while him You have created of dust'" (Qur'an, 7:12). Earth is steady and calm, while fire is unsteady, rising and burning. The result of anger is hatred, because of which a man is ruined.

The harms of anger

The Qur'an

Allah says, "When those who disbelieved harboured in their hearts (feelings of) disdain, the disdain of (the days of) ignorance, but Allah sent down His tranquillity on His Messenger and on the believers ..." (Qur'an, 48:26). Allah rebuked the unbelievers for their disdain, which arose out of baseless anger, and praised the believers, as He sent down solace and consolation on him.

Ḥadīth

One day, a man came to the Prophet (ṣ) and said, "O Prophet of Allah, order me to do a short action." He said, "Do not be angry." Ibn 'Umar said, "I told the Prophet (ṣ), 'Give me a short piece of advice by dint of which I may hope for good.' He said, 'Do not be angry.'" Once, 'Abdullāh ibn 'Amr asked the Prophet (ṣ), "What will save me from the wrath of Allah?" The Prophet (ṣ) replied, "Do not express your anger." The Prophet (ṣ) once asked some of his Companions, "Whom do you consider among you a strong man?" They replied, "Him who men cannot take down." He said, "That is not so. He is the strong man who can control his passion at the time of anger." Similarly, he said, "He who has physical strength is not a stronger man than him who can control his passion."

The Prophet (ṣ) said, "Allah keeps the secret affairs of a man secret who can swallow anger." Sulaymān, the son of Dāwūd, said, "O dear son, save yourself from excessive anger, as excessive anger makes the heart of a patient man light." Concerning Allah's words "Honourable and chaste" (Qur'an, 3:39), 'Ikrimah said an honourable person is someone who cannot be defeated by anger. Abū al-Dardā' said, "I said, 'O Messenger of Allah, teach me an action which can take me to Paradise.' He said, 'Do not be angry.'"

The prophet Yaḥyā told 'Īsā, "Do not be angry." 'Īsā said, "I can't help but be angry. I am merely a man." Then Yaḥyā said, "Do not amass wealth." 'Īsā said, "Yes, I can do this." The Prophet (ṣ) said, "Anger destroys faith like a condiment destroys honey." He also said, "If a man gets angry, he roams near Hell." Once, a man asked the Prophet (ṣ), "What is hard?" He replied, "Anger." He asked, "What will keep me away from Allah's wrath?" He replied, "Do not express anger."

Ja'far ibn Muḥammad said, "Anger is the key to every evil." In a similar vein, a Madīnan Helper (*Anṣārī*) said, "Anger is the root of foolishness and its guide." Mujāhid said, "Satan said, 'The son of Adam cannot baffle me in three matters. When any man is intoxicated, we fix a rope in his nose and direct him to whichever direction we like and make him do whatever we like. When he gets angry, he utters words unknown to him and does things he regrets later. When he is miserly with something which is under his control, we engage him in work beyond his strength.'"

A wise man said, "Appease your anger, as it may lead to the disgrace of explanation." 'Abdullāh ibn Mas'ūd said, "Look at the patience of a man at the time of his anger and at his trust at the time of his greed. If he does not get angry, why would you need to know about his patience? If he is not greedy, why would you need to know about his trust?" 'Umar ibn 'Abd al-'Azīz wrote to one of his governors, "Do not punish at the time of your anger. When you get angry at any man, keep him in detention. When your anger is appeased, give him punishment in proportion to his crime. And do not inflict on him more than fifteen lashes at the time of punishing him."

'Alī ibn Yazīd said, "A man of the Quraysh used harsh words against 'Umar ibn 'Abd al-'Azīz, who remained silent for a long time and then said, 'You wish that Satan arouses in me the pride of a caliph and that I treat you so rudely that you can take revenge tomorrow on me.'" A wise man said to his son, "O dear son, wisdom does not remain safe at the time of anger, just as life does not remain safe in a burning fire. He who gets the least angry is the most intelligent among them. If anger concerns any matter of the next world, it is called 'wisdom' and 'patience.' If it concerns any matter of this world, it is called 'deceit' because people say that anger is the enemy of the intellect and a danger." 'Umar used to say in his sermon, "Those of you who are safe from greed, passion and anger gets salvation."

Al-Ḥasan said, "The signs of a Muslim are the following: He has strength in religion, discretion in lenient matters, faith in sure matters and knowledge of patience. He pays his dues, adopts a middle course in riches and has patience in times of danger. His anger does not overcome him, his excitement does not throw him into danger, his passion does not prevail over him, his stomach does not disgrace him, his greed does not make him light and his intention does not make him mean. He helps the oppressed and shows kindness to the weak. He is not extravagant in expense and does not misuse his money. He pardons if oppressed or an ignoramus gives him trouble. People remain safe at his hands."

A prophet told his followers, "Is there anybody among you who can promise me that he will never get angry? If so, he will gain my rank, reside with me in Paradise and be my successor. A young man got up and said, "I" and observed this during his lifetime. When the Prophet (ṣ) died, the young man became his successor and was named Dhū al-Kifl, a name meaning 'he fulfilled his promise truly.' Wahb ibn Munabbih said, "There are four elements of infidelity: anger, passion, greed and foolishness."

Definition of "anger"

Know that Allah Most Merciful first created an animal in such a way that for some of his internal and external ingredients, his destruction was inevitable. Then Allah gave him weapons for a fixed time to save him from that destruction. The internal ingredients with which his body was formed are heat and cold, which He set up against each other. In order to save himself from external dangers, he has been given weapons, one of which is anger. It arises from his mind and removes destructive elements. So Allah created the passion of anger from fire and kept it concealed in the human heart. Whenever anything stands against his wishes, anger is enhanced in such a way that the blood of the heart spreads through all of his veins and as a result his eyes become red and his face reddish. The birth place of anger is the heart. The food of anger is revenge and greed. Anger is not appeased without these two things.

Three kinds of men

Mankind is divided into three classes according to the degree of anger: those with no anger, those with extreme anger and those with moderate anger.

Regarding the first class of men, they are no good because they lack anger. These people are called "men of impotence." Al-Shāfi'ī said, "He whose anger cannot be aroused is an ass, and he who has lost his strength of anger is a man of very short intellect." Allah praises the Companions of the Prophet (ṣ), saying, "Firm of heart against the unbelievers, compassionate among themselves" (Qur'an, 48:29). Similarly, Allah said to His Prophet, "Strive hard against the unbelievers and the hypocrites and be unyielding to them" (Qur'an, 9:73). This hard treatment is the result of the excitement of anger."

Excessive anger is harmful and prevails over good qualities. A man with excessive anger first loses his intellect, religion and worship; then his sense of right and wrong and the power of right and good thinking, then his power of freedom. Finally, he becomes a man afflicted with danger.

The cause of excessive anger is an inborn nature and also the result of habit. There are men who are naturally inclined to anger: They have a sense of anger in their inborn nature. The Prophet (ṣ) said, "The coldness of nature appeases anger and breaks up its nature."

Anger arising from habit

There are men who say, "I shall not bear any kind of deceit. I will not bear any harsh words." He who hears this helps him in arousing his anger. Thus, when his anger is aroused, he becomes blind and deaf to advices and counsels. The man of thoughts is brave. Anger him as the steam of heated blood rises to his brain. Sometimes it covers even the mind of sight. As a result, the eye become blood, and to him the whole world becomes dark. Fire burns in him, and the light of the intellect is extinguished. As a result, his figure changes, his eyes become red and his nostrils change. If he could see his body patiently at the time of anger, he would become ashamed of it.

Verbal signs of anger include the use abusive language. Physical signs include attack, assault and murder. The person attacks any man before him, and his opponents flee from him. Out of wrath, he cuts his clothes, slaps his own face, beats the ground with his hands and feet and sometimes runs like a wild man, breaking plates and utensils. The effect of wrath on the heart is hatred, envy, gloating over his adversaries' sorrows and sadness about their happiness.

The Prophet (ṣ) said, "Sa'd has wrath, and I have more wrath than him, and Allah's wrath is more than mine." He said, "He who is firm in religion among my followers is good." Allah says, "Let not pity for them detain you in the matter of obedience to Allah (Qur'an, 24:2). He who has no wrath is unable to bear hardships for the progress of the soul. Anger which rises at the hint of the intellect and religion is good. Intellect arouses anger where it is necessary and appeases anger where patience is necessary. The best way is to keep anger on the line of moderation, and Allah enjoins man to stand on this border line. The Prophet (ṣ) said, "The middle way is the best of all actions." So the two extremes must be avoided in order not to become angry at all or excessively angry. This is the straight path.

Is it possible to root out anger?

Man loves things and dislikes things. So there is no alternative for him but to be angry. Things occur according to his nature, and things occur opposite to his nature. What agrees with his nature is loved by him, and what disagrees with his nature is disliked by him. When an object of love is snatched away from him, he becomes angry, and when a disliked thing is given to him, he becomes angry.

There are three kinds of things which a man loves. The first is things he needs, such as food, clothes, housing and physical health. If any man wants to strike your body, it is natural for you to get angry at him. If anybody wants to take your clothes or make you naked, it is natural for you to get angry at him. The second is things he does not need, such as fruits, abundant riches, servants, birds and beasts. Gold and silver are loved and hoarded, so if anyone steals them, it is but natural to get angry at him. The third is things which are special to a person, such as books for the learned man. If anybody takes away his books, for example, be becomes angry at him. This is the case for the implements of expert industrialists and businessmen.

The Prophet (ṣ) said with regard to the necessary objects of love, "He who rises in the morning with a safe dwelling place, sound body and the provisions of his day has been given the world with its treasures." Nobody should get angry except about the three kinds of things enumerated above.

With regard to these three objects of love, we shall discuss the controlling of anger.

Regarding the first object, absolutely necessary things, anger should be kept under control and expressed according to the rules of Sharī'ah. However, to root out anger from the heart is impossible and unnatural. Regarding the second object, unnecessary things, it is possible to get out of anger by practice and habit, as it is possible to remove from the heart love for unnecessary things.

This can be done in the following way. Understand that the grave is your dwelling, the next world your permanent abode and this world a resting place or a bridge over which you will have to walk to get to the next world. So take what is absolutely necessary with you to cross the bridge and leave what is not necessary. So you will have to leave the world and give up its love. Anger comes out of love, and if such habits are formed, anger can be brought under control.

The Prophet (ṣ) used to have anger, but would say, "O Allah, I am only a man and have anger as a man does. Take my anger as a blessing, purification and nearness from me to any Muslim whom I rebuke, curse or assault." 'Abdullāh ibn 'Amr ibn al-'Āṣ said, "O Messenger of Allah, I write everything you say in anger and in content." The Prophet (ṣ) said, "Write! For by Him who sent me with the truth, nothing but truth comes from it" pointing to his tongue. The Prophet (ṣ) did not say, "I have no wrath." Rather, he said that anger could not take him out of the limits of truth. In other words, he would not do anything at the behest of anger.

Similarly, 'Ā'ishah once got angry, and the Prophet (ṣ) asked her, "What is the matter with you?" She replied, "Does not Satan come to you?" He said, "Yes, he comes. But because I have invoked Allah, He made me prevail over him, and he has submitted to me, enjoining me only to the good." He did not say, "Satan does not come to me."

'Alī said, "The Prophet (ṣ) did not get angry at any action of the world. When any true matter charmed him, nobody knew it, and nobody took revenge on his anger. He got angry for the truth, which was evident in his actions. Once, a man rebuked Salmān, who then said, "If my deeds are less in the scale, I am more heinous than your rebuke. If, however, my deeds are heavy in the scale, I will not suffer harm from your rebuke." He said this because the affairs of the next world kept him engaged. Likewise, a man once rebuked Abū Bakr, who replied, "My faults Allah has kept secret from you are more heinous than your rebuke." A woman called Mālik ibn Dīnar a hypocrite, whereupon he said to her, "Nobody has come to know me better than you." The insult did not enrage him. Once, a man rebuked al-Sha'bī, who responded, "May Allah pardon me if you have spoken the truth, and may He pardon you if you have spoken a lie." These examples show that sages did not get angry because they were engaged in the affairs of the next world.

There are three causes of not getting angry: being more engaged in more necessary things, being immersed in Allah's oneness and knowing that Allah does not love anger, and so more love for Him extinguishes the fire of anger. This is possible when the love of the world is ousted from the heart.

Causes of anger and its medicine

Know that you have learnt that the medicine of a disease is to remove the root cause of that disease. It is therefore necessary to know the root cause anger. Yaḥyā once asked 'Īsā, "What is difficult?" 'Īsā replied, "Allah's wrath." Yaḥyā then asked, "What brings one close to the wrath of Allah?" 'Īsā replied, "Anger." Yaḥyā asked him, "What grows and increases anger?" 'Īsā replied, "Pride, prestige, hope for honour and haughtiness." The causes which grow anger are self-conceit, self-praise, jest and ridicule, argumentation, treachery, too much greed for too much wealth and name and fame. If these evils are united in a person, his conduct becomes bad and he cannot escape anger.

So these things should be removed by their opposites. Self-praise is to be removed by modesty; pride by knowing one's own origin and birth; greed by remaining satisfied with necessary things; and miserliness by charity. The Prophet (ṣ) said, "A strong man is not he who defeats his adversary in wrestling. Rather, a strong man is he who controls himself at the time of anger."

We shall now discuss the medicine for anger after one gets angry. The medicine is a mixture of knowledge and action.

Medicine based on knowledge

The medicine based on knowledge is of six kinds.

- The first medicine of knowledge is to ponder over the rewards and punishments of appeasing anger that have been mentioned in the verses of the Qur'an and words of the Prophet (ṣ). Your hope for getting rewards for appeasing anger will restrain you from taking revenge. Mālik ibn Aws ibn al-Ḥadathān said, "'Umar was once enraged with a person and ordered that he be assaulted. Then I said, 'O Commander of the Faithful, 'take to forgiveness and enjoin good and turn aside from the ignorant' (Qur'an, 7:199).' So 'Umar would say, 'Take to forgiveness and enjoin good and turn aside from the ignorant' (Qur'an, 7:199).'" So it was his habit to ponder over this verse after he released the man. Once, 'Umar ibn 'Abd al-'Azīz ordered that a man be whipped. But when the latter recited the verse "Those who restrain (their) anger" (Qur'an, 3:134), 'Umar said to his slave, "Leave him."

- The second kind of medicine based on knowledge is to fear the punishment of Allah and to know that Allah's punishment of you is greater than your punishment of another. In other words, if you take revenge on a man out of anger, Allah will take revenge on you on Judgement Day. Allah said in one of the earlier scriptures, "O son of Adam, when you get angry, remember Me. Then, when I get angry, I will not include you in those whom I will destroy." One day, the Prophet (ṣ) sent a servant on an errand. When he returned very late, he said to the servant, "I would assault you if revenge were not taken for it in the next world." It was said that there was a king among the children of Israel who had a minister. When the king got angry, the minister showed him a piece writing in which was written, "Fear death and remember the next world." He used to read it until his anger was appeased.
- The third kind of medicine for anger based on knowledge is to take precautions of the punishment of enmity and revenge on yourself. You feel joy in seeing your enemy sorrowful in your presence, yet you yourself are not free from that danger. You should fear that your enemy may take revenge against you in this world and in the next.
- The fourth kind of medicine for anger based on knowledge is to think about the ugly face of the angry man, which resembles that of a ferocious beast. He who appeases anger looks like a sober and learned man. So which figure do you like to take: the figure of a beast or that of a learned man?
- The fifth medicine of anger based on knowledge is to think that Satan will advise you, saying, "You will be weak if you do not get angry." Do not listen to him.

- The sixth medicine is to think of the reason why you are angry and remember that what Allah has wished has occurred.

Medicine based on action

When you get angry, say "I seek refuge in Allah from the accursed Satan. The Prophet (ṣ) ordered us to say thus. He also said this at the time of his anger. When 'Ā'ishah got angry, he dragged her by the nose and said, "O dear 'Ā'ishah, say, 'O Allah, you are the Lord of my Prophet Muḥammad. Forgive my sins, remove the anger of my heart and save me from misguidance.'"

If anger does not go by this means, you should sit down if you are standing, lie down if you are sitting and bring yourself close to the ground, as you have been created of earth. Thus, make yourself calm like the earth. The cause of wrath is heat, and its opposite effect is to lie down on the ground and to make the body calm and cool.

The Prophet (ṣ) said, "Anger is a burning coal which burns in the heart. Do you not see your eyebrows wide and eyes reddish? So when one of you feels like that, let him sit down if standing and lie down if sitting. If the anger still does not stop, perform ablution with cold water or take a bath, for it cannot be extinguished without water." He said, "When one of you gets angry, let him perform ablution with water, as anger arises out of fire." Another narration reads, "Anger comes from Satan, and Satan is made of fire, and fire can be extinguished by water. So when anybody among you gets angry, he should perform ablution."

The Prophet (ṣ) said, "When you get angry, be silent." Abū Hurayrah reported that when the Prophet (ṣ) got angry, he sat down if he was standing and lay down if he was sitting, whereupon his wrath was appeased." The Prophet (ṣ) said, "Be careful! Anger is a burning coal in the heart of the son of Adam. Have you not looked at his reddish eyes and wide eyebrows? When any of you see it signs, let him attach his face to earth" indicating we should prostrate and keep the most honourable place among the limbs attached to the earth and keep it calm.

It was reported that when 'Umar got angry one day, he wanted cold water to snuff and said, "Anger comes from Satan, and water removes anger." When 'Urwah ibn Muḥammad was appointed governor of Yemen, Ubayy said to him, "When you get angry, look to the heavens above and the earth below and consider the supremacy of the Creator of both. It was related that Abū Dharr said to a man, "O son of a red mother (son of a maidservant)." News of this reached the Prophet (ṣ), who said, "O Abū Dharr, I heard that you have backbitten about your Muslim brother, mentioning his mother." He said yes and at once went to the man to please him, but the man came to him first and greeted him. When news of this reached the Prophet (ṣ), he said, "O Abū Dharr, raise your head and look and know that you are not better than a red or a black man. Superiority is acquired only by action." Then he said, "When you get angry, sit down from a standing posture and lie down straight from a sitting posture."

Merits of appeasing anger

Allah says, "Those who restrain (their) anger" (Qur'an, 3:134), praising them.

The Prophet (ṣ) said:

Allah keeps his punishment from one who appeases anger. Allah pardons the faults of one who confesses his sins to his Lord. Allah conceals the hidden faults of one who controls his tongue.

He who is victorious over his passions at the time of anger is strong among you. He who pardons, having power, is more patient among you.

Whoever appeases anger, though having the will to translate his anger into action, Allah will fill his heart with contentment on Resurrection Day.

Another narration reads, "Allah will fill his heart with belief and peace."

Nobody swallows a bitterer pill than that of anger for the pleasure of Allah.

There is a special door in Hell through which no sinner other than one who gets angry unlawfully will enter.

Whoever restrains his anger, having power to translate it into action, Allah will tell him to select any hour in the presence of all His creatures.

The gulp of anger a man takes is dear to Allah. Whoever resists this gulp of anger, Allah will fill his heart with faith.

Traditions from Companions and early Muslims

'Umar said, "He who fears Allah cannot commit sin by his anger. He who fears Allah cannot do what he likes. Were it not for Judgement Day, it would be otherwise." Ayyūb said, "A moment's patience removes many evils." Sufyān al-Thawrī, Abū Khuzaymah al-Yarbūʿī and al-Fuḍayl ibn ʿIyāḍ were once discussing renunciation of the world. They said unanimously that patience at the time of anger and forbearance at the time of greed are the best acts of worship. Muḥammad ibn Kaʿb said, "The faith of one who has three is perfect. He has faith in Allah, His satisfaction does not arise out of false matters, and his anger cannot remove him from truth. When he has strength, he does not accept what is not for him."

Merits of patience

Know that patience is better than the appeasement of anger, as patience is necessary for controlling anger and requires great effort. If one is accustomed to control anger, it becomes a habit, and eventually anger will not arise. If it arises, he does not experience much difficulty in controlling it. This is the sign of a perfect intellect. The Prophet (ṣ) said, "Knowledge is acquired by effort. He who seeks good deeds gets them. He who saves himself from sin is secure." It appears from this that it is by effort that patience is gained. It is acquired like knowledge. The Prophet (ṣ) said, "Seek knowledge and with it peace and patience. Behave modestly with those who acquire knowledge and from whom you learn. Do not be included among haughty scholars, otherwise your ignorance will prevail over your patience."

The Prophet (ṣ) used to say in his invocation, "O Allah, make me fortunate with knowledge, adorn me with patience, honour me with God-fearingness and increase my dignity with tranquillity." He said, "Seek a high rank with Allah." The Companions asked, "O Prophet of Allah, what is it?" He replied, "Maintain ties with one who severs them with you and give one who deprives you." He said, "Prophets have five traits: shame, patience, being treated cupping, cleansing the feet and using perfume." He said, "A Muslim gains the rank of fasting the whole year and praying all the nights by dint of patience. A man is written as an oppressor and a haughty man, but his power does not extend beyond his family members."

Abū Hurayrah said, "A man came to the Prophet (ṣ) and said, 'O Prophet of Allah, I have relatives I treat well, but they treat me evilly. I am good to them, but they are bad to me. They hold me in contempt, but I remain patient.' The Prophet (ṣ) said to him, 'If you stick to what you have said, you are filling their bellies with the fire of ashes, and as long as that fire remains in them, you will have a helper from Allah.'"

A Muslim prayed, "O Allah, I have no money to give in charity. If any man mars my honour, consider it my charity." Allah then revealed to the prophet of the time, "Tell him I have forgiven his sins." The Prophet (ṣ) once asked, "Can nobody among you be like Abū Ḍamḍam?" The Companions asked, "Who among your predecessors is Abū Ḍamḍam." The Prophet (ṣ) replied, "He used to pray at dawn, 'O Allah, I've given my honour to whoever opposes me.'"

Concerning Allah's words "When the ignorant address them, they say, 'Peace'" (Qur'an, 25:63), al-Ḥasan said that Allah speaks here of those who are patient: If they are held in contempt, they do not hold in contempt. ʻAṭā' ibn Abī Rabāḥ said the phrase "in humbleness" (*hawnan*) in the verse "They who walk on the earth in humbleness" (Qur'an, 25:63) means patience. When they pass by useless talks, they pass honourably. Mujāhid said that when they are given trouble, they forgive.

The Prophet (ṣ) said, "O Allah, let me not reach the age, nor let the age reach me, in which people do not follow the learned, are not embarrassed before the patient and whose hearts will be foreign while their tongue is Arabic." The Prophet (ṣ) said, "There are people among you now with me who are patient and forbearing, then their successors, then their successors. Do not hold differing opinions which will separate your hearts, and be careful of the dangers of markets." The Prophet (ṣ) once said to Ashaj, who came as a deputation to him, "O Ashaj, you have two traits Allah and his Prophet love." He said, "O Messenger of Allah, my parents be sacrificed for you. What are they?" The Prophet (ṣ) replied, "Patience and gravity. These two traits Allah gave you."

The Prophet (ṣ) said, "Allah Most Merciful loves the patient, the shameful, those who love freedom, those who refrain from begging, even though they have large families, and the God-fearing. He hates the hardhearted, beggars with earnestness and fools." He said, "The spiritual works of a man who has not one of the three qualities will not be accepted: God-fearingness which restrains him from sinful acts, patience which restrains fools and conduct with which he can live among people."

The Prophet (ṣ) said, "When Allah assembles all creatures on Judgement Day, a proclaimer will proclaim, 'Where are the people of rank?' Then a party will run towards Paradise hurriedly. When questioned why by angels, they will say, 'We remained patient when oppressed, and we pardoned when held in contempt. Then they will be told, 'Enter Paradise. How good the rewards of the doers of good are!'"

Traditions from Companions and early Muslims

'Umar said, "Acquire knowledge and seek peace of mind and patience for learning." 'Alī said, "There is no good in the increase of wealth and children, but there is good in the increase of knowledge and patience and not boasting about spiritual works. When you do good, praise Allah. When you commit sin, beg forgiveness of Allah." Al-Ḥasan said, "Acquire knowledge and adorn it with gravity and patience." Aktham ibn Ṣayfī said, "Patience is the root of wisdom and all affairs."

Abū al-Dardā' said, "I saw people as leaves without thorns, and now I am seeing them as leaves with thorns. If you are acquainted with them, they ridicule you. If you give them up, they will not give you up." They asked, "How should we treat them?" He replied, "If anybody rebukes you, do not respond to him. When you are poor on Resurrection Day, it will benefit you."

Mu'āwiyah said, "A man will not reach the rank of one qualified to issue expert legal opinion (*mujtahid*) until his patience prevails over his ignorance and forbearance over his low desires, and he will not be able to reach that rank without the strength of learning." Mu'āwiyah asked 'Amr ibn al-Ahtam, "Who is the bravest man?" He replied, "One who removed his ignorance by his patience." He asked him, "Who is the most charitable man?" He replied, "One who spends his world for the good of his religion."

Regarding Allah's words "He between whom and you was enmity would be as if he were a warm friend" (Qur'an, 41:34), Anas ibn Mālik said, "His brother rebuked him, then said, 'If you tell lie, Allah may forgive you. If you speak the truth, Allah may forgive me.'"

Mu'āwiyah said to 'Arābah ibn Aws, "O 'Arabah, how did you become chief of your people?" He replied, "O Commander of the Faithful, I remain patient with the treatment of the ignorant, give their beggars charity and help them in their needs. He who works like me is like me, and I am better than him."

'Alī ibn al-Ḥusayn ibn 'Alī said, "One day, a man rebuked me. I gave him clothes to put on and ordered that he be given a thousand dirhams." Al-Khalīl ibn Aḥmad said, "It is well known that if you benefit a man who ill-treats you, there occurs in the mind of the latter thoughts which prevent him from doing further ill-treatment." Wahb ibn Munabbih said, "He who shows kindness is shown kindness. He who keeps silent remains safe. He who holds in contempt is defeated. He who makes haste commits mistakes. He who wants to do evil deeds does not remain safe. He who does not give up quarrels and disputes is rebuked. He who does not hate sins commits sins. He who hates sins becomes sinless. He who follows the instructions of Allah is safe. He who takes Allah as a friend becomes the friend of all. He who does not invoke Allah becomes needy. He who does not fear the punishment of Allah becomes disgraced. He who invokes the help of Allah gains the upper hand."

A man once told Mālik ibn Dīnar, "I heard you have backbitten about me." He said, "Then you are more honourable than me. If I have done so, I have given my spiritual works to you." Luqmān said, "There are three people who cannot be known except at three times: A patient man cannot be known except at the time of anger; a brave man cannot be known except at the time of battle; and a friend cannot be known except at the time of need."

When is revenge punishable?

Know that to treat an oppression with oppression is unlawful. To backbite for backbiting, to spy for spying and to rebuke for rebuking are unlawful. This is the case for all sins. But to take revenge or retaliation is allowed according to the rules of Sharī'ah. The Prophet (ṣ) said, "If any man insults you for who you are, do not insult him in return for who he is." He said, "If two men rebuke each other, the sin is his who first rebuked, so long as the rebuked man does not exceed the limit. Two mutual rebukers are devils, accusing each other falsely."

One day, a man was rebuking Abū Bakr al-Ṣiddīq, who remained silent for a long time. When he began to take revenge, the Prophet (ṣ) got up. Abū Bakr said, "O Messenger of Allah, you were silent when the man was rebuking, but when I began to take revenge, you stood up." The Prophet (ṣ) replied, "An angel was defending you when you were silent, but when you began to retaliate, the angel went away and Satan came. So I cannot remain where Satan comes."

Classes of men in the matter of anger

There are four classes: men who quickly get angry and quickly get appeased, men who get angry late and get appeased late, men who get angry late and get appeased quickly—this class is the best—and men who get angry quickly and it get appeased late—this class is the worst.

The Prophet (ṣ) said, "A believer gets angry quickly and appeased quickly." Al-Shāfi'ī said, "He who does not get angry when aroused is an ass, and he who is given pleasure but is not pleased is a devil." The Prophet (ṣ) said, "Beware. Men have been created of different natures. Some of them get angry late and appeased quickly. Some of them get angry quickly and appeased quickly. One compensates for the other. Some get angry quickly and it appeased late. Beware. He who gets angry late and appeased quickly is the best, while he who gets angry quickly and appeased late is the worst."

'Umar did not punish a man when he found him intoxicated with wine, as it would have been inflicted out of anger. He said, "I do not like to whip a Muslim out of anger." When a man aroused the wrath of 'Umar ibn 'Abd al-'Azīz, the latter said to him, "If you had not excited my anger, I would have certainly punished you."

2
Hatred

Know that when a man wishes to take revenge at the time of anger, it creates hatred in the heart. Hatred is the prevalence of the effect of anger in the heart. The Prophet (ṣ) said, "A believer has no hatred."

There are eight evils arising out of hatred: envy, gloating over another's sorrows, non-cooperation, contempt, backbiting, ridicule, assault and refusal to give a loan. If a person is free from hatred, he is free from all these eight sins.

Misṭaḥ was a relative of Abū Bakr and was adopted by him. He took part in the Battle of Uḥud and spoke of the slander against 'Ā'ishah. Abū Bakr heard what he said and took an oath not to spend on Misṭaḥ or help him. Allah then sent this revelation: "And let not those of you who possess grace and abundance swear against giving to the near of kin and the poor and those who have fled in Allah's way, and they should pardon and turn away. Do you not love that Allah should forgive you?" (Qur'an, 24:22). Abū Bakr said, "Yes, we love it." Then he began to spend for him. This is the rank of the truthful.

The states of the hated

A hated person can be in one of three states when not under compulsion. The first is that his mind remains steady in spite of the hatred. In other words, he receives his kindness just as he used to get it before from him. The second is that the man cherishing hatred pardons the hated man, treating him well. The third is that he oppresses the hateful person. The first state is that of the religious, the second that of the faithful and the third that of the worst..

The merits of good treatment

Pardoning means not to take revenge when one has power to do so. Allah says, "Take to forgiveness and enjoin good and turn aside from the ignorant" (Qur'an, 7:199) and "It is nearer to righteousness that you should relinquish" (Qur'an, 2:237).

The Prophet (ṣ) said, "By Him in whose hand is my life, if I were someone who often swore, I would swear three things: that wealth does not decrease by charity, so give charity; that if a man pardons the faults of another for the pleasure of Allah, He will honour him more on Resurrection Day; and that if a man opens for himself the door of begging, Allah will open for him the door of poverty." He said, "Modesty increases only progress, so be modest and Allah will exalt you; pardon increases only honour; and charity increases only wealth, so give charity and Allah will show you mercy."

'Ā'ishah said, "I never saw the Prophet (ṣ) take revenge for any wrong as long as nobody did what Allah has forbidden. When someone did so, he was the angriest. And when he was given a choice between two, he would choose the easier one as long as it was not a sin." 'Uqbah said, "Once, I met the Prophet (ṣ) and shook his hand hastily out of respect, and he said, "O 'Uqbah, shall I not inform you of the best character traits of the people of this world and the next? Maintain family ties with whoever severs them, give charity to whoever deprives you of something and pardon whoever does any wrong to you." He said, "When the Lord Most Merciful raises all the creatures on Resurrection Day, a proclaimer will proclaim thrice from underneath the Throne, 'O followers of Allah's oneness, Allah has forgiven you, so forgive one another.'"

Abū Hurayrah reported, "After the conquest of Makkah, the Prophet (ṣ) prayed two *rak'ahs* of prayer within the Ka'bah after circling it. Then he entered the Ka'bah, placed his hand on its door and said to Quraysh, 'What do you see, and what kind of treatment do you expect?' They replied, 'We are your brothers and children of your patient and kind uncle,' repeating this thrice. The Prophet (ṣ) then said, 'I will tell you what Yūsuf said to his brothers: '(There will be) no reproof against you this day. Allah may forgive you. He is the most merciful of the merciful' (Qur'an, 12:92).' They then went away as if they had arisen from graves. Afterwards, they all accepted Islam."

Suhayl ibn 'Amr said, "When the Prophet (ṣ) came to Makkah, he placed his two hands on the door of the Ka'bah and was surrounded by the people. He said, 'There is no deity but Allah, alone, without partner. He has proved His promise true. He has helped His servant and routed the combined forces of the enemies.' Then he said, 'O assembly of Quraysh, what do you say, and what kind treatment do you expect?' I said, 'O Messenger of Allah, we pray for good and pardon from you. You are our honoured brother and the son of our kind uncle. Now all powers are in your hands.' The Prophet (ṣ) said, 'I will say what my brother Yūsuf said: '(There will be) no reproof against you this day. Allah may forgive you' (Qur'an, 12:92).'"

The Prophet (ṣ) said, "When all people are waiting on Judgement Day, a proclaimer will proclaim, 'Let whoever whom Allah owes rewards arise and enter Paradise.' It will be asked, 'Whom does Allah owe rewards?' He will say, 'Those people who used to pardon men.' Then thousands and thousands of people will arise, and He will admit them into Paradise without reckoning."

The Prophet (ṣ) said, "When a guilty man is brought before any judge, he is not bound to punish him. Allah loves pardon and is forgiving." Then he read this verse: "Pardon and turn away" (Qur'an, 24:22). He said, "He who has three qualities with belief will enter Paradise by whichever door he likes and will marry any black-eyed houri he likes: He who pays his dues secretly, he who recites Sūrah al-Ikhlāṣ (Qur'an, 112) eleven times after each obligatory prayer and he who exempts his murderer from the charge of his murder." Abū Bakr asked, "O Messenger of Allah, will the rewards be obtained if there is only one quality? The Prophet (ṣ) said, "Yes, even if there is only one quality in him."

Traditions from Companions and early Muslims

Yazīd ibn Maysarah said, "If you invoke against a man who has done you wrong, Allah says, 'Someone you have wronged will also invoke against you. If you wish, I will put off answering your prayer until Resurrection Day and forgive you.'" A Christian monk came to Hishām ibn 'Abd al-Malik, who asked him, "Do you think Dhū al-Qarnayn was a prophet?" The monk replied, "He was not a prophet, but was given four qualities: He used to pardon, having had power to do otherwise; he used to fulfil promises when he promised; he used to speak the truth; and he did not use to put off his day's work until the following day."

Merits of kind treatment

Kind treatment is good, and its opposite is harsh and cruel treatment. The result of anger is harsh treatment, and the result of good conduct is kind and good treatment. The cause of cruel treatment is anger, and the cause of anger is too much greed and love for influence. For this reason, the Prophet (ṣ) praised kind treatment highly.

The Prophet (ṣ) said:

> O 'Ā'ishah, he who has been given the gift of kind treatment has been given an abundant portion of the good of this world and the next. He who has been deprived of kind treatment has been deprived of an abundant portion of the good of this world and the next.

When Allah loves the members of a family, He gives them the quality of kind treatment.

Allah does not give for benevolence what He gives for kind treatment. When Allah loves a man, He gives him the quality of kind treatment. The members of a family who are deprived of kind treatment are deprived of the love of Allah.

Allah is kind and loves kind treatment. He gives for kind treatment what He does not give for harsh treatment.

O 'Ā'ishah, give kind treatment, as Allah intends to honour my household. So show the path towards the door of kind treatment.

He who has been deprived of kind treatment has been deprived of all good.

Do you know for whom hellfire has been made unlawful? Every modest man of pleasant tongue, easy and near (to Allah).

On Judgement Day, Allah will treat kindly the ruler who gave kind treatment and was modest.

Kind treatment is the sign of fortune, and foolishness is the sign of misfortune.

Delay comes from Allah, and hastiness from Satan.

When you wish to do a thing, think of its result. If it is easy, do it, otherwise refrain from doing it.

O 'Ā'ishah, give kind treatment, as it adorns a thing in which there is kind treatment and it disgraces a thing from which it is taken off.

Traditions from Companions and early Muslims

'Umar once heard some complaints against one of his governors, so he called the people and addressed them thus: "O people, it is your duty to advise me in my absence and help me in my good deeds, whoever you may be. Know that there is nothing dearer to

Allah than the patience and kind treatment of a ruler, and there is nothing more displeasing to Allah than the ignorance and foolishness of a ruler. Know that whoever pardons those among him will be pardoned by those below him."

A *ḥadīth* states that learning is the friend of a believer, patience his minister, wisdom his proof, spiritual works his protector, good treatment his father, modest treatment his brother and patience the commander of his forces.

A wise man said, "How nice is faith? Learning makes it nice. How good is learning? Action makes it good. How good is action? Kind treatment makes it beautiful. Just as patience makes learning beautiful, one thing makes another thing beautiful." 'Amr ibn al-'Āṣ asked his son 'Abdullāh, "What is kind treatment?" He replied, "A ruler's kind treatment to his subordinate officers." 'Amr asked, "What is foolishness?" The son replied, "To oppose your leader and to be modest to one who does you harm."

Sufyān once said to his disciples, "Do you know what kindness is?" They replied, "Tell us, O Abū Muḥammad." He said, "To put everything in its proper place, to give good treatment in its proper place, to use the sword in its proper place and to whip in the proper place." It appears from this that it is necessary that there should be harsh treatment with modesty and kind treatment with harshness. So it is best to take the middle course between kind and harsh treatments.

3
Envy

There are many statements from the Prophet (ṣ) regarding envy. He said, "Just as fire destroys fuel, so envy destroys spiritual works." He said, "Do not envy one another, do not forsake one another, do not hate one another, do not trade over the trade of another. O servants of Allah, be brothers to one another." Anas said, "Once we were seated near the Prophet (ṣ), who said, 'Soon, one of the inhabitants of Paradise will pass by this way.' It was then found that a Madīnan Helper (*Anṣārī*) was coming.' 'Abdullāh ibn 'Amr ibn al-'Āṣ told him what the Prophet (ṣ) had said about him and asked him how he had earned such a rank. He said, 'I do not envy any Muslim for any gift Allah has given him."

The Prophet (ṣ) said, "No man escapes from three: bad conjectures, envy and evil omens. I will teach you how to get rid of these things. When there is a bad conjecture, do not believe it. When you find an evil omen, do not believe it. When you are envious, do not hate." He said, "The disease of earlier generations have crept into you: envy and hatred. Hatred shaves. I do not say that it shaves hairs, but it shaves the religion. By Him in whose hand is the life of Muḥammad, you will not enter Paradise until you believe, and you will not believe until you love one another. Shall I not tell you what will establish that for you? Spread peace among you."

The Prophet (ṣ) said, "Poverty is nearly infidelity, and envy nearly overcomes fate." He said, "The behaviours of the other nations will soon afflict my people." The Companions asked,

"What are the behaviours of other nations?" He replied, "Pleasures and enjoyments, heedlessness, abundant wealth, rivalry in the world because of envy, to think one another as distant, to envy one another, rebellion and to live in dangers and calamities." He said, "Do not express joy at the sorrows of your brothers. Perhaps Allah may forgive him and inflict you with that calamity."

It was related that Mūsā went to meet his Lord and found a man under His Throne. He seeing his high rank, there grew a spirit of rivalry in his mind, and he asked his Lord, "What is the name of this man?" Allah did not communicate his name but said, "I will inform you about his three good deeds: He does not envy anyone because of a gift Allah gave him; he does not disobey disobedient his parents; and he does not go about with slander." The prophet Zakariyyā said, "Allah says, 'An envious man is an enemy of My gifts, dissatisfied with My decree and dissatisfied with the division of My gifts I have distributed among My servants.'"

The Prophet (ṣ) said, "The greatest fear I have for my followers is the increase of their wealth, for which they will envy one another and quarrel with one another." He said, "Pray for help with the fulfilment of secret necessities, as every wealthy man is an object of envy." He said, "Six people will enter Hell one year before judgement." The Companions asked, "O Prophet of Allah, who are they?" He said, "A ruler for his oppression, a Bedouin for his unjust love for his tribe, a rich man for his pride, a village man for his foolishness and a learned man for his envy."

A story of envy

A man approached a king and said, "Treat the religious man well for his good works and release the wicked, as his evil deeds suffice as a punishment for him." A courtier of the king grew envious of him and complained about him to the king, saying that he had defamed the king because his mouth smelled very offensive. The king said, "How can I know that this is true?" He said, "You will know when he places his hand on his nose." The courtier then invited the man to his house and gave him fresh onions to eat with the meal. After eating, the man went to the king and, fearing that the king would smell the odour of the onions, placed his hand on his mouth and nose. The king was then convinced of the truth of the courtier's statement and sent him with a letter to his governor to put him to death. On the way, the courtier asked the man to hand over the letter to him, thinking that it contained words of rewards. Accordingly, the letter was handed over to him, who then took it to the governor. When the governor received the letter, he at once put him to death. The man went the next day to the king as usual, but the latter was surprised to see him alive and asked him about his letter. He said that he handed it over to another man. The king asked him why he closed his mouth and placed his hand over his nose at the time of his interview with him. He said that the courtier had invited him over for a meal and gave him fresh onions. So for fear of the bad smell, he placed his hand over his mouth and nose. The king said, "The wrong deeds of a person suffices as his punishment."

What is envy

There is no envy except for gifts. When Allah showers gifts on any person, two states may arise in your mind. The first is that you do not love those gifts for him and wish he would lose them. The second is that you do not wish that he would lose the gifts, but rather that those gifts may be bestowed on you also. This is rivalry or competition in good works and gifts. The Prophet (ṣ) said, "A believer makes effort based on competition, but a hypocrite envies."

Envy is unlawful under all circumstances, and there is no distinction between Muslims and non-Muslims in matters of envy. Allah has distributed His gifts among His servants in the world, to envy them is to express displeasure at His distribution. So there is no reason to envy.

Allah says, "If good befalls you, it grieves them, and if an evil afflicts you, they rejoice at it" (Qur'an, 3:120). This rejoicing is glee, and glee and envy are interconnected. Allah also relates the story of Yūsuf and also the envy of his brothers towards him. They said out of envy, "Slay Yūsuf or cast him (forth) into some land, so that your father's regard may be exclusively for you" (Qur'an, 12:9).

Ibn 'Abbās said, "When the Jews fought with a people before the prophethood of Muḥammad, they used to pray, 'O Allah, we invoke You by the prophet you have promised to send and by the book You have promised to reveal.' As a result, they used to be victorious. But when the Prophet (ṣ), a descendant of Ismā'īl, was sent to them, they recognised him, yet refused to believe in him. In this connection, Allah says, 'Aforetime they used to pray for victory against those who disbelieve, but when there came to them (Prophet) that which they did not recognize, they disbelieved in him, so Allah's curse is on the unbelievers. Evil is that for which they have sold their souls—that they should deny what Allah has revealed, out of envy' (Qur'an, 2:89-90)."

To compete is not unlawful but commendable. It is an effort towards further progress and advancement. Allah says, "For that let the aspirants aspire" (Qur'an, 43:86) and "Hasten to forgiveness from your Lord" (Qur'an, 57: 21). They are like two servants who both try to please their master and hope to defeat the other in this matter.

The Prophet (ṣ) said, "There is no envy for two people: someone whom Allah gave wealth as well as the power to spend it in the path of truth, and someone whom Allah gave knowledge and who acts on it and teaches it to people." He explained this further in the *ḥadīth* of Abū Kabshah al-Anmārī, saying, "This nation is like four people. It is like the person whom Allah gave wealth and learning and who spends wealth in useful ways according to his learning. It is like the person whom Allah gave learning and not wealth, yet he says, 'O Allah, if I had wealth like so-and-so, I would spend it as he spends.' They will get equal rewards. The rewards a rich man will get by spending money will be equal to those which a poor man will get only by cherishing the desire to spend it. This nation is like a person whom Allah gave wealth and not learning and who spends it on sinful acts. It is also like the person whom Allah did not give learning or wealth and says, 'If I had wealth like so-and-so, I would spend it on sinful acts as he does.' They are equally sinners." The Prophet (ṣ) rebuked people who intend to commit sins. He also said, "No believer is saved from three matters: envy, bad conjectures and bad omens." These are their outlets. When you feel envy, do not pursue it.

Stages of envy

There are three stages of envy according to status. The first stage is that the envious person loves that wealth and gifts should leave the person envied and that they should not come to him again. This is unlawful and the worst state to be in. The second stage is that the envious person wishes to have the gifts of the envied person, such as to have a beautiful house like his, to have a beautiful wife like his and to have power like him. This is lawful, but not commendable. The third stage is that the envious person wishes to have not identical things for himself but similar things. This is blameworthy in some cases and not in others. Allah says, "Do not covet that by which Allah has made some of you excel others" (Qur'an, 4:32).

Causes of envy

There are seven causes of envy arising out of seeing the fortunes of another.

- The first is enmity which is the worst cause. As he is your enemy, you do not wish that he should have gifts and riches and other things of the world, and such a person likes that these gifts of Allah should leave him. The object of God-fearing men is the opposite. They do not envy anybody for these things. Allah mentions the envy of the unbelievers for the believers in this verse: "If good befalls you, it grieves them" (Qur'an, 3:120).

- The second cause is dislike another's good. An envious man greatly dislikes the welfare and good of another, and it gives him too much pain. He cannot bear when the person envied gets any power, recognition or honour.
- The third cause is pride. The envious man takes pride over the envied man and holds him in contempt. Allah says unbelievers ask, "Are these they upon whom Allah has conferred benefit from among us?" (Qur'an, 6:53).
- The fourth cause is to express wonder. The unbelievers say, "Shall we believe in two mortals like ourselves?" (Qur'an, 23:47). They expressed wonder at the Prophet's claim to prophethood and cherished hatred for him, seeing his influence and power.
- The fifth cause is fear of failure. For instance, two men have the same goal in mind, but one of them envies the other, fearing he will fail. This is like the envy of two co-wives.
- The sixth cause is greed for name and power. This is also a cause of envy between two people. This applies in all spheres of life—worship, industry, beauty, wealth, power and so on.
- The seventh cause is narrow-mindedness. One becomes rejoices at another's loss and wishes that all blessings and gifts should be bestowed on him alone.

True religious men have no envy. The real cause of envy is love of the world. Those who love the world envy one another's wealth, riches, power and name and fame. The religious have no such greed and as such have no envy. They desire the next world and its comforts, which does not constitute narrow-mindedness. The religious also do not envy one another in matters of religious advancement

Treating envy

Envy is a very serious disease of the heart and cannot be cured without knowledge and action.

Medicine for envy, based on knowledge

The first medicine is to know that envy is injurious in this world and the next. Envy does not harm the person envied but rather benefits him. When you know it by deep insight, you will consider it your enemy and injurious to you.

The second is to know that envy is injurious to your world. The fire pangs of envy burn your heart, filling your mind with sorrows and difficulties.

The third is to know that the envied person suffers no harm in this world or the next. Allah gives possessions and wealth to a person for a certain term, and there is a decree for every age. A prophet complained to Allah about the oppression of a queen's administration. Allah then revealed to him, "As long as her rule continues, live elsewhere and flee from her." In other words, "What I have decreed for her will not change, so be patient until the end of her time." If by envy, gifts could go, Allah's gifts would not be bestowed on you or anybody in the world. The unbelievers envied the Muslims for the gift of faith. Allah says, "Many of the followers of the Book wish that they could turn you back into unbelievers after your faith, out of envy from themselves" (Qur'an, 2:109).

The fourth is to know that the envied person benefits in this world and the next world. The envied person will gain benefit by your envy, but you think that he is oppressed. The envied person, if backbitten about, will get the spiritual works of the envious person. The worldly anxieties of the envious person, then, are a benefit to the envied person. A Bedouin asked the Prophet (ṣ), "O Prophet of Allah, what is your opinion about a person who loves a people without seeing them?" The Prophet (ṣ) said, "He is with the one he loves."

Another Bedouin asked the Prophet (ṣ) during his sermon, "O Prophet of Allah, when will the Resurrection occur?" He replied, "How have you prepared for it?" The man said, "I neither pray much for it nor fast much, but I love Allah and His Prophet." The

Prophet (ṣ) said to him, "You will be with the one you love." Anas said, "The Muslims did not feel as much joy after their conversion to Islam as they did on that day." It appears from this that to love the Messenger of Allah was great matter to the Muslims. Anas said, "We began to love the Prophet (ṣ), Abū Bakr and 'Umar, and although we could not do spiritual works like them, we cherished hope to live with them."

Abū Mūsā asked the Prophet (ṣ) about a man who loves those who pray, but does not himself pray, and who loves those who fast, but does not fast himself. The Prophet (ṣ) replied, "He will be with the one he loves." A man told 'Umar ibn 'Abd al-'Azīz, "Every man says from the beginning, 'If you can be learned, be a learned man. If you cannot be a learned man, be a student. If you cannot be a student, love him. If you cannot love him, do not hate him.' Glory to Allah! Allah has made a way for us."

The Prophet (ṣ) said, "Three types of man are inhabitants of Paradise: a man who does good deeds, a man who loves him and a man who refrains from harming him." So you should not exclude yourself from these three by taking recourse to envy and hatred. Satan has entered your mind and keeps you out off them. Moreover, evil returns to you, as Allah says, "The evil plans will not beset any save the authors of it" (Qur'an, 35:43). Many a time it happens that the snare which was laid for an enemy catches the person who contrived it.

Medicine for envy, based on action

To do an action opposite to the cause for which envy arises is its medicine, be it with words or with actions. If your object is to mention the sins of the envied person out of envy, then the medicine to remove it is to praise him. If the cause is pride, its medicine is to treat with him with humility. If envy advises you to destroy another's property, its medicine is to help him.

Envy is an evil of the mind and not of any body part. Allah says, "Those … do not find in their hearts a need of what they are given" (Qur'an, 59:9), "They desire that you should disbelieve as they have disbelieved, so that you might be (all) alike" (Qur'an, 4:89) and "If good befalls you, it grieves them" (Qur'an, 3:120). Envy is expressed through backbiting and falsehood. So a person will sin for entertaining envy in his mind. When it is expressed physically, seeking pardon for it becomes obligatory.

Book 6
Attachment to the world

Introduction

All praise is due to Allah, who discloses the merits and demerits of the world to His friends, who weighed its benefits and harms on the scale and found that its harms outweigh its benefits.

The world is like a beautiful unchaste woman who attracts people towards her by her beauty, but she has secret diseases which destroy whoever goes to her. If you do good to the world for one hour, it does you harm for one year. If you do business with worldly people, you gain nothing but loss. Whoever seeks the world faces many dangers and difficulties which cannot be enumerated. Whoever wants it, it flees from him, whoever does not want it, it goes to him.

The world is an enemy because it is an obstacle to spiritual works. Because Allah created the world, he keeps an eye on it. The world is an enemy of the friends of Allah, for it presents itself with its best grandeurs, like an unchaste woman dressed clad in beautiful clothes. The world is also an enemy of the enemies of Allah, as it entraps them in its net of love after deceiving them and opens its door of love for them. They are deceived by its love and grow attached to it. Consequently, they are dishonoured and disgraced and eventually leave it. Their hearts are pierced on separation from it, and fortune bids, them adieu forever. There is no limit to their remorse, so they seek refuge in Allah. They have purchased this world for the price of the hereafter.

Since the harms of the world are many, we should know its snares and charms and then save ourselves from its deceptions and love.

1

Evils of the world

There are innumerable verses in the Qur'an regarding the evils of the world. The goal of the Prophet (ṣ) was to turn people away from the evils and harms of the world, so there is no need to cite verses from the Qur'an about it. Instead, I shall cite some *ḥadīths*.

Ḥadīth

It was related that the Prophet (ṣ) was once passing by a dead goat when he said to his Companions, "Do you not see the dead animal? Its owner is now looking at it with hate. By Him in whose hand is my life, just as this dead goat is more an object of hate to its owner, the world is likewise more an object of hatred to Allah. If the value of the world were like that of the wing of a mosquito, He would not have given a draught of water to an unbeliever to drink."

The Prophet (ṣ) said, "The world is a prison to a believer and a paradise to an unbeliever." He said, "The world is cursed and all the things in it are cursed." He said, "Whoever loves the world injures his hereafter, and whoever loves his hereafter injures his world. So take what will last forever by giving up what will not last." He said, "Love of the world is the root of all sins."

Zayd ibn Arqam reported, "We were once with Abū Bakr al-Ṣiddīq, who asked for water and honey, which were brought to him. When he lifted them to drink, he began to weep. Asked why, he said, "Once, I was with the Prophet (ṣ) and saw him wiping something from his body. I asked him, 'O Prophet of Allah, what are you wiping off?' He replied, 'This is the world. It came to me with a beautiful face. I said, 'Be off!' The world said, 'You have saved yourself from me, but those who will come after you will not be safe from my hand.'"

The Prophet (ṣ) stood by a rubbish dump and said to the people, "Would you like to look at the world?" He then took a tattered rag and decayed bones and said, "This is the world." He said that the wealth and pleasures of the world will be ruined like the rag and all the people will decay like the decayed bones.

The Prophet (ṣ) said, "This world is sweet and fresh, and Allah made you His representatives therein. He is watching how you act therein."

When the children of Israel were given enormous wealth, and when they were engrossed therein, they were attached to worldly pleasures, love of women and precious scents and clothes. 'Īsā said to them, "Do not take the world as your Lord. If you do so, it will make you slaves. Hoard up your wealth with Him who will not destroy it. Guards of wealth in this world cannot be relied on, but you can rely on the guards of Allah."

'Īsā said, "O my disciples, I have overturned the world for you, so do not revive it after me. One of the evils of the world is that people commit sins therein. Another evil of the world is that the next world cannot be acquired unless this world is given up. So pass through the world and do not dwell therein. Know that the root of all evil is attachment to the world. Many a time, greed for the present becomes the cause of man's calamities."

'Īsā said, "The world lies behind you, and you sit on it. Therein, kings and women stand as stumbling blocks against you. Do not dispute with kings regarding this world, as they will not stand in your way if you give up your connection with them and their affairs. Save yourselves from women by fasting and prayer."

'Īsā said, "The world seeks people, and people seek the world. The world seeks someone who seeks the next world as long as his provisions do not become complete for him. The next world seeks someone who seeks the world until his death. Thereafter, it catches his neck and climbs him." The Prophet (ṣ) said, "Allah created nothing so obnoxious to Him as the world. He has not even looked at it since the day He created it."

It was reported that Sulaymān, the son of Dāwūd, was roaming in the air, and birds were giving him shade and men and jinn were on his right and left sides. He met a hermit of the children of Israel on the way who said to him, "O son of Dāwūd, Allah Almighty has given you reign and power." Sulaymān responded, "A single praise of Allah in a believer's book of deeds is more superior than my reign, as what has been given to the son of Dāwūd will end, whereas the praise will remain."

The Prophet (ṣ) said, "Excessive wealth has kept you forgetful. The son of Adam says, 'My wealth! My wealth!' Do you have any other wealth than what you have eaten and finished, what you have put on and worn out, what you have given in charity and perpetuated?" He said, "Whoever has no abode takes the world as his abode. Whoever has no wisdom becomes its enemy. Whoever has no power of doing justice covets it. Whoever has no sure faith strives for it." He said, "Whoever gets up at dawn with the world as his object of thought is not God-fearing in any matter, and Allah attaches to his heart four things: endless anxiety, limitless engagement, poverty that can never make him rich and perpetual hope."

Abū Hurayrah reported, "The Prophet (ṣ) said to me, 'O Abū Hurayrah, shall I show you what obnoxious things there are in this world?' I said, 'O Prophet of Allah, show me.' Then he caught my hand, took me to a valley of Madīnah and showed me a place full of carcasses, stool and urine, rotten clothes, bones and hide. He said, 'O Abū Hurayrah, there were in their heads greed like your greed and hopes like you hopes, but today those are with rotten remains and will be consumed by earth after some days. All these are of the world. If you can weep at the sad plight of the world, then weep.' Then we began to weep."

Dāwūd ibn Hilāl reported that it is written in the scripture of Ibrāhīm, "O World, how ignoble you are to religious men. You have presented yourself to them with your adornments, but hatred for you has been cast into their hearts, so they have turned away from you. There is nothing so obnoxious to Me as you. Every act of yours is mean and comes to destruction. I have recorded for you on the day I created you that you will not stay with anybody forever and that whoever loves you will be a miser. Thanks to those pious men who seek Me with pleasure in their hearts, those in whose hearts there is truth and who stand on the right path. Happy are they, as they will get rewards for what their hands have acquired. When they come to Me from the graves, light will move forward in front of them and the angels will surround them. They will get mercy, as they all hoped for it from Me."

The Prophet (ṣ) said, "On Resurrection Day, there will appear people whose merits will be high as the hillock of Tihāmah, but they will be ordered to go to Hell." The Companions asked, "O Prophet of Allah, did they observe prayers?" He replied, "Yes, they observed prayers and fasts and prayed also at night, but whenever anything of the world came to them, they jumped on it."

The Prophet (ṣ) said in a sermon, "A believer will live with two fears. One fear is for his fate, which has passed and in which he does not know what has been recorded. Another fear is his book of deeds, which yet remains and in which he does not know what Allah has recorded for him. So a servant should take provisions from himself for himself, from his world for his hereafter, from his life for his death and from his youth for his old age, as the present world has been created for your good, and you have been created for the next world. By Him in whose hand is my life, there is no field for labour except Paradise and Hell, and there is no abode after the world."

'Īsā said, "Love of both this world and the next cannot coexist in the heart of a believer, just as water and fire cannot coexist."

Jibrīl asked the prophet Nūḥ, "O one having a very long life, how have you found the world?" He replied, "It is like an abode having two doors. I have entered through one door and come out of another."

'Īsā was asked, "Why do you not construct a house to live in?" He replied, "The abode of our predecessors is sufficient."

The Prophet (ṣ) said, "Beware of the world, as it is a sorcerer greater then Hārūt and Mārūt."

Al-Ḥasan said, "Once, the Prophet (ṣ) went out to his Companions and said, 'Who among you would wish to see after being blind? Beware! The more a person is attached to the world and the longer his hopes are, the more Allah makes his heart blind. And the more he gives up the world and curtails his hopes, the more Allah gives him wisdom without education and guides him without guidance. Beware! There will come a people after you whose kingdom will not be without pride and miserliness and who will not love except passion. Beware! Whoever reaches that age and endures poverty, even though he can acquire wealth; endures hatred, even though he can earn love; remains patient with dishonour, even though he can earn honour; and has no other object for these things than the pleasure of Allah, will get rewards of fifty truthful men."

It was reported that 'Īsā was seeking refuge after getting caught in a thunderstorm when he found a tent, into which he went. But when he found a beautiful woman therein, he left. Thereafter, he came to a cave, in which was a tiger. He placed his hand on the ground and said, "O Lord, you have given shelter to everything but me." Allah then revealed to him, "Your shelter is Allah's mercy. On Resurrection Day, I shall marry you to a hundred houris whom I have created with My hands. Your marriage ceremony will continue for four thousand years, one day of which is equal to the age of this world. I will order a proclaimer to proclaim, 'Those who were religious and ascetic will join this marriage ceremony.'"

'Īsā said, "Woe to him who is addicted to the world. How can he die after leaving the world and its fortunes? How does the world deceive him, and how can he trust it? The world is treacherous with him, but he does not live in fear of it. What he does not love comes to him, and what he loves leaves him. What has been promised to them must come. Woe to him whose only object of thought is this world and whose actions are sins. How can he appear tomorrow with sins?"

It was reported that Allah revealed to Mūsā, "O Mūsā, why do you need the abode of the sinners (the world)? It is not your abode. Drive out your thoughts from it and remain aloof on the strength of your wisdom. What a bad house it is! It is only a good abode for one who does good therein. O Mūsā, I am searching for someone who commits oppression secretly therein so that I may take his good deeds and give them to someone oppressed."

It was reported that the Prophet (ṣ) once sent Abū 'Ubaydah to the province of Bahrain. He went there and returned with enormous wealth from the inhabitants and placed it before the Prophet (ṣ). The Madīnan Helpers (*Anṣār*) came to know of it and assembled for the morning prayer in the mosque. After the prayer, the Prophet (ṣ) said, "You have perhaps heard about the riches brought by Abū 'Ubaydah." Then he said, "I fear not that you will become poor, but that you will get enormous wealth like our previous nations did. They acquired enormous wealth and engaged in quarrels with one another. Just as they were destroyed by this wealth, you will likewise be destroyed by it."

The Prophet (ṣ) said, "I fear that you will be given the blessings of the world." When asked, "What are the blessings of the world?" he replied, "The riches and treasures of the world." He said, "Do not keep your mind engaged in thoughts about the world."

'Īsā said to his disciples, "In order to attain peace in this world as well as in the next, it is more preferable to eat bread with only salt, to wear a gunny sack and to sleep in stables."

Anas reported that the Prophet (ṣ) had a she-camel named "al-'Aḍbā'," which defeated all other camels. One day, a Bedouin came with a camel which defeated it. The Muslims were grieved to see this, and the Prophet (ṣ) said, "It is a duty of Allah to not raise up a thing without lowering it."

'Īsā once said, "Is there anyone who can construct a house on the currents of a sea? That is the world. Do not make it your permanent abode." It was once said to him, "Give me a short piece of advice by which Allah will love us." He said, "Hate the world and Allah will love you."

The Prophet (ṣ) said, "If you knew what I know, you would laugh little and weep much. Hate the world and love the next world." Abū al-Dardā' said, "Had you known what I know from the Prophet (ṣ), you would go out to every elevated place and weep for the salvation of your soul and give up the riches and treasures of the world except what is essential."

'Īsā said, "O my disciples, be satisfied with little of worldly riches but with greater spiritual works, as the worldly addicted man remains satisfied with few acts of worship but greater worldly riches." He also said, "It is of greater virtue to give up the world for those who seek the world for religion."

The Prophet of Islam said, "The world will be made vast for you after me, but will consume your faith as fire consumes dry wood."

Allah revealed to Mūsā, "O Mūsā, do not be addicted to the world, as you will not come to me with a greater sin than this." Once, Mūsā passed by a man who was weeping. He found the man in the same condition when he was returning. Then Mūsā prayed to Allah, "O Lord, your servant is weeping for fear of you." Allah said, "O son of 'Imrān, if his tears flow over his head and he keeps his hands raised until they fall down, I shall not forgive him, for he loves the world."

Traditions from Companions and early Muslims

'Alī said, "Whoever has six virtues is not lacking anything for seeking Paradise and for salvation from Hell: obeying Allah after knowing Him, following truth after knowing it, disobeying Satan after knowing him, saving oneself from falsehood after knowing it, giving up the world after knowing it and seeking the next world after knowing it.

Al-Ḥasan said, "Allah shows mercy to him who competes with another in matters of religion and He throws him on his neck who competes with you in matters of the world."

Luqmān advised his son, "O son, the world is a deep sea and many people are drowned therein. Make God-fearingness your boat, faith your oar and trust in God your sail so that you may get salvation. Otherwise, I see no cause for your salvation."

Al-Fuḍayl said, "We should ponder deeply over the Qur'anic verse 'Surely We have made whatever is on the earth an embellishment for it, so that We may try them (as to) which of them is best in works. And most surely We will make what is on it bare ground without herbage' (Qur'an, 18:7-8)."

A hermit was asked, "What do you think about time?" He answered, "Time destroys the body, creates new hopes, draws death near and makes hopes distant." A sage said, "Success in the world means failure, cleanliness therein means uncleanliness and its dwellers remain in fear of loss of wealth, calamity and impending death."

A man said to Abū Ḥāzim, "I have no abode in the world, yet I complain to you about my attachment to the world." He said, "Look at the wealth Allah granted you. Do not take except what is lawful. Do not spend except on things you should spend on. If you conduct yourself in such a way, attachment to the world will not harm you."

Al-Fuḍayl said, "If the transient world were made of gold and were everlasting, and the hereafter of clay, it would be our duty to choose the clay hereafter over the gold world. How futile it is to love a transient earth-made world rather than an everlasting, gold hereafter."

Luqmān said to his son, "O son, sell your world for your next world and you will then get the benefit of both worlds. But do not sell your next world for this world, for you will be a loser in both worlds."

Ibn 'Abbās said, "Allah divided the world into three parts: one part for the believers, one part for the hypocrites and one part for the infidels. A believer gathers his provisions therein, a hypocrite adorns it and an infidel enjoys himself therein."

Abū Umāmah al-Bāhilī said, "After the Prophet (ṣ) became the messenger of Allah, the armies of Satan came to him and said, 'A prophet has appeared, and a nation has emerged. What shall we do now?' Satan asked, 'Do they love the world?' They said yes. Satan said, 'I have no worries about them, even though they do not worship idols, provided they love the world. I will come to them morning and evening with three pieces of advice: acquire wealth unjustly, spend money in improper areas and be a miser in areas where expenditure is necessary. All sins arise out of these three matters.'"

'Alī was once asked about the world and said that accounts will be taken of lawful things in the world and punishment will be given for unlawful things.

Abū Sulaymān al-Dārānī said, "When the next world is in the mind of a man, the world stands before him. When the world is in his mind, the next world does not enter because the next world is honourable, whereas the world is an object of hatred." Mālik ibn Dīnār said, "The thoughts of the world will leave your mind in proportion to your sorrows for the next world." 'Alī said, "This world and the next world are like two co-wives. A co-wife will be dissatisfied in proportion to your giving satisfaction to another co-wife."

Al-Ḥasan said, "I saw men to whom this world was more an object of hatred than trodden mud. They did not care whether it was day or night, or whether the world favoured this person or that."

Once, 'Umar went to visit Syria when Abū 'Ubaydah was its governor. He came riding on a she-camel to receive 'Umar. The she-camel had a rope tied to her nose. 'Umar conversed with him and then came to his abode but found nothing therein except a sword, a shield and a wooden stand for placing the Qur'an therein. 'Umar asked him, "Why have you not kept other necessary things in your house?" Abū 'Ubaydah replied, "O Commander of the Faithful, these things will carry me to the place of questions and answers (the grave)."

Luqmān said to his son, "O son, you have been drifting away from this world since the day you were born and advancing towards the next world. The abode to which you are proceeding is better than the abode from which you are drifting away."

Someone said, "Strange is he who roams merrily even though he knows that death is inevitable. Strange is the man who laughs even though he knows that Hell is a truth. Strange is the man who remains satisfied with the world even though he knows that it is transient. Strange is the man who keeps himself engaged in earning wealth even though he knows that fate is true."

Once, a two-hundred-year-old man came to Mu'āwiyah, who asked him what he wanted from him. The old man replied, "I wish to get from you the life that has passed and to remove the death which is near." Mu'āwiyah said, "I have no power to do that." The old man said, "Then I have nothing to ask of you."

Al-Ḥasan said, "The life of a man will not leave the world without regret for three things: not being able to enjoy with satisfaction what be hoarded, not being able to fulfil what he hoped to fulfil and not being able to do what he ought to have done for the next world."

A sage was asked, "For whom is this world?" He replied, "For those who give up this world." When asked, "For whom is the next world?" he replied, "For those who want it."

Yaḥyā ibn Mu'ādh said, "The intelligent are three: whoever gives up the world before the world gives him up, whoever keeps himself prepared for his grave before he enters it and whoever keeps Allah satisfied before he meets Him."

'Alī said, "The following six things are the world: food, drinks, clothes, conveyance, women and scents. Honey is the best of foods and comes from the mouths of bees. Water is the best of drinks. Both the virtuous and sinners enjoy it. Silk clothes are the best of clothes and come from the saliva of worms. Horses are the best of conveyances, and the Prophet (ṣ) fought riding on one. Women are the best of things coveted by men, who take pleasure in inserting their genital organs into the female vaginal canal, making the vagina the most coveted thing in a woman. And musk is the best of scents and is the blood of deer."

Al-Ḥasan al-Baṣrī once wrote to 'Umar ibn 'Abd al-'Azīz, "This world is transient, not everlasting. Adam was sent to the world as a sort of punishment. O Commander of the Faithful, fear the world. Giving up the world means gathering provisions from the world for the next world. To remain in want in the world means to posses wealth in the hereafter. Every moment of the world destroys a man. Whoever honours the world is humiliated by it. Whoever hoards up for the world is thrown into want. The world is like poison. Whoever is unfamiliar with it, eats it, and therein lies his destruction. Live in the world like the person who treats his wound and bears hardship for a time for fear of suffering and keeps patient with bitter pills for fear of too many medicines. So fear this abode of deception, deceit and treachery. The treasures of the world were presented to our Prophet and, although it would not have diminished him by a mosquito's wing, he refused to accept them."

According to a *ḥadīth qudsī*, Allah said to Mūsā, "When you see some wealth coming to you, tell it, 'The punishment for sin will soon come.' When you see poverty coming to you, say, 'Welcome, O Mark of the Religious!'"

'Īsā used to say, "Hunger is my condiment, God-fearingness is my sign, wool is my raiment, the sun rays of winter are my provision, the morning is my lamp, my feet are my conveyances, what the earth grows is my food. I spend nights having nothing, and spend my days having nothing. Who is richer than me?"

Wahb ibn Munabbih said, "When Allah sent Mūsā and Hārūn to Fir'awn, He said, 'Do not fear him; his forelock is in My hand. He cannot move his tongue or breathe without My permission.'"

'Alī said in a sermon, "O people, know that you are dead and you will be resurrected after you die. Let not the life of this world deceive you. It is surrounded by dangers and difficulties, and its destruction and treachery are well known to all. All that is therein will pass away along with the world, and the world will roam in the midst of its votaries."

2

Similes about the world

The world is moving towards destruction. The world promises that it is lasting, but breaks its promise immediately after. Look at the world: It is motionless and steady, but really always moving.

Similes

The world is like a shade. Outwardly, a shade seems to be steady, but it is really moving and constantly drifting.

The world is like a dream and the different ideas in a dream. The Prophet (ṣ) said, "The world is like a dream and the happiness and punishment in a dream." Yūnus ibn 'Ubayd said, "I found myself like a sleeping man in the world, who sees what he likes and does not like, then wakes up in this condition. In like manner, people are asleep and will wake up at death."

The world is like an unchaste woman. The world at first treats us well, but then destroys us. The world dresses itself like an unchaste woman and calls people to herself, but when she takes people into her house, she ruins them. 'Īsā saw the world in his mind's eye like an old woman dressed nicely and asked her, "How many husbands have you taken?" She said, "Countless." He asked, "Did all of them die during your lifetime, or did they divorce you one after another?" The woman replied, "I have ruined all of them." 'Īsā said, "Woe to your remaining husbands. They do not learn a lesson after seeing the condition of your previous husbands.

They do not take precautions, even though you have ruined them one after another."

The world is like an ugly old woman. The outer form of the world is one thing, and its inner form is another. Its outer form is nice, but its inner form is ugly and poisonous. So the world can well be compared to an old and ugly woman. Abū Bakr ibn 'Ayyāsh said, "In a dream, I saw the world as an ugly woman with dishevelled hair. She was beating a drum with her hands, many people dancing behind her. When she came forward, she said, 'If I can win you over, it will be good. I will deceive you as I have deceived these people.'" Then Abū Bakr wept, saying, "I saw this woman before I came to Baghdad."

Know that a man has three states. The first is that he was nothing at one time; this was before his birth. The second is that he will not see the world after his death until resurrection. The third is the period between these two times: the time of life. This is one's lifespan. Now compare this short time with the endless time before and after. For this reason, the Prophet (ṣ) said, "I am in this world like a sojourner who travels in the scorching rays of the sun, then sleeps for a time under the shade of a tree on the way, then awakens and walks." Whoever sees the world from this perspective cannot become addicted to it. He cannot see how his days pass by, whether in sorrows, difficulties, joy or happiness. He does not construct a building or a house of wood up to his death.

One day, the Prophet (ṣ) saw a Companion constructing a house of wood and said, "I see that death is faster than this house." 'Īsā said, "The world is like a bridge. Cross it, but do not live in it." This is a clear illustration that the life of this world is drifting towards the next world. The beginning of this bridge is the birth place and the end is the grave. To construct houses on the road and to adorn them is extreme foolishness, as they will be hard to cross.

At first, it seems that there is joy and happiness in the world, but it is difficult to get out of it safely. 'Alī wrote to Salmān al-

Fārisī, "The world is like a snake which is smooth on touch but whose poison is destructive. So be careful of what seems to be to your liking. When you are certain that you will have to part with it, you should give up all thoughts about it. The more you enjoy the objects of happiness in the world, the more it will be the cause of your sorrows."

The Prophet (ṣ) said, "The worldly addicted man is like one who walks on water. Can he walk on water without getting his feet wet?" This is a lesson for those who think that their souls are pure, though their bodies are in worldly happiness. Worldly attachment becomes a stumbling block to deriving pleasure from spiritual works.

'Īsā said, "I tell you in truth that the worldly addicted man does not derive pleasure from spiritual works, just as a diseased man cannot taste delicious foods. I tell you in truth that if you do not control your riding animal, its nature will change and you will find it difficult to ride. Such is the case for the mind. If you cannot keep the mind under control by constant acts of worship and remembrance of death, it will become hard and harsh."

The Prophet (ṣ) said, "There are difficulties and dangers in the world. The good work of any of you is like a pot. If its upper portion is clean, its inner portion is also clean, and if its upper portion is unclean, its inner portion is also unclean." He also said, "The world is like a cloth torn from top to bottom. The bottom of the cloth hangs by a thread which will soon be torn."

'Īsā said, "He who seeks the world is like he who drinks seawater. The more he drinks the saltwater of the sea, the more his thirst will increase, and ultimately he will meet his end."

The temptations and greed of the world are conducive to happiness, as greed for food is enjoyable to the stomach. Everyone will see his greed of the world malodorous and an object of hatred at the time of his death, for the delicious foods become obnoxious in the stomach. The more the food is delicious and tasteful, the more the stool gives an obnoxious smell. Similarly, the more temptations are delicious to the heart, the more they will become troublesome at the time of death. And the more a man has worldly riches, the greater are his pangs of separation at the time of his death. What is the meaning of death except the leaving of worldly riches? The Prophet (ṣ) said, "Allah likened the world to the food of man and likened the food to the world."

The Prophet (ṣ) said, "What is this world in comparison with the next world? This world is like that small amount of water a finger catches when it is put into a sea."

Know that worldly men are like people in their carelessness who got on a boat, and the boatman stopped at an island and asked the passengers to relieve themselves. Some of them returned soon after, and some sat on the island, heartily enjoying the songs of birds and watching the beautiful birds and beasts and other charming things of the island. They returned after sometime only to find their places on the boat were made too narrow. Some of them completely forgot the boat and settled on the island without heeding the boatman's words that they should return soon to their boat. As a result, they stayed on the island and died soon after, having no food or drinks. This is like the world. Those who forgot their permanent abode and are engrossed in worldly enjoyments meet with spiritual death and destroy themselves. Nothing will go with them at the time of their death except good deeds.

Al-Ḥasan reported, "I heard that the Prophet (ṣ) advised his Companions, "The world is like a company of people who were travelling through a desert. Their provisions ran short, and they faced death. While in this state, they found a man coming towards them from a distance. When he came, he said to them, 'If I can take you to a fountain and a good garden, will you obey me?' They said 'Yes, we shall not disobey you. We swear in the name of Allah.' He then took them to a fountain and a garden full of vegetables and fruits. Thus, they saved their lives after eating them. The man said, 'O people, now you may go.' Some of them obeyed him and went away from that place. Those who disobeyed were soon caught by enemies and were either killed or made captives."

This world is like a guest or rest house built for travellers and not for permanent residence therein: The rest house is to be enjoyed only temporarily. This world is likewise a rest house for travellers to the next world, who will benefit therefrom for their permanent residence.

Special knowledge of the world

What is the world? What of the world is to be accepted and what is to be rejected? What is good in the world and what is bad? This world and the next world are two states of your mind. Everything before death is the world, and everything after death is the next world. What gives you pleasure before death, increases your greed and gives you pleasure is the world to you; what gives you pleasure after death is the next world.

Things not of the world

Things not of this world are three. The first is knowledge and actions. The objects of knowledge are Allah, His attributes, His actions, His sovereignty over the heavens and earth and so on. "Actions" means actions done for the sake of Allah and His pleasure. The learned man is whoever possesses these two attributes. To him knowledge of the former is the greatest, so he gives up eating, drinking and even marriage, as the happiness of the former is greater than that of the latter. Knowledge is a portion of the world, yet it cannot be called the "world," for it is included in the next world.

A sage said, "I fear death, as it will destroy my night prayers." Another sage said, "O Allah, give me strength in the grave to pray, to bow and to prostrate." The Prophet (ṣ) said, "Three things of the world are dear to me: women, perfume and prayer." Even prayer was considered part of the world. Everything which can be perceived by the five senses is of this world. Because prayer is performed by bodily movements, it is part of the world.

The second is what is absolutely necessary for man in this world. In contrast, what is not absolutely necessary is part of the world. Further, what is not done for the next world is part of the world and not the next world, just as to enjoy the lawful in excess of necessity, silver, gold, horses, cattle, property, houses, buildings, clothes and a variety of delicious foods is part of the world.

It was reported that 'Umar appointed Abū al-Dardā' as governor of the province of Homs. The governor erected a latrine for two dirhams. Receiving news of this, 'Umar wrote to him, "From 'Umar, Commander of the Faithful, to Abū al-Dardā'. You have ample worldly adornments in the buildings of Persia and Byzantium, but Allah intends to destroy them. When this letter of mine reaches you, you and your family must go to Damascus and stay there until death." 'Umar thought the adornments unnecessary.

The third is everything between the two above. This is to work with the object of doing other-worldly actions, such as eating and drinking to remain alive, wearing coarse clothing only to cover the private parts and doing things from which there is no escape. So such actions as eating and drinking to remain alive and healthy are not of the world.

What man will take with him upon dying

Man will take three things with himself when he dies: purity of heart, satisfaction arising out of the remembrance of Allah and engagement of the heart in divine love. Purity of heart cannot be attained if one cannot control his worldly passions and temptations. Satisfaction cannot be gained unless there is constant remembrance of Allah and patience. These three things are the causes of satisfaction.

The existence of man does not end with death. Rather, he returns to Allah after parting with what he holds dear of the world.

Thus, it is known that a traveller to the next world must necessarily possess three qualities: remembrance of Allah, and meditation and pious actions which prevent him from worldly greed. To such a man, the enjoyments of the world are bitter. If he has neither health, clothes nor home, he cannot attain these qualities. So these things are also necessary. If he takes these things to the proportion of necessity with the object of the next world, he cannot become addicted to the world. For him the world is a seed ground for the future.

Such things can be divided into two: lawful and unlawful. Unlawful things lead to punishment in the next world, and lawful things are obstacles to higher ranks. To wait for judgement on Resurrection Day is a sort of punishment itself. The Prophet (ṣ) said, "There is judgement for the lawful things of the world and punishment for the unlawful things." He also said, "There is also punishment for the lawful things, but this punishment is lighter than that for unlawful things."

So everything in the world is cursed, small or great, lawful or unlawful. What contributes to God-fearingness is not of the world. He whose knowledge of Allah is strong takes great care of the world. 'Īsā once was sleeping with his head on a stone. Satan came to him and said, "You have become attached to the world." With that, he threw the stone at him." Sulaymān would feed his people various dishes, yet he himself ate wheat husk. Our Prophet was presented with the treasures of the world, but kept himself hungry for some days and bound stones to his stomach to reduce the pangs of hunger. Prophets and friends of Allah were given the most severe trials so that they might enjoy eternal happiness in the next world. So what is not done for the sake of Allah is called the "world," while what is done for His sake is not of the world.

But what is for the sake of Allah? Everything can be divided into three: what is not done for the sake of Allah, such as sins, prohibited things and unnecessary lawful things—all these are of the world; what is done for the sake of Allah; and worldly actions done for the sake of Allah, such as eating, drinking and marrying. The second can again be sub-divided into three: meditation about the creation of Allah, remembrance of Allah and abstinence from worldly greed and passions. When these are done for the sake of Allah and not for show, they fall into the third category, which includes eating, drinking and marrying. If they are done for the sake of Allah, they are other-worldly actions. But if they are done merely for satisfaction, they are worldly.

The Prophet (ṣ) said, "Whoever seeks the lawful things of the world to get glory or boast will meet Allah while He is enraged. But whoever seeks the world to abstain from begging and to save himself will come on Resurrection Day with a face bright as a full moon." Allah says whoever "forbids the soul from low desires, then surely the garden—that is the abode" (Qur'an, 79:40-41).

Vain desires

Passion or vain desire is composed of five things. Allah speaks of them in the following verse: "Know that this world's life is only sport and play and gaiety and boasting among yourselves, and a vying in the multiplication of wealth and children" (Qur'an, 57:20). In another verse, vain desires are seven: "The love of desires, of women and sons and hoarded treasures of gold and silver and well-bred horses and cattle and tilth, is made to seem fair to men; this is the provision of the life of this world" (Qur'an, 3:14).

Now you have come to know what the world is and what it is not. Food, clothes and houses to the extent of near necessity, and if done to please Allah, are not of the world. What is in excess of these is the world. There are things which are absolutely necessary and things which are simply necessary, and between the two is a middle course, which is best; the middle course nears the borderline of absolute necessity.

Uways al-Qaranī was regarded by his countrymen as a madman, as he subjected himself to strict rigours of life. They constructed for him a hut, which he visited once a year or once in two or three years. He used to leave before the call to the morning prayer and returned home after the nightfall prayer. His food was the seeds, and he used to put on torn pieces of cloth, which he gathered from heaps of refuse in markets, after sewing them. Often the boys threw stones at him, whereupon he would tell them to throw small stones because if large stones were thrown at him, he would bleed and his ablution would be annulled.

The Prophet (ṣ) said, "I feel the breath of Allah from the land of Yemen" hinting at Uways. Upon becoming caliph, 'Umar delivered a sermon, in which he said, "O people, let the inhabitants of Iraq stand up, and let the others sit down." A party of men stood up. Then he said, "Let the inhabitants of Kūfah stand up, and let the others sit down." When they did so, he said, "Let those of the Murād clan remain standing, and let the others sit down." He said afterwards, "Let the inhabitants of Qaran remain standing, and let the others sit down." All except one sat down. Then 'Umar said to him, "Do you know Uways ibn 'Āmir al-Qaranī?" He said, "I do, O Commander of the Faithful. Why do you ask about him? By Allah, there is nobody more insane, stupid and foolish than him." 'Umar began to weep and said, "I heard from the Prophet (ṣ) that because of his intercession, as many people as the clans of Rāb'iah and Muḍar will get salvation."

Haram ibn Ḥayyān said, "When I heard this from 'Umar, I went to Kūfah, searched for Uways and found him at noon washing clothes at the bank of the Tigris. I found him strong and stout, with a bald head, thick beard and broad face. I asked him, 'How are you, Uways?' and he replied, 'O Haram ibn Ḥayyān, how are you? Who gave you my address?' I said, 'Allah.' Wondering how he came to know my name when he never saw me before, I asked him, 'How have you come to know my name and the name of my father?' He replied, 'The Almighty gave me this information. My soul recognised your soul when I talked with you. Similarly, a believer can recognise another believer.'

"I said, 'Tell me a *ḥadīth* of the Prophet (ṣ).' He said, 'I was never a Companion of the Prophet (ṣ), but I saw some of his Companions and heard some traditions from them.' Then he recited the Qur'anic verse 'We did not create them both but with the truth, but most of them do not know' (Qur'an, 44:39) and continued until 'Surely He is the Mighty, the Merciful' (Qur'an, 44:42), at which point he shrieked and said, 'O Haram, your father Ḥayyān has died, and you will soon die. Adam, his wife Ḥawwā', Nūḥ, Mūsā, Dāwūd and even Muḥammad, the messenger of the Lord of the Worlds, died. Abū Bakr died, and my friend 'Umar has also just expired. Alas, O 'Umar. Alas, O 'Umar.' I said, "Umar has not died. I saw him alive when I left him.' He said, 'My Lord has just now given me news that 'Umar has expired. Walk in the path of Allah's Book, believers and the pious. News of your and my death have come. Do not be unmindful, even for the twinkling of an eye. When you return to your people, give sermons to them. Do not take a single step outside the majority of the Muslims. Pray for me and for you. Haram, I entrust you to Allah. May Allah shower mercy on you. You will not see me again. I am going this way, and you that way.'"

Definition of "this world" and "the next world"

It should be clear to you from what has been described above that whatever the sun casts its rays on and whatever the earth grows are included in the definition of "this world." What is done for the sake of Allah and what is contrary to the above are part of the next world. Whatever is absolutely necessary to gain strength for spiritual works is an action of the next world if done in accordance with the wishes of Allah. If a pilgrim is on his way to perform the pilgrimage and takes care of things necessary for his pilgrimage, such as his provisions and conveyance, his pilgrimage is not nullified thereby, as he is engaged in actions connected with the pilgrimage. Similarly, the body is the carrier of the soul and walks the distance of life. So efforts to gain and preserve strength for the body to acquire knowledge and good works are called not "the world" but "the next world."

Al-Ṭanāfisī said, "I was at the Banū Shaybah door of the Ka'bah for seven days. On the eighth day, I heard an unknown voice say, 'Be careful! Allah makes his internal eye blind who takes from the world things in excess of what is necessary for him.'"

3
The reality of the world

Types of world

Know that the world consists of what exists in the world, what man has a connection with and the adornments in which man is engaged.

The things which exist in the world are the earth and the things that are on it. Allah says, "Surely We have made whatever is on the earth an embellishment for it, so that We may try them (as to) which of them is best in works" (Qur'an, 18:7). The earth is a bed for the children of Adam and for their rest.

Whatever is grown is divided into three: mineral substances, plants and animals. Animals are men, birds and beasts. Man wants to subdue birds, beasts and even men, called "slaves," and he also wants women for enjoyment. These are the world. Men love women, children, gold, silver, crops and quadrupeds.

Man has two connections with these things: internal and external. The internal connection is to love these things with the heart, engage with them in enjoyment and turn all thoughts to them. His heart then becomes addicted to the world like a slave. For this reason, all evils, such as pride, treachery, ostentation, hatred, name and fame, flattery and love of wealth enter the heart. This is the internal connection with the world.

The outer connection is that of the body to take recourse to business and industry. So the connection of the heart is with love, and the connection of the body is with things. All the things are for the food of the body, but the food of the soul is the intention with which food is eaten for the sake of Allah. For the man who forgets his goal and soul, living in the world is like the pilgrim who remains always engaged with his conveying animal and forgets his pilgrimage. The pilgrim to the next world remembers his goal and does only what is necessary to take him to the destination.

Reasons for engagement in the world

There are three reasons for engaging in the world: food, clothing and housing. Food is for preservation of the body, clothes are for protection of the body from heat and cold and housing is for protection of the body and to keep away what destroys lives and wealth. Allah created these things for the benefit of mankind.

Man needs five things to form the basis of industry and the main causes of his engagement: cultivation, grazing, hunting, weaving and construction. Cultivation is for growing crops and food stuffs. Grazing is for maintaining beasts and quadrupeds. Weaving is for making cloth and clothes. Construction is for making houses for habitation. For smooth living, administrative work, judicial work and military work are necessary. In this regard, mankind is divided into three classes: cultivators and industrialists, soldiers and government workers.

Religious men are of different classes. One class think that this world is a house of dangers, difficulties and labour, and they also think that they will be owners of fortune in the next world, whether or not their actions were good or bad. Another class of religious men think that natural passions must be uprooted for salvation and that it is not sufficient merely to bring them under control. Another class think that it is impossible to observe religious rules and that Allah has no need for people's spiritual works. Another class think that pious deeds are not necessary, as it is sufficient to have knowledge of Allah. Still another class of men rightly think that there is salvation in following the prophets, especially the last prophet of Arabia. They neither give up the world nor uproot their passions. They take from the world whatever is absolutely necessary for them.

The Prophet (ṣ) said that out of many parties, only one party will get salvation. The Companions asked, "O Prophet of Allah, who are they?" He replied, "The People of the Sunnah and Community (*Ahl al-Sunnah wa al-Jamā'ah*)." When asked, "Who are the People of the Sunnah and Community?" he replied, "Those who tread my path and the path of my Companions, who took the world not for its sake but for religion, who did not give up the world but renounced it, who adopted a middle course in their actions and did not go to extremes."

Book 7
Love for wealth

Introduction

There are many dangers and difficulties in the world and the greatest danger is that of wealth. One of the dangers of wealth is that it cannot satisfy anybody and that nobody is safe even if he possesses enormous wealth and riches. If he loses his wealth, he becomes poor, and poverty leads to infidelity. If his wealth becomes enormous, it leads him to irreligiousness. Its ultimate result is loss.

In short, wealth has benefits and harms. Its benefits lead a person to salvation and its harms lead him to destruction. It is very difficult to distinguish its good and evil. Only those who are experienced know them. Man is tried by two states: solvency and poverty. Furthermore, whoever has no wealth meets with one of two states: satisfaction or greed. Satisfaction is good, and greed is bad. Greed also has two states: greed for what people have and engagement in different businesses and industries. The rich man meets also with one of two states: hoarding wealth or spending it. The former is bad, while the latter is good. Whoever spends wealth in two states is either extravagant or moderate. The former is bad, whereas the latter is good. We shall describe below these states in detail.

1

Condemnation of love for wealth

Evidence

The Qur'an

Allah says:

O you who believe, let not your wealth or your children divert you from the remembrance of Allah; and whoever does that, these are the losers. (Qur'an, 63:9)

Your possessions and your children are only a trial, and Allah it is with whom is a great reward. (Qur'an, 64:15)

Whoever desires this world's life and its finery, We will pay them in full their deeds therein, and they will not be made to suffer loss in respect of them. (Qur'an, 11:15)

No, man is most surely inordinate, because he sees himself free from want. (Qur'an, 96:6-7)

Abundance diverts you. (Qur'an, 102:1)

Ḥadīth

The Prophet (ṣ) said, "Love for wealth and greed for power breed hypocrisy just as rain grows grass in the earth."

He said, "As two hungry tigers cause harm to goats by entering their fold, so also love for riches and greed for power and for name and fame cause destruction by entering the religion of a Muslim."

He said, "Those who have enormous riches are ruined, but those who spend it for the good of the people are happy. They are few in number."

He was once asked, "O Prophet of Allah, who among your followers are bad?" He replied, "The rich."

He said, "After you, there will appear people who eat various delicious dishes, ride a variety of good conveyances, marry beautiful women and wear expensive clothes. Their bellies are not satisfied with a little food, not even with sufficient food. They spend their energy on earning money, worship deities other than Allah and follow their low desires. By Muḥammad, the son of 'Abdullāh, if your successors or those who after them met them, they would neither greet them, treat them in their illnesses, attend their funeral prayers nor honour their elders. Whoever does the above aids in the destruction of Islam."

He said, "Leave the world to the worldly addicted. Whoever takes from the world in excess of what is necessary for him takes the path of destruction without his knowledge."

He said, "The son of Adam says, 'My wealth! My wealth!' What connection do you have with your wealth? You have destroyed what you have eaten. You have rendered old what you have put on. What you have given in charity is gone and has become permanent."

One day, a man said to the Prophet (ṣ), "O Prophet of Allah, I do not love wealth. What is the reason?" He replied, "Do you have any wealth?" The man said, "O Prophet of Allah, I do." The Prophet (ṣ) said, "Send your wealth in advance, as the heart of a believer is attached to his wealth. If he leaves that wealth in this world, his mind will wish to remain with it in this world."

He said, "The son of Adam has three kinds of friends: One kind of friend remains with him until his death; another kind of friend goes with him up to his grave; and the third kind of friend remains with him up to Resurrection Day. The friend who remains with him up to his death is his wealth. The friend who goes with him up to his grave is his relatives. The friend who remains with him up to Resurrection Day is his good works."

The disciples of 'Īsā asked him, "How can you walk on water?" He replied, "What value do you attach to gold and silver?" They said, "To us they are most valuable?" He said, "To me gold and silver are the same as earth."

Salmān al-Fārisī wrote to Abū al-Dardā', "O dear brother, do not accumulate things from the world for which you will not be able to express gratefulness, as I have heard the Prophet (ṣ) say, 'The worldly man who spends wealth in obedience to Allah will be brought on Resurrection Day with his wealth. When he is hanging on the Bridge, his wealth will tell him, 'You may go, as you have paid Allah's dues.' Then the worldly man who did not spend wealth according to the injunction of Allah will be brought, and his wealth will be placed around his neck. When he is hanging on the Bridge, his wealth will say to him, 'Woe to you. You did not pay Allah's dues. You will remain in this condition.' His wealth will then lead him to destruction.'"

The Prophet (ṣ) said, "When any man dies, the angels say, 'What wealth has he sent in advance?' But people say, 'What wealth has he left behind?'"

He said, "Do not acquire landed property. If you do, you will love the world."

A man badly treated Abū al-Dardā', who said, "O Allah, keep the body of the man who ill-treats me sound, give him a long life and increase his wealth. For if these three things coexist in a person, disaster befalls him."

Al-Ḥasan said, "By Allah, Allah makes him loud and humiliated who loves wealth." He also said, "When gold and silver were prepared, Satan lifted them, placed them on his forehead and kissed them out of love, saying, 'Whoever loves you will truly be my slave.'"

Yayḥā ibn Mu'ādh said, "Gold and silver come to one like a snake. Do not attempt to catch it without learning beforehand its charms, for when it touches you, its venom will destroy you." He was asked, "What are its charms?" and replied, "Earning it in a lawful manner and spending it moderately for Allah."

Maslamah ibn 'Abd al-Malik went to 'Umar ibn 'Abd al-'Azīz when the latter was dying and said to him, "O Commander of the Faithful, you have done good works which nobody before has done. You are leaving thirteen sons and daughters, but have left no possessions for them." 'Umar said, "Bring them to me." When they came to him, he said to Maslamah, "You have told me that I am leaving nothing for my sons and daughters. I have not prevented them from taking their dues, nor have I given them what is due to others. My issues belong to either of two classes. If they are obedient to Allah, Allah is sufficient for them, for Allah gives power to the pious. And if they are disobedient to Allah, I do not care what happens to them."

Muḥammad ibn Ka'b al-Quraẓī once acquired enormous wealth. People requested that he leave it for his sons, but he refused and said, "I will hoard it for myself with Allah and leave Allah for my sons."

Yaḥyā ibn Mu'ādh said, "Two calamities appear before a rich man at the time of his death. The predecessors and successors will find no more danger than these two." He was asked, "What are these two calamities?" He said, "All his wealth is separated from him, and he knows that he will be held accountable for all his wealth."

2

The benefits of wealth

Evidence

The Qur'an

In many place in the Qur'an, Allah mentions wealth as "*khayr*" (good). For example, He says, "If he leaves behind wealth (*khayr*)" (Qur'an, 2:180). He also says, "Your Lord desired that they should attain their maturity and take out their treasure, a mercy from your Lord" (Qur'an, 18:82) and "Help you with wealth and sons, and make for you gardens, and make for you rivers" (Qur'an, 71:12).

Ḥadīth

The Prophet (ṣ) said, "Lawful wealth is good for pious people" and "Poverty nearly became infidelity." Thus, wealth is good in a way and bad in another. When it is good, it is praiseworthy, and when it is bad, it is blameworthy. But wealth is not wholly bad or wholly good. Rather, it is an instrument of good and bad. The Prophet (ṣ) was once asked, "Who is the most honourable and wise?" and replied, "Whoever remembers death much and becomes most prepared for it."

Modes of spiritual fortune

There are three: the gift of the soul is knowledge and good conduct, the gift of the body is health and safety and the gift of the world outside the body and soul is wealth, air and light. Of all the above three gifts, the gift of the soul is the greatest. The gift of the body is less than that and the gift of the outer world is bad. Out of these gifts, the worst is the gift of wealth, and still more worse is the gift of gold and silver, as they are slaves having no value of their own but are utilised for gaining other gifts.

The soul is the most valuable gift. Its object is to attain virtues and good conduct and knowledge of Allah. The body is the carrier and slave of the soul. It perfects the soul, and the purity of the soul is possible because of knowledge and good conduct. Whoever knows this mode knows the function of wealth, which is necessary for maintaining the body, which is necessary for maintaining the soul.

Is wealth good or bad?

Intention is what determines whether wealth is good or bad. If the intention is good, wealth is also good. If it is bad, wealth is bad. The Prophet (ṣ) said, "Whoever acquires wealth in excess of what in necessary for him unknowingly draws his own destruction."

Wealth supplies materials to a man who follows his evil desires. For that reason, prophets used to seek refuge in Allah from excessive wealth. Our Prophet used to pray, "O Allah, supply the provision of the family of Muḥammad according to their requirements." He also used to pray, "O Allah, keep me alive as a poor man, take my life as a poor man and resurrect me in the company of the poor."

The prophet Ibrāhīm prayed, "Save me and my sons from worshipping idols" (Qur'an, 14:35). By this he meant the worship of gold and silver, as gold and silver are deities to people. The status of prophethood is so high that he had no fear of idol worship, but the worship of gold and silver was a possibility. The Prophet (ṣ) said, "The owners of gold are ruined, and the owners of silver are ruined." So it appears that whoever loves gold and silver worships stones and idols.

There are two kinds of polytheism. One kind is subtle, for which Hell is not the permanent abode, and another kind is open, for which Hell is the permanent abode.

3

Benefits and harms of wealth

Know that wealth is like a snake which has both a poison and an antidote. Whoever knows its antidote and poison can avoid its harms and enjoy its benefits.

Benefits of wealth

The benefits of wealth are worldly and other-worldly. The worldly benefits are known to all, whereas the other-worldly benefits are of three kinds.

The first is of spiritual works, such as spending wealth on pilgrimage and jihad, for without money these virtuous acts cannot be performed. A poor man is deprived of these virtues. The strength required for acts of worship is gained from food, dress, abode, marriage and other necessities of life. These things without which pious deeds are not possible are also pious deeds to the extent of necessity.

The second benefit of spending is in good works, which are four: charity, spending for hospitality, spending to preserve honour and remuneration for work. The benefits of charity are no secret. It appeases the wrath of Allah. Spending for hospitality includes spending on entertainment, feeding, presents, help and giving satisfaction to the minds of honourable men. Through this spending, brotherhood and friendship are established and the attribute of generosity is born. The benefit of preserving honour is to save oneself from the attack of fools, to uproot jest and the like. The Prophet (ṣ) said, "An act of charity is written for whoever saves his honour by spending money." The benefit of paying wages and remunerations is a kind of charity itself.

The remembrance of Allah is the highest stage of a religious traveller. Whoever has no wealth has to do many things by his own hand, making him uselessly spend a great deal of time, which could otherwise be engaged in the remembrance of Allah. Whoever is rich can engage others to do things which he would otherwise have to do himself.

Another benefit of wealth is continuous charity. It is spent not on a particular man, but for the good of the general public, such as the construction of a mosque, a bridge, a rest house, an orphanage, a home for the destitute and helpless, a charitable hospital and the like. Because of this, the soul benefits even after death. These are the religious benefits of wealth. Besides these, a person with wealth can save himself from the humiliation of begging and poverty.

Harms of wealth

Wealth has two harms: worldly and religious. The religious harms are of three kinds. The first is wealth leads to sins and opens doors to sins, thus ruining one. The second is it leads to the happiness of enjoying lawful things, which is the first step to the path of sin. Does a rich man use coarse clothes and rice? Can he give up various kinds of delicious food? Sulaymān was able to give up the fineries of the world in spite of his rule over vast territories. Another harm of wealth is heedlessness of Allah, a danger from which no one is free. Man forgets Allah in his engagement in maintaining his fortune and wealth. The thing which keeps a man forgetful of Allah is harmful. 'Īsā said, "Wealth has three harms. It is acquired even if it is not lawful." He was asked, "If wealth is taken from lawful things?" He replied, "Even then, he spends it in an illegal way." He was asked, "And if he spends it in a legal way?" He replied, "Even then, it keeps him forgetful of Allah because he engages himself in maintaining and guarding it."

This is a serious disease, as the root and life of spiritual works is the remembrance of Allah and to ponder over His glory and His wonderful creations. For this, the mind should be free from thoughts other than Allah. A man having wealth thinks of the success of his disputes, his accounts, his quarrels with co-sharers regarding boundaries, clashes with government officials, peasants and workers and a thousand other things concerning his property, businesses and industries.

We have mentioned in the book "Poverty" that poverty is good provided one remains content with it and does not develop a greed for earning wealth. The Prophet (ṣ) said, "If the son of Adam had two mountains full of gold, he would surely search for a third. His stomach cannot be filled up except with earth. Allah accepts the repentance of one who repents." Abū Mūsā al-Ash'arī said, "A *sūrah* like Barā'ah (Qur'an, 9) was revealed and then abrogated later on. Of it, this was memorised: 'Allah will surely help this religion through men who have no share therein. If a son of Adam had two mountains full of gold, he would search for a third one full of gold, but nothing can fill the stomach of man except earth. Allah accepts the repentance of him who repents.'" The Prophet (ṣ) said, "There are two coveted things which cannot be satisfied: desire for knowledge and greed for wealth." He also said, "The son of Adam gets old, but two things of his remain young: hope for a long life and greed for wealth."

4

The merits of satisfaction with poverty

Allah and His Prophet praised one who remains satisfied with poverty.

Ḥadīth

The Prophet (ṣ) said, "Glad tidings of Paradise to him who is guided to Islam and remains satisfied with necessary provisions for removing his wants." He said, "There is no such man, rich or poor, who would not like to say on Resurrection Day that only necessary food was sufficient for him in the world." He said, "There is no real contentment in enormous wealth. Real contentment is that of the mind." He said, "O people, take care and seek power in a legal manner, as man will get nothing except what has been decreed for him. No man will leave the world until he enjoys fully the provision Allah has prescribed for him."

Mūsā once asked Allah, "O Lord, who is the richest man among Your servants?" He replied, "The man who remains satisfied with what has been given to him." Mūsā asked, "Who among them is the best judge?" He replied, "The man who is the best judge of himself."

The Prophet (ṣ) said, "Jibrīl inspired my soul, "No man will die until he fully enjoys his provisions."

Abū Hurayrah reported that the Prophet (ṣ) said to him, "O Abū Hurayrah, when you are extremely hungry, take a piece of bread and a cup of water and strike the world away with your feet."

The Prophet (ṣ) said, "Fear Allah and you will become the most religious man. Remain satisfied with little and you will become the most grateful man. Love for others what you love for yourself and you will become a real believer." He said, "When you pray, pray as if you are leaving the world. Do not utter a word for which you will have to offer an excuse on Resurrection Day. Do not be greedy for the things in possession of men." He said, "Will you not give allegiance to the Prophet of Allah?" The Companions replied yes. He said, "Do acts of worship, not setting up partners with Him and pray five times a day. Hear and obey." Then he secretly said, "Do not beg people." The narrator of the *ḥadīth* said, "After that day, nobody among us required anybody to lift even a stick when it fell down."

Traditions from Companions and early Muslims

'Umar said, "Greed is poverty, despair is wealth. Whoever does not wait to receive from the people is not deprived."

A wise man said, "What is wealth? Little hope and satisfaction with necessary things.

Muḥammad ibn Wāsi' used to eat dry bread soaked in water and say, "Whoever is satisfied with this food does not rely on others."

Sufyān said, "The world is good for you as long as you do not face danger and calamities in the world. What leaves your hands is the best of things to try you."

Ibn Mas'ūd said, "There is not a day on which an angel does not proclaim, 'O son of Adam, a small amount of necessary provisions is better for you than misguidance by enormous wealth.'"

It is related that Allah said, "O son of Adam, if the whole world were given to you, nothing would be yours except what is necessary for you. Therefore, when I give you necessary food and entrust your accounts to others, you think that I am merciful to you."

A sage said, “I see an envious man the most distressed, a contented man the happiest, a greedy man the most impatient at the time of distress, a man who has renounced the world the most joyful and a transgressing learned man the most repentant.”

Once, a Bedouin rebuked his brother for greed and said, “O brother, what do you seek and what seeks you? You cannot avoid him who seeks you (death). The necessary things you seek must come to you. The thing concealed from your eyes (death) is not secret to you now, but rather open. The condition in which you are now must change. You have thought that a greedy man is never dependent and a sage who has renounced the world does not get his sustenance. This is only your conjecture.”

Al-Sha‘bī reported that a hunter caught a bird which said, “What will you do with me?” He said, “I shall eat your meat.” The bird said, “Will you be satisfied if you eat my meat? I will teach you three bits of information which will be better for you than my meat. I can tell you the first while I am in your hand, the second if you let me go and the third when I am sitting in the valley.” He said, “Tell me the first.” The bird said, “Do not grieve over the past.” Then the hunter released the bird, which took shelter in a tree and said, “Do not believe an impossible thing.” The bird then sat on the valley and said, “Woe to you! If you had killed me, you would have found two jewels in my stomach, each weighing twenty *mithqāls*.” The man became much grieved and said, “Tell me the third.” The bird said, “How can I tell you the third? Have I not told you that you should not grieve over the past or believe an impossible thing? My blood, meat and wings are no more than twenty *mithqāl*s. How can I have two jewels weighing twenty *mithqāl*s each in my stomach?” Then the bird flew away. This story is related to show how blind man becomes when he has greed, thus believing impossible things.

‘Abd al-Wāḥid ibn Zayd said, “I was passing once by a Christian monk and asked him, “Where does your sustenance come from?” He said, “Whoever created the crushing wheel in me brings wheat therein for crushing” and pointed at his teeth.

5
Medicine for greed

The medicine for greed is prepared with three ingredients: patience, knowledge and action. During the use of this medicine, the ingredients come through five prescriptions.

The first prescription for removing greed is to adopt a middle path to earning a living and to cutting expenditure. Whoever wishes to get the honour of contentment should shut all the doors of expenses as far as possible and spend what is absolutely necessary. If his expenses are too much, it is impossible for him to earn the quality of contentment. If he remains single, he should remain content with coarse clothes, whatever food he gets and however little curry. If he has a family, each should take a like proportion of things. The middle course is the root of achieving contentment in livelihood.

The Prophet (ṣ) said, "Allah loves the middle course in all affairs." He said, "Whoever spends moderately does not become needy." He said, "There is salvation in three: fearing Allah openly and secretly; adopting a middle course in expense, poverty and solvency; and justice in happiness and wrath." He said, "Adopting a middle course, good treatment and true guidance are a little over one-twentieth of prophethood." He said, "Allah saves moderate spenders from depending on others, throws the extravagant into want and loves him who remembers Him." He said, "If you wish, delay a thing until Allah makes a way out and a means for you. And to delay in spending is very necessary."

The second prescription for removing greed is that a person should not be anxious for fortune if he has everything he needs. Rather, he should curtail his hope, having faith that the provision which has been pre-decreed will come to him. Greed does not draw sustenance. He should put faith in the following verses of the Qur'an: "There is no animal in the earth but on Allah is the sustenance of it" (Qur'an, 11:6) and "Satan threatens you with poverty and enjoins you to be niggardly" (Qur'an, 2:268).

A sage said, "Once, two sons of Khālid came to the Prophet (ṣ), who said to them, 'Do not despair of livelihood as long as your heads move. Man is born from his mother's womb without any defect, and before his birth Allah prescribed his sustenance.'"

The Prophet (ṣ) once passed by Ibn Mas'ūd and, finding him troubled in mind, said, "Do not worry much. What has been decreed must come to pass." He said, "O people, seek your livelihood in a just manner, as nobody will get except what has been decreed for him. Nobody will leave the world until that portion of the world which was destined to be his goes to him unwillingly."

Nobody will be free from greed until he believes firmly in the good management of Allah regarding the measure of sustenance. That can be earned if sought after well. He should know that Allah provides him with sustenance from where he does not even conceive. Allah says, "Whoever is careful of (his duty to) Allah, He will make for him an outlet and give him sustenance from whence he thinks not" (Qur'an, 65:2-3). When one door of his livelihood is closed, another door is opened up for him. The Prophet (ṣ) said, "Allah provides a believer with provision from a place he cannot even conceive."

Sufyān said, "Fear Allah. I have never found a God-fearing man fall in want." In other words, Allah provides the God-fearing man with his necessities and does not abandon him. Allah instils in the minds of Muslims the feeling that His sustenance will arrive to them. Abū Ḥāzim said, "I see two things about the world. One of these two is that the combined strength of the heavens and earth will not be able to bring before its due time what has been decreed for me. The other thing is for others. I did not get it in the past, nor can I hope to get it in the future. I will never get what has not been decreed for me. What has been decreed for me must come to me. I do not know in which of these two things my life will end."

The third prescription for removing greed is to know what merits there are in contentment, what honour there is in not depending on others and what disgrace there is in greed. When knowledge of these things grows, eagerness for contentment will grow, as there is difficulty in greed, but in contentment there is not difficulty but patience.

The Prophet (ṣ) said, "The honour of a believer lies in not depending on others." Thus, there is freedom and honour in contentment. A sage said, "You will become an equal to whomever you wish unless you depend on him, and you will become the slave of whomever you wish if you depend on him. If you benefit whomever you wish, you will become his master."

The fourth prescription for removing greed is to think about the wealth of the irreligious people of the Jews, Christians and Bedouins, consider the prophets and friends of Allah and their sayings and wise counsels and then adopt a way for yourself. You will then say to your intellect, "Will you be like the prophets and the friends of Allah or like irreligious and low-class people? If you feel happiness in filling your stomach with food, an ass is happier than you in that respect, as it eats more than you. If you feel happiness in copulation, a swine is happier than you in that respect. If you feel happiness in clothes, buildings and conveyances, Jews are happier than you in those respects. If you feel happy in having little, you will have a status lower than others except the prophets and friends of Allah."

The fifth prescription for removing greed is not to hoard wealth and riches. If wealth is hoarded, there is fear of theft and looting. If the hands remain empty, there is security and leisure.

A rich religious man will enter Paradise five hundred years after a poor religious man. One should look to those who are superior to one in religion and to those who are inferior to one in worldly riches. Abū Dharr said that the Prophet (ṣ) gave him this instruction: "Look to your inferiors in worldly matters and do not look to your superiors. The root of all affairs is to have patience, to curtail hopes and to know that one will have enjoyment if one keeps patient for a few days in this world."

6
The merits of generosity

If a man has no wealth, he should remain contented and curtail his greed. If anybody has wealth, he should be generous and benevolent and keep away from narrow-mindedness and miserliness, as generosity is the conduct of prophets and is the root of salvation.

Ḥadīth

The Prophet (ṣ) illustrated this when he said, "Generosity is a tree of Paradise whose branches hang towards the earth. If a man catches a branch therefrom, it will take him to Paradise." He said, "Jibrīl told me that Allah said, 'This religion I have proposed for Myself. Generosity and good conduct increase its grandeur. So honour Islam with these two qualities.'" He said, "Allah does not accept as His friend someone who lacks generosity and good conduct."

The Prophet (ṣ) was once asked, "O Prophet of Allah, which action is good?" He replied, "Patience and generosity." He said, "Allah loves two qualities: good conduct and generosity. Allah hates two conducts: bad conduct and miserliness. When Allah wishes good for a man, He engages him in good works of public utility."

It was once said to the Prophet (ṣ), "Tell me of an action which will take me to Paradise." He replied, "Actions which give power are feeding others, spreading peace and good words." He said, "Generosity is a tree of Paradise. Whoever is generous takes hold of one of its branches and does not give it up until he enters Paradise. Miserliness is a tree of Hell. Whoever is a miser takes hold of one of its branches and does not leave it until he enters Hell." He said, "Allah says, 'Seek good from My kind people and you will live under their care, as I have placed My mercy among them. Do not seek good from those who are hard-hearted, as I have placed My displeasure among them.'"

The Prophet (ṣ) said, "Forgive the faults of the benevolent man, as Allah conceals his faults with His hands." He said, "On a man who gives food mercy descends so soon that a knife cannot be inflicted on the neck of a camel with greater speed." He said, "Allah is benevolent and loves good conduct and hates bad conduct."

Anas reported that if any person begged anything of the Prophet (ṣ) in the name of Islam, he gave it to him. One day, a man begged something of the Prophet (ṣ), who ordered goats for him. The open space between two valleys was filled with *zakāh* goats. He gave all the goats to him. He came back to his clan and said, "O my clan, accept Islam. Muḥammad gives charity as if he has no fear of poverty." The Prophet (ṣ) said, "Allah makes some men prosperous with riches so that they may do good to people. Whoever shows miserliness in doing good to people, Allah takes it from him and gives it to others."

The Prophet (ṣ) said, "Everything has its fruit, and the fruit of benevolence is salvation." He said, "The food of a benevolent man is treatment, whereas the food of a miser is disease." He said, "Whoever is a giver of excess gifts bears the sufferings of many people." 'Īsā said, "Take such thing in excess which cannot be destroyed by the fire of Hell." He was asked, "What is it?" He said, "To do good."

The Prophet (ṣ) said, "Paradise is the abode of the generous." He said, "The charitable man is near Allah, near people, near Paradise and distant from Hell. The miser is distant from Allah, distant from people, distant from Paradise and near Hell." He said,

"Do good to all, whether in want or not. If you do good to people, you will remove your wants. If you do not, you will fall into want." He said, "The *Abdāl* of my nation will not enter Paradise for only prayer and fasting, they will enter Paradise for their generosity, purity of heart and the benefit of advising people." He said, "Allah created some matters for the good of the people. He made dear to people the doing of good to others, he made dear to people those who do good to others and he turned the faces of those who want good to those who do good. They give charity to them without difficulty just as rain water falling on some dry place brings it and its inhabitants back to life."

The Prophet (ṣ) said, "Every good act is an act of charity. What a man spends for himself and his family is regarded as an act of charity. Whoever saves his honour is an act of charity. It becomes the duty of Allah to give rewards to one who spends." He said, "Every good act is charity, and whoever guides to a good act will get the rewards of one who does that good act." He said, "To do good to a man, rich or poor, is an act of charity." It was revealed to Mūsā, "Do not kill al-Sāmirī, for he is a charitable man."

Traditions from Companions and early Muslims

A sage said, "Spend worldly riches when it comes to you, as it will not finish." Al-Ḥasan ibn ʿAlī said in response to a question Muʿāwiyah asked, "The meaning of manhood is to save one's life and religion, to treat a guest well, to argue in a good manner and to proceed to one's duty. The meaning of courage is to remove the sufferings of a neighbour and to have patience where it is required. The meaning of generosity is to do good before asking, to give charity on time and to treat a beggar well." He also said, "He is not a benevolent man who gives in charity when asked. Rather, the benevolent man is whoever, in obedience to Allah's command, pays the dues of those to whom they are due before asking and is not eager for their gratitude, as he believes firmly that he will get full rewards from Allah."

Al-Ḥasan al-Baṣrī was asked, "What is generosity?" He replied, "Your charity of wealth in the way of Allah is considered generosity." He was asked, "What is miserliness?" He replied, "Not to spend your wealth in the way of Allah is miserliness." He was asked, "What is the misuse of money?" He replied, "To spend out of greed for passion is misuse."

Ja'far al-Ṣādiq said, "There is no greater wealth than wisdom, no greater danger than ignorance and no greater helper than mutual consolation. Beware! Allah says, 'I am generous and honourable. No miser can come near Me.' Miserliness is included in infidelity, and infidels are in Hell. Benevolence and honour are a part of faith, and believers are in Paradise." Al-Ḥasan said, "It is the height of generosity to give in charity from one's hard-earned money."

Stories of generosity

Mu'āwiyah once sent in two loadfuls of a hundred and eighty thousand silver coins to 'Ā'ishah as a present. She accepted them and distributed them all to the people. At dusk, she said to her maidservant, "Bring my meal." She took a piece of bread and some olive oil and said to 'Ā'ishah, "We could have broken our fast with meat if you had kept a dirham of those you distributed today. 'Ā'ishah said, "If you had reminded me, I could have given something to you therefrom."

Once, Mu'āwiyah went on a pilgrimage. When he was passing by Madīnah, al-Ḥusayn ibn 'Alī told his older brother al-Ḥasan not to meet him and not to greet him. When Mu'āwiyah left Madīnah, al-Ḥasan informed him that they were in debt, and his people paid him eighty thousand dinars. Before this, the people of Mu'āwiyah went in advance, and all that was left was a camel, which was given to al-Ḥasan along with the money it was carrying.

The Prophet (ṣ) once said to al-Zubayr ibn al-'Awwām, "O al-Zubayr, know that the key to the sustenance of men is placed before the Throne. Allah gives to every man in proportion to his expenditure. He gives him more sustenance whose expense is much. He gives him less sustenance whose expense is less."

Once, a man complained of his wants to al-Ḥasan ibn ʿAlī, who said, "I do not have enough wealth to satisfy your needs. If I give much in charity, it seems little to me." The man said, "I will accept whatever you give me." He ordered his officer to count the money he had, which amounted to three hundred thousand dirhams and five hundred gold coins. He gifted away all the sums he had at that time to him."

Ibn ʿAbbās was once governor of Basra. One day, some learned men of Basra said to him, "One of our neighbours prays all night and fasts all day long. He has a daughter to be given in marriage, but for want of money he cannot." Then Ibn ʿAbbās got up and gifted six bags full of coins to him and said, "I will not give him so much money as can divert him from his prayer and fasting."

ʿAbd al-Ḥamīd ibn Saʿd was once the governor of Egypt. One year, during his reign, there was a drought. Consequently, the prices of food stuffs became high. He began to meet the demands of the people, so much so that he fell into debt for two hundred thousand dirhams. He mortgaged the ornaments of his family members to the merchants for the debt, ornaments which valued at fifty million dirhams. When he could not buy back the ornaments, he wrote to the merchants, "Sell those ornaments, and whatever remains after paying my debts should be given to those who did not get anything from me."

When Maʿn ibn Zā'idah was the ruler of the two Iraqs, a poet came to see him but could not have an interview with him. One day, the ruler entered a garden having a canal and sat at the end of this garden by the side of the canal. The poet saw him, wrote on a plank this couplet and floated it into the canal:

> O Generosity of Maʿn, free me from my wants.
> Who other than you will speak for me to Maʿn?

Maʿn lifted the plank and read the couplet. He ordered that the poet be brought to him and gave him ten thousand dirhams. On the second day, he read the couplet, then called the poet and gave him a hundred thousand dirhams. The poet did not like to receive it, but he had to accept it. On the third day, the poet was sought for but could not be found. Thereupon, Maʿn said, "It is my duty to give him charity until not a dinar remains in my treasury."

Once, al-Ḥasan, al-Ḥusayn and ʿAbdullāh ibn Jaʿfar set out for pilgrimage from Madīnah with a camel loaded with all their foods, drinks and luggage. When it was lost on the way, they grew fatigued due to hunger and thirst. They then took shelter in a house wherein was an old woman. She gave them milk from her only goat. They wanted food, but there was nothing with her except the goat. She slaughtered the goat and fed them. When they were leaving, they said to the woman, "We belong to Quraysh and we are making a pilgrimage. When we return to Madīnah, you will see us. We will help you at that time." Thereafter she fell into extreme poverty and came to Madīnah, where she gathered camel dung and sold it to maintain herself. One day, she was passing by a lane when al-Ḥasan, who was sitting in his house, saw her and recognised her. He then purchased a thousand *zakāh* goats and gave them to her along with a thousand dinars. He also sent her to al-Ḥusayn, who gave her a similar amount. Then al-Ḥusayn sent her to ʿAbdullāh, who gave her two thousand goats and two thousand dinars. Then this woman went with four thousand goats and four thousand dinars to her husband.

ʿAbdullāh ibn ʿĀmir purchased a house situated in the midst of a market belonging to Khālid ibn ʿUqbah ibn Abī Muʿayṭ for ninety thousand dirhams. When it was night, he heard the cries of the family members of Khālid. Upon inquiring, he learnt that they were crying for the house sold to him. He said to his servant, "Tell them that the house along with the money belongs to them."

Hārūn al-Rashīd once sent a present of five hundred dinars to Mālik ibn Anas. When al-Layth ibn Saʿd heard, he sent to Mālik a thousand dinars. When Hārūn learnt of this, he was enraged and called al-Layth, who said, "I earn daily no less than a thousand dinars, and I felt ashamed to give in charity less than a day's income." It was reported that al-Layth did not have to pay *zakāh* because of this and that he did not talk with anybody before giving three hundred and sixty poor men charity daily."

Sa'īd ibn Khālid was a charitable man. One day, he went to Sulaymān ibn 'Abd al-Malik, who asked him, "Do you need anything?" He replied, "I have debts." Sulaymān said, "How much?" He replied, "Thirty thousand dinars." Sulaymān said, "I will give you this sum for the payment of your debts in addition to a like amount."

When al-Shāfi'ī was on his death bed, he gave instructions that a certain man wash him. When he died, the man was brought and the written instructions were given to him. He read it and learnt that he left a debt of seventy thousand dirhams. He paid all his debts and explained that it was what he meant by washing.

It was reported that Ṭalḥah was indebted to 'Uthmān for fifty thousand dirhams. One day, Ṭalḥah said to 'Uthmān, "I have collected money to settle your debts." 'Uthmān said, "O Abū Muḥammad, I give it in charity to you owing to your religious tendencies." Sa'dā bint 'Awf said, "I went to Ṭalḥah and found him in a pensive mood. I asked him why he was so and he replied, 'I have some money about which I am thinking. Call my people.' Then his people were called and he distributed the money among them. I asked his servant, 'How much did he spend today on charity?' He said, 'Four hundred thousand dirhams.'"

Once, a Bedouin came to Ṭalḥah, introduced himself as his relative and wanted some money. Ṭalḥah had landed property, which he sold to 'Uthmān for three hundred thousand dirhams, so he gave the money in charity to the man.

7
Condemnation of miserliness

The Qur'an

Allah says:

> *Whoever is preserved from the niggardliness of his soul, these it is that are the successful ones.* (Qur'an, 59:9)
>
> *Let not those who are niggardly in giving away that which Allah has granted them out of His grace deem that it is good for them. No, it is worse for them. They will have that whereof they were niggardly made to cleave to their necks on Resurrection Day.* (Qur'an, 3:180)
>
> *Those who are niggardly and bid people to be niggardly and hide what Allah has given them out of His grace.* (Qur'an, 4:37)

Ḥadīth

The Prophet (ṣ) said, "Be careful of miserliness because the nations before you were destroyed for miserliness. Miserliness encouraged them to shed blood among themselves, and they considered unlawful things lawful." Similarly, he said, "Keep away from miserliness, as people before you shed blood among themselves, considered unlawful things lawful and severed blood ties owing to its incitement."

He said, "The miser, the wrongdoer, the treacherous man and whoever mistreats people under his control will not go to Paradise." He said, "There are three destructive things: miserliness which is obeyed, passion which is followed and self-praise which is considered good." He said, "Allah is displeased with three people: an old fornicator, a miser who causes troubles and a proud man with a big family." He said, "Two traits do not coexist in a believer: miserliness and bad conduct."

He prayed, "O Allah, I seek refuge in You from miserliness. I seek refuge in You from cowardice. I seek refuge in You from extremely old age." He said, "Save yourselves from miserliness, for nations before you were destroyed by it. Miserliness enjoined them to speak falsehood, so they spoke falsehood. Miserliness enjoined them to oppress, so they oppressed. Miserliness enjoined them to sever family ties, so they severed them." He said, "Man has two extreme evils: extreme miserliness and extreme cowardice."

One man was killed at the time of the Prophet (ṣ). A woman was weeping for him, saying, "Where is my martyr?" The Prophet (ṣ) said to her, "Who told you that he has become a martyr? Perhaps he uttered a word which he did not need to utter or was miserly when spending was necessary."

Jubayr ibn Muṭ'im reported that when the Prophet (ṣ) was returning home after the siege of Khaybar, some Bedouins drove him to a place full thorns after begging him for something. The Prophet (ṣ) said to them, "By Him in whose hand is my life, if I had wealth equal in amount to these thorns, I would distribute it among you and you would not have found me a miser, liar or coward."

He said, "No man has miserliness and faith coexisting in his mind." He said, "No believer should be a miser or a coward." He said, "You say that an oppressor is more disliked by Allah than a miser. What oppression is greater to Allah than the oppression of miserliness? Allah says with His glory and honour, 'No narrow-minded man or miser will enter Paradise.'"

Once, the Prophet (ṣ) was circumambulating the Ka'bah and found a man clinging to the cover of the Ka'bah, saying, "O Allah, forgive me by virtue of this holy Ka'bah." The Prophet (ṣ) said, "Tell me your sin." The man said, "My sin is greater than a mountain, a sea, the sky and the Throne." The Prophet (ṣ) asked, "Is your sin greater than Allah?" He replied, "Allah is the greatest." The Prophet (ṣ) said, "Tell me your sin." He said, "I had enormous riches, and beggars used to come to me to beg. Then I saw that they were approaching me with sticks of fire." The Prophet (ṣ) said, "Be off from me lest I should be consumed by fire. By Him who sent me with guidance, if you prayed for two hundred thousand years standing between the Corner and the Station of Ibrāhīm, then wept so much that your tears formed a river, as a result of which trees grew, then died in a state of miserliness, Allah would throw you in Hell. Woe to you! You know that miserliness is infidelity, and infidelity is in Hell. Do you not know that Allah says, 'Whoever is niggardly is niggardly against his own soul' (Qur'an, 47:38) and 'Whoever is preserved from the niggardliness of his soul, these it is that are the successful ones' (Qur'an, 59:9)."

Traditions from Companions and early Muslims

Muḥammad ibn al-Munkadir said, "It is well known that when Allah does not wish good for a people, He gives power to the impious of them to rule over them and places their sustenance in the hands of the misers of them."

Once, a woman was praised before the Prophet (ṣ). They said that she fasts all year round and prays the whole night, but she has miserliness." The Prophet (ṣ) said, "Then what good does she possess?"

Bishr said, "The heart becomes hard when one looks at misers, and trouble enters the hearts of believers when they meet them."

Yaḥyā ibn Mu'ādh said, "Love grows in the heart for charitable people, and hatred grows in the heart for misers, even if they are virtuous."

The prophet Yaḥyā once saw Satan in his own form and said to him, "O Satan, tell me who the dearest and the most hated to you are." Satan replied, "The dearest to me is the miserly believer, and the most hated to me is the charitable sinner." Asked why, he said, "The miserliness of the miser is sufficient for me. But if a charitable man commits a sin, I fear lest Allah show mercy to him for his generosity."

8
The merits of self-sacrifice

There are degrees of generosity and miserliness. Self-sacrifice is the highest stage of generosity. It is to give in charity a thing required by the charitable person himself. So he does not regard his own inconvenience, but gives a thing which he badly needs in order to satisfy the needs of another. The utmost limit of benevolence is to satisfy the needs of another in spite of the fact that he requires the thing very badly. The utmost limit of miserliness is to be a miser to oneself in spite of the fact that he requires it. He falls ill, but does not undergo medical treatment. He has greed for many things, but does not purchase them, as they are dear in the market.

Allah praised the Companions of the Prophet (ṣ) for their self-sacrifice in spite of the fact that they required the things they sacrificed. Allah says, "Prefer (them) before themselves though poverty may afflict them" (Qur'an, 59:9).

The Prophet (ṣ) said, "If a man has a desire for anything, but fulfils the desire of another with that thing, leaving his own desire unfulfilled, Allah forgives his sins."

'Ā'ishah said, "The Prophet of Allah could not eat to his heart's content for three consecutive days until his death. We could have eaten to our heart's content if we had wished, but we left our wants unfulfilled and fulfilled the wants of others."

Once, a guest came to the Prophet (ṣ). He could not gather food for him from his wives. Then a Madīnan Helper (*Anṣārī*) came there and took the guest to his house. He placed food before his guest and told his wife to extinguish the lamp. In darkness, the host pretended to eat with his guest, as there was not sufficient food for the guest. The guest ate to his heart's content. When it was dawn, the Prophet (ṣ) said to him, "Allah is pleased with you, for you treated your guest well last night, and it was revealed, 'Prefer (them) before themselves though poverty may afflict them' (Qur'an, 59:9)." Benevolence is an attribute of Allah, and self-sacrifice is its highest degree. The Prophet (ṣ) had such a high degree of self-sacrifice that Allah called it "sublime," saying, "Most surely you conform (yourself) to sublime morality" (Qur'an, 68:4).

Sahl ibn 'Abdullāh al-Tustarī said, "Mūsā said, 'O Allah, show me the superiority of Muḥammad and his followers.' Allah said, 'O Mūsā, you have no power to see their superiority. But I will show you a superiority of his I have given you and all the people.' Allah then disclosed the heavenly region to him. Mūsā saw a rank which nearly destroyed him owing to its dazzling light. Mūsā said, 'For what action did he get this rank?' Allah said, 'For a trait I have ordered him especially to have, which is self-sacrifice. O Mūsā, I feel ashamed to take account of any of his followers who make self-sacrifices even once in his lifetime. He will be given any place in My Paradise he wishes.'"

It is reported that 'Abdullāh ibn Ja'far went to see a garden of his, and on the way he entered a garden of grapes belonging to another. He saw a black slave with food in the front, and a dog was present there. The slave threw a piece of bread in front of the dog, which ate it. Then he gave the dog another piece of bread, which it ate. Thereafter, he gave a third piece of bread to the dog, which it ate. 'Abdullāh was looking at it and asked the slave, "How much food do you get daily?" He replied, "I get what you saw." He asked, "Why have you fed the dog without fulfilling your own need?" He said, "There are no dogs in this region. This dog has come from a distance and is hungry, so I did not wish to eat the bread." He asked, "How can you survive today?" He said, "I will bear the hunger." 'Abdullāh thought to himself, "People tell me that I am a philanthropist, yet I see this slave a more philanthropic man." Then he gave the garden to this slave and purchased his freedom.

'Umar said that when a Companion of the Prophet (ṣ) was presented with the head of a goat, he said, "The need of my Muslim brother is greater than mine" and sent it to him. The latter also thought likewise and sent it to a third Muslim. Thus, the head of the goat went to seven houses and returned to the first man.

One day, some Qurayshite youths surrounded the house of the Prophet (ṣ) in order to kill him. 'Alī, in order to save his life, thought his life insignificant and went to the bed of the Prophet (ṣ). Allah then addressed Jibrīl and Mīkā'īl, saying, "I have established brotherhood among you and gave you an equal period of life. Who among you can sacrifice his life for another?" Each of them preferred to save his own life. Allah then said to them, "Why could you not be like 'Alī? I have established brotherhood between him and Muḥammad, and he is spending the night lying in the bed of Muḥammad in order to save the life of the latter. Go to the earth and save him from his enemies." Jibrīl began to protect him, keeping near his head, and Mīkā'īl near his feet. Jibrīl said to 'Alī, "Blessed you are! Blessed you are! There is no comparison with you. Allah boasts of you before the angels." Allah then revealed, "Among men is he who sells himself to seek the pleasure of Allah; and Allah is affectionate to the servants" (Qur'an, 2:207).

More than thirty pious people lived with al-Ḥasan al-Anṭāqī. Once, they stayed in a village within the province of al-Rayy with some pieces of bread which were insufficient to feed everyone. They broke their bread into pieces, extinguished the light and sat to eat. When the cloth was lifted, it was seen that the bread was as before: None had eaten of it. Everybody showed self-sacrifice, giving an opportunity for his comrades to eat.

Ḥudhayfah al-'Adawī reported, "Many Muslims were martyred in the Battle of Yarmūk. I was trying to give water to my cousin in the battlefield. When I found him, I gave him water to drink. Just then, a man by his side cried, 'Water! Water!' My cousin told me to give water first to that man. When I came to him with water, I recognised him: He was Hishām ibn al-'Āṣ. I said, 'I am giving out water. Just then, another man cried, 'Water! Water!' Hishām then indicated that the man should first be given water. Before I came to him with water, he breathed his last. Then I came to Hishām with water only to find that he also had expired. Then I came to my cousin with water only to find that he also had expired."

'Abbās ibn Dihqān reported, "Man cannot go out of the world in the condition in which he came into the world, except for Bishr ibn al-Ḥārith. At the time of his death, one man came to him and complained about his wants. He gifted his only shirt to him, put on another after borrowing it from someone and then expired."

9

Definition of “charity” and “miserliness”

One party says that “not to spend on what Sharīʿah orders us to spend on” is the definition of “miserliness,” and that whoever pays what is obligatory for him is not a miser. Another party says that a miser is someone who feels pain when giving charity.

Similarly, there are differences regarding the definition of “charity.” Some say that the definition of “charity” is that which is given without rebuke. Some say that charity is what is given without asking. The fact is that wealth has been created with a special object, namely to remove the wants of men. Not to spend where expense is obligatory is miserliness. To spend where it is not obligatory is extravagance. The middle course between these two extremes is good. Allah says, “Do not make your hand shackled to your neck nor stretch it forth to the utmost (limit) of its stretching forth” (Qur’an, 17:29) and “They who when they spend are neither extravagant nor parsimonious, and (keep) between these the just mean” (Qur’an, 25: 67).

So to spend wealth proportionately and to save money to the extent which is obligatory is generosity. This is not sufficient if it is given by bodily limbs, but satisfaction of the heart is necessary without any dispute or argument.

There are two kinds of obligatory spending: obligatory according to Sharīʿah and obligatory to preserve honour, dignity and manliness. A benevolent man does not hesitate to spend according to the requirements of Sharīʿah as well as chivalry. If he does not spend as described above, he will be regarded as a miser.

Whoever does not spend according to the dictates of Sharī'ah is a more miserly man. For instance, if a man does not pay *zakāh* or does not spend for the maintenance of his family, he is a more miserly man. If he feels pain in this expenditure, he is a miser by nature. To spend for chivalry and honour is also charity, just as narrow-mindedness is an evil thing. This difference is according to the economic condition and personality of a man.

If miserliness is shown to a wealthy man, it is more reprehensible than that shown to a poor man. Miserliness shown to family members and relatives is more reprehensible than that shown to strangers. Miserliness shown to neighbours is more reprehensible than that shown to strangers. Miserliness shown in entertainment is more reprehensible than that shown to strangers. Miserliness shown in food, clothing, feasts and presents is worse than that shown in other respects. So want of expenditure where expenditure is necessary is miserliness. It is obligatory according to Sharī'ah or gentlemanly behaviour. The definition of *miserliness* is not to spend on necessary things and in proper places. It is better than hoarding riches. So he who does not pay *zakāh* is a miser. To spend out of chivalry is more necessary than to save money.

There remains another stage, which is this: A man spends money on his obligatory duties and acts of chivalry if he has surplus wealth and does not give it in charity. He entertains the thought of hoarding, which is miserliness according to pious men, though it is not miserliness according to the general public. Whoever spends money according to Sharī'ah and chivalry is not termed a miser, but he cannot be considered a generous and benevolent man until he spends beyond the optional duties for gaining a higher rank in religion. Thus, a man is considered philanthropic if he spends in charity beyond what is obligatory for him.

Spending on good works

Whoever spends on good works can be considered philanthropic provided he gives in charity with a contented heart and is under no pressure or hopeful of any service or reward. A female saint went to Ḥabbān ibn Hilāl, who was at that time surrounded by his disciples. The woman asked them, "What is philanthropy?" They replied, "Charity and self- sacrifice." The woman said, "It is worldly charity with satisfaction of the heart without being dissatisfied in spiritual works." She asked, "Do you not hope for a reward for it?" They replied, "Allah has promised to give ten rewards for one act of charity." The woman said, "If you get rewards in exchange for an act of charity, how can it be considered philanthropy? The meaning of 'philanthropy' to me is 'to give charity with pleasure of the heart in obedience to Allah's commands without hoping for a reward.'" Another woman said "philanthropy" means "the sacrifice of life along with spending money." Al-Muḥāsibī said, "The meaning of 'charity' in religion is 'to sacrifice one's life for Allah voluntarily, not under compulsion, and without hoping for any reward.'"

10
Medicine for miserliness

Know that miserliness arises out of love for wealth, which again appears for two reasons. The first is to satisfy passions and desires which cannot be fulfilled without wealth and hope for a long life. Hope for a long life is conjoined with the existence of children and is also a cause of miserliness. The Prophet (ṣ) said, "Children are the cause of a man's miserliness, cowardice and ignorance."

The second cause of love for wealth is love for wealth itself. There are men whose habit is to hoard money and not to spend, even though they have sufficient wealth to cover their necessities for the rest of their lives. We find people with no children in their old age, but they have enormous wealth. In spite of this, they do not pay *zakāh* and do not undergo treatment for their diseases. Rather, they worship money and love it for itself. They even bury their money underground, although they know that after death the money will be destroyed. This is extreme misguidance.

The medicine of every disease is to apply its opposite to the root cause of the disease. The medicine of greed is satisfaction with little and patience. The medicine of prolonged hope is much remembrance of death and to think of the sudden death of contemporaries. In addition, it is to remember its condemnation by the Qur'an, Ḥadīth and wise men and to spend money in charity, without which the disease of miserliness cannot be removed.

Another method of removing it is to remove one evil by another evil. In other words, spend money to acquire name and fame and to be known in society as a great philanthropist. Though the motive is evil, it will habituate you to spend money. So acquire the will of show by removing the evil of miserliness. So a lesser evil is sometimes good to remove a greater evil. The weak evil becomes the food of the strong evil until there remains only one strong evil after all the evils are crushed. This is similar to the case of worms eating the dead body of an animal. After the meat is finished, the strong worms eat the small worms until there remains only one strong worm, which also dies in the end for want of food. Miserliness commands to the hoarding of wealth. When it is not hoarded but rather spent again and again in spite of unwillingness, miserliness dies and spending becomes the habit and no difficulty is felt in spending.

The medicine of miserliness is based on knowledge and action. To know the evil of miserliness and rewards of charity and generosity is the medicine based on knowledge. To give in charity in spite of unwillingness is the medicine based on action. A king was once presented a most valuable cup made of rare pearls. The king was greatly pleased to get it and asked a wise courtier how he liked it. The courtier replied, "I consider it a great danger and, perhaps, it will throw you into want and distress." The king asked, "How?" The courtier replied, "If it breaks, it will be an object of great regret, as the like of it will not be found. If it is stolen by a thief, you will sense its absence very keenly." As it happened, the cup was broken or stolen. The king then felt very much worried and said that the words of the wise courtier were correct. This event is applicable to all things of the world.

11

Duties concerning wealth

For the above reasons, wealth is good from one point of view and bad from another point of view. Wealth is like a snake: The charmer takes out its venom after catching it. A layman, on the other hand, may be poisoned by its venom if he catches it without knowing its charms. So if someone attempted to catch the snake of wealth before knowing its charms, it would become an object of ruin.

The venom of wealth has four charms, which every rich man should know.

The first charm is to appreciate the benefit of wealth, the reason it was created, its need and the reason it should be earned. These should be known beforehand along with the fact that wealth beyond necessity should not be kept.

The second charm is to seek a mode of earning wealth. Unlawful earning is to be given up like poison. This includes accepting bribes, begging, stealing and the like.

The third charm is the proportion of earning wealth. Earning excess wealth should be avoided. Wealth should be earned only when necessary. Only what is needed of food, clothes and housing should be earned. Each of these has three stages: low, middle and high. So long as you remain near the low stage and near the necessary limit, you are in the right. When you cross that limit, you will fall in the lowest Hell.

The fourth charm is to be honest and have good motives in earning money, in expenditure and in saving. Earning money is necessary to gain ease in worship. If money is acquired with this intention, it will to harm you. 'Alī said, "If one becomes the owner of all the things of the world and thereby wishes to have the pleasure of Allah, he can be considered a man who has renounced the world. If one, however, renounces all wealth but does not wish to have the pleasure of Allah, he cannot be considered so. So in all your actions and movements, confine yourself to worship and those things which assist it. The actions which are nearest to worship are eating and satisfying the needs of relieving yourself. If by these actions your object is to worship, they are considered acts of worship. So every worldly action, if done to please Allah, is an act of worship. Your wearing clothes, your sleeping, your eating, your drinking—these are all acts of worship if done with that object. What you earn beyond what is necessary should be spent for the good of the people when they require it. A poet said:

> The world is like a serpent which pours venom,
> But the snake greets him who knows its charms.

12
Condemnation of wealth and praise of poverty

Traditions from al-Ḥārith al-Muḥāsibī

ʿĪsā said, "O dishonest learned man, you fast, pray and pay *zakāh*, but you do not do what you were ordered and you say what you do not do. What you utter is very bad. You repent with your mouth, but you follow your passions with your heart. Your repentance with your mouth is of no use. You keep your outer appearance neat and clean, but you keep your heart polluted and unclean. I say in truth that you should not become like a sieve. Subtle things come out of a sieve, and only outward forms remain. Words of wisdom come out of your mouth, but hatred and evils remain in your heart. O worshippers of the world, how can you gain the fortunes of the next world when there is no end to your greed and temptations? I tell you in truth that your hearts are weeping seeing your actions. You have placed the world under your tongue and actions under your feet.

"I tell you in truth that you have destroyed your next world. Earthly good is dearer to you than the good of the next world. Who are greater losers than you? Had you known, you would have gained for yourselves. You show the path to the travellers, but remain misguided in the same place. You tell worldly people to give up those things for you. Stop! Stop! Woe to you! What is the use of keeping a lamp on top of a dark house? Likewise, what is the use of keeping the lamp of education in your mouth?

"O worshippers of the world, you are not like pious men, like free, respected men. It is a wonder that the world will sever your roots, throw them over your faces and then into your nostrils. Then it will throw you into Hell."

Al-Ḥārith said, "O brethren, three evil learned men are the demons of the people and their trials. They are attached to the wealth of the world and eager for worldly advancements. They have preferred worldly treasures to those of the next world and humiliated religion for the world. They are owners of a high rank in this world, but losers in the hereafter.

"Do you not see that the Prophet (ṣ) said, 'Do not hoard wealth' when it was claimed that a Companion of the Prophet (ṣ), 'Abd al-Raḥmān ibn 'Awf, was a great, rich man during the time of the Prophet (ṣ). When he died, Ka'b said that he earned money lawfully and left lawful wealth. When the Companion Abū Dharr heard this, he grew enraged with Ka'b, found him with 'Uthmān and asked him, 'O Ka'b, you think there is no fault in the wealth left by 'Abd al-Raḥmān? The Prophet (ṣ) took me one day to the mountain of Uḥud and said, 'O Abū Dharr, the rich will become poor on Resurrection Day, except those who spend to their right, left, front and back, and their numbers are small. O Abū Dharr, if my wealth were equal to the mountain of Uḥud, it would not be good for me if I left therefrom even two *qīrāṭs* at the time of my death. You wish to have greater wealth, but I wish to have little.'

"Abū Dharr said to Ka'b, 'You say that there is no fault in the wealth left by 'Abd al- Raḥmān.' Then he left. We heard that there was a great row when several camel loads of 'Abd al-Raḥmān's merchandise arrived in Madīnah. 'Ā'ishah asked, 'Why the row?' She was told that merchandise had come. Then she said, 'I heard the Prophet (ṣ) say, 'I saw Paradise and saw poor Emigrants entering it. I saw no rich man entering it except 'Abd al-Raḥmān, who was going there crawling.' 'Abd al-Raḥmān said, 'I donate in the way of Allah all this merchandise, and I give liberty to all the male and female slaves along with it so that I can enter Paradise with them running.' The Prophet (ṣ) said to 'Abd al-Raḥmān, 'You will be the first among my rich Companions to enter Paradise, but you will enter it crawling.'"

The riches of the Companions

It is true that some Companions of the Prophet (ṣ) had riches. But these riches were for spending on those who were unable to earn and in the way of Allah and His Messenger. They earned lawfully, spent lawfully, ate lawful foods, paid *zakāh* and were not misers. They spent almost all their riches in the way of Allah and preferred poverty for themselves. They felt sorry when wealth came to them and thought that punishment for their sins was approaching them. When they saw poverty coming to them, they welcomed it.

A Companion used to say, "I feel joy when there remains nothing in my house at dawn, and the Prophet (ṣ) is my ideal. I become grieved when there is something in my house, as the Prophet (ṣ) is my ideal." The Prophet (ṣ) said, "Those whose bodies grow by luxurious enjoyments are the worst among my people." He said, "Whoever is grieved at the loss of his earth in the world comes one month near Hell." He said, "Love for the next world goes away from the heart of a man who loves the world and delights in it."

The Companions of the Prophet (ṣ) saved themselves from lawful things more than the way you save yourselves from unlawful things. What is now not a fault with you was a destructive fault for them. They used to consider a miser's sins to be as great as you regard great sins. What you regard as lawful wealth was considered by them to be doubtful. They used to fear the non-acceptance of their good works just as you fear it now for your bad deeds. Your fasts are like their non-fasts. Your efforts in acts of worship are like their waking up and their sleeping. Your entire good deeds are like one of their sins.

A Companion said, "I have given up seventy sources of lawful earnings lest I fall in an unlawful thing." The Prophet (ṣ) said, "Who dares to accept doubtful things?" A sage said, "Do you not know that to give up one dirham for fear of Allah is better for you than to give in charity one thousand gold coins whose lawfulness is doubtful?"

A Companion said, "It does not seem good to me that I earn a thousand dinars lawfully and spend it in the way of Allah, for which I lose the prayer of congregation." The people asked him why. He said, "The reason is that I will not be able to absolve myself from judgement of such a nature on Resurrection Day. Allah will say, 'O My servant, where have you earned this money from, and in what way have you spent it?'"

In spite of the wealth being lawful, they gave it up for fear of judgement. In some cases, when a Companion received inheritance, he gave it up for fear that it might harm his heart. The Prophet (ṣ) said, "Whoever faces reckoning will get punishment." He said, "On Resurrection Day, a man who earned wealth illegally and spent it illegally will be brought for judgement. It will be said, 'Take this man to Hell.' Another man will be brought. He hoarded lawful wealth and spent it legally. He will be told, 'Wait! Wait! Perhaps you could not pray on time in search of it and could not prostrate well." He will say, 'O Lord, I have earned lawful wealth. I did not ruin your obligatory duties.' He will be told, 'Perhaps by boasting of your wealth, you rode on a good conveyance, wore expensive clothes and were proud.' He will say, 'O my Lord, I have not boasted.' Allah will say, 'You have perhaps not carried out your duties towards your relatives, orphans, the poor and travellers.' He will say, 'I did not neglect my duties. I earned lawfully and spent lawfully.' He will be told, 'Show gratitude for the food, drinks and other dubious things that I gave you.' Thus Allah will question him."

The Prophet (ṣ) said, "Poor Emigrants will enter Paradise five hundred years before rich Emigrants. He also said, "Poor believers will enter Paradise before rich believers. They will be engaged in enjoyments of eating and drinking while the rich are down on their knees. Allah will say, 'I have questions to ask you. You have wielded power over men. You were kings and rulers over them. Now inform me what actions you have done with the gifts I gave you?'"

Once, Abū Bakr was thirsty and a cold drink with honey was brought to him. He drank it, but soon after, he began to weep profusely. Asked why, he said, "Once, I was with the Prophet (ṣ), and there was nobody else. He was throwing away something from his body, saying, 'Leave me.' I said, 'May my parents be sacrificed for you. I do not see anybody before you. Whom do you address?' He said, 'The world. It extended its hands and neck towards me and said, 'O Muḥammad, take me,' so I said, 'Leave me.' The world then said, 'O Muḥammad, though you have saved yourself from me, your successors will not be able to save themselves from me.' I feared lest I be that man."

A pious successor of the Companions was asked about the better of two men. One man seeks wealth in a lawful manner, shows kindness to relatives and spends on good works. The other man gives up wealth and does not seek it. The successor said, "By Allah, there is a great deal of difference between them. Whoever gives up wealth is better, and there is between them the distance between the east and west."

The Prophet (ṣ) said, "The chiefs in Paradise among believers will be those who could not procure their dinner after their breakfast, who did not get a loan when asked to, who had no clothes except what they had to cover their shame and who could not procure even their necessities, yet they were satisfied with their Lord at all times. They are those people on whom Allah showered His blessing—prophets, the truthful, martyrs and the religious. How good they are as companions."

Having read these traditions, if you want to hoard up wealth and promise that you will do it for good works, your word will not come true. In this age, we are deprived of lawful things. How can we expect to live on lawful food and lawful clothes? Abū Umāmah al-Bāhilī reported that Tha'labah ibn Ḥāṭib once asked the Prophet (ṣ), "O Prophet of Allah, pray to Allah that He may grant me wealth. He said, "O Tha'labah, to express gratefulness for little wealth is better than enormous wealth, for which gratefulness cannot be expressed." Tha'labah said, "O Prophet of Allah, pray that Allah grant me wealth." He said, "O Tha'labah, will you not adopt an ideal? Are you not satisfied to be like the Prophet (ṣ) of Allah? Beware! By Him in whose hand is my life, if I wished, this mountain would be filled with gold and silver." Tha'labah said, "By Him who sent you as a true prophet, if you pray that Allah grant me wealth, I will pay everyone's dues and I will do this and that work." The Prophet (ṣ) prayed, "O Allah, give sustenance to Tha'labah." He then got some goats, which began to increase like worms. He began to live with those goats in the suburbs of Madīnah He could not pray in congregation except for the noon and afternoon prayers. When the goats increased a great deal, he could not pray in congregation except for the Friday prayer. When the goats still increased, he left the Friday prayer also. One day, the Prophet (ṣ) enquired of him when he did not find him in the congregation. The people said, "He is engaged in grazing goats in the outskirts of Madīnah." The Prophet (ṣ) said, "O Tha'labah, woe to you." Then the following verse was revealed: "Take alms out of their property, you would cleanse them and purify them thereby, and pray for them; surely your prayer is a relief to them" (Qur'an, 9:103). This was the first verse about *zakāh*.

The Prophet (ṣ) then engaged two people to collect *zakāh* from Muslims. They both went to Tha'labah and asked for the *zakāh* from him in accordance with the order of the Prophet (ṣ). He said, "It is nothing but a poll tax. Show me your letter of appointment." When it was shown, he said, "It is the sister of the poll tax." They returned to the Prophet (ṣ) and informed him of it. Then Allah revealed this verse: "And there are those of them who made a covenant with Allah: If He give us out of His grace, we will certainly give alms and we will certainly be of the good. But when He gave them out of His grace, they became niggardly of it and they turned back and they withdrew. So He made hypocrisy to follow as a consequence into their hearts till the day when they will meet Him because they failed to perform towards Allah what they had promised with Him and because they told lies" (Qur'an, 9:75-77).

At that time, there was a relative of Tha'labah with the Prophet (ṣ), and he informed Tha'labah of this verse. Then Tha'labah came to the Prophet (ṣ) and asked him to take the *zakāh* from him, but he said Allah prohibited him to take it. He then began to besmear dust on his face, whereupon the Prophet (ṣ) said, "This is your action. I enjoined you, but you did not obey me." Then Tha'labah returned to his house. After the demise of the Prophet (ṣ), he came to Abū Bakr, who also refused to accept his *zakāh*. Thereafter, he went to 'Umar, who also refused to accept it. And during his caliphate, Tha'labah died.

The Prophet (ṣ) preferred poverty for himself and his family members. 'Imrān ibn Ḥuṣayn said that he had rank and honour before the Prophet (ṣ). One day, the Prophet (ṣ) asked him, "O 'Imrān, will you go with me to see the illness of Fāṭimah, the daughter of the Prophet (ṣ) of Allah?" He replied, "O Prophet of Allah, I will go with you." When they arrived at the house of Fāṭimah, the Prophet (ṣ) knocked on the door and sought permission to enter the house. Fāṭimah asked the Prophet (ṣ), "Who is with you?" He replied, "'Imrān ibn Ḥuṣayn." Fāṭimah said, "By Him who sent you as a prophet with the truth, I have nothing to put on except an old blanket, which does not cover my whole body." The Prophet (ṣ) said, "Cover your head with a piece of cloth." After receiving permission, the Prophet (ṣ) entered with 'Imrān. When questioned about her health, she said, "By Allah's mercy, I am in pain. I also have nothing to eat. Hunger bothers me."

At this, the Prophet (ṣ) wept and said, "O darling, have patience. I am more honourable to Allah than you. If I prayed to my Lord, He would give me food, but I prefer the next world to this world." Then he placed his hand on the shoulder of Fāṭimah and said, "Rejoice! By Allah, you will be the queen of women in Paradise." Fāṭimah asked, "Then where will be Āsiyah, the wife of Fir'awn, and Maryam, the daughter of 'Imrān?" He said, "Āsiyah will be the queen of her contemporary women, Maryam will be the queen of her contemporary women and Khadījah will be the queen of her contemporary women. You will all reside in buildings made of jewels, where there will be no sorrow." Then he said to Fāṭimah, "Remain satisfied with the son of your paternal uncle. By Allah, I married the king of this world and of the next." See, then, how the Prophet (ṣ) preferred poverty for his beloved daughter.

A man wished to accompany 'Īsā in his travels. They both came to the bank of a river and sat to eat their morning meal with three pieces of bread. Each of them ate one piece, so there remained one piece. 'Īsā then got up and drank water from the river. Upon returning, he did not find the remaining piece of bread there and asked his companion, "Who has eaten the bread?" He said, "I do not know."

Then they both went on their journey until they found a deer with two fawns. They caught one, sacrificed it and ate its meat. Then 'Īsā said to the fawn, "Rise with the permission of Allah." It arose alive. He asked his companion, "By Him who showed you this miracle, tell me who ate the remaining piece of bread?" He said, "I do not know." Both came to the bank of a river, and 'Īsā caught the hand of his companion and crossed it by walking over it, then asked him, "By Him who showed you this miracle, I ask you, 'Who ate the remaining bread?'" He replied again, "I do not know." Then they reached a region full of dust. 'Īsā gathered a heap of sand and said, "Be gold by the permission of Allah." Then 'Īsā divided it into three portions and said, "One portion is for myself, another for you and another for that man who ate the remaining piece of bread." Then the man said, "I ate the remaining piece of bread." 'Īsā said, "All the divisions of gold are for you." Then he parted from him and went away.

The man met in that place two other men, who saw the heaps of gold and wished to get them all by killing the man. They sent the man to purchase food for them. The man thought to kill the two people, and so he went to purchase bread. He purchased poison and bread, mixed them together and went to the two men. The two men thought that they should kill the other man when he comes with the bread and appropriate the heaps of gold. When the man came with the food mixed with poison, they at once killed him. They then ate the bread mixed with the poison and soon expired. The dead bodies of the three people lay there. 'Īsā returned by that way and saw the dead bodies and said to his companions, "It is the world, so fear the world."

Once, Dhū al-Qarnayn came to a people who had no wealth. They dug graves and prayed therein. They also used to eat grass like lower animals. Dhū al-Qarnayn called the chief of them, who refused to come, saying, "I do not need to go to him." Dhū al-Qarnayn himself went to him and said, "I find you in a condition in which I have found no man. You have nothing of this world. Do you not use gold and silver?" They said, "We hate these two things, and whoever gets them wants them more. We want what is better than that." He asked them, "Why do you pray in graves?" They said, "When we see the graves, the world cannot attract us." Dhū al-Qarnayn asked, "Why do I not see you eating food?" They said, "We hate to make our bellies graves for meat. Rather, grass and leaves are our staple food. This is sufficient for the children of Adam. All things become equal when they enter the stomach, be they delicious foods or leaves."

Then he took a skull from behind Dhū al-Qarnayn and asked, "O Dhū al-Qarnayn, do you know who he was? He was the king of a vast empire, but he began oppression. When Allah saw it, He caused his death and dug his skull underneath the ground." Thereafter, he dug out an old skull and said, "O Dhū al-Qarnayn, do you know who he was? He came after the former king. He treated his subjects well and did good and established justice.

Allah will reward him on Resurrection Day." Then he took a skull with two horns and said, "O Dhū al-Qarnayn, look at this man having two horns like you." Dhū al-Qarnayn said, "Can I live with you, and can I have you as my friend and member?" He said, "We cannot live together in the same place, as all men are your enemies, whereas they are our friends." Dhū al-Qarnayn asked why. He said, "They are your enemies because you have a vast empire and enormous wealth, and they are our friends because we have nothing in this world. Then Dhū al-Qarnayn left that place.

Book 8
Love for power and ostentation

Introduction

The Prophet (ṣ) said, "The greatest of what I fear most for my followers is ostentation and hidden greed. It is subtler than the movements of black ants on a smooth stone in the darkest night." For that reason, experienced scholars have become baffled as to how to save themselves from its harms. Thereby, religious men are tried, as they want to gain respect from people for their learning and piety. They wish to receive praise and respect in meetings. Given that ostentation is a subtle disease and a great window for Satan, its causes should be known. We shall divide this book into two chapters:

1. Love for power, name and fame
2. Ostentation

1

Love for power, name and fame

Know that the lover of name and fame is bad and that to live in an unknown state is good. But if name and fame spread unintentionally, it is not bad.

The Prophet (ṣ) said, "It is sufficiently evil for a man to be pointed at with fingers because of his temporal or spiritual state. But he is saved whom Allah saves." He said, "Allah looks not at your figures, but at your hearts and actions."

'Alī said, "Spend, but do not disclose it. Do not elevate yourself to attract the attention of others. Rather, conceal yourself and remain silent and you will remain safe. The pious will be satisfied with you, and the impious will be dissatisfied."

Ibrāhīm ibn Adham said, "Whoever loves name and fame does not know Allah to be true."

Similarly, Ayyūb al-Sakhtiyānī said, "By Allah, a man does not know Allah to be true until he knows well that his address should not be known by anybody."

When many people gathered in the invocational assembly of Khālid ibn Ma'dān, he used to leave it.

Once, ten people were walking with Ṭalḥah, who said, "It is the wing of greed and the bed of Hell." Ibn Mas'ūd was once coming out of his house when a host of men were following him. He said to them, "Why do you walk behind me. By Allah, if you knew why I keep my door closed, two of you would not follow me." Al-Ḥasan once came out followed by a group of people. He said to them, "Do you need anything from me? If so, it is okay, or else it is not good for this feeling to remain in the heart of a believer." Ayyūb once came out, and many people followed him. He said, "Had I not known that Allah knows that I hate your following me, I would have feared the dislike of Allah."

Al-Thawrī said, "The wise men of yore hated clothes which drew people's attention. Once, a man requested Bishr to advise him. He said, "Whoever loves name and fame will not get a taste of the next world."

Merits of anonymity

The Prophet (ṣ) said, "There are many a man whose body is besmeared with dust, whose hair is dishevelled, whose clothes are torn and who is disregarded by men, but fulfils his promise made in the name of Allah. If he says, 'O Allah, I seek from you Paradise,' Allah will grant him Paradise. When he seeks anything of the world, He does not give it to him."

He said, "Shall I not inform you of the dwellers of Paradise? Every weak and neglected man. If he makes an oath in the name of Allah, He makes him fulfil it. Shall I not inform you of the inmates of Hell? Every proud, haughty and harsh man."

He said, "Those who have dishevelled hair are dust ridden, are clad in tattered clothes, are hated by people, are not given permission to go to the ruler when they ask, are not given girls in marriage when they seek it, are not heard when they talk and whose wants and complaints are extinguished in their hearts—they are the dwellers of Paradise. If their light is distributed among people on Resurrection Day, it would be sufficient for them."

He said, "There is a man among my followers who is not given gold coins when he begs, is not given silver coins when he begs and is not given a piece of cloth when he begs. But he is given even Paradise by Allah when he prays to Allah for it, and if he wants from Him anything of this world, He does not give it to him. Do not think that Allah is dissatisfied with him because Allah does not give him anything of the world. Many men there are dressed in tattered clothes, men who, if they make an oath in the name of Allah, are made to fulful it by Allah."

Once, 'Umar entered the mosque and saw that Mu'ādh ibn Jabal was weeping by the side of the grave of the Prophet (ṣ). When asked why he was weeping, he replied, "I heard the Prophet of Allah say, 'A little ostentation is ascribing partners to Allah. Allah loves religious men who are not sought for when absent, who are not taken notice of when present, whose hearts are lighted by the light of providence and who are free from all sorts of darkness and dirtiness.'"

There was once a famine in Madīnah. There was a religious man there whom the people considered mean. He stayed in the mosque of Madīnah. When people were engaged in prayer to Allah to ward off famine, a man with tattered clothes came there, prayed two short *rak'ahs* and then began to invoke Allah with his hands spread out, "O Lord, I ask that you shower rain now." Not long after he raised his hands and his invocation ended, the entire sky was filled with clouds and it rained. It was so profuse that the dwellers of Madīnah feared drowning. Then he prayed, "O Allah, you know best that it is sufficient for the people, so stop the rain." Then the rain stopped. The religious man followed the man who prayed for rain and recognised his abode. At dawn, he went to him and said, "I have come to you on account of a necessity." He said, "Tell me your necessity." He said, "Oblige me by accepting my invitation." He said, "Allah is pure. It is a wonder that I would oblige you by accepting your invitation." Then he said, "How did you acquire the rank I saw?" He said, "I obeyed Allah's commands and prohibitions, so I invoked Him and He accepted my invocation."

Ibn Mas'ūd said, "Be a fountain of learning, be a light of guidance, be a lamp of the night, be a jewel of the heart and wear old clothes and you will be known to the dwellers of heaven and live unknown to the dwellers of this world."

The Prophet (ṣ) said, "Allah says, 'The object of envy is that a believer who makes light the burden on himself delights in prayers, perfects his worship of his Lord, worships in secrecy, lives behind the eyes of men, is not pointed at with fingers and keeps patient.' The Prophet (ṣ) then made a sound with his hands and said, "His death is quick, his inheritance is very little and his mourners are very few."

'Abdullāh ibn 'Umar said, "The dearest servants of Allah to Allah are the strangers." The people asked, "Who are the strangers?" He replied, "Whoever flees from society with his religion and assembles with 'Īsā on Resurrection Day."

Al-Thawrī said, "I wish to see myself with the poor of Madīnah who live in want of necessary food and with difficulty."

Al-Fuḍayl said, "If you can make yourself such that people do not know you, it is better."

You should be in such a condition that nobody can know you and nobody praises you. It does not matter if you become mean in people's eyes, but good to Allah.

One might ask, "Is there anyone more famous than the prophets and learned men? Have they lost the rewards of not remaining anonymous?" The answer is that seeking name and fame is bad, but if name and fame comes from Allah, without seeking it, it is not bad. It is true that it is harmful for the weak and not for the strong. The weak man is like a drowning man with whom many men are about to drown. Nobody among them should help him, as they themselves are drowning, and nobody can help another. The drowning man should introduce himself to the strong man so that he may rescue him and get rewarded.

Condemnation of love for power

Allah says:

> *(As for) that future abode, We assign it to those who have no desire to exalt themselves in the earth nor to make mischief.* (Qur'an, 28:83)

> *Whoever desires this world's life and its finery, We will pay them in full their deeds therein, and they will not be made to suffer loss in respect of them. These are they for whom there is nothing but fire in the hereafter, and what they wrought in it will go for nothing, and vain is what they do.* (Qur'an, 11:15-16)

The Prophet of Allah said:

> Wealth and power grow hypocrisy in the heart as rain grows herbage.
>
> Just as two hungry wolves do harm by entering the pen of goats, so fame and wealth destroy the good qualities of a believer by entering his religion.
>
> To follow the dictates of passion and greed for praise destroys mankind.

Meaning of "love for power"

Know that wealth and love for power are two worldly things. "Wealth" means "beneficial things," and "love for power" means "exercising power over those from whom allegiance, obedience and honour are sought." Just as a rich man meets his objects and necessities by owning gold and silver, so the possessor of power keeps the hearts of the public subdued in such a manner that they do whatever he wishes them to do. Man's heart cannot to subdued without belief and knowledge, and physique and wealth are subservient to the heart.

If the heart can be subdued, physique and wealth can also be subdued along with the heart. The state of mind is, again, the result of faith, knowledge and thought. As a man loving wealth likes to be the owner of servants and slaves, so whoever loves power to subdue free people and to obtain their services loves to be the owner of their hearts.

Causes of love for power

The cause of love for power is the same as that for which gold and silver are loved. In fact, love for power is more than that. Gold and silver are loved not for their own sake, but for the fact that therewith necessary things can be purchased. The same is true for love for power, as it brings the heart of another under one's control. There are three causes for which power is more loved than wealth.

The first cause is that to get wealth by power is easier than to get power by wealth. If a kind man or a man who has renounced the world wishes to earn money, it is easier for him because the wealth of those whose hearts have been brought under control is under his control. So power is a weapon to earn money. If there is power, wealth comes, but if there is wealth, power does not come in all circumstances. For this reason, power is more liked than wealth.

The second cause is that wealth is easily ruined and thieves and dacoits can steal it. Oppressors may have greed for getting it, and there arises the necessity of keeping guards to save it and thoughts in the heart to maintain it. When a man becomes the owner of human hearts, these calamities do not appear. Power is a wealth over which thieves have no control and oppressors have no power. Moreover, power is safe from theft and plunder.

The third cause is that the right over the heart increases gradually without effort, as when the hearts of people fall into the snare of respect for a man, in which case the superiority of his actions and knowledge is proclaimed by endless mouths and his name and fame spread. As a result, many hearts bend down to show respect to him. On the other hand, wealth does not increase without effort.

The heart is not free from love for wealth and power for two reasons. One reason is open and another secret. The open reason is the removal of fear. A man possessing enormous wealth hopes to get more wealth, and there is no limit to it. For this reason, the Prophet (ṣ) said, "Two greeds cannot be satisfied: greed for knowledge and greed for wealth." Love for power is like that disease. He wishes that people from distant places will come and show respect to him. The second cause is more powerful. The soul of man is included in the commands of Allah. Allah says, "They ask you about soul. Say, 'It is a command from my Lord'" (Qur'an, 17:85). It is therefore part of the spiritual world and may not be explained, as the Prophet (ṣ) himself did not explain it.

The soul has four natures: an animal nature, bestial nature, demonic nature and divine nature. The soul's animal nature is eating, drinking and copulation. Its bestial nature is to kill, assault and harm. Its divine nature is to boast, seek honour, power, love of lordship and the like. As there is a divine command in the soul, it loves the divine nature, which means full knowledge of the oneness of Allah and His being without equal. The perfection of the sun is in its uniqueness. Had there been another sun, there would have been a threat to the sun or retained power, as it would not been unique in shedding its lustre. Allah is unique in His existence, as there is no existence besides His. Whatever exists besides Him is a sign of His power and has no independent existence. Everything exists by His existence, and He expresses Himself through His creations. He has no equal. The sun suffers no loss because of its shedding rays throughout the world. Just as rays exist within the sovereignty of one sun and cannot be separated from it, so too is the case with Allah, who dominates everything in the world and without whom there is no existence. Whatever exists in the world is lighted through His radiant light.

Every man is an object of love by nature, as he is unique in his attributes. Fir'awn said, "I am your lord, the most high" (Qur'an, 79:24). There is no man in whose heart this does not exist, but he does not express it. Slavery is obligatory in nature, but power is dear. As man's soul has a connection with Allah, it is natural for him to seek power and lordship.

All things are divided into three classes: things which are naturally unchangeable, for man cannot see things such as Allah's existence and attributes; things which are changeable and over which creatures have no power, such as the sky, stars, angels, jinn, demons, mountains, rivers, seas and the wonders beneath mountains, rivers and seas; and things which can be changed by men, such as earth, metal and trees. So there are principally two kinds of things: things which can be changed by men, such as things made of earth, and heavenly things which cannot be changed by men, such as the existence of Allah, angels and jinn.

Man loves the sky, as he wishes to extend his power of research and investigation into its secrets. The thing that comes within the preview of knowledge is included within knowledge, and wise men rule over them. For this reason, man loves knowledge about Allah, angels, stars, the sky and the wonders underneath the oceans and mountains. It is a part of power and lordship.

Another kind of things is underneath the ground. Man has power over it. This is also of two kinds: material and immaterial. Material things are wealth, gold, silver and so on. Man wants to lord over them and loves to hoard, spend and give them in charity. It is termed "power" and is included within the supreme power of Allah. It is naturally dear to men. Immaterial things are the hearts of men. Men love the power to lord over the hearts of people. So the object of the mind is full and complete progress in knowledge and power.

Progress has different degrees. There are real and unreal progresses. Unreal progress arises out of three causes. The first cause is that the knowledge of Allah is limitless, while man's wisdom is limited. So if the knowledge of man increases, he becomes much nearer to Allah. The second cause is the connection of Allah's knowledge with the objects of knowledge and the full expression of the objects of knowledge. Since man's knowledge is limited, the more knowledge he has of Allah, the near he draws to

Allah. The third cause is that Allah's knowledge is everlasting and eternal, without any loss or decrease. So if a person's knowledge is not changed with regard to the object of knowledge, he becomes very close to Allah.

The objects of knowledge are of two kinds: changeable and unchangeable. Knowledge of changeable things is described below. You know that Zayd is in a house. This knowledge is not perfect, as Zayd may not be in that house and might have gone out. This knowledge is faulty and not sufficient. This applies to everything in the world. Knowledge about unchangeable things is that of Allah, His attributes, His creations and His management of the heavens and earth and their arrangements. Whoever acquires knowledge of these things comes near to Allah and this knowledge remains with his soul even after his death. It will serve as a light in front of him and to his sides. They will say, "O my Lord, perfect our light." This knowledge will be a valuable asset at that time. This is a secret lamp. Whoever has no such secret lamp cannot expect the perfection of his light. Whoever has no basic spiritual knowledge of Allah cannot expect to get that light and will remain in a darkness from which there will be no outlet. It will be the darkness of the fathomless bottom of the sea.

No benefit will be derived without such spiritual knowledge. Knowledge of literature or poetry or science will be of no avail on that day. Knowledge of Arabic, the Qur'an and Ḥadīth will be a helping hand to that knowledge. These are materials to purify the soul. Allah says, "He will indeed be successful who purifies it" (Qur'an, 91:9) and Allah says, "And (as for) those who strive hard for Us, We will most certainly guide them in Our ways" (Qur'an, 29:69). Therefore, there are helpers to spiritual knowledge. Whoever knows that everything in the world is the action of the Almighty and that his will, strength and wisdom are His creations, gains perfect knowledge of Allah. These have no connection with the exercise of power, ostentation and so on.

Power

No man can have full power, but he can have real knowledge. Full, unlimited power belongs to Allah only. Full and perfect knowledge remains with the soul even after man's death, but his power ends after his death. Power should be exercised to acquire spiritual knowledge, and if it is bereft of that, it has no value. Whoever regards this temporary taste of power as full progress is a fool. The majority of men are immersed in that idea and thus ruined. They forget the knowledge which takes them near Allah. That progress arises out of knowledge and freedom. This knowledge implies knowledge of Allah, and freedom implies freedom from passions and low desires, which the angels enjoy. Their nature then becomes like the nature of angels.

Qualities of full progress

Full progress has three qualities: no change of anything owing to greed; result not without perfection, like full progress of knowledge; and full progress of freedom from passions and other worldly desires. If a man possesses full power, it shows the path towards full knowledge and full freedom. Power dies with his death, but spiritual knowledge remains with his soul to gain full perfection. Now see how fools think that full power can be gained by wealth and lordship.

The ignorant purchase the world at the price of the next world. Allah says, "Wealth and children are an adornment of the life of this world; and the ever-abiding, the good works, are better with your Lord in reward and better in expectation" (Qur'an, 18:46). So knowledge and freedom are everlasting good works which will go with the soul, but wealth and power will vanish. Allah illustrates this as follows: "The likeness of this world's life is only as water which We send down from the cloud, then the herbage of the earth of which men and cattle eat grows luxuriantly thereby, until when the earth puts on its golden raiment and it becomes garnished, and its people think that they have power over it, Our command comes to it, by night or by day, so We render it as reaped seed; produce, as though it had not been in existence yesterday; thus do We make clear the communications for a people who reflect" (Qur'an, 10:24).

It is understood from the above that wealth and power are considered progress arising out of ignorance, which has no root. Whoever seeks it takes the life of this world as his goal. Abū al-Ṭayyib said, "Whoever loses time in earning wealth for fear of poverty creates wants. What he earns for what is necessary leads him to real progress."

Advantages and disadvantages of power

I have already said that "lordship" means "to subdue human hearts and to exercise power over them." Thus, the rules which are applicable to wealth are also applicable to lordship, as they end with the start of death. This world is a seed ground for the next world. Whatever is done in the world is a provision of the next world. As eating, drinking and clothing oneself are necessary to the limit of necessity, so also some power is necessary for the maintenance of men. As food is necessary for life, so servants are necessary for work and friends are necessary to show him the path of religion. Guides are necessary for the same purpose, and kings and rulers are necessary for his protection from bad people. So love for servants, friends, spiritual guides, rulers and kings is not bad.

Like riches, power is a means to achieve an ultimate goal. This love is not for itself, but for achieving a goal. This love should be such that a man loves toilets for relieving himself or loves his wife for the satisfaction of his sexual desire at his sweet will. When he has no sexual passion, he leaves his wife. Such is the case for wealth and power. One should love these two things with an ultimate object.

Objects of seeking name and fame

There are three objects of seeking name and fame. Of them, two are lawful. The object which is unlawful is to seek rank after creating belief in the hearts of people, even though he is not qualified with that qualification. He tells them that he is high in pedigree, that he is a real learned man or that he is a pious and God-fearing man.

One of the objects which are lawful is to seek rank by the qualities which a man has. Yūsuf said, "Place me (in authority) over the treasures of the land; surely I am a good keeper, knowing well" (Qur'an, 12:55). He knew that he was a trustworthy treasurer and as such sought this rank. Another lawful object is to try to conceal one's sins and faults so that they may not come out. This is lawful, as to conceal evil things is allowed, and it is unlawful to disclose sinful acts. One of the prohibited things is to pray well before people with the object of gaining their respect and good opinion. This is deception. It is unlawful to seek name and fame in this way. This is like earning wealth illegally.

The causes of love for praise and hatred for backbiting

There are four causes of love for praise. The first cause is an appreciation of one's own qualities. This is a strong cause. Owing to praise from others, one thinks that he has all qualities. The praise with which a man is praised is either clear, open or appreciable. If you tell someone he is handsome, he derives pleasure. If the praise is of a doubtful thing, it is more pleasurable. If a man is praised, for example, for his complete knowledge or perfect God-fearingness, he experiences more pleasure. Moreover, it is more pleasurable when it comes from a learned or God-fearing man.

The second cause is a deep appreciation of one's own influence. It appears from the praise that the heart of the praised man has come under the control of the praiser. To subdue man's heart is a covetable thing, and there is a great pleasure in it. For this reason, he finds great joy if the praise comes from powerful men—rulers, kings or great men.

The third cause is the joy of the increase in the number of praises. The hearers of the praise also fall into this trap.

The fourth cause is an appreciation of power and influence. Praise shows the power and influence of the praised man. It is understood from the praise of the praiser that he praises a proud man after being subdued by the latter. He either willingly praises him or is compelled to praise.

Medicine for love for praise

There are four medicines for these four causes. The medicine of the first cause, which is an appreciation of one's own qualities, is to remove the praise by recognising that the praise is not true. If a man says you are a generous man, a great scholar or a great God-fearing man, while you find that you do not have those qualities, the taste of praise goes away, as you do not believe in those assertions.

The medicine for the second cause, which is a deep appreciation of one's influence, is this. The feeling of power and influence of the praised man over the praiser can be removed if he knows that the praise was a joke, for which the taste of praise goes away.

The medicine for the third and fourth causes is the following. The third cause is joy in the increase in the number of praises, whereas the fourth cause is an appreciation of one's influence. The medicine for both is to remove the causes.

Medicine for the love of power

The medicine is mixture of knowledge and action. The medicine of knowledge is to know that the end of power is death and that it does not pertain to everlasting good works. Those who wielded great power had to fall victim to death or downfall. You will also meet the same fate. He whose goal is the next world considers it valueless, as he sees death imminent and considers earthly things insignificant. His state is like that of al-Ḥasan al-Baṣrī, who wrote to 'Umar ibn 'Abd al-'Azīz, "It is as if you are the last person who will die." 'Umar's reply to him was in the same vein: "Think that you are no more in the world and will live forever in the next world."

The objects of these people were the next world. With this belief, they performed good deeds with fear of Allah. So they considered early rule, honour and wealth insignificant. Allah says, "Rather, you prefer the life of this world, while the hereafter is better and more lasting" (Qur'an, 87:16-17) and "But you love the present life and neglect the hereafter" (Qur'an, 75:20-21). Whoever has the disease of greed for power must remove it from his heart by applying this medicine arising out of this knowledge, as this disease is very dangerous and ruinous. He should ponder the state of those who wielded power and influence, their fall and their being always in fear of losing power and control.

Whoever wishes to live in the hearts of men is like someone who builds a house on the waves of the sea. Whoever is busy controlling the hearts of men to preserve power, to remove the envy of those who envy and to remove enmity remains in worldly thoughts and anxieties and immersed in the abyss of the pleasure of power. There is no end to his worldly hopes and aspirations. This is the medicine based on knowledge.

The medicine of action is to make yourself the object of rebuke. In order to remove love for praise, you should do an act for which you may be rebuked for and respect for you leaves the hearts of people. Love to remain aloof from people and not to meet them. In a certain city, there lived a learned and pious man: The ruler of that country, who was charmed by his praise, came to see him. When the hermit saw the ruler, he began to eat food and curry in big morsels. The ruler saw this manner of eating, and the respect he had in his heart for the hermit went away and he departed. The pious man said, "All praise is due to Allah, who removed you from me."

Another pious man used to drink lawful drinks in a cup whose colour resembled the colour of wine. Seeing this, people thought that he was drinking wine, and so their respect for him decreased. This is allowed according to Sharī'ah. These pious men take sure medicine for the purification of their souls, which jurists do not mention. A other pious man observed that his name spread because of his renunciation of the world and that people were coming to him. He then entered a bathroom, put on another's clothes, came out and waited on the road. People caught him as a thief and beat him. When they came to know of this, they stopped coming to him. The best way of preventing fame is to leave one's own place. When his name and fame spread, he should live in a distant land where nobody knows him.

Causes of love and praise and their medicine

The first cause is an appreciation of one's own qualities. Its medicine is this. Ask yourself whether you have the quality for which you are praised? If you have that quality, ask whether you are fit to be praised for it or not. The quality for which you are fit to be praised is that of learning or God-fearingness. That for which you are not fit to receive praise is your wealth, power and influence. If you are praised for worldly riches, its joy is like that of grass: wind will blow it away. So man should not feel joy at worldly riches. If he feels delighted at his wealth, he should not feel joy at the praise of men. If you are praised for your God-fearingness or your learning, you still should not feel happy, as you do not know what will be your condition at the time of death—whether it will be good or bad. The world is an abode of sorrows and anxieties and not an abode of joy and rejoice.

The second cause is that the heart of the praiser becomes under the control of the praised man. Its medicine is to seek a rank with Allah and not from men. Your knowing that you seek a rank from Allah is also its medicine, so it cannot be the cause of your joy.

The third cause is joy at the echo of the praise of the praiser. Its medicine is this. The praise is connected with your present power, which has no stability, so it cannot be an object of joy. You should hate it, as it makes you anxious. A sage said, “Satan makes his abode in the heart of whoever feels joy at praise.” Another sage said, “When you are told, ‘How good a man you are!’ you should say, ‘How bad you are. By Allah, you are really a bad man.’”

Once, a man praised another man before the Prophet (ṣ) for his good works. With that, the Prophet (ṣ) said, “If your praised man were present and liked what you uttered or died in that condition, he would be a dweller of Hell.” The Prophet (ṣ) once said to a praiser, “Woe to you! You have broken his back. If he heard your praise, he would not have salvation until Resurrection Day.” He also said, “Beware! Do not praise one another. When you see praisers, throw dust on their faces.”

A caliph once asked a man something, and the latter replied, “You are better and more learned than me.” He got enraged at this and said, “I have not told you to proclaim my purity.” Likewise, a man said to a Companion, “So long as Allah keeps you alive, people will continue good works.” The Companion got enraged at this praise and said, “I think you are an inhabitant of Iraq.” The praises of men were objects of hatred to the Companions.

Medicine for criticism

The person who criticises you falls into one of three categories: What he says might be true, and he does so for your own good; what he says might be true, but his object is to hurt you and reveal your faults; or what he says might be untrue.

With regard to the first, if he criticises you by way of admonition for your good, you should neither rebuke him nor be enraged at him. Rather, you should be delighted to hear it, as you can remedy your defects.

With regard to the second, if his object is to hurt you, you should consider it a benefit, as he has informed you of your defects. This can be clearly explained by the following illustration. You wish to go to the court of an emperor, but there is impurity and stool and urine on your clothes. If one shows you the filth on your clothes, you should be thankful to him because you have been saved from being put to disgrace by the emperor. Similarly, evil traits are ruinous in the next world. You can know these from your enemies. It is a gift to you, even though the object of your enemies is to hurt you.

With regard to the third, if a defect you do not have is attributed to you, you should not hate or rebuke whoever criticised you. Instead, you should consider three things. The first is that if you are free from that defect, there may be another defect like that in you—what Allah keeps concealed is greater. In fact, you should express gratefulness to Allah that He did not disclose all your faults. The second is that his criticism will be an expiation for your remaining faults and sins and that the critic's good deeds will be transferred to you. Whoever praises you cuts your back, so why would you feel joy at the cutting of your back and be sorry for getting rewards which will draw you near to Allah? The third is that the critic falls from the eyes of Allah, as he destroys his religion and destroys himself by his false accusations and calls for self-destruction. You should pray, "May Allah correct him, accept his repentance and show mercy to him."

When the teeth of the Prophet (ṣ) fell out and his face was wounded by the attack of the enemies and the enemies killed his uncle Ḥamzah, he prayed, "O Allah, forgive my people. O Allah, give guidance to my people, as they do not know." Once, a man wounded the head of Ibrāhīm ibn Adham, who prayed for the forgiveness of his sins. Asked why, Ibrāhīm said, "I know that I will be rewarded for that and that there will remain nothing for me from him but good. So I do not want him to be punished for me."

In short, if you can give up the trouble of rebuke, it will be easy for you because his accusation will not be able to exercise any influence on your heart. The root of religion is contentment, which cuts greed for wealth and love for power. Love for power and praise will remain in your heart as long as there remains in your heart greed and passion.

Classification of men in terms of praise and condemnation

Whoever praises and whoever accuses have four states. The first state is that the praised man expresses gratefulness to the praiser for his praise and wishes to take revenge on whoever accuses him. This is the state of people in general. This class of men are the worst.

The second state is that the accused man hates the accuser in the heart, yet keeps his tongue and limbs from taking revenge. He becomes pleased with the praiser, but does not express his satisfaction. There is harm in it, but this state is better than the first one.

The third state is the highest stage. For this class of God-fearing people, praise and condemnation are equal, as condemnation cannot make them sorry, and praise cannot give them joy. This indifferent attitude has signs: His heart remains the same if he stays with the accuser and the praiser; the joy in the removal of the praiser's wants is the same as in the removal of the accuser's wants; the grief he feels at the death of the praiser is the same as that at the death of the accuser; he feels the same agony if a calamity befalls the praiser and accuser. The pious deeds of a person who does not enquire about the machination of Satan and the impulse of passions are lost both in this world and the next world. Allah says, "Say, 'Shall We inform you of the greatest losers in (their) deeds? (These are) they whose labour is lost in this world's life and they think that they are well versed in skill of the work of hands'" (Qur'an, 18:103-104).

The fourth state is the highest stage of those with great faith. They do not love praise or the praiser, as they know that praise puts them to trial, breaks their backs and destroys their religion. They love, on the other hand, an accuser, as they know that he reveals their faults, shows them the necessary path and gives them his good deeds. The Prophet (ṣ) said, "God-fearingness is the root of humility and the expression of hatred for praise of virtuous acts." He said, "Woe to him who fasts all year round. Woe to him who prays the whole night. Woe to the owner of wool except for him who ..." The people asked, "Except for whom?" The Prophet (ṣ) replied, "The religious man who keep himself separate from the world, hates praise and loves accusation."

2
Ostentation

Condemnation of ostentation

The Qur'an

Allah says, "So woe to the praying ones, who are unmindful of their prayers, who do (good) to be seen" (Qur'an, 107:4-6).

Mujāhid said the people of which Allah speaks in this verse are ostentatious people: "And (as for) those who plan evil deeds, they will have a severe chastisement; and (as for) their plan, it will perish" (Qur'an, 35:10).

Allah instructs us to say, "We only feed you for Allah's sake; we desire from you neither reward nor thanks" (Qur'an, 76:9).

Allah praises those who are sincere in their intentions and removes the pleasure of others besides Allah: "Therefore whoever hopes to meet his Lord, he should do good deeds, and not join anyone in the service of his Lord" (Qur'an, 18:110).

Ḥadīth

A man asked the Prophet (ṣ), "O Prophet of Allah, in which action is there salvation?" He replied, "There is salvation in not wishing to incur the pleasure of men in serving Allah. Allah will question three people—a martyr in the way of Allah, a philanthropist and a man learned in the Qur'an—and they will reply. He will say to the philanthropist, 'You have spoken falsehood, but your intention in giving charity was that people should see you as a great philanthropic man.' He will say to the martyr, 'You have spoken falsehood. Rather, your intention was that people should call you a great hero.' He will say to the learned man, 'You have spoken falsehood. Your intention was that people should call you a great learned man.' The Prophet (ṣ) said they were not rewarded and that ostentation destroyed their good deeds. He said, "Allah will mete out the same treatment to whoever does acts of worship for ostentation. Allah will also mete out the same treatment to whoever seeks fame." Another version reads, "Allah will say to the angels, 'This man did not do acts of worship for Me, so take him to Hell.'"

The Prophet (ṣ) said, "I do not fear anything for you more than small polytheism." The Companions asked, "O Prophet of Allah, what is small polytheism?" He replied, "Ostentation. Allah will say on Resurrection Day, 'O man of ostentation, go to those people for whom you did divine service and get from them your rewards.'"

The Prophet (ṣ) said, "Seek refuge in Allah from Jubb al-Ḥuzn." The Companions asked, "What is that?" He replied, "It is the name of a well in Hell which has been made for the learned who act ostentatiously."

The Prophet (ṣ) said, "Allah says, 'I give the worship of whoever ascribes a partner to me in My worship to the partner. I become free from it, more so than an independent man.'"

'Īsā said, "When a day of fasting comes to one of you, let him rub oil on his head and beard and wipe his two lips so that people may not know that he is fasting. Let his left hand not know when his right hand gives in charity. When he prays, let the screen of his door hang, as Allah distributes praises in the same way he distributes sustenance."

The Prophet (ṣ) said, "Allah does not accept an action in which there is the slightest degree of ostentation." He said, "I do not fear for anything as much as I fear for you ostentation and hidden passion." He said, "On the day when there will be no shade except the shade of the Throne, a man will remain under its shade who gives charity with his right hand, keeping it concealed from his left." He said, "The merits of hidden acts of worship are seventy times more than those of open acts of worship." He said, "A polytheist will be addressed on Resurrection Day thus: 'O treacherous man, O man of ostentation, your good deeds have been lost and your rewards have become void. Go and get rewards from whomever you worshipped.'"

Shaddād ibn Aws reported, "I saw the Prophet (ṣ) one day weeping, so I asked him, 'O Prophet of Allah, why are you weeping?' He replied, 'I fear polytheism most for my followers. Beware! They will not worship idols, the sun, the moon or stones, but they will worship ostentatiously.'"

The Prophet (ṣ) said, "When Allah created the earth, it was tossing to and fro with its inhabitants. Then he created mountains and placed them on it as nails. The angels said, 'Our Lord did not create anything harder than mountains.' Then He created iron, which is so powerful that it can cut a mountain into two pieces. Then He created fire, which is still more powerful, as it can melt iron. Then He created water, which can extinguish fire. Then He created wind, which can remove water. The angels asked their Lord, 'O Lord, what is the strongest thing you have created?' He replied, "I have not created anything stronger than the heart of a man who gives in charity with his right hand, keeping it concealed from his left.'"

Mu'ādh ibn Jabal said, "I heard the Prophet (ṣ) say, 'Allah created seven angels before He created the seven heavens and the earth, and He placed one angel as a guard for each heaven. The angel who presents actions raises men's actions from morning to evening. When he reaches the first heaven with a man's actions, the guard of this heaven says to him, 'I am the examiner of backbiting. My Lord has ordered me not to lift the actions of a man who has backbitten.' Then the angel leaves behind this bad action and takes the rest of his good actions to the second heaven. The guard of the second heaven says to him, 'My Lord has prohibited me from allowing those actions to go up which have been done for worldly purposes.' The angel then leaves those actions and takes the rest upwards. The guard of the third heaven says to the angel, 'I am the angel of pride. My Lord has ordered me not to allow up actions which have been done with pride because of some acts of worship in an assembly of men.' Then he leaves such actions and takes the rest towards the fourth heaven. The guard of the fourth heaven says to him, 'My Lord has prohibited me from allowing up actions which have been done with self-praise, for I am the angel of self-praise.' Then the angel leaves those actions and takes the rest towards the fifth heaven. The guard of the fifth heaven says to the angel, 'I am the angel of hatred and have been ordered not to allow up those actions of men which have been done with hatred.' Then he leaves those actions and takes the rest towards the sixth heaven. The guard of this heaven says to him, 'My Lord ordered me not to allow up actions of a man who did not show kindness to My servants when they were in danger and calamities. I am an angel of kindness.' Then the angel leaves those actions behind and takes the rest towards the seventh heaven. The guard of this heaven says to the angel, 'My Lord ordered me to allow up only those actions which have been done to please Him or for His sake, not for name and fame or for ostentation.' Then this angel leaves those actions behind and takes the rest towards the seventh heaven and to Allah, who says, 'You are presenting the actions of My servants. I am the guard of man's heart. I know that some of these actions were not done to please Me, so My curse is on him.' The angels and the seven heavens curse him as well."

Then the Prophet (ṣ) instructed Mu'ādh, "Do not allow others to hear your sins. Bear them yourself. Do not think yourself pure by backbiting others or placing yourself above them. Do not allow your worldly actions to enter your other-worldly actions. Do not boast in any assembly of yours. Do not talk secretly with another in the presence of other men. Do not feel pride before people and do not boast before them. Do not joke with people lest the dwellers of Hell joke with you on Resurrection Day."

'Umar saw a man looking downwards to appear pious. He said to him, "O brother, raise your neck. Humility rests in the heart and not in the neck."

'Alī said, "An ostentatious man has three signs: When he is alone, he exhibits idleness in acts of worship, but when he is among others, he prays well; when he is praised, he does more acts of worship; and when he is dispraised, he does fewer acts of worship."

Definition of "ostentation"

Know that the real meaning of "ostentation" is "to show good conduct in order to attract respect from people." Attracting people's hearts by acts other than those of worship produces power and honour. Ostentation, on the other hand, is expressed only in acts of worship according to habits. It is wishing to show acts of worship to people. Religious people, then, are the ones who are ostentatious.

There are fives ways to be ostentatious: by the limbs, by signs and gestures, by words and actions, by having many followers and by outward causes. Worldly men are also ostentatious in these ways.

The first way is by the limbs. A pious man shows people that he is making an effort in his worship by appearing pale or appearing before people with dishevelled hair or with yellow clothes. 'Īsā said, "When anybody among you fasts, let him rub oil on his head and apply antimony to his eyes." He recommended this to rid people of ostentation.

The second way is in demeanours and clothes: to appear with dishevelled hair, to clip off the moustache, to lower the head when walking, to walk in a pensive and thoughtful way, to keep traces of prostration on the forehead, to put on coarse clothes, to put on

Sufi clothes or to put on torn clothes. By these acts, one shows that he is a pious man.

The third way is by words. Such a religious man delivers lectures and gives sermons using verses of the Qur'an and *ḥadīths* after committing them to memory in order to show that he is a great learned man. He gives his utmost in reading invocations when among people, gives advice to people, angrily prohibits them from doing evil deeds, expresses great grief at the sins of people, recites verses of the Qur'an in a pleasant tone and is ostentatious in a thousand other ways.

The fourth way is by actions, such as standing for a very long time in prayer and in bending and prostration.

The fifth way is by having a great number of disciples and visitors. Such a man says, "Such a great religious man has come to see me. I have so many disciples ..."

The lawfulness of ostentation

Ostentation can be unlawful, detested and lawful depending on the circumstances and conditions. The object of ostentation is to seek name, fame and influence by acts of worship. If ostentation is done by actions other than religious ones with the object of earning wealth, it is lawful. Just as earning wealth in an illegal manner is unlawful, so gaining power in an illegal manner is also unlawful. To earn very necessary things is good, so a little power to save oneself from dangers and difficulties is good. Yūsuf said, "Surely I am a good keeper" (Qur'an, 12:55). Just as there are harms and benefits in riches, there are also harms and benefits in power. And just as too much riches makes a man a sinner and keeps him away from the remembrance of Allah, so too much power is ruinous.

A man may adorn himself when going out. The proof is the following *ḥadīth*. The Prophet (ṣ) once intended to go to his Companions, and so he straightened his turban and his hair. 'Ā'ishah asked, "O Prophet of Allah, are you doing this?" He replied, "Yes. Allah loves the actions of His servant who refines his body in order to meet his friends and brothers. So it is lawful to be ostentatious in an action which is not included within acts of worship.

In prayer, fasting, jihad and the like, the ostentatious man can have two states. One is that he does that only for ostentation and not to get any merits or virtues. This spoils the act, as man's action is judged by his intentions. He commits a sin by this act, as he is deceiving others. The second is that he jokes with Allah. Qatādah said, "When a man shows off in his worship, Allah says to His angels, 'Look at him. How does he joke with Me?'" This is a destructive element. No ostentation is free from minor or major sins.

Types of ostentation

There are various types of ostentation, some more heinous than others. There are three basic elements of ostentation which account for this difference: motive, subject matter and reason.

Motive

There are four degrees of ostentation according to motive. The first is the worst if the motive is for committing sins and evil deeds without the motive of getting rewards for an act of worship. Take, for example, a man who prays before people, but not when he is alone. He prays often without ablution with people. His only object is to show off. This is hated by Allah. As another example, a man pays *zakāh* for fear of condemnation by men, but does not hope for a reward at the time of the payment. When he is alone, however, he does not pay. This is the highest degree of ostentation.

The second degree is that a man has the intention to earn rewards, but it is weak, for when he remains alone, he does not do it. This is similar to the first degree.

The third degree is that the intentions of getting rewards and of ostentation are equal, as without them he gets no encouragement for acts of worship. As result, his acts of worship are not wholly good, neither to his advantage nor his disadvantage.

The fourth degree is that the intention of earning rewards is strong and that of ostentation is weak. In other words, he gets encouragement in acts of worship before people, but does not give it up when alone. He would not pray if his object was solely ostentation. The Prophet (ṣ) said, "Allah says, 'I am free from polytheism.'"

Subject matter

The second basic matter of ostentation has three stages in divine service.

The first degree is ostentation in faith, which is the worst, and as result of which a man will live in Hell forever. He utters the Testification of Faith (*shahādah*) openly, but does not believe it inwardly. He openly says that he is a Muslim, but inwardly does not believe in Islam. The Qur'an mentions this class of hypocrites in many places. Allah says:

> *When the hypocrites come to you, they say, "We bear witness that you are most surely Allah's Messenger." Allah knows that you are most surely His Messenger, and Allah bears witness that the hypocrites are surely liars.* (Qur'an, 63:1)

> *And among men is he whose speech about the life of this world causes you to wonder, and he calls on Allah to witness as to what is in his heart, yet he is the most violent of adversaries. And when he turns back, he runs along in the land that he may cause mischief in it and destroy the tilth and the stock, and Allah does not love mischief-making.* (Qur'an, 2:204-205)

> *When they meet you they say, "We believe," and when they are alone, they bite the ends of their fingers in rage against you.* (Qur'an, 3:119)

> *They do it only to be seen of men and do not remember Allah save a little. Wavering between that (and this), (belonging) neither to these nor to those; and whomsoever Allah causes to err, you will not find a way for him.* (Qur'an, 4:142-143)

The second degree is that the basic principles of religion are believed, but there is ostentation therein. This is of a lower degree than the first. For Instance, a man prays in congregation, but does not pray when alone. He fasts among people, but does not fast when alone. He does this for fear of men. This is ostentation along with basic faith. He believes that there is no deity but Allah. If he is ordered to worship others, he does not do it.

The third degree is that there ostentation not in obligatory duties, but in additional or optional duties. If optional duties are given up, there is no sin, but on account of idleness, it is not done when alone, such as to pray in congregation, to see a patient, to pray the night vigil and to fast on days other than those of Ramaḍān.

Reason

In terms of the reasons for ostentation, there are three degrees. The first degree is that ostentation is expressed by actions which, if given up, will harm acts of worship, such as to bow and prostrate in a poor manner when alone but in a good manner when with others.

The second degree is that ostentation is done by an action which, if given up, does not harm one's acts of worship but makes it perfect, such as to prolong bowing and prostration.

The third degree is that ostentation is done in an action which is not included in *sunnah* duties, such as to come before all others for the Friday prayer and to join the first row. If he remains alone, he does not do that.

Objects of ostentation

There are three degrees.

- The first degree is the worst kind of ostentation. The object of it is to commit a sin by showing off in worship. For example, one prays more optional prayers to show one's piety in order to get a higher appointment of trust and responsibility and thereby misappropriate money.
- The second degree is that a man takes recourse to ostentation to gain something lawful, such as gaining lawful wealth or marrying a beautiful woman.
- The third degree is that he intends by ostentation not to marry a beautiful woman or the like, but to ward off the low estimation of people about him or to gain respect from them.

Secret ostentation

Ostentation is of two kinds: open and secret. Open ostentation is expressed in actions. Secret ostentation, on the other hand, does not give encouragement to do good works, but reduces it. For instance, a man has the habit of praying the night vigil prayer, which he finds difficult. But to pray it before people is easy for him. There is a more subtle ostentation than this. It does not affect his good works, but it lies concealed like fire in iron. It is to feel pleasure in doing acts of worship before people, although he has the intention of sincere worship.

'Alī said, "Allah will ask Qur'anic scholars, 'Did people not sell things to you at a reduced price? Did they not greet you first? Did they not work for you free of wages? Now you have no reward. You received your reward already.'"

It is reported that Wahb ibn Munabbih said that a hermit said to his disciples, "We have given up our wealth and children for fear of transgression, but we fear there may enter our acts of worship a greater transgression than that of the rich. Some of us may like the fact that people should show respect to them, do their jobs and sell their goods to them at reduced prices." This news reached the king of that country, who came to the hermit with many people. When the hermit knew that the king had come, he said to his servant to bring curry, olive oil and fruits and he began to eat them. When the king saw this, he went away from the hermit. The hermit said, "All praise is due to Allah, who removed you from me." Thus a sincere religious man used to fear secret ostentation. They tried their best to remain free from it in their religious duties because they knew that Allah would not accept anything other than sincere acts of worship on Judgement Day. So there are countless forms of secret ostentation.

Ostentation which ruins pious deeds

When a man decides to do a good deed with a pure intention and then the pleasure of ostentation enters his mind, he experiences three states in three stages: at the beginning of the act of worship, in the middle and at the end. If the pleasure of ostentation comes at the beginning of an action, and if it is not disclosed, it does not spoil the act of worship, as the action began already with a pure intention. After the beginning of an action, if ostentation comes, it is expected that it will not affect the good work, and there is no harm if Allah discloses it. His pleasure enters his heart without an outward expression. If he discloses it after the end of his act of worship and discusses it with others, it is a matter of fear. It appears from a *ḥadīth* that it will be useless and void. A man said to the Prophet (ṣ), "O Prophet of Allah, I have fasted all along." The Prophet (ṣ) replied, "You have neither fasted nor broken it." This he said as he disclosed his act of worship. The Prophet (ṣ) also said, "An act of worship is like a pot. If its bottom is good, its top is also good."

The medicine of ostentation

Know that ostentation is a great evil hated by Allah. One should take utmost care to remove it. There is no cure for this disease without bitter pills. All religious men are compelled to make efforts to remove it. Boys are naturally attracted to this virulent disease, as they are prone to imitate people. When they grow mature, they can understand that this disease is destructive, but at that time it finds a firm footing in their hearts. There are two modes of treatment for this disease. One mode is to uproot it, and the second mode is to remove from the heart what arises therein. The root of ostentation is greed for rank and power.

There are three causes of greed for rank and power: love for praise, fleeing from the agony of accusation and wishing to have what is in the possession of others. For these reasons, ostentation is sought.

A Bedouin once said to the Prophet (ṣ), "O Prophet of Allah, one man fights to save himself from dishonour, another fights to establish his position and yet another fights for praise. What do you say about them?" The Prophet (ṣ) replied, "Whoever fights to keep the word of Allah high is on the path of Allah." 'Umar said, "People say, 'So-and-so is a martyr.' Perhaps he has loaded his conveyance with two purses of silver coins." The Prophet (ṣ) said, "Whoever fought to get the nose-string of the camel got what he wanted."

We shall now discuss the medicine for ostentation.

Medicine based on knowledge

Man wishes to acquire something because he thinks that it is useful for him at present or in the future. If he can find that it is delicious at present but heinous in the end, his greed can easily be cut off for that thing. He knows that honey is sweet, but when he knows that there is poison in it, he refrains from eating it because it is injurious in the end. This greed for power is to be cut in this way because there is harm therein. On Resurrection Day, it will be proclaimed before all people, "O sinner, O treacherous man, O man of ostentation, are you not ashamed that you have purchased the temporary things of the world at the price of pure worship, looking to the hearts of men; that you have joked with worship; that you have sought the pleasure of men by incurring the displeasure of Allah; that you have sought honour from people by becoming dishonoured by Allah; that you have sought nearness to men by becoming distant from Allah and that you have sought praise from men by incurring the displeasure of Allah? Have they now come to do you benefit?"

For the greed of wealth, the remedy is as follows. Know for certain that earning wealth is in the hand of Allah. There is no sustenance except what is given by Allah. Whoever has greed for wealth from men is not free from despair and neglect. You will not get beyond what has been decreed for you by Allah. If you are a dweller of Paradise, people cannot send you to Hell: Men are all powerless and cannot do you benefit. There is no birth, death or resurrection in their hands. If these things are engraved in your hearts, your hopes can be brought under control. If anybody knew that you are ostentatious in worship, he would hate you. You will also be an object of anger of people. This is the medicine based on knowledge.

Medicine based on action

Do acts of worship secretly and close your doors. Do not be satisfied without acts of worship. A certain disciple of Abū Ḥafṣ spoke ill of the world and its dwellers, so the latter said, "You have disclosed what you ought to have concealed: You will not be able to remain with us."

So there is no other alternative for ostentation than to conceal acts of worship. At first, it will seem very difficult, but ultimately it will be easy. Allah does not change the state of a people unless they change their own state. The duty of man is to make a sincere effort in acts of worship, and it is the duty of Allah to give him guidance. People will knock at the door of Allah, and Allah will open it. Allah does not spoil the rewards of a pious man. If he does one act of virtue, He increases it manifold and gives him ample rewards.

Thoughts that beget ostentation are three, and the modes of removing them are as follows. Sometimes the three thoughts occur together in the heart, and it seems that they are the same current of thought. Sometimes one thought comes after another. The first thought that arises in the heart is that people should know your good works. The second thought is to hope that those who come to know of it should think it good. The third thought is to believe firmly that it is good when people praise it and think it good.

Firstly, when you know that people have come to know of your good works, remove your greed for informing people of your good deeds. Tell your heart, "Why do you need people to know it? Allah knows your condition best. Man has no hand in your affairs." If the second thought arises in your mind, remove it by thinking that Allah will hate it on Resurrection Day. When the third current of thought arises in your heart, remember that in the next world, the man of ostentation will suffer humiliation. Only sincere effort in act of worship will be taken into account. If acts of worship are spoilt because of ostentation, there will be great remorse on Resurrection Day. This fear will dispel the thought of ostentation of the third kind.

Jābir said, "Under the tree, we took an oath of allegiance to the Prophet (ṣ) that we shall not flee from fight, but in the Battle of Ḥunayn we forgot it. Then the Prophet (ṣ) said, 'O those who promised under the tree.' Immediately, we returned to the battlefield, and our hearts were filled with fear." Once, some Companions of the Prophet (ṣ) complained to him, saying, "Sometimes there enters our hearts such thoughts that we feel that, rather than disclosing it, we should fall to the ground or that wind should lift us up and blow us away to inaccessible places." The Prophet (ṣ) asked, "Do you feel it now?" They said yes. Then he said, "This is open faith." They hated it by thinking that it is an evil thought. But the Prophet (ṣ) considered it open faith, as they had hated it. The Prophet (ṣ) said, "All praise is due to Allah, who turned the contrivance of Satan to evil designs."

Freedom from baseless thoughts of ostentation

If baseless thoughts of ostentation arise in the heart, man goes into one of four states. The first is that he drives away Satan, thinks him a liar and engages himself in arguments with him. This is not good, as instead of engaging himself in the service of the Lord, he is busy with thoughts of Satan. This is just like an engagement with a robber on the way instead of going towards the destination. The second state is that he does not engage in arguments with Satan, but rather goes on his way towards his destination. The third state is that he does not call Satan a liar, but rather hates ostentation and walks away. The fourth state is that a man gets enraged at Satan when he finds that the cause of ostentation has arisen in his heart, increases his sincere wish and engages in the remembrance of Allah and acts of worship. Disappointed, Satan leaves him and does not come to him again.

Al-Fuḍayl ibn Ghazwān was once informed that a person backbit about him. He said, "By Allah, I am displeased with whoever ordered him to do so." He was asked, "Who ordered him to do so?" He said, "Satan." Then he said, "O Allah, forgive him who backbit about me. I will make Satan disappointed by doing more good works. When Satan comes to know of this, he will keep himself quite aloof from such a man."

Ibrāhīm al-Taymī said, "Do not respond to Satan if he calls you from any door of sin, but rather engage in good works. When he finds you in that condition, he will leave you. He also said, "When Satan finds you in doubt, he feels tempted towards you. When he finds you doing good works for a long time, he becomes disappointed and goes away from you."

Al-Ḥārith al-Muḥāsibī explained the condition of these four people by an illustration. He said that these four people are like four students who intended to go to an assembly of the learned in a distant land to acquire knowledge of Ḥadīth and guidance. Envious, a misguided liar came to a student and prohibited him from going there, ordering him to join the misguided. He refused to join him and engaged with him in arguments. When he called a second student towards misguidance, he did not engage himself in arguing with him, but rather waded on his way. The misguided man was a little pleased with him, as he spent some time in misuse by stopping him. Then he went to a third student who did not at all listen to him, but waded on his journey. The misguided man was utterly disappointed at this. Then he went to a fourth student, who grew enraged at him and waded quickly on his way. The misguided man may return to them on their way back, but he will not come near the fourth student.

Allah says:

> *O children of Adam! let not the Shayṭān cause you to fall into affliction as he expelled your parents from the garden.* (Qur'an, 7:27)

> *He surely sees you, he as well as his host, from whence you cannot see them.* (Qur'an, 7:27)

From beginning to end, the Qur'an warns people of Satan. So how can we be safe from him? This is possible only by obeying what Allah has ordered us to do and refraining from what He has prohibited us from doing.

> *Let a party of them stand up with you, and let them take their arms.* (Qur'an, 4:102)

> *Prepare against them what force you can and horses tied at the frontier.* (Qur'an, 8:60)

If you should be cautious of unbelievers, then, *a fortiori*, you should be even more cautious of Satan.

The Prophet (ṣ) said, "Surely, Satan roams about the four corners of my heart." Moreover, the Prophet (ṣ) relied firmly on Allah, yet he took precautions against unbelievers by taking recourse to arms and ammunition and even digging trenches, none of which contradicts reliance on Allah.

The mind is like a well. If the accumulated filth at the bottom of a well is cleared, pure water will emerge therefrom. Similarly, if a heart is cleared of evil thoughts, pure ideas will emerge therefrom. When one is busy with Satan, one accumulates filth in the bottom of the mind, rather than remaining busy clearing it.

The permissibility of disclosing good deeds

If an act of worship is kept secret, the benefits of sincere intention and freedom from ostentation can be obtained. But if it is done openly, the benefits of following can be gained and encouragement for doing good deeds is given to people.

Al-Ḥasan said, "Muslims know that secret acts of worship are safe, but there are benefits from open acts of worship. For this reason, Allah praises both secret and open acts of worship, saying, 'If you give alms openly, it is well, and if you hide it and give it to the poor, it is better for you' (Qur'an, 2:271)."

An open act of worship is of two kinds. The first kind encourages others to follow suit. For example, giving charity among people encourages others to give charity. It was reported that a Madīnan Helper (*Anṣārī*) gave in charity a purse full of money. Seeing this, the people began to give charity. Then the Prophet (ṣ) said, "Whoever introduces a good custom and acts on it gets the rewards of that action and the rewards of those who follow him." This is also true in the case of prayer, fasting, pilgrimage, jihad and other acts of worship.

The second kind pains people. For example, if an act of charity is disclosed, it may pain the recipient. If such is the case, it is better to keep it secret, as to give pain to a heart is unlawful. If it does not give pain, there is a difference of opinion among jurists. A party of them says that in this circumstance, secret charity is better than open charity. Another party says that open charity to encourage others is better than secret charity. It appears that Allah ordered prophets to do open acts of worship. Allah gave them this status for the rank of their prophethood. The Prophet (ṣ) said, "Secret acts of worship have seventy times more rewards than those of open acts of worship.

Open acts of worship followed by others is seventy times better than secret acts of worship there is no ostentation and they are done with a sincere intention. So whoever does an open act of worship should observe two things. One thing is that he should disclose it in a place where he knows others will follow it, as there are some people whose family members would follow him, but not his neighbours, or whose neighbours would follow him, but not the entire community. A kind man is a person who is followed by all people. An ignorant man, on the other hand, cannot expect to have this benefit, and so he should keep secret his acts of worship.

Another matter is that there should not be any ostentation in acts of worship. Generally, people say upon completion of their acts of worship, "I have done such and such." But strictly pious men do their actions not with ostentation, but for public benefit.

Sa'd ibn Mu'ādh said, "Ever since I became a Muslim and observed prayers, I have not thought without prayer. When I buried a man, I did not think of anything except what he will be asked. When I heard a *ḥadīth* from the Prophet (ṣ), I believed it firmly to be true." 'Umar said, "I do not fear any action, whether it is difficult or easy, if I can understand that it is good for me." 'Uthmān said, "Ever since I pledged allegiance to the Prophet (ṣ), I have not sung, lied or touched my private parts with my right hand." Shaddād ibn Aws said, "Ever since I accepted Islam, I have not uttered a word without thinking." Abū Sufyān said at the time of his death to his family members, "Do not weep for me, as I have not committed any sin since I accepted Islam." 'Umar ibn 'Abd al-'Azīz said, "Allah has not destined anything for me except that I was pleased that nothing other than it was destined. I feel pleasure that Allah has placed me in a proper place."

These words cannot be uttered unless one is in a good state. These are words of advice giving encouragement to do good works, as these words are fit to be followed and came out of the pure mouths of the leaders. Thus, it is allowed to disclose acts of worship on the part of those who are strong in faith, but it is not for those who are weak in faith.

Rules for concealing a sin

Know that open and secret acts of worship, in order to be equal, must have as their the root pure and sincere intention. For this reason, 'Umar said to a man, "Be careful of open acts of worship." The man then asked, "O Commander of the Faithful, what is an open act of worship?" He replied, "That action about which you feel no shame if it is disclosed to you." Abū Muslim al-Khawlānī said, "I do not do anything considered by people to be bad if it is disclosed to them." This is a high rank and everyone cannot attain it, as nobody is safe from the sins of his heart and bodily limbs.

Reasons for concealing a sin

The first reason is that if Allah conceals the sin of a truthful man with a pure motive who does actions without ostentation, he becomes pleased. When He discloses it, he becomes displeased and fears that He will disclose it on Resurrection Day. The Prophet (ṣ) said, "If anybody commits any sin and Allah conceals it in this world, He will conceal it in the next world." This thought comes from the strength of faith.

The second reason is that he knows that Allah hates the disclosing of sin and loves concealing it. The Prophet (ṣ) said, "If anybody commits any sin out of these sins, let him conceal it, as Allah conceals it. If he disobeys Allah by committing any sin, let him not keep his heart empty of what Allah loves."

The third reason is to save oneself from the rebuke of people. This sinner becomes sad if he hears rebuke, which takes his heart and intellect away from the act of worship. For this disease, praise is also to be hated, as it diverts the heart from the remembrance of Allah. This is also a sign of the strength of faith.

The fourth reason is to save oneself from the harms of men, as rebuke troubles the heart in the same way the body feels pain if beaten. Fear for pain in the heart owing to rebuke is not unlawful.

The fifth reason is to hate rebuke. This is because the rebuker commits sin by rebuking and because hating it is a part of faith. Moreover, just as you feel pain in your heart if anybody rebukes you, so also you should feel pain if you rebuke another. This is a sign of hate.

The sixth reason is so that it may not be committed again.

The seventh reason is shame. To feel shame is also a matter of sorrow and is good. The Prophet (ṣ) said, "Shame is a part of faith," "Shame does not bring but good" and "Allah loves the shameful and patient." Whoever commits sin and does not feel ashamed of disclosing it brings his own ruin. Shame is a trait which begets good conduct.

The eighth reason is that others may become encouraged to commit a similar sin and may follow him. For this reason, it is good to disclose acts of worship and to conceal sins. This is the conduct of the leaders whom people follow.

Abandoning acts of worship for fear of ostentation

There are many men who abandon acts of worship for fear of ostentation. This is a mistake and the work of Satan. Good deeds are of two kinds. One kind of good deeds is naturally good, having no connection with people, such as prayer, fasting, pilgrimage and jihad. This is because these acts of worship entail hardship. When people praise that, it gives pleasure. Another kind of good deeds are connected not only with the body, but also with people, such as administration, judicial work, power, teaching, spending on others and other good deeds.

The first kind of good deeds are obligatory duties connected with the body and not with people. These duties have no pleasure of their own. Examples include prayer, fasting and pilgrimage. There are three kinds of ostentation in these acts of worship. Ostentation of the first kind appears before the act of worship. This kind of good deed should be given up, as it is really a sinful deed, as respect is sought through the medium of the act of worship. It is necessary to remove this motive for ostentation from the heart. The second kind of ostentation is that which appears in the middle of an act of worship, though it is begun with a sincere intention. Such ostentation should be avoided. The third kind of ostentation is also to be avoided by turning one's undivided attention to acts of worship and not to people.

The second kind of good deeds is connected with people and is fraught with dangers and difficulties. The greatest of such deeds are the administration of a country, the administration of justice, admonition and teaching and the spending of riches. With regard to the administration of a country, if it is done with a pure intention and for the administration of justice, it becomes the greatest act of worship. The Prophet (ṣ) said, "One day of a just ruler is more than sixty years of worship." He said, "Three people will enter Paradise first," and mentioned a just ruler as one of them." He said, "The invocation of three people is not rejected," and likewise mentioned a just ruler as one of them. He said, "The man who will be in my companionship most on Resurrection Day is a just ruler." So to rule as the vicegerent of Allah is the greatest act of worship.

Administration of a country

In administrative work, passions rise and the pleasure of exercising power grows strong. It is the greatest pleasure in this world. When power becomes dear, the ruler tries to live in comfort and enjoyment and conducts himself according to his sweet will. It is then he falls in the mouth of destruction. One day of an oppressive ruler is greater than sixty years of sin.

The Prophet (ṣ) said, "Whoever rules over ten people will appear on Resurrection Day with his hands tied to his neck. Either his justice will untie him or his injustice will ruin him."

Ma'qil ibn Yasār said that when 'Umar wanted him to be appointed as governor, he said, "O Commander of the Faithful, you should consult with me in this affair." 'Umar said, "If you entrust me in this affair, sit near me and keep your consultation with me concealed."

Al-Ḥasan said that when the Prophet (ṣ) wanted to appoint a man as governor, the man asked, "Is it good for me?" The Prophet (ṣ) replied, "Sit down."

The Prophet (ṣ) said to 'Abd al-Raḥmān ibn Samurah, "O 'Abd al-Raḥmān, do not be a candidate for administration, for if it is given to you without your seeking it, you are helped therein, but if it is given to you after seeking, it is entrusted to you."

Abū Bakr said to Rāfi' ibn 'Umar, "Do not accept a government post, even if it is to rule over two people." After that, when Abū Bakr was invested with rulership, Rāfi' said to him, "Did you not say to me, 'Do not accept a government post, even if it is to rule over two people'? But you have become the caliph of the followers of the Prophet of Allah." Abū Bakr replied, "Yes, I told you that and still tell you that. Curse is on that leader who cannot do justice."

Very few people with deep insight can understand the great good and great harm in administrative matters. Those people who are firm in religion and strong should respond to take over administrative charges, but those who are weak in faith should not come near it and ruin themselves. The former people have given up the world and stay out of the public eye and engage themselves in the progress of their souls. They have become victorious over their passions and subdued their demons. They are fit to hold power. It is unlawful for those who have no such qualities to take charge of power. In doubtful places, charges of power should not be undertaken, as human nature is deceptive. It promises just administration, but finds it difficult in the end. Such people promise to do good works, but as soon as they get power they forget their promises. The Prophet (ṣ) said, "We shall not appoint him who wants administrative charges."

Administration of justice

Although placed below the caliphate and administrative work, it has no less responsibility. Justice, if administrated fairly, has unlimited rewards, but in the case of injustice, there is grievous punishment. The Prophet (ṣ) said, "There are three classes of judges. Two classes will go to Hell and only one class of judges will go to Paradise." He said, "Whoever prays for being appointed as a judge is sacrificed, even without a knife."

When an administrator or a ruler is an oppressor, a judge under him should not deviate an inch from doing justice. If unable to do so, he should resign his post. Strong judges are necessary in an oppressive reign. If injustice is done by any judge, his place is in Hell.

Admonishing and teaching

In teaching, giving sermons, admonition, giving decisions on legal matters and other jobs in which there is honour, power, name and fame, there are dangers and difficulties like those of administrative matters. Whoever delivers lectures and sermons wishes to hear praise from people. He arouses their tears by his lectures. When this state becomes strong in his heart, he wants to adorn his speeches with ornamental words and phrases so that it may become pleasant to the audience, although there may not be any truth at all in what he says. When he finds these dangers, he should give up giving lectures.

The Prophet (ṣ) prohibited the seeking of administrative powers. He said, "You will have greed for administrative powers, which will be a cause for regret and sorrows on Resurrection Day. Only he who fulfils it in truth will be saved."

He said, "Whoever suckles is good, and whoever refrains from suckling is bad." From this it is understood that if there is no reign and rule, worldly effects and religion will be in camouflage, people will be loggerheads, peace will be distant, towns and villages will be destroyed and there will be a shortage of provisions. So why would the Prophet (ṣ) prohibit rule and reign?

'Umar once saw that Ubayy ibn Ka'b was followed by a host of men, and so he assaulted him, though he knew him as one of the leaders of Muslims. Ubayy used to read out to him the Qur'an, but still 'Umar prohibited people from walking behind Ubayy and said, "Whoever is followed is tried, and whoever is tried is disgraced."

A man once wanted 'Umar's permission to deliver sermons after the dawn prayer, but 'Umar refused. The man asked, "Do you prohibit me from delivering sermons?" 'Umar replied, "There has entered your brain an air which I fear will carry you up into the sky." He saw in him a desire for lectures. But there should be some people who deliver lectures and do good for Islam, though they may not strictly follow religious principles. The Prophet (ṣ) said, "Allah will help this religion by men who have no share of Islam in them." People should be careful of irreligious scholars, however.

'Īsā said, "O dishonest scholars, you advise people to pray, fast and give charity, but you do not do that. You do not do what you ask people to do. You advise people, but you do not take your own advice. This is indeed bad. You say, 'Repentance! Repentance!' with your mouth, yet you act according to your desires. What benefit will you get from this? You keep your body neat and clean, but you keep your heart impure. I tell you in truth: Do not be like a sieve, from which fine things come out, but only husk remains therein. Similarly, orders come out of your mouth, but hatred and jealousy remain in your heart. O worshippers of the world, how can you earn the next world when you cannot give up earthly desires and cut off your greed?

"I tell you in truth that your souls are weeping having seen your actions. You have placed the world under your tongue and your works under your feet. I tell you in truth that you are destroying your next world in benefitting your world; the good of this world is better to you than the good of the next. If you knew your troubles, how good it would be! How long will you guide those who wander in darkness and stand by those who are misguided? It seems that you are calling worldly addicted men with the object that they may give up their wealth to you. Do you not think that if a lamp is placed on a roof, it will not do any good to a house full of darkness?

"Similar is the lamp of learning, which is burning in your mouth, but your mind is full of darkness. So what benefit will you derive from such an education? O people addicted to the world, you are not like religious men, like fully independent men. If the world cuts you off from your wealth, you will fall on your faces and nostrils. Then your sins will catch you by your forelocks, your knowledge will be thrown on your backs and you will be brought naked before the Almighty. You will have to wait before Him for your sins, and you will be punished for your sins. What wonder is there in this?"

It might be argued that, although the dangers of bad and irreligious learned men are obvious, great benefit is derived from their sermons. For the Prophet (ṣ) said, "If Allah gives guidance to a single man through you, it is better than the world and everything therein" and "Whoever calls to guidance, and it is followed, will get its rewards and the rewards of those people who follow it."

Knowledge has merits and demerits, as is the case with administration and public affairs. Owing to the harms of knowledge, we shall not say to someone, "Give up learning," for there is harm only in being ostentatious and not acting according to one's knowledge.

Ostentation has degrees. The first degree is ostentation in administrative matters. Because of this danger, the sages of the past gave up these charges.

The second degree is in prayer, fasting, pilgrimage and jihad. Ancient sages did not love to give up acts of worship owing to the dangers therein.

The third degree is the middle course between the above two degrees, which includes being candidates for delivering lectures, sermons, giving legal decisions, teaching traditions and other matters. The dangers that are in these affairs are less than those in administrative matters, but greater than the internal dangers of prayer. For fear of ostentation, those who are weak in faith should not give up prayer. Rather, they should give up the sudden thoughts of ostentation in prayer.

The fourth degree is to earn wealth and distribute it to those who are in want with the hope of receiving praise. Al-Ḥasan was asked about two people: one who seeks his necessities and another who seeks beyond his necessities and then gives it in charity. He said that the first person is better, as he knows that there is very little safety in the world and that if the world is given up, proximity to Allah is attained. Abū al-Dardā' said, "If I earn fifty gold coins daily and give them in charity standing on the staircase of the mosque of Damascus, I will not consider it good. I do not make buying and selling unlawful, but I wish to be one of those people whom merchandise and trade cannot divert from the remembrance of Allah."

'Īsā said, "O worshippers of the world, your renunciation of the world is a more meritorious work than seeking rewards." He said, "In doing good through wealth, a little drifting from the remembrance of Allah is bad, for the remembrance of Allah is the greatest and best."

There are some signs which show whether a man delivers sermons with a divine motive. The first sign is that he does not hate whoever gives better lectures than him and is praise by men. Sa'īd ibn Abī Marwān said, "I was once seated near al-Ḥasan, who was giving sermons. Suddenly, the tyrannical governor al-Ḥajjāj came to us through a door of the mosque escorted by his guard and mounted on a horse. He came near the assembly of al-Ḥasan, got down from the horse, came to him and sat. Al-Ḥasan continued his sermon as before. When he finished his sermon, al-Ḥajjāj placed his hand on the shoulder of al-Ḥasan and said, 'You have spoken well. You will follow those instructions and form your character and conduct, as I heard from the Prophet (ṣ) that an assembly for the remembrance of Allah is a garden of Paradise. Had we not been engaged in the affairs of men, you would not have sat in such a place longer than myself.' Then al-Ḥajjāj began to deliver good lectures which charmed the audience.

"When he went to Syria, a man came to al-Ḥasan and said, 'O Muslims, I am in charge of horses, asses and tents. I have three hundred dirhams people have given me, and I have seven daughters.' He began to complain about his wants. When he finished, al-Ḥasan said, "What has become of administrators? May Allah ruin them. They made the servants of Allah slaves, took up the treasures of Allah as their own and fight for money. When they engage in jihad against Allah's enemies, they live in comfortable beds and ride on fast horses. When they send other Muslims to jihad, they keep them hungry and thirsty.' A man who heard this went to al-Ḥajjāj and informed him of the rebuking of al-Ḥasan. After some time, a man came from al-Ḥajjāj to al-Ḥasan and told him to see al-Ḥajjāj. Al-Ḥasan went accordingly and came back smiling. He said, 'Nobody says to a flame of fire what has been said to him in confidence. When I went to al-Ḥajjāj, he said, 'Do not say such things in the future. Do you instigate people against me? I do not care for it. I do not care for your sermons. You should control your tongue.' Thus Allah removed me from him.' Then a-Ḥasan started for his house, but many people followed him. He said to them, 'Do you need anything from me? If you do not, then please get away from me.'"

'Alī ibn al-Ḥusayn used to pray, "O Allah, I seek refuge in You from the fact that my open acts of worship are good to people and my secret acts of worship are bad to You when I separate myself from people. I seek refuge in You from the fact that I should perform my acts of worship in a good manner when I am with You and I should approach you with sin when I become separate from You."

So the religious man treading the path of Allah should always seek the pleasure of Allah. It cannot be attained if he fears any other thing than Allah and depends on Him. Whoever fears another and depends on him hopes that his good works should be known to him. He should know it to be bad on the strength of his wisdom, as Allah's wrath may follow him.

Shaqīq al-Balkhī said, "Once, I gave an article of clothing to Sufyān al-Thawrī as a gift, but he returned it to me. I said to him, 'O Abū 'Abdullāh, I did not hear *ḥadīths* from you. Why do you return it?' He said, 'I know, but your brother has heard *ḥadīths* from me. I fear lest my mind incline to him more than it inclines to others.'"

Once, a man came with two purses to Sufyān. His father was a friend of Sufyān who used to go to him often. He said to him, "O Abū 'Abdullāh, this is money from my father to you." Sufyān said, "May Allah shower mercy on your father." When he went away, he called his son and said to him, "Return this money to him." When he went to him, he said, "My desire is that you should take back your money." The reason is that he remembered afterwards that his friendship with his father was for the pleasure of Allah, so he declined to receive the money. Sufyān's son complained to his father for not accepting the money, and the latter replied, "You will enjoy this money with pleasure, but I will be questioned for that on Resurrection Day." So everybody should seek the pleasure of Allah and show the right path to people.

Ibrāhīm ibn Adham said, "I gained knowledge of Allah from a Christian named Sam'ān. I asked him, 'How long have you lived in this house?' He replied, 'For seventy years.' I asked, 'What is your food?' He replied, 'What do you need?' I said, 'I wish to learn.' Sam'ān then answered the question. 'O monotheist, one chickpea every night.' I asked, 'Do you think one chickpea is enough?' He replied, 'Can you see the monastery by you?' I said, 'Yes.' He said, 'The monks (of that monastery) come to me once a year. They roam round this prayer place and show respect to me. Whenever I become tired of acts of worship, I remember their respect. I do acts of worship for one year but get respect for just one day. O monotheist, endure the hardship of a moment for everlasting glory.'

"So he caused knowledge to appear worthy in my heart. Then he asked, 'Is this sufficient for you, or do you want more?' I replied, 'I want more.' He said, 'Get down from the praying place.' I got down, he handed me a pot with twenty chickpeas in it and said, 'Enter the monastery as the people saw what I have given you.' When I entered the monastery, the Christians assembled near me and asked, 'O monotheist, what has been given to you by this hermit?' I replied, 'He has given me a portion of his food.' They asked, 'What will you do with it? We are more entitled to it.' They asked me to accept money in exchange for it and gave me twenty dinars. I then went back to the hermit, who asked me, 'O monotheist, what have you done?' I replied, 'I sold it to them.' He asked, 'For how much?' I replied, 'For twenty dinars.' He said, 'You have made a mistake. They would have given you twenty thousand dinars. This honour is for what you do not worship. Now look, O monotheist, at the respect for that man who worships Allah. O monotheist, advance to your Lord and give up wandering.'"

It was reported that the rich used to feel dishonoured in the assembly of Sufyān al-Thawrī. He used to seat them in the back row and the poor in the front row; even the rich wanted to be poor in his assembly. The poor are more respectable to Allah than the rich. But the case is otherwise with us. We show more respect to the rich, and there is ostentation in it because of the greed for wealth. Keep your passion within your control. Do not be satisfied with your passion, which will lead you to Hell and which will perish with you. Live in the world in the same way a king passes the remaining days of his life, having being afflicted with a serious disease. He takes bitter medicine for treatment and gives up all delicious foods. This leads him gradually to health. If he does not observe this, his disease will worsen.

Similarly, the traveller in the path of religion gives up all the things harmful to his next world in order to get everlasting peace and happiness of the next world. In other words, he gives up worldly enjoyments and remains satisfied with little. He prepares himself for the happiness of Paradise. He knows that Allah helps whoever helps himself with acts of worship. Allah makes his actions easy, removes idleness from him, makes patience easy for him and makes acts of worship dear to him. The pleasure of intimate discourse with Allah is his sustenance. That is more than all pleasures and stronger in removing passions.

Allah says, "I advance one cubit towards the man who advances half a cubit towards Me." He also says, "The desire of religious men to meet Me is still greater." So everyone should proceed towards His mercy, blessing and nearness.

Book 9
Pride and self-praise

Introduction

The Prophet (ṣ) said, "Allah says, 'Pride is My shirt and greatness is My garment. I destroy whoever takes something of them.'" He also said, "There are three destructive things: miserliness which is obeyed, passion which is followed and self-praise." So pride and satisfaction owing to self-praise are bad and destructive diseases of the heart, and such a heart is greatly diseased and an object of hatred to Allah.

1
Condemnation of pride

The Qur'an

I will turn away from My communications those who are unjustly proud in the earth. (Qur'an, 7:146)

Thus does Allah set a seal over the heart of every proud, haughty one. (Qur'an, 40:35)

They asked for judgement and every insolent opposer was disappointed destroyed. (Qur'an, 14:15)

He does not love the proud. (Qur'an, 16:23)

Surely those who are too proud for My service will soon enter Hell abased. (Qur'an, 40:60)

There are many verses about pride in the Qur'an.

Ḥadīth

The Prophet (ṣ) said, "Whoever has in his heart a mustard seed's weight of pride will not enter Paradise, and whoever has in his heart a mustard seed's weight of faith will not enter Hell."

He said, "Allah will throw Hell over the face of one whose heart has the slightest pride."

Sulaymān once addressed the birds, beasts, animals and men, "Go out in procession." Thereupon, two hundred thousand men and two hundred thousand beasts joined the procession, and the wind took them upwards. He rose to such a height that he heard the sound of angels in the sky glorifying Allah. Then he descended into the bottom of the sea and heard this advice from heaven: "If the least sign of pride was found within the heart of your friend Sulaymān, he would be destroyed at the bottom of sea before he rose to the sky."

The Prophet (ṣ) said, "A long neck will have two ears to hear, two eyes to see and a tongue to speak. It will say, 'I have been entrusted with three people: every proud and insolent man, every man who worships others along with Allah and every maker of pictures.'"

He said, "Paradise and Hell once quarrelled with each other. Hell said, 'I have been entrusted with the proud and oppressors.' Paradise said, 'The weak, the destitute and the helpless will enter me.' Allah said to Paradise, 'You are Allah's mercy. I will give you, out of My mercy, those whom I wish.' He said to Hell, 'You are My punishment. I will punish those whom I wish by you. I will fill you both.'"

He said, "Whoever is an oppressor and exceeds the limit, having forgotten the Almighty, is hated. Whoever is engaged in fruitless talk and lives forgetful of grace and destruction is hated. Whoever is disobedient and lives forgetful of the First and the Last is hated."

He was once informed that a man was very proud and asked, "Will he not die after this?" When the death of the prophet Nūḥ drew near, he called his two sons and said, 'I am giving you two injunctions and two prohibitions. I prohibit you from being proud and ascribing partners to Allah. I order you to say, 'There is no deity but Allah' and 'Glory to Allah' and 'All praise is due to Allah.' If the heaven and earth were placed in one scale pan and 'There is no deity but Allah' in the other, the latter pan would be heavier.'"

'Īsā said, "He is good whom Allah taught the revealed Book and who does not die an oppressor."

The Prophet (ṣ) said, "Every passion-loving man, every proud man, every hoarder and every hypocrite are dwellers of Hell. Every poor and weak man is a dweller of Paradise."

He said, "Whoever is best among you in conduct will be the dearest and nearest to me in the next world. The most distant from me among you, and the object of the most hatred, are those people who are talkative, troublemakers and hypocrites." The Companions asked, "Who are the hypocrites?" He replied, "The proud."

He said, "The proud will be raised on Resurrection Day as dwarves. People will tread on these dwarves with their feet. The figure of everything will be taller than their figures. They will then be driven to a hell named Būlas. Their food will be the fire of Hell, and their drink will be the blood and puss of the dwellers of Hell." Similarly, he said, "On Resurrection Day, the proud and the oppressed will be presented in Hell as dwarves, and people will tread on them as they were toys of Allah." He also said, "There is a palace in Hell where the proud will be admitted and then it will be shut.

He used to pray, "O Allah, I seek refuge in you from the pride of the proud."

He said, "He from whose body life has gone out and is saved from three matters—pride, debt and deceit—will enter Paradise."

Words attributed to the Companions

Abū Bakr al-Ṣiddīq said, "No Muslim will hold in contempt another Muslim, as whoever is small among Muslims is great with Allah."

Wahb said, "When Allah created Adam, He looked at him and said, 'You are unlawful for every proud man.'"

Muḥammad ibn al-Ḥusayn ibn 'Alī said, "Whenever something of pride enters into the heart of a man, small or great, his wisdom is reduced in that proportion."

Sulaymān was once asked, "Is there any sinner whose rewards do not do him any benefit?" He replied, "A proud man."

Demerits and signs of pride

The Prophet (ṣ) said:

> Allah will not look at him who drags his garment out of pride.
>
> Once, a man was feeling delighted by his own clothes, and Allah ordered that he be drowned underneath the earth until Resurrection Day.
>
> When my followers walk with pride, and their servants are the inhabitants of Persia and Byzantium, Allah will appoint some of them to rule over others.
>
> Whoever thinks himself great and discloses pride in his behaviour will meet Allah in His enraged state.

Allah says:

> *Do not go about in the land exultingly, for you cannot cut through the earth nor reach the mountains in height.* (Qur'an, 17:37)

Merits of modesty and humbleness

The Prophet (ṣ) said, "Allah increases the honour of a man by virtue of his pardon, and He elevates whoever is modest for His sake."

He said, "There is no such man with whom there are not two angels who fix a reign to his mouth. When he raises his head, they lower it. When he is modest, they say, "O Allah, raise his head."

He said, "Whoever is powerful yet modest, spends what he earns lawfully, shows kindness to the helpless and the destitute and keeps the company of the wise and the learned is blessed."

He said, "Allah humiliates him who is proud. Allah makes him solvent who takes a middle course in spending. Allah makes him poor who is extravagant. Allah loves him who remembers Him most."

The Prophet (ṣ) was once having a meal with some of his Companions when a beggar came and stood at his door. The beggar was crippled, having been afflicted with paralysis, and people began to hate him. The Prophet (ṣ) gave him permission to come in and kept him seated on his thigh and said, "Have some food." A man of the Quraysh saw this and prohibited him, being greatly hateful to him. When the beggar later died of his disease, the Prophet (ṣ) said, "My Lord gave me two options: slavery with the office of prophethood or reign with the office of prophethood. I could not decide which of these two I should choose and therefore raised my head towards my friend Jibrīl, who said, 'Be humble to your Lord.' I said, 'I choose slavery with prophethood.'"

Allah revealed to Mūsā, "I accept the prayer of whoever humbles himself before My glory, who does not boast to My servants, who keeps My fear attached to his heart, who spends the day in My remembrance and who deprives himself of passions and desires for My sake."

The Prophet (ṣ) said, "There is honour in God-fearingness, pedigree in humility and real wealth in faith."

'Īsā said, "Those who are humble in this world are blessed. They will gain a high rank in the highest heaven on Resurrection Day. Those who keep their minds pure in this world are blessed. They will gain the sight of Allah on Resurrection Day."

The Prophet (ṣ) said, "When Allah gives a servant the guidance of Islam, beautified his figure, does not put him to any place of dishonour and gives him the quality of humility, he becomes dear to Allah."

He said, "Modesty does not increase but progress. So be modest and Allah will bestow mercy on you."

Once, he was having his meal when a black man suffering from small pox and trembling came before him. The neighbouring men went away from him, but the Prophet (ṣ) kept him seated by his side.

He said, "Allah gives four qualities to a man whom He loves: silence in worship, reliance on Allah, modesty and renunciation of the world."

He said, "Allah raises him to the seventh heaven who takes recourse to modesty."

He said, "Whoever carries the necessities of his family destroys his pride."

He once asked his Companions, "Why do I not get from you the pleasure of acts of worship?" They replied, "What is the pleasure of worship?" He said, "Modesty."

He said, "When you find the humble among my followers, be humble to them. When you find the proud, treat them with pride, for they will feel humiliated and humble."

Traditions from Companions and early Muslims

'Umar said, "When a man takes recourse to modesty for Allah, He raises his wisdom. When he takes to pride and enmity, He drowns him underneath the earth. It is then ordered, 'Be off! Allah has removed you.' He is great to himself, but small to people. He is even worse to them than a pig."

Yūsuf ibn Asbāṭ said, "God-fearingness is sufficient for more acts of worship, and a little modesty is sufficient for great labour."

Ibn al-Mubārak said, "To modestly treat a person who is inferior to you in wealth is the root of modesty. The latter will then understand that superiority is insignificant to you. Treat with superiority whoever is superior to you in worldly riches and he will understand that worldly superiority is insignificant to you."

Allah revealed to 'Īsā, "When I give you wealth, I will give it to you in full if you accept it humbly."

Ka'b said, "If Allah gives a man worldly wealth, for which he expresses gratefulness in order to please Allah and becomes humble, He will give him its benefit in the world and will increase his rank in the hereafter."

'Abd al-Malik ibn Marwān was asked, "Who is good?" He said, "That person who is modest in spite of his power, who gives up his low desires and who pardons in spite of his strength."

Ibn al-Sammāk went to Hārūn and said, "O Commander of the Faithful, the modesty which you show in spite of your unsullied power is more honourable than the honour of your lordship." Hārūn replied, "What a good word you have uttered?" Ibn al-Sammāk said, "O Commander of the Faithful, if one who has been given by Allah the beauty of physique, the quality of modesty, wealth and prosperity acquires the quality of God-fearingness, removes the wants of others by his wealth and earns the attribute of modesty, his name is written along with the friends of Allah in the special record of Allah." Hārūn kept these instructions written by his own hand.

It was the habit of Sulaymān to receive at dawn the rich and the honourable and then sit with the poor and say to them, "Whoever is poor sits with the poor."

A sage said, "The more one is humble to himself, the more he is raised to Allah. The more one is great to himself, the more he is mean to Allah."

Ziyād al-Namirī said, "An ascetic without humility is like a tree without fruits."

Al-Fuḍayl said, "Whoever loves power will never be successful."

Al-Shiblī said, "My humility has made the humility of the Jews void."

A sage said, "Whoever considers himself an asset has nothing of humility in him."

Abū Yazīd said, "So long as one thinks that others are worse than him, he can be called a proud man." He was asked, "When will he be modest?" He said, "When he does not find for himself any rank or honour."

'Urwah ibn al-Ward said, "Modesty is a means of earning pedigree. There is an envious person for every gift except modesty."

A sage said, "It is good for every man to take to modesty, but it is better for a rich man. To take pride is bad for everyone, but it is worse for a poor man."

A sage said, "Whoever thinks himself modest for the pleasure of Allah, there is honour for him. There is progress for whoever is modest for the pleasure of Allah. There is safety for whoever fears Allah Almighty. There is gain for him who sells himself for Allah."

Abū 'Alī al-Jurjānī said, "The ego is filled with pride, greed and envy. Allah deprives one of modesty, admonition and contentment whom He wishes to destroy, and He gives those qualities to one for whom He wishes good."

Al-Junayd said that the Prophet (ṣ) said, "The worst men will be leaders in the latter days."

Abū Bakr al-Ṣiddīq said, "We have found honour in God-fearingness, contentment in firm faith and pedigree in modesty. We pray for Allah's mercy."

The reality of pride

Pride is of two kinds: open and secret. Secret pride is a feeling of superiority. When it is expressed in actions, it is open pride. A feeling of superiority in the heart is self-conceit (*kibr*), but when it is expressed in actions it is pride (*takabbur*). So self-conceit is the root of pride. Self-conceit is content in thinking that one is superior to others.

Self-conceit has three elements: the person with pride, the person to whom pride is shown and the object for which it is felt. Self-praise (*'ujb*) has only one element, namely the people who have pride, while self-conceit has three. An appreciation of one's own trait is not by itself self-conceit. However, if he firmly believes he has this trait, feels joy at it and thinks himself superior to others, it is to be understood that there are elements of self-conceit in him.

For this reason, the Prophet (ṣ) said, "I seek refuge in You from the breath of the proud." 'Umar said to a person who sought his permission to deliver a lecture, “I fear for you the blow of pride.” This feeling of superiority is self-conceit. Ibn ‘Abbās described it as a feeling of superiority over others. If it is expressed in words or behaviour, it is pride, which is the outward expression of self-conceit.

Harms of pride

The Prophet (ṣ) said, “Whoever has an atom of pride in him will not enter Paradise.” A proud man cannot love for others what he loves for himself, as there is pride in him. He cannot give up hatred, as there is pride in him. He cannot be truthful, as there is pride in him. He cannot control his anger, as he has pride in him. He cannot accept admonitions, as there is pride in him. He is not safe from the accusations of people, as there is pride in him. The worst harm of self-conceit is to receive no benefit from knowledge, not being able to recognise truth and not being able to follow it.

Allah says:

> *Enter the gates of Hell to abide therein; so evil is the abode of the proud.* (Qur'an, 39:72)
>
> *Then We will most certainly draw forth from every sect of them him who is most exorbitantly rebellious against the Beneficent Allah.* (Qur'an, 19:69)
>
> *So (as for) those who do not believe in the hereafter, their hearts are ignorant and they are proud.* (Qur'an, 16:22)
>
> *Surely those who are too proud for My service will soon enter Hell abased.* (Qur'an, 40:60)
>
> *I will turn away from My communications those who are unjustly proud in the earth.* (Qur'an, 7:146)

It has been explained that the understanding of the Qur'an will be taken out of their hearts. It has also been said that Allah will throw a screen over their hearts. Ibn Jurayj said in the explanation of the above verse that Allah will keep them away from thoughts of the unseen world and from the acceptance of sermons.

Thus, 'Īsā said, "Crops grow in soft earth. They do not grow in a hard ground." In like manner, wisdom arises in a modest or soft heart, not in a hard heart. Do you not see that the head of whoever lifts it to the roof is crushed and the head of whoever keeps low is saved. The Prophet (ṣ) said, "Whoever is heedless of the truth and a backbiter is proud."

Objects of pride

Such objects are of three types: the Creator, then His prophets, then people in general. Man has been created an oppressor and ignorant because sometimes he is arrogant towards Allah's creatures and sometimes even to the Creator.

First type

It is pride to Allah, which is the worst. Its cause is utter ignorance and infidelity, as the infidelity of Namrūd and Fir'awn. It occurred in the heart of Namrūd that he should fight with Allah. Fir'awn and others also claimed also godhood. Fir'awn said, "I am your lord, the most high" (Qur'an, 79:24). For this reason, Allah says, "Surely those who are too proud for My service will soon enter Hell abased" (Qur'an, 40:60); "The Messiah does by no means disdain that he should be a servant of Allah, nor do the angels who are near to Him, and whoever disdains His service and is proud, He will gather them all together to Himself" (Qur'an, 4:172); and "When it is said to them, 'Prostrate to the Most Merciful,' they say, 'And what is the Most Merciful? Shall we prostrate to what you bid us?' And it adds to their aversion" (Qur'an, 25:60).

Second type

It is pride to prophets. The reason is that a person thinks himself greater than prophets and therefore does not follow them. Out of ignorance, he thinks that his words are true. A man said to the Prophet of Allah, "Shall we believe in two mortals like ourselves" (Qur'an, 23:47) and "Why has not an angel been sent down to him" (Qur'an, 6:8). Allah says about Fir'awn, "He was unjustly proud in the land, he and his hosts," (Qur'an, 28:39). He was proud to Allah and to all His messengers. Fir'awn said, "I will consult Hāmān in this matter. He then consulted with Hāmān, who said, "You are our Lord. People worship you. If you proclaim faith in Allah, you will be a slave and a worshipper of another." Then Fir'awn refused to worship Allah and to follow Mūsā.

Allah informs us that Quraysh said, "Why was not this Qur'an revealed to a man of importance in the two towns?" (Qur'an, 43:31). Qatādah said that the "man of importance" was al-Walīd ibn Mughīrah and Abū Mas'ūd al-Thaqafī. They said, "How has Allah sent an orphan over us? Then Allah revealed, "Will they distribute the mercy of your Lord?" (Qur'an, 43:32). Quraysh said to the Prophet (ṣ), "How can we sit near you when these mean people are sitting round you?" referring to the poor Muslims. Then Allah revealed this verse: "Do not drive away those who call their Lord in the morning and the evening. They desire only His favour; neither are you answerable for any reckoning of theirs" (Qur'an, 6:52). Allah says, "Withhold yourself with those who call on their Lord morning and evening desiring His goodwill, and let not your eyes pass from them, desiring the beauties of this world's life" (Qur'an, 18:28). Allah speaks of their punishment in the following verse: "They will say, 'Why do we not see men whom we used to count among the vicious?'" (Qur'an, 38:62). By "vicious" they meant Bilāl, 'Ammār, Suhayb, al-Miqdād and other Companions of the Prophet (ṣ).

Third type

It is pride to people in general. To think oneself greater than other people and to look on them with contempt is to be proud to them. Consequently, such a person keeps himself away from others. It is bad for two reasons.

The first reason is that pride and superiority are due only to the Lord Most High. Man, naturally helpless, is not able to do anything. How can he claim pride under the circumstances? Whenever a man wants to be proud, he wants to ascribe partners to the attribute of Allah, which he cannot do. If any slave wears the crown of a king and sits on the throne, he becomes an object of wrath and hatred of the king. How is he punished for this treason? For this reason, Allah says, "Pride is my garment and glory is my shirt. Whoever quarrels with me about these two matters, I destroy him." Another version reads, "Whoever claims to be vested with an attribute which is solely Mine is ruined." Whoever shows pride to the servants of Allah disobeys Him. If an officer of the king is humiliated by anybody, he is said to oppose the order of the king. Whoever wears the crown of the king and sits on his throne becomes an object of utmost hatred and extreme anger of the king, for which he gets the highest punishment for treason.

The second reason is that pride encourages one to disobey the injunctions of Allah, as a proud man declines to hear sermons from anybody. Allah says, "Those who disbelieve say, 'Do not listen to this Qur'an and make noise therein; perhaps you may overcome'" (Qur'an, 41:26). Furthermore, it is the habit of the unbelievers and the hypocrites not to accept the truth, as Allah says, "When it is said to him, 'Guard against (the punishment of) Allah, pride carries him off to sin" (Qur'an, 2:206). 'Umar said that when he had recited the verse "Surely we are Allah's and to Him we shall surely return" (Qur'an, 2:156), a man stood up and began to deliver a sermon, but was soon killed. Another man then got up and said, "Do you kill those who tell people to establish justice?" Whoever opposed the proud man was killed by him. The Prophet (ṣ) once said to a man, "Eat with your right hand." He said, "I am unable to." The Prophet (ṣ) said, "May you be unable to!" His pride prevented him from eating with his right hand. It was reported that afterwards his right hand became paralysed.

Satan is the best example of this pride. He was driven out of Paradise by Allah, as he was proud and did not prostrate before Adam in obedience to Allah's command. He said, "You created me of fire, while him you created of dust" (Qur'an, 7:12). This finished Satan once and for all. The Prophet (ṣ) said, "Whoever rejects the truth and backbites about people is a proud man." In another *ḥadīth*, he said, "Whoever denies the truth and holds people in contempt is a proud man."

The second harm of pride is to reject the truth. Whoever thinks that he is better than another Muslim and holds him in contempt and sees him small, rejects truth knowingly and is proud to people. Whoever does not like to be humble to Allah, obey His commands and follow His Prophet is proud to Allah and His Messenger.

Subjects of pride

Pride is shown in religious and earthly matters. Religious matters include education, acts of worship and honesty. Earthly matters include pedigree, beauty, power, wealth and lordship. In these matters, there arises pride.

Education

The first cause of pride is education, as the learned take pride in their learning. The Prophet (ṣ) said, "The danger of education is pride." A learned man easily takes pride in his learning. He thinks himself great on account of the excellence of learning and perfectness and holds other men in contempt. He considers others to be beasts, illiterate and ignorant. He believes that he is the most respectable man among them. A man, however, can know himself and his Lord by real education and know the dangers at the time of death. Though there are great dangers in education, real education increases God-fearingness, modesty and other qualities. Abū al-Dardā' said, "The more a man is wise, the more is his responsibility."

There are two reasons why learning begets pride. The first is that he does not receive a real education by which Allah is known and which engages the heart in other-worldly duties. This develops God-fearingness and modesty. Allah says, "Those of His servants only who are possessed of knowledge fear Allah" (Qur'an, 35:28). Other fields, such medicine, mathematics, language, poetry and law are technical education and not real education. Real education provides knowledge of the godhood of Allah and the slavehood of man.

The second reason is that vain arguments are made by education, arguments which pollute the heart, change motives and breed bad conduct. Wahb cited an illustration of this learning. He said, "Education is like rain which comes down pure from the sky. Trees, plants and leaves drink that water through their roots. That water then assumes different natures according to the different kinds of trees and leaves. Water increases bitterness in a plant which is bitter and sweetness in a plant which is sweet. Similar is the condition of education. People acquire education and change it according to their conduct and desires, for which pride in the hearts of the proud and humility in the hearts of the humble are generated. The man whose object of learning is to boast increases his boasting by education. The man whose object is to increase God-fearingness increases his God-fearingness by his education. He knows that there is no need for proof, as it is well established for him. Hence, Allah said to His Prophet, "Be kind to him who follows you of the believers" (Qur'an, 26:215) and "Had you been rough, hard hearted, they would certainly have dispersed from around you" (Qur'an, 3:159). Moreover, Allah describes His friends as being "lowly before the believers, mighty against the unbelievers" (Qur'an, 5:54).

The Prophet (ṣ) said, "Soon there will come a people who will recite the Qur'an, but it will not go beyond their throats. They will say, 'We have recited the Qur'an. Who is better in reciting the Qur'an than us?'" Then he said to his Companions, "O followers of mine, these people will come from among you. They are fuel for Hell."

'Umar said, "Do not be one of the proud scholars. Your education will not be able to remove your ignorance in that circumstance." For this reason, when Tamīm al-Dārī sought his permission to deliver lectures, 'Umar refused and said that it was equal to murder.

Once, Ḥudhayfah led people in prayer and said after it, "Pray behind another imam, as there occurred in my heart the thought that there is nobody among my people better than me." If a reputed Companion such as Ḥudhayfah is unsafe from this, then what about us?

Those who had a perfect education passed away in the first and second centuries of Islam. The Prophet (ṣ) said, "Soon there will come a time in which a man doing one-tenth of what you do will attain salvation." But for this good news, people of this age would be ruined.

Acts of worship

The religious are not free from pride. The form of pride of a man regarding worldly matters is that he thinks that people should come to him and not to others, that they should stand up for him to show respect and that they should broadcast his piety among the general public. The form of pride of a man in religious matters is that he thinks that he alone has salvation and others are ruined.

The Prophet (ṣ) said, "When you hear a man say, 'Men are ruined,' know then that he is ruined among them." He also said, "It is sufficiently wicked for a man to debase his Muslim brother."

It was reported that there was a man called the "profligate of the children of Israel," who was a great sinner among them. One day he passed by a man over whose head was a cloud giving him shade. The profligate thought while passing by him that Allah would show mercy to him if kept his companionship. When he went to him, the religious man thought, "I am a religious man, and this man is a sinner. How can he sit with me?" Therefore, he said to him, "Go away from me!" Allah then revealed to the prophet of that age, "Tell them both to perform acts of worship afresh. I have forgiven the great sinner and erased the rewards of the religious man." In another version of the *ḥadīth*, the cloud drifted away from the religious man and went above the head of the sinner. Know from this that Allah examines the heart of a religious man. When a sinner becomes humble to Allah and has the most God-fearingness, he becomes obedient to Allah with all his heart.

Once, a man struck a hermit on his neck with his foot and then fell at once in prostration. The hermit said, "Raise your head and Allah will forgive you." Allah then revealed to the prophet of that time, "Tell the hermit that he is proud, and Allah will not forgive his sins."

A man was once praised before the Prophet (ṣ). When he came to the Prophet (ṣ), they said, "O Messenger of Allah, we praised this man." The Prophet (ṣ) said, "I can sense the smell of Satan from the mouth of this man." The man came, greeted the Prophet (ṣ) and stood by him. The Prophet (ṣ) said to him, "I ask you in the name of Allah: Do you think you are the best man in your tribe?" The man replied, "Yes, I think so." The Prophet (ṣ) saw the impurity of his heart by the light of prophethood, and that was reflected on his face.

Pedigree

Whoever is honourable in pedigree and ancestry holds others in contempt, even though the latter may be superior to him in acts of worship and education. Abū Dharr said, "There was an altercation between me and another man in the presence of the Prophet (ṣ). I said to him, 'O son of a negro.' At once, the Prophet (ṣ) said, 'O Abū Dharr, one *ṣā'* is equal to another *ṣā'*. A pretty woman is not superior to a black woman.' I grew ashamed and said to the man, 'Rise and slap my face.'" Thus the Prophet (ṣ) brought him to his senses. He thought himself superior because he was handsome.

Two men once began to boast of their ancestry. One man said to the other, "I am the descendant of so-and-so. Who are you? You have no mother." The Prophet (ṣ) said, "Two men quarrelled thus before Mūsā. One man said, 'I am the son of so-and-so,' showing his lineage up to the ninth degree. Allah then revealed to Mūsā, "O Mūsā, tell that proud man, 'Your ancestors up to the ninth degree have gone to Hell. You are the tenth person among them.'" The Prophet (ṣ) said, "Some men boast of their ancestors, but they are reduced to ashes in Hell or are worse to Allah than the worms of cow dung."

Beauty

Pride about beauty is found mostly in women. 'Ā'ishah said, "A woman once came to the Prophet (ṣ), and I indicated with my hand that she was short. The Prophet (ṣ) then said, 'You have backbitten about her.'"

Wealth

This includes the wealth and riches of the kings and rulers, the merchandise of merchants, the land of peasants and the clothes and conveyances of the luxurious. As a result of pride, such people hold the poor in contempt.

Power

If there is strength in the body, it generates pride. A strong man feels pride before a weak man.

Lordship

If there are many disciples, helpers, students or relatives, pride crops up in the heart. Similarly, rulers and kings take pride in the number of their soldiers, arms and ammunitions.

Causes of pride

Know that self-conceit is a secret disease, and if it appears in conduct and actions, it is called "pride." There are three causes for the expression of pride. One is connected with the proud man, another is connected with the man to whom pride is shown and another is connected with things other than the two above. The first is self-praise (*'ujb*), the second is hatred towards the one to whom pride is shown and the third is ostentation. From this point of view, there are four causes of pride: self-praise, hatred, envy and ostentation. Self-praise generates self-conceit, which, if expressed in words, actions and conduct, is called "pride."

Signs of pride

The first sign of pride is expressed by conduct, such as looking askance, keeping the head downward, sitting cross-legged and sitting leaning against. It is also expressed in conversation, gestures, movements and actions. 'Alī said, "If anybody wishes to see one of the inmates of Hell, let him see a sitting man in front of whom people remain standing." Anas said, "None was so dear to people than the Prophet (ṣ). When they saw him, they did not stand to show respect to him, as they knew that the Prophet (ṣ) did not like it."

Another sign of pride is that a proud man does not walk alone. He likes that others should follow him. Abū al-Dardā' said, "If people follow a man, he is removed from Allah." 'Abd al-Raḥmān ibn 'Awf could not be distinguished from his servants, as there was no distinction between him and them outwardly. Once, a party of men were following al-Ḥasan al-Baṣrī and he prohibited them from following him. The Prophet (ṣ) sometimes said to his Companions to walk in front of him.

Another sign of pride is that a proud man does not like to meet with others. It is reported that when Sufyān al-Thawrī came to Makkah, Ibrāhīm ibn Adham sent to him a man who said, "Come to us to read *ḥadīths*." When he came, Ibrāhīm was asked, "O Abū Isḥāq, why have you sent a man to call him?" He said, "I desired to test his modesty."

Another sign of a proud man is that if the poor sit by him, he does not allow them to come very close to him. This is contrary to modesty. Ibn Wahb said, "Once I sat near 'Abd al-'Azīz ibn Abī Rawwād, and his thigh touched mine. As a result, I moved aside. He dragged my garment and said, 'Why do you treat me as you treat the proud? I do not know anyone among you worse than myself.'" Anas said, "Even an ordinary woman of Madīnah would catch hold of the hand of the Prophet (ṣ), and he would not take if off until she took him to whatever place she wished."

Another sign of a proud man is that he saves himself from associating with the diseased and the ill, keeping away from them. Such conduct is included in pride. Once, a man came to the Prophet (ṣ) trembling, as he had small pox. At that time, the Companions were eating with the Prophet (ṣ). When he sat near one of the Companions, he went away from him. But the Prophet (ṣ) drew him near and made him sit.

Another sign of a proud man is that such a man does not give charity with his own hand. One night, a guest came to 'Umar ibn 'Abd al-'Azīz, who was writing, and the light of the lamp was about to be extinguished. The guest said, "I shall take the lamp and fix it." Thereupon, 'Umar said, "To engage a guest in any work is against chivalry." The guest said, "I will wake up your servant." 'Umar said, "The servant has just now gone to sleep." Then he himself filled the lamp with oil. The guest said, "O Commander of the Faithful, are you yourself doing it?" He replied, "Before the oil was brought, I was the same 'Umar as I was after. I will not decrease in honour. Whoever is humble to Allah is the best."

Another sign of pride is that the person does not carry his things to his house. This is opposed to the habit of the humble. The Prophet (ṣ) used to take recourse to the path of modesty. 'Alī said, "The perfection of a perfect man is not reduced if he carries something to his house." When Abū 'Ubaydah ibn al-Jarrāḥ was the commander-in-chief, he used to carry his own water pitcher to the bathroom. Thābit ibn Abī Mālik said, "I saw the Companion Abū Hurayrah carrying a load of firewood from the market, though he was then the governor of Marwān. He said, 'O Ibn Abī Mālik, make way for your governor.'" Al-Aṣbagh ibn Nubātah said, "It is as if I am seeing 'Umar with a bushel of meat in his left hand and the staff of administration in his right hand roaming in the market." A sage said, "I saw 'Alī with a bag of meat, which he purchased for a dirham, carrying it to his house. I said to him, 'O Commander of the Faithful, let me carry it.' He said, 'No. The head of the family is fit to carry it.'"

Another sign of pride is in clothes and adornments. The Prophet (ṣ) said, "Ordinary clothes belong to faith." Zayd ibn Wahb said, "I saw 'Umar once going to the market with the staff of administration in his hand and wearing a loin cloth with fourteen patches, some of which were of old skin." 'Alī was once asked about short clothes and said, "I put on clothes which soften my heart." 'Īsā said, "Pride comes into the heart if good clothes are worn."

It was reported that 'Umar ibn 'Abd al-'Azīz once purchased a garment for a thousand dirhams before he became caliph and said, "How good it would be if it was not rough." When he accepted the caliphate, he purchased a garment for five dirhams and said, "How good it would be if it was not so thin." He was asked, "O Commander of the Faithful, where are your clothes, conveyances and scents?" He said, "My ego was desirous of the constant enjoyment of happiness. I enjoyed them once in the world and do not desire to enjoy them again. I like to enjoy happiness which is greater than that. Even though I enjoy the happiness of rule, which is the highest worldly pleasure, there is still a greater enjoyment with Allah, which I now want to enjoy."

Once the caliph 'Umar ibn 'Abd al-'Azīz was leading the Friday prayer wearing clothes with stitches in the front and back. A man said to him, 'O Commander of the Faithful, Allah has given you wealth. It would be better if you put on good clothes." He replied, "The time of wealth is the best time for good actions, and the time of power is the time of pardon."

The Prophet (ṣ) said, "Whoever gives up adornment for the pleasure of Allah gives up fine clothes, being modest to Him for His pleasure, it becomes a duty of Allah to dress him with fine clothes in Paradise." He said, "Eat and drink, put on clothes and give charity, but do not be extravagant and do not be proud. Allah loves that the traces of his gifts be visible on His servant."

'Īsā said, "What has become of you that you come to me wearing the clothes of a hermit while your heart is like a ferocious beast? Wear the clothes of kings, but make your hearts soft with God-fearingness.

Another sign of pride is that when anyone rebukes you, gives you trouble or realises his dues, you do not keep patient. Abū Sa'īd al-Khudrī said, "Eat for the pleasure of Allah, drink for pleasure for Allah and dress for pleasure of Allah. If there is ostentation and name and fame in these things, there will be sin. Keep in your house habits which the Prophet (ṣ) had in his house. He used to give food to animals with his own hands, sweep his house, milk his goats, put on shoes, sew his sandals, sew his clothes, eat food with servants, help them when they became tired, purchase necessities from the market, carry necessities, help his wives with their work, shake hands with everyone, rich or poor. He used to greet those who appeared in front of him, young or old, white or black, slave or master. When anybody invited him, he did not feel shame in accepting it, even if it came from someone with dishevelled hair and laden with dust. He did not reject invitations. He would not hate the food served to him. He did not hoard dinner for the next morning. He remained satisfied with little food. He was modest and his heart was kind. His face was pleasant. He used to smile, not laugh. He became sorry without despair, stern without harshness, modest without meanness, charitable without misuse and kind to his relatives and Muslims. He never ate to his heart's content."

'Ā'ishah corroborated Abū Sa'īd's words, saying, "I tell you that the Prophet (ṣ) never ate to repletion and did not complain of hunger to anybody. Poverty was dearer to him than solvency and wealth. If he remained hungry at night, he fasted the next day. If he prayed to his Lord, he could have been given the treasures of the world, but he rejected them all. Many a time, I pitied him, seeing him hungry. I passed my hand over his stomach and said, 'May I be ransomed for you! If only you received what is sufficient for your hunger!' He replied, 'O 'Ā'ishah, the great messengers of patience before me had greater patience than this. They died in this condition and drew near their Lord. They are now living in the most honourable places. I would feel ashamed to have a lower rank for engaging in worldly enjoyments. I would rather have patience for these few days than to have a lesser rank in the next world. I do not consider anything more valuable than to live with my brethren and friends.' Hardly had one week passed after these talks when Allah took his life."

You will find the conduct of a modest man in the above ways of his life. So whoever wants to be modest should follow him. Whoever considers himself greater than the Prophet (ṣ) and is not pleased with what the Prophet (ṣ) remained pleased with is a great fool. The Prophet (ṣ) is the owner of the greatest rank both in this world and in the next. There is no honour or progress except in following him. For this reason, 'Umar said, "We are a people who have been honoured by the religion of Islam, so we should not seek honour by following others." When 'Umar entered Syria, he uttered the above words when a man objected to his humility and modesty.

Abū al-Dardā' said, "Know that there are friends of Allah called the *Abdāl*, who are the vicegerents of the prophets. They are the pegs of the earth. When prophethood ended, Allah made them the prophets' successors, who appear before Muslims with true God-fearingness, pious intentions and sound souls and give them sermons, although they may not pray and fast and dress better than most people. Thereby, they seek Allah's pleasure with patience, without cowardice and humility, without meanness. Allah prefers them and gives them special qualities. They are thirty to forty truthful people in number. In their hearts, there is faith firm and strong as that of Ibrāhīm. None of them dies without being replaced by another by Allah. O brother, know that they do not curse anything, do not inflict trouble on anything, do not hold anything in contempt, do not have enmity towards anybody and do not envy anybody. They are the best of people and best in actions, and their conduct is best in terms of modesty and charity. Benevolence is their song, modesty is their habit and safety is their attribute. They are not such that today they fear Allah and tomorrow they are heedless. They are in the same condition outwardly. No storm or cyclone can ruin them in divine matters, and no running horse can surpass them. Their hearts rise to Allah eagerly, merrily and progressively in good works. They are the party of Allah. Allah says, 'Now surely the party of Allah are the successful ones' (Qur'an, 58:22)."

The narrator said, "O Abū al-Dardā', I have never heard of more beautiful qualities than these. How can I obtain them?" He said, "If you would like to obtain these attributes, hate the world, for when you hate the world, you will love the next world. Take recourse to renunciation of the world in proportion to your love of the next world. You will find things benefitting you in your renunciation. Listen to what Allah says, 'Surely Allah is with those who guard (against evil) and those who do good (to others)' (Qur'an, 16:128)."

Treatment of pride and how to attain modesty

Know that pride is harmful. Every man has some pride. It is incumbent or compulsory to remove it. It cannot be removed by mere wish, but it should be placed under treatment to uproot it. There are two stages of treatment. The first stage is that the root of pride is removed. The second stage is that the impediments or the causes which generate pride are removed.

First stage

The medicine for uprooting pride is knowledge and action together.

Medicine for pride based on knowledge

You have to know yourself and know your Lord. If a man knows his real origin, he will know that he is most heinous and not fit for anything except dishonour and disgrace. When he knows his Lord, he can appreciate that nobody is fit for pride except the Lord. To know Him, His glory and His superiority is the end of spiritual knowledge. Hark to what the Qur'an says about man's origin in the verse "Cursed be man! How ungrateful he is! Of what thing did He create him? Of a small seed. He created him, then He made him according to a measure, then He made the way easy (for him), then He causes him to die, then He assigns to him a grave, then, when He pleases, He will raise him to life again" (Qur'an, 80:17-22). In these verses, attention has been drawn to the origin, end and intermediate states of man so that he may appreciate his own position.

Man's origin

He was not even a thing to be mentioned, even. He was in the realm of nothingness for a long, long time. What is a more heinous thing than his inexistence? Then Allah created him of the most obnoxious thing. He created him first from earth, then from semen, then his bones were covered with flesh. Then he came into existence. First, he could not see, hear or talk, so he began his being with death before life, weakness before strength, blindness before sight, deafness before hearing, dumbness before speaking, misguidance before guidance, poverty before solvency, frustration before power. This is the meaning of Allah's words "Of what thing did He create him? Of a small seed" (Qur'an, 80:18-19). This is also the meaning of the verse "There surely came over man a period of time when he was a thing not worth mentioning. Surely We have created man from a small life-germ uniting (itself): We mean to try him" (Qur'an, 76:1-2).

Allah has given man the power of sight and hearing and showed him the two ways— infidelity and gratefulness. He came into being from non-existence and was given life after death, the power of speech after being dumb, the power of sight after blindness, strength after weakness, guidance after misguidance and solvency after poverty. So how can man be proud?

There are strong diseases, dangers and calamities in his lifetime in spite of his willingness or unwillingness. He becomes ill by compulsion. He dies by compulsion. He cannot do good or harm to himself. He cannot get what he desires. He moves within the circle of the machinations of Satan and cannot control his ego. He is helpless and hopeless. How can he be proud?

Man's ultimate end

Allah says, "Then assigns to him a grave, then when He pleases, He will raise him to life again" (Qur'an, 80:21-22). In other words, He will rob him of all his powers—the power of speech, the power of seeing, the power of hearing, the power of smell, the power of knowledge. These things become non-existent as they were in the beginning. Nothing remains in him after his death. His body becomes a corpse from which an obnoxious smell comes out. His bones are crushed, and his flesh becomes the food of worms and insects. So the best way for him is to become dust, with which pots and utensils and buildings are made.

Then he becomes nothing and goes into non-existence after a brief existence. If man ended in dust, it would be better, but for him are a punishment for sins and rewards for good deeds. He will be raised again into a new world on Resurrection Day and will have to be held accountable for all his deeds, which two angels had already recorded. They did not miss even the most minor detail. So how can he be proud? How can he boast?

Medicine for pride based on action

The medicine of pride based on action is to conduct oneself very humbly before people and to follow the conduct of the humble and the modest. The Prophet (ṣ) said, "I am only a servant. I eat as a servant eats." Salmān was once asked, "Why don't you put on new clothes?" He said "I am merely a slave. I would put on new clothes if I had hope for a single day." Modesty does not become perfect without actions. For this reason, those who were proud were ordered to have faith and to pray, as prayer is the pillar of religion, therein is intimate discourse with the Creator and therein is humility. The Arabs who were haughty were ordered to be humble through prayer. They did not bow down or prostrate to anybody, so they were ordered to crush their pride by bowing and prostrating.

Second stage

In this stage, one of the seven reasons mentioned above come into light. We shall describe the treatment for these seven causes by a mixture of knowledge and action.

Medicine for pride in pedigree

If a person takes pride in his pedigree, let him treat this disease of his heart by understanding two things. One of the two things is that he should know that he is gaining respect not for his own quality, but for that of another. For this reason, a poet says:

> If you take pride in pedigree, though it be may true,
> Ponder what you have been created of.

If a proud man of pedigree is vile in himself, what benefit will he derive from the honour of his ancestors? If his predecessors were alive, they would say, "Honour is mine! Who are you? You are merely a worm created from my urine." But do you think a worm created from human urine is superior to a word created from horse urine? Far from it. Honour is due to man not for this worm alone but for his soul, which comes from Allah.

Second, he cannot know his real ancestors. His father was created of an obnoxious matter, and his earliest ancestor was created of earth. Allah says, "Who made good everything that He has created, and He began the creation of man from dust. Then He made his progeny of an extract of water held in light estimation." (Qur'an, 32:7-8). So man's origin is earth, which is trodden on. How can he boast of his ancestry?

Medicine for pride in beauty

This medicine is to consider your internal impurity. Consider your insides, which are filled with urine and stool. You have stool in your intestine, urine in your bladder, spittle in your mouth, blood in your veins, a foul odour underneath your genital organ, sweat underneath your armpits and the stench of stool on your hand as a result of your washing away the stool with your hand. These are signs of your impurity. Your origin is from obnoxious semen mixed with the impure blood of menstruation. Ṭāwūs said to 'Umar ibn 'Abd al-'Azīz, "Can one whose insides are full of stool and urine be proud?" This was uttered before he became caliph.

Medicine for pride in strength

It is to know a disease which is strong. If a gland of your head gives you pain, you lose all your strength. If a fly takes something from you, you cannot recover it from it. If a mosquito enters your nostril or an ant your ear, you may die. If you are afflicted with fever for one day, you lose such strength as cannot be recovered for many days. So when you have no strength, when you cannot recover a minor thing from a fly, should you take pride in your strength? Nobody is stronger than an elephant, a tiger or a camel.

Medicine for pride in wealth and power

This is the worst kind of pride. Whoever takes pride in wealth is like that man who takes pride in his conveyance and house. If the conveyance is lost, or if the house collapses, he grieves over it. How, then, can a rich man take pride in wealth? The Jews are the richest people in the world, but are kicked out of every land. It is foolishness to boast about these things. You are merely a slave, and nothing is under your control.

Medicine for pride in education

A learned man cannot remove his pride unless he knows two things. The first thing is that Allah's judgement of the learned man will be most strict. His patience with a learned man is not even a tenth of His patience with an unlearned man, for whoever commits sin knowingly commits a heinous offence. The Prophet (ṣ) said, "On Resurrection Day, a learned man will be driven to Hell. His entrails will be cut to pieces, and he will roam with that as an ass roams round an oil mill. The dwellers of Hell will ask him, 'What did you do?' He will say, 'I advised people to do good works but I myself did not do them. I prohibited people from doing evil deeds but I myself did them.'"

Allah compares those who do not act according to their knowledge with a load-bearing ass, saying, "The likeness of those who were charged with the Torah, then they did not observe it, is as the likeness of the ass bearing books" (Qur'an, 62:5). In this verse, the learned of the Jews are spoken of. Allah revealed the following verse regarding Bal'am ibn Bā'urā': "Recite to them the narrative of him to whom We give Our communications, but he withdraws himself from them, so the Shayṭān overtakes him, so he is of those who go astray. And if We had pleased, We would certainly have exalted him thereby. But he clung to the earth and followed his low desire, so his parable is as the parable of the dog. If you attack him he lolls out his tongue; and if you leave him alone he lolls out his tongue" (Qur'an, 7:175-176). Ibn 'Abbās said, "Bal'am was given knowledge, but he satisfied his passions and therefore has been likened to a dog."

Second, the learned man knows that Allah alone can take pride, so when he takes pride, he becomes an object of Allah's wrath. Allah says to him, "You will be honoured by Me so long as you do not honour yourself. If you honour yourself, you will not be honoured by Me." So do what Allah loves, then pride will leave you.

Medicine for pride in God-fearingness and devotions

This pride is a great trial for people. The medicine for it is that such a man should sow the seed of modesty in his heart. This means that if a learned man comes to him, he should not be proud. Allah says, "Are those who know and those who do not know alike?" (Qur'an, 39:9). The Prophet (ṣ) said, "The superiority of a learned man over a religions man is as my superiority over my Companions."

There are many verses in the Qur'an regarding the merits of learning. Wahb ibn Munabbih said, "The wisdom of a man does not become perfect until acquires ten qualities" describing the tenth as "to think everyone as better than oneself." To him mankind is divided into two groups. One group are better than him, and the other group are worse. But he behaves modestly and humbly towards these two groups, as he thinks everyone is better than him.

Allah shows the path to good conduct in the following verse: "Those who give what they give (in alms) while their hearts are full of fear that to their Lord they must return" (Qur'an, 23:60). In other words, they worship, but they remain fearful of its acceptance. Allah says of His angels that they remain always fearful of Him, though they are free from sins and engaged always in acts of worship. He says, "They glorify (Him) by night and day; they are never languid" (Qur'an, 21:20). Thus, pride of the heart can be removed.

How to know if you have pride

1. You will know that you have pride when, in an altercation with your friend, you do not accept his opinion, though it is correct. Fear Allah and treat your disease of pride.
2. When you meet with your friends or other people, seat them in places higher than you or in front of you. If you find this difficult, you have pride, and so you should take the appropriate medicine and seat them in a higher place.
3. Accept invitations from the poor and go shopping for relatives and friends. If you find this hard, you have pride and must try to remove it.
4. Carry your items from the market, and also those of your friends. If your ego prohibits you from carrying them, know that you have pride and there is impurity in your heart. Try to remove it by remembering this verse: "The day on which property will not avail, nor sons except, him who comes to Allah with a heart free (from evil)" (Qur'an, 26:88-89). 'Abdullāh ibn Salām was once carrying a load of firewood when it was said to him, "O Abū Yūsuf, your servant is sufficient for that." He said, "Yes, that is true, but I wish to see whether my ego is ready to carry them or not." Similarly, a tradition reads, "Whoever carries fruits or something else is free from pride."
5. Wear ordinary clothes. If you want to appear before people wearing nice clothes, it is ostentation, and if it seems good to you when alone, it is pride. 'Umar ibn 'Abd al-'Azīz had a coarse garment he used to put on at night. In addition, the Prophet (ṣ) said, "Whoever tethers a camel and puts on wool

is free from pride." He also said, "I am a mere servant. I wear wool, tether camels, lick my fingers after eating and accept the invitation of a slave. Whoever turns away from my ways does not belong to my party."

Acquiring modesty

Know that modesty has, as other traits, two extremes. Humility which reaches the extreme limit is pride, and humility which reaches the limit of loss is meanness. The middle course in humility is modesty. The best is modesty without meanness or pride. Whoever walks in front of friends is a proud man, and whoever walks behind them is modest. The good man to Allah is whoever adopts the middle course and pays dues to whom they are due. Do not hold in contempt any man of the market, as you do not know your ultimate end.

Know that self-praise has been condemned by Allah and His Prophet. Allah says:

> *On the day of Ḥunayn, when your great numbers made you vain, but they availed you nothing.* (Qur'an, 9:25)

> *They were certain that their fortresses would defend them against Allah; but Allah came to them from where they did not expect.* (Qur'an, 59:2)

> *They think that they are well versed in skill of the work of hands.* (Qur'an, 18:103)

Man feels self-satisfaction even when he does something wrong. The Prophet (ṣ) said, "There are three harmful things: miserliness which is followed, passion which is obeyed and self-praise." He said to Abū Tha'labah regarding his latter followers, "When you see miserliness followed, low desires obeyed and each man following his own opinion, you should go on doing your duties." Ibn Mas'ūd said, "There are two injurious things: despair and self-praise." He mentioned the two together because a man of despair gives up effort, but fortune cannot be acquired without effort, labour and care. The man of self-praise thinks that his object has been successful owing to his efforts, and so he gives up effort. Thus, whoever has self-praise has no effort. A man of self-praise thinks that he has attained fortune, so he does not strive to achieve it.

Allah says, "Therefore do not attribute purity to your souls" (Qur'an, 53:32). Commenting on this verse, Ibn Jurayj said, "When you do a good deed, do not say, 'I have done it.'" Zayd ibn Aslam said, "Do not call yourself religious." This is self-praise—considering oneself better. Ṭalḥah guarded the Prophet (ṣ) in the Battle of Uḥud. He received wound after wound in defending the Prophet (ṣ) and dedicated his life to him. 'Umar said that because of this, Ṭalḥah felt some self-praise. Ibn 'Abbās said to 'Umar at the time of consultation, "Where are you in comparison with Ṭalḥah?" 'Umar said, "There is self-praise in him. When a man like him was not saved from self-praise, then what about us?"

Muṭarrif said, "Self-satisfaction from saying at dawn, 'I have done enough,' after spending two whole nights in prayer, is worse to me than spending two whole nights in sleep and then repenting in the morning." The Prophet (ṣ) said, "If you did not commit sins, I would fear for you a more heinous crime: self-praise." He termed it a "heinous" evil. 'Ā'ishah was once asked, "When does a man do an evil deed?" She answered, "When he thinks that he is a man of good deeds."

Harms of self-praise

The harm of self-praise is great, as it breeds pride and is a cause of pride. Self-praise with the attributes of Allah makes a person forgetful of his sins. Whoever does not understand the harm of his actions, almost all his efforts go in vain. Whoever has more God-fearingness than self-praise inquires into all things. Whoever has self-praise is cheated by his own opinion. His self-praise takes him to such an extent that he praises himself and thinks himself pure. He gets satisfaction at seeing his wisdom, good deeds and opinions. He considers his opinion good. If he does not believe his opinion and receives light from the Qur'an, seeks help from experts in religion and follows those who have deep insight, he can reach the real truth. So self-praise is injurious.

The reality of self-praise

Self-praise arises out of the realisation of the perfection of good deeds, learning and other qualities. There are three conditions. One condition is that if he fears its loss, it cannot be called self-praise. The second condition is that if he thinks it is a gift of Allah, it cannot be called self-praise. The third condition may be called self-praise provided there is no fear of self-satisfaction and persistence in it.

Self-praise arises out of the following thoughts: I am a perfect man, I am gifted, I am good, I am intelligent and so on. He does not feel joy at the gifts of Allah, but considers them his own and as such takes pleasure in them. He deems these attributes to be his self-acquired attributes and not the gifts of Allah. If, after giving charity to a man, a person wants compensation and thinks that he has done a good deed, he commits self-praise, as Allah says, "O you who believe, do not make your charity worthless by reproach and injury" (Qur'an, 2:264). The Prophet (ṣ) said, "The prayer of a man who does it for a return does not rise above his head. To weep seeking a return for your good deeds is worse than to laugh after recognising your sins." There is hope for compensation behind self-praise, and nobody expects a return except him who praises himself, as that arises from a feeling of superiority.

Medicine for self-praise

Know that the medicine of every disease is its opposite. Self-praise arises out of ignorance. So its medicine is the knowledge opposite of ignorance. Self-praise arises out of acts which are in one's control, such as acts of worship, charity, jihad, administration or public service. Sometimes it arises from acts which are not under one's control, such as beauty, strength, pedigree and so on. The first is stronger than the second.

The causes of self-praise arising out of the first qualities are that the person thinks he possesses these qualities by dint of his own efforts. Its medicine is to think as follows: All gifts are given by Allah. Strength, will, limbs and other causes are also gifts of Allah and not one's own earned possessions. So Allah, and not oneself, is to be praised for all the actions done with the help of strength, will and limbs. If an emperor gives a gift to one of his many servants or officers, the recipient of the gift should not think that it has come because of his own qualities. It is true that your power, the movement of your limbs, your will and all your other attributes are creations of Allah. So when you work, you do not work. When you pray, you do not pray. Allah says, "You did not smite when you smote (the enemy), but it was Allah who smote" (Qur'an, 8:17). It is true, also, that this is clear to those who are experienced in hearts. Allah created you and your limbs and gave you strength, health, wisdom, intellect and will. Then He created the movement of your limbs. He also created your heart.

Second, you perform an action because of your strength. But where has your strength come from? By your existence, this action would not have assumed form. Your will, strength and other causes of your action come from Allah, not from you. If any action is done with the help of strength, this strength is its key, and the key is in the hand of Allah. When the key has not been given to you, it is not possible for you to act.

Acts of worship are the most valuable, and fortune is gained by it. The key of these acts of worship is strength, will and knowledge, which are in the hand of Allah. Consider a jewel kept in a fort. Is not its key in the hand of the treasurer? If you sit round the doors and walls of that fort for thousands of years, it will not be possible for you to see the jewel within it. If you are given its key, you can take it after opening the door of the greatest treasury of the world.

Allah created your strength and gave you lordship over your will, gave your limbs, the power of movement and your hands to remove barriers and obstacles. All these come from Allah and not from you. So whoever gave you the key is the root cause of your actions. To open the door and take the jewel is insignificant.

He gave you the key to do good works. The treasury of acts of worship is closed to sinners. Allah has made strong the causes of sins for sinners and removed them from you. He made strong for them the urge to sin and removed it from you. He gave them implements of worldly enjoyments and removed them from you. Therefore, doing good works becomes easy to you and difficult to sinners. He preferred good works for you and sins for sinners.

Having understood this, how can you praise yourself for your actions? Rather, you should express gratefulness to Allah that He has given you the impulse to do good actions. There is no doer of deeds except Allah, and there is no creator except Him. Whoever is given wisdom but not riches says in wonder, "How could He not give me the sustenance of even one day when He gave me wisdom, and how could He give this ignorant man riches but not wisdom?" He is about to say that Allah did injustice. But this proud man does not know that if he was given wisdom and riches together, it would have been an open act of injustice. Then the ignorant poor man would have said, "O Lord, you have given him both wisdom and riches, but have deprived me from them. Why have you not given me both?" 'Alī was once asked, "Why do the intelligent become poor?" He replied, "Intelligence is considered part of one's sustenance."

The prophet Dāwūd said, "No time passes during the night or day in which a member of the family of Dāwūd does not worship by means of prayer, fasting or invocations." Allah then revealed to him, "O Dāwūd, how can they do that? It would not be so if I did not give them the opportunity. If I did not help you, you could not have the strength. Now I will entrust you to yourself and you will see what calamity befalls you." Dāwūd then began to have endless troubles.

Ayyūb said, "O Allah, You are trying me by this calamity, but I did not complain once against Your will. I am satisfied with Your will." Then he was addressed by ten thousand voices from a cloud, "O Ayyūb, from whom did you get that attribute of patience?" Then he became repentant, besmeared his head with dust and said, "O Lord, I got it from You."

For this reason, Allah said, "Were it not for Allah's grace on you and His mercy, not one of you would have ever been purified" (Qur'an, 24:21). The Companions of the Prophet (ṣ) were most pious and religious. The Prophet (ṣ) said to them, "None of you is such that his good deeds can give him salvation." They asked, "O Messenger of Allah, not even you?" He said, "Not even me, but Allah has covered me with His grace." After this, the Companions wished to be changed to earth, brick and birds, although their works were pure and their hearts were clean. This is a great medicine for uprooting self-praise. When God-fearingness fills your heart, self-praise will vanish.

Types of self-praise

There are different causes of self-praise, which have been mentioned above. Sometimes there is self-praise in a matter in which there is no pride, for instance, a mistaken opinion which seems good to an ignoramus. In this regard, self-praise is of eight types.

The first is self-praise for physical beauty, health, strength, the constitution of the body and a good voice. A man praises himself for the beauties of his physique and forgets that they are vanishing every moment. The remedy to remove it is to think of his contemptible origin, how his face was made beautiful by clay and how it will be rotten and melted in the grave.

The second is self-praise for strength and power. Take the example of the tribe 'Ad, who said, "Who is stronger than us?"

Moreover, a strong man lifted a mountain over his head and threw it down on the soldiers of Mūsā to crush them, but the Merciful had it lifted by the beak of a bird and thrown on his neck. A believer sometimes takes pride. For instance, Sulaymān once said, "I shall this night cohabit with my one hundred wives and beget children." But Allah deprived him of his wish, and he did not beget any child.

The third is self-praise for wisdom and intellect for worldly and religious affairs. He holds his own opinion, thinks another who is opposed to him a fool, does not consult with others and hears the sermons of the learned. The medicine for the above is that he should be grateful to Allah for the wisdom that Allah has given him, think that it may be destroyed by a small disease and think that he has not been given but a little intellect as the Qur'an says.

The fourth is self-praise for pedigree, such as the self-praise of people from the dynasty of Hāshim. Some of them think that they will get salvation for respecting their ancestors, that their sins will be forgiven and that all others are their slaves and servants. Its medicine is to know that your character and conduct are different from those of your predecessors. If you follow them, you cannot have any self-praise, but think that there is real honour in God-fearingness, piety and good conduct. So follow the actions for which they were honoured. To them, every dynasty was equal, and they did not boast about pedigree or ancestry. Allah says, "O men, surely We have created you of a male and a female, and made you tribes and families that you may know each other; surely the most honourable of you with Allah is the one among you most careful (of his duty)" (Qur'an, 49:13). It appears that the origin of all is the same.

The Prophet (ṣ) was once asked, "Who is the most honourable and most intelligent among men?" He did not say that he is the one born of his dynasty. Rather, he said, "The most honourable is whoever remembers death the most and becomes the most prepared for it." The above verse was revealed when Bilāl proclaimed the call to prayer in the Ka'bah on the day of the conquest of Makkah. At that time, al-Ḥārith ibn Hishām, Suhayl ibn 'Amr and Khālid ibn Usayd said, "This black slave is proclaiming the call to prayer!" Then Allah revealed, "Surely the most honourable of you with Allah is the one among you most careful (of his duty)" (Qur'an, 49:13). The Prophet (ṣ) said, "Allah removed from you the pride of the dark age. You all are the children of Adam, and Adam was created of dust."

The Prophet (ṣ) said, "O assembly of Quraysh, let it not be that people come on Resurrection Day with their actions, and you come with the world on your necks, crying, 'O Muḥammad! O Muḥammad!' as I will say thus," meaning he will turn his face away from them. It appears from this that they will be addicted to the world, and their ancestry will be of no use to them.

Allah says, "Warn your nearest relations" (Qur'an, 21:214). When this verse was revealed, the Prophet (ṣ) called all the tribes of Quraysh, saying, "O Fāṭimah bint Muḥammad, O Ṣafiyyah bint 'Abd al-Muṭṭalib, take care of your own actions, as I am not responsible to Allah for any of your actions."

The fifth is the self-praise for oppressive rulers and kings. The medicine is as follows. They should think that they are disgraceful. They will be the object of Allah's extreme hatred for their oppression of people and creation of disturbance in the land. The angels on Resurrection Day will throw Hell on their faces.

The sixth is self-praise for many children, slaves and servants, relatives, friends, helpers and disciples. The unbelievers said, "We have more wealth and children" (Qur'an, 34:35). Consider how they were destroyed. The Muslims thought in the Battle of Ḥunayn that they were superior in number, and as such they fled from the battle field at the first instance. Allah says, "How often has a small party vanquished a numerous host by Allah's permission" (Qur'an, 2:249). So how can you boast of your number? When you are dead, you will be alone, bereft of your friends, relatives and helpers, who will come of no use to you. Then will leave you to be eaten by snakes and worms in graves. They will flee on Resurrection Day from you, the day when you will be in utmost distress.

The seventh is self-praise for riches. The Prophet (ṣ) once saw a poor man sitting by the side of a rich man. The rich man moved away from him, and the Prophet (ṣ) said, "Do you fear his poverty will come to you?" Its medicine is to think that there are many dangers in wealth, rich men have many duties and there are endless rewards for the poor. The poor will enter Paradise long before the rich. Wealth comes and goes; there is no fixity.

The eighth is self-praise for wrong opinions. Allah says, "Is he whose evil deed is made fair-seeming to him so much so that he considers it good?" (Qur'an, 35:8) and "They think that they are well versed in skill of the work of hands" (Qur'an, 18:103). The Prophet (ṣ) said there will appear among his latter followers mistaken notions for which earlier nations were ruined, having split themselves up into different tributes, each satisfied with its own opinion and "each part rejoicing in that which is with them" (Qur'an, 23:53). This is the condition of those who introduced ideas and practices into the religion and take pleasure in that. Its medicine is that his opinion is not free from defect and is not consistent with the Qur'an and Sunnah. The best course is to follow the ways of sages and saints and have faith in Qur'anic verses and traditions and the ways of the Messenger of Allah.

Book 10
Condemnation of delusions

Introduction

Those whose hearts lie in delusion lie in darkness in the bottom of a fathomless ocean. They have no light, as Allah has not given them any. Allah opened to Islam the breasts of those whom He guided to the straight path, and He straightened the hearts of those who are deluded.

Delusions are of four types: delusions of the learned, delusions of the religious, delusions of the Sufis and delusions of the rich. Allah says, "Let not this world's life deceive you, nor let the arch deceiver deceive you in respect of Allah" (Qur'an, 31:33). The Prophet (ṣ) said, "How good is the restraint of the wise from sleep and food. How they defraud the sleeplessness and labour of fools. A mustard seed's weight of God-fearingness and faith are better than an earth full of the works of the deluded."

The Prophet (ṣ) said, "A wise man is someone who humbles himself and does good deeds for what will occur after death, and a fool is someone who follows his low desires and hopes Allah will save him."

Delusion is a kind of ignorance, which to believe a thing but see it as contrary to what it is. The traditions regarding ignorance, therefore, are applicable to delusion. Although delusion is a kind of ignorance, not every kind of ignorance is delusion. Delusion is what brings peace of mind consistent with low desires. Nature is inclined to it, entertaining doubt and falling in Satan's snares. Whoever believes out of vain doubt that he is on the good path of worldly and other-worldly matters is full of delusions. Many men think that they are on the right path, but are in delusion and live in a fool's Paradise. Their delusions, however, are of different classes and degrees.

1
Delusions

Delusions of unbelievers

The life of this world keeps the unbelievers in delusion. They say, "Cash is better than credit," with "cash" being this world and "credit" the next world. What they mean is that this world, which is certain, is better than the next world, which is uncertain and doubtful, as this world's joys and enjoyments and wealth and riches are objects of certitude, whereas the other-worldly gifts are objects of doubt. We shall thus not forsake what is certain for what is doubtful and uncertain. This is a belief of Satan, who said he was better than Adam because he was created of fire, while Adam was created of dust. Allah says of this delusion, "These are they who buy the life of this world for the hereafter, so their chastisement will not be lightened nor will they be helped" (Qur'an, 2:86).

The medicine of this delusion is faith and proof. The medicine of faith is to believe in Allah's words "What is with you passes away and what is with Allah is enduring" (Qur'an, 16:96), "Whatever is with Allah is better" (Qur'an, 28:60), "The hereafter is better and more lasting" (Qur'an, 87:17), "The life of this world is nothing but a provision of vanities" (Qur'an, 3:185) and "Let not this world's life deceive you" (Qur'an, 31:33).

The Prophet (ṣ) told the unbelievers this, with the result that some of them became believers in these principles without wanting proof from him, as they believed that he was the prophet and messenger of Allah. This is similar to a child's blind belief in the words of his father "To go to school is better than sports and games." A boy who does not believe his father is ruined.

The medicine of proof

Proof is another medicine of this delusion, for a thing is known by proof. Every proof is a kind of idea in the mind, an idea which generates peace of mind, although without one's awareness.

There are two basic ideas which Satan gives to people. One is that this world is cash and the next world is credit, which is correct. Another is that cash is better than credit, an idea which should be enquired into. If cash is equal to credit, then credit is better. The misguided unbeliever spends one coin to get credit for ten. He does not say that cash is better than credit and why he should give up one coin for ten. Similarly, if a physician prohibits a patient from eating delicious food and fruits, the patient refrains from enjoying them for fear of future trouble. It appears from this that he remains satisfied with future affairs, forsaking the present, or with credit after forsaking cash.

Merchants travel to many countries by sea for commercial profit in the future. To them, ten rupees in the future are better than one rupee in the present. In like manner, the treasures and enjoyments of the present world are less and are more short lived than those of the next world. Man can expect to live a hundred years at most, which is not even a ten-millionth of the hereafter. It appears from this that we should take one ten-millionth after foregoing one.

Now if you look at the enjoyments of this world, you will find them mixed with troubles and calamities, whereas the enjoyments of the next world are without any trouble or calamity. So the unbeliever's saying that cash is better than credit, or the present is better than future, is erroneous and deceptive. The cause of this delusion is that he believed this upon hearing it from others. Moreover, he thinks that certainty is better than doubt and that this world is certain and the next world is doubtful. But both of these are false, as a sure matter is better than a doubtful matter if they are equal. If it is contrary, the matter stands otherwise.

Merchants, for instance, undertake labour on sure faith, but are not sure about profit. Similarly, a learned man undertakes efforts on sure faith, but is uncertain about gaining a rank in learning. A hunter is certain about hunting, but uncertain about getting game. So to forsake a sure thing to get a doubtful thing becomes necessary. For example, a merchant says, "If I do not carry on trading, I will remain hungry and my loss will be great. If I carry on trading, I may suffer loss, but gain much." A patient likewise swallows bitter pills, uncertain whether he will recover from illness, but he is certain about the bitterness of the medicine. He says, "The bitterness of the medicine is better than fearing death because of illness."

This rule is applicable to the uncertainty of the next world. The days of patience in the world are less in comparison with those of the next world and will last until the end of life. One should thus say, "If people lie about the next world, I will suffer no loss, but my solace in the words will be lost. If what they say comes true, I will remain in Hell for ever without end." In this connection, 'Alī said, "If what they say is true, you and I will suffer no loss. But if what I say is true, I will get salvation and you will be destroyed."

The second basic argument of unbelievers is that the next world is doubtful, which is also erroneous. To believers, the next world is certain and sure for two reasons. One of them is that they believe the words of the prophets and the learned. This is the belief of people in general, who are like a patient who does not know the medicine of his disease, while the physicians and experts prescribe for him a medicine which he takes and which cures him. He does not go about enquiring whether the medicine works and whether there is any proof that it works. Rather, he believes their words and acts, whereas a misguided madman takes their words as erroneous. If he follows the madman and forsakes the prescribed medicine of the experts, he falls into delusion and ruins himself.

The second reason is to know the next world in the revelation of prophets and inspiration in the minds of the friends of Allah. Do not think that in matters of the next world and religion, the Prophet (ṣ) accepted all he heard from Jibrīl just as you accept what you hear from the Prophet (ṣ). His knowledge of things and your knowledge are not the same. Your blind faith is not equal to his knowledge of things. The prophets saw with their inner eyes the true nature of everything in the same way you see with your external eye the material world. The cause is that the real nature of the soul becomes vivid and clear to them. The soul is a spiritual thing coming from the command of Allah. It does not mean that it is opposed to the prohibition of Allah, as it is not the command of world, and the soul is not the world.

The world is of two kinds: material and spiritual, both of which belong to Allah. The material world has length, breadth and space. That which is free from length and breadth belongs to the spiritual world. Its details are secret matters of the soul, and there is no permission to describe it, as delving into the details of predetermination is prohibited.

Whoever has come to know the secrets of the soul has come to know himself. When he knows himself, he knows Allah. When he does not know himself through knowing the secrets of the soul, he does not know Allah. The soul is a stranger to this material world. Its descent into this world was an affair opposed to its nature. When Adam disobeyed Allah, he opposed his own soul, forgetting himself and Allah, so his soul was sent to a world opposed to its nature. When a kernel comes out of its cover, it is said the kernel *fasaqa*, which is the same verb used in the Qur'an to describe the disobedient to Allah. Thus, those who know Allah take out the original smell or odour of the soul and remain satisfied, but those who have little intellect remain satisfied only with hearing words and not with the odour, as it does them harm in the same way the smell of roses does dung worms harm and sunlight does bats harm.

The opening of this door from the secrets of the soul to the spiritual world is called "*ma'rifah*" and "*wilāyah*." Whoever acquires these is called an "*'ārif*" and "*walī*," respectively. These are the first stations of prophets, the last stations of whom are the first stations of the friends of Allah.

The delusion of Satan is that the next world is doubtful. This delusion can be removed by sure faith. When believers disobey the injunctions of Allah and engage themselves in sins, they become partners with unbelievers in this delusion, as they prefer this world to the next. They know that the hereafter is better than the present world, but they prefer the comforts of this life. So faith alone is not sufficient for them for their satisfaction. Allah says, "Most surely I am most Forgiving to him who repents and believes and does good, then continues to follow the right direction" (Qur'an, 20:82). Allah says, "Surely the mercy of Allah is nigh to those who do good (to others)" (Qur'an, 7:56). He says, "I swear by the time most surely man is in loss, except those who believe and do good, and enjoin on each other truth, and enjoin on each other patience" (Qur'an, 103:1-3). So faith alone is not sufficient, and good works are necessary.

The following are examples of the delusions of unbelievers and great transgressors.

Delusions of unbelievers

Some of the unbelievers thought that there were better men than the prophet to receive revelation. Allah has told us that one of two men who were arguing said, "I do not think the hour will come, and even if I am returned to my Lord I will most certainly find a returning place better than this" (Qur'an, 18:36).

This verse is about an unbeliever who created a place for a thousand dinars, and prepared a garden therein for another thousand. He purchased servants and slaves for another thousand and married a beautiful woman for another thousand. A believer then advised him concerning every one of these items, saying

"You have built a building in a garden which will fall to ruin. You have purchased a garden which will fall to ruin. Why did you not purchase a garden in a paradise where there is no destruction? Why did you not purchase servants who cannot fall to ruin and who will not die? Why did you not marry a houri with black eyes who will not die?" The unbeliever said in reply, "Where is this Paradise which people talk about? They speak falsehood. If it exists, I will get in Paradise that which is better than this."

Likewise, Allah describes al-'Āṣ ibn Wā'il as saying, "I shall certainly be given wealth and children" (Qur'an, 19:77). In refuting him, Allah says, "Has he gained knowledge of the unseen, or made a covenant with the Beneficent Allah? By no means!" (Qur'an, 19:78-79). These utterances are the promptings of Satan.

Worldly wealth and comforts are harmful and keep one away from Allah. Out of love for His religious servants, Allah saves them from the world in the same way a man saves his patient from undesirable food and drink. Allah says:

> *Do they think that by what We aid them with of wealth and children, We are hastening to them of good things? No, they do not perceive.* (Qur'an, 23:55-56)
>
> *We draw them near (to destruction) by degrees from whence they know not.* (Qur'an, 7:182)
>
> *We opened for them the doors of all things, until when they rejoiced in what they were given We seized them suddenly, then lo, they were in utter despair.* (Qur'an, 6:44)
>
> *We grant them respite only that they may add to their sins.* (Qur'an, 3:178)
>
> *Do not think Allah to be heedless of what the unjust do; He only respites them to a day on which the eyes will be fixedly open.* (Qur'an, 14:42)

So whoever believes in the above verses, other verses of the Qur'an and the words of the Prophet (ṣ) is saved from delusions. He turns his attention to Fir'awn, Qārūn, Hāmān, Namrūd and others to take lessons from the punishment meted out to them by the Almighty, who says, "But none feels secure from Allah's plan except the people who will perish" (Qur'an, 7:99) and "They devised plans and Allah too had arranged a plan; and Allah is the best of planners" (Qur'an, 8:30).

Delusions of transgressing believers

They say, "We expect mercy from the merciful Allah." They rely on this and neglect their acts of worship, thinking that this expectation is a good religious station and that Allah's mercy is all-encompassing.

This is their delusion about Allah. The fact is that Allah loves the religious and hates sinners. The Prophet (ṣ) said, "A wise man is he who humbles himself and performs deeds for what comes after death, and a fool is he who follows his passions with the hope that Allah will save him." Allah explains this hope, saying, "Surely those who believed and those who fled (their home) and strove hard in the way of Allah—these hope for the mercy of Allah" (Qur'an, 2:218). The cause is that the meaning of virtues in the next world is rewards for actions, as Allah says, "A reward for what they did" (Qur'an, 32:17) and "You will only be paid fully your reward on the Resurrection Day" (Qur'an, 3:185).

So it appears that the condition of reward is good works. Allah promised this and will not break His promise. Al-Ḥasan was once said, "People say, 'We cherish hope,' but they are ruining their good deeds." He replied, "That is not so. It is their vain desire. Whoever fears a thing flees from that thing."

Muslim ibn Yasār said, "Last night I prostrated in such a way that two of my front teeth broke." A man said to him, "I cherish hope in Allah." Muslim replied, "That is impossible. Whoever desires a thing searches for it, and whoever fears a thing flees from it. If a man desires a child but does not marry, or marries but does not cohabit with his wife, or cohabits but does not eject semen into her uterus, he is considered mad. Similarly, whoever hopes for the mercy of Allah but does not have faith, or has faith but does not do good deeds, or does good deeds but does not forsake sins, is a fool.

Whoever marries, cohabits with his wife and ejects semen into her uterus cannot still be certain of a child, but should depend on the favour of Allah. Such a man is an intelligent man. Likewise, a wise man has faith, does good works, gives up evil deeds, stands between fear and hope, fears whether his own deeds are accepted or not, fears that his ultimate end may not be good and hopes that Allah will show mercy to him. Everyone other than such a man is in delusion. When they see the punishment of erroneous people, they will say, "Our Lord, we have seen and we have heard. Therefore send us back and we will do good; surely (now) we are certain" (Qur'an, 32:12). In other words, "We have come to know that Allah is perfect and that He does beget without marriage and without cohabitation. He does not create crops without cultivation and the sowing of seeds. He does not give rewards in the next world without good deeds. Send us back to the world and we shall do good deeds there. Now we have come to know that Your words are true and 'that man will have nothing but what he strives for and that his striving will soon be seen' (Qur'an, 53:39-40)."

Hope for good on two occasions

When repentance crosses the mind of a great sinner, there is a good place for hope. Satan says to him, "Will your repentance be accepted?" at which time he should root out despair by hope and remember that Allah forgives all sins. Allah says, "Say, 'O my servants who have acted extravagantly against their own souls, do not despair of the mercy of Allah. Surely Allah forgives faults altogether. Surely He is the Forgiving, the Merciful" (Qur'an, 39:53). He also says, "Most surely I am most forgiving to him who repents and believes and does good, then continues to follow the right direction" (Qur'an, 20:82).

A man who hopes for forgiveness with repentance is a man of hope, but whoever hopes for forgiveness without turning away from sin lives in delusion. The Prophet (ṣ) said, "Delusions will prevail over the minds of my people in latter days." He said, "People of the first century will be busy with acts of worship, will give in charity from what they have been given, will have fear upon thinking that they will return to Allah, and will engage day and night in worship." He also said, "There will come a time when people will think that the Qur'an is an old book, just as a piece of cloth gets old if used on the body. They will have greed in all their affairs and no fear of Allah. If anybody does any good works, he will say, 'It will be accepted from me.' If he does any evil deed, he will say, 'It will be forgiven, for Allah says, 'For him who fears standing before his Lord are two gardens' (Qur'an, 55:46).'" This will be for that person who fears Allah, the warnings of Allah, and the Qur'an from beginning to end.

2
Categories of the deluded

Delusions occur among four kinds of people:

Religious scholars

There is a party of Islamic scholars who become experts in Sharī'ah. They take pride in their education and expert knowledge, hoping that Allah will not punish them. If they looked with the eye of insight, they would see that knowledge is of two kinds: secular and spiritual. Spiritual learning is about Allah and His attributes and actions. Secular knowledge is of lawful and unlawful things, good and bad habits and so on. Such knowledge is not acquired except through works, without which it has no value.

As an illustration, consider the case of someone with different kinds of diseases which cannot be treated without a mixture of medicines known only to an expert physician. He goes to him, gets a prescription and returns home. He constantly reads it without taking the medicines. A cure in his case is impossible. However, if he takes the medicine, there is hope for a cure.

Similar is the case of a religious scholar who issues rulings on legal matters but does not apply them himself, gives instructions to forsake sins but does not forsake sins himself, learns how to acquire good conduct but does not acquire it. He therefore lives in gross delusion.

Allah says that whoever makes his soul pure will get salvation. He does not say that whoever knows how to make his soul pure and teaches it to others will get salvation. Allah says that a learned man without action is like a dog, or like an ass which bears loads. The Prophet (ṣ) said, "Whoever gains much knowledge without much guidance increases in distance from Allah. He said, "Such a learned man will be thrown into Hell and his intestines will come out. He will roam like the roaming of an ass round a crushing mill." He also said, "The worst man is a dishonest scholar." Abū al-Dardā' said, "There is only one woe for an illiterate man, for Allah can make him learned if He wills. But there are a hundred woes for a scholar who does not benefit by his learning and who will be given the greatest punishment." Whoever has spiritual knowledge but does not act on it is roaming in delusion, which is worse. He is like a person who wishes to serve a king and then learns about the king's character and conduct and all of his matters, but gives up what the king likes and does what he dislikes. Such a person cannot go near the king.

If one knows Allah with true knowledge, he will fear Him. It is impossible for a wise man not to fear a tiger. Allah revealed to Dāwūd, "Fear Me as you fear a tiger." Whoever knows Allah, knows His attributes and that all people are under His control. Allah says, "Those of His servants only who are possessed of knowledge fear Allah" (Qur'an, 35:28). The beginning of the Psalms reads, "Fear of Allah is the root of knowledge." Ibn Mas'ūd said, "God-fearingness is sufficient for knowledge, and lack of it is sufficient for ignorance." Al-Ḥasan said, "A learned man is whoever prays all night, fasts all day long and renounces the world." He said at another time, "A learned man is someone who enquires, does not dispute with others and spreads the wisdom of Allah. If someone obeys him, he praises Allah. If someone disobeys him, he also praises Him. He knows Allah, knows His commands and prohibitions and knows His chosen and unchosen matters."

A second kind of religious scholar is he who acts according to his knowledge. He is engaged in open acts of worship and gives up sins, but does not take care of his mind. He does not remove from his mind evils like pride, hatred, show, bad treatment and desire for name and fame. He does not pay heed to the words of the Prophet (ṣ), who said, "A little show is shirk"; "Whoever has pride equal to the weight of a mustard seed will not enter Paradise"; "Hatred destroys all virtues just as fire burns fuel"; and "Greed for honour and wealth generate hypocrisy just as water grows crops." Such a learned men forgets the *ḥadīth* "Allah looks not at your figures but at your hearts and actions." They know outward acts of worship, but not inward qualities.

The heart is the root, as nobody will get salvation unless he has a sound one. Such a man is like a well of stool of which the outer cover is good but whose interior smells obnoxious. Or like a house on the roof of which a lamp is lit but whose interior is full of darkness. Or like a man who adorns the door of his house to receive the king but spreads out stool in its interior. This is his delusion. As an illustration, consider a man who sows seeds of corn of which corn and weeds grow. He orders that the weeds be taken out and keeps the corn plants. But his men cut only the top portion of the weeds. As a result, they grow stronger with many branches. Similarly, the evils of the mind are the root of sins. Whoever does not purify his soul from these evils, his divine service does not become perfect.

The third kind of religious scholars are those who know that these internal evils are bad, but owing to their self-praise they think that they are free from these evils and that Allah will not try them for this. When their pride is expressed, they say that it is not pride, but it is disclosing the honour of learning. They say that their dishonour is the dishonour of Islam. They should remember the case of 'Umar, who, when he went to visit Syria, was wearing course clothes, which the people disliked. He said to them, "We are a people who have been honoured by the religion of Islam. We are not seekers of honour from other peoples."

The fourth kind of religious scholars are those who gain knowledge, purify their limbs and adorn themselves with acts of worship. They forsake open sins and purify their minds from show, hatred, pride and other evils, yet they entertain delusions and keep away from meditation, seeking name and fame instead. They also write books to get praise and accuse others of bad writing, and they copy the writings of others with amendments.

Religious scholars of unnecessary knowledge

We have mentioned above the conditions of religious scholars who acquire necessary knowledge. Now we shall describe those who remain satisfied with unnecessary branches of knowledge after giving up necessary knowledge. Some of them acquire education of administration and worldly laws and regulations. They are misguided in actions and knowledge. Regarding their erroneous actions, they are like the patients who learn and teach the prescription of medicines. Moreover, they are like the patient who remains in the mouth of destruction owing to insanity, but learns of the medicine for the disease arising out of menstruation and reads it day and night.

In like manner, love of the world is strong in the mind of jurists who are always engaged in the laws of divorce and other laws. Then Satan leads them to erroneous paths. From the point of view of delusions about knowledge, he learns only to give *fatwās* that he has learnt. He does not learn the Qur'an and Ḥadīth, nor does he even want to learn them. He gives up the learning of divine knowledge, with which Allah and His attributes are known and which lead to God-fearingness and piety. True knowledge of Islamic law increases one's fear of Allah, for Allah says, "Why should not then a company from every party from among them go forth that they may apply themselves to obtain understanding in religion, and that they may warn their people when they come back to them that they may be cautious?" (Qur'an, 9:122).

Another group of religious scholars learn scholastic theology (*'ilm al-kalām*). Among them, one group are guided and another misguided. Those who do not guide towards the ways of the

Prophet (ṣ) are the misguided ones, while those who guide towards the ways of the Prophet (ṣ) have found guidance. But both of them are in delusion. The latter thinks that arguments are necessary and the best to acquire the nearness of Allah. They also think that religion does not become perfect until arguments are learnt and that those who have faith without proof are not perfect men. Their whole life is spent in argumentation. The Prophet (ṣ) said, "The nation which is firm on a true path is never misguided except for mutual quarrels." One day, the Prophet (ṣ) went to his Companions and saw that they were quarrelling with one another. He grew angry at them and said, "Have you been ordered to set one verse of the Qur'an against another? Look what you have been commanded and act accordingly and refrain from what you have been prohibited."

Another group of religious scholars remain busy in sermons and invocations. Those among them who deliver sermons regarding character and conduct, God-fearingness, patience, gratefulness, reliance on Allah, sure faith and other attributes are placed high in rank. Nevertheless, such people still have some delusions, as they do not act according to all of their instructions. They love self-praise, thinking that they are the embodiment of all virtues and that they are sincere workers for religions. In them is a subtle desire for show.

Another group of religious scholars drift away from their sermons. When delivering them, they discuss wonderful stories unrelated to Sharī'ah and knowledge. Some of them deliver sermons in ornamental language, poetry and love episodes. They deal with separation and the unity of lovers and beloveds. In addition, they mix falsehood with truth.

Another group of religious scholars condemn the world and recite the verses and traditions relating to the condemnation of the world, but they do not follow those teachings.

Another group spend their time learning Ḥadīth. They collect chains of transmission and travel to collect them.

Another group of religious scholars remain busy with grammar, poetry and many foreign tongues. They erroneously believe that Allah will forgive them for being preservers of the Qur'an and Ḥadīth and for guiding Muslims. They ought to know that the best kernel is actions, and that knowledge of actions is like the cover of a kernel.

Another group wrongly hold that Allah will judge men just as the judges of the world pass judgement. Take for instance, a scholar who gives *fatwās* that if a wife waives her dower, her husband will not get any punishment. This is a delusion because the wife often foregoes the dower owing to his cruel treatment of her. Allah says, "If they of themselves are pleased to give up to you a portion of it, then eat it with enjoyment and with wholesome result" (Qur'an, 4:4). The above remission was made by compulsion and not voluntarily.

The religious

There delusions are regarding prayer, the recitation of the Qur'an, pilgrimage and so on. A class of religious men forsake compulsory duties and remain busy with additional duties. Doing so is the result of the whisperings of Satan. Another group of religious men go to extremes in stating the intention of the prayer, another in the pronunciation of the words and another in the recitation of the Qur'an. Another group do not go on the pilgrimage after paying the dues of others and do not get the parents' permission. And another group seek name and fame in their renunciation.

The delusions of the Sufis are strong. There are many kinds of Sufis. One kind adopts the habits of real Sufis in dress, character and conduct, yet inwardly they have delusions. They think they have become real Sufis, although they cannot purify their minds.

One class of Sufi walk in the ways of divine knowledge, and when they see any light in their minds they stop then and do not proceed further thinking that they have attained perfection. This is a delusion. They are just like a man who goes to serve the king, but halts at seeing a beautiful garden and spends all the time without going to the place of the king. There are seventy screens of Allah. If he reaches only one screen, he thinks he has attained his object.

The Qur'an says of Ibrāhīm, "So when the night over-shadowed him, he saw a star. He said, 'Is this my Lord?' So when it set, he said, 'I do not love the setting ones'" (Qur'an, 6:76). What was meant by "Lord" was not the star, as Ibrāhīm had been seeing it from his earliest years and had come to know that it is not a deity to be worshipped. What was meant, rather, is a screen of light. A sojourner in the paths of religion sees so many screens of light, which they cross in order to see the divine light, as Allah says, "Thus did We show Ibrāhīm the kingdom of the heavens and the earth and that he might be of those who are sure" (Qur'an, 6:75).

The first screen which falls between a servant and Allah is the screen of the soul, which is one of the lights of Allah, also called "the essence of the heart" or "subtle thing" (*laṭīfah*). In it are reflected the full particulars of the soul. It can also entertain the world, as it reflects the true nature of everything.

The rich

One group among the rich have greed for constructing mosques, schools, bridges and other works of public utility, so that men can see such works and their names are remembered even after death. This belief is pardonable. Another group of rich men spend their lawful earnings on the construction of mosques, but fall into delusion for two reasons. The first reason is that they do it for show and praise from others. The second reason is that they embellish the mosque with paintings and pictures which are prohibited, as the attention of those who pray may be diverted from their prayers. The punishment for this goes to the builder, who lives in the delusion that he does pious acts. The sages of yore would hesitate to enter such a mosque.

The disciples of 'Īsā once said, "Look at what this church is like?" 'Īsā replied, "I tell you in truth that my followers will construct lofty buildings and churches, and Allah will destroy all of them for the sins of the builders."

The gold and silver and bricks of the mosque which you consider good have no value to Allah. The dearest thing to Allah is the hearts of pious men, which are immersed in the love of Allah.

The Prophet (ṣ) said, "When you embellish your mosques with variegated workmanship, and the Qur'an with gold and silver, your condition will be deplorable." Al-Ḥasan said that when the Prophet (ṣ) wished to construct the mosque of Madīnah, Jibrīl came to him and said, "Make its roof a cubit higher than the head, and do not embellish it with different kinds of workmanship."

Another class of rich man give charity to the poor and beggars, but in a place where people gather. Moreover, they choose poor men who express their gratitude for charity and broadcast their charity. They make one pilgrimage after another, but they do not give in charity to hungry neighbours. Ibn Mas'ūd said, "There will be people in latter times who will make pilgrimage without cause." Once, a rich man sought Bishr al-Ḥāfī's advice about making pilgrimage, and the latter asked him, "Why do you wish to make additional pilgrimages?" The man replied, "To seek the pleasure of Allah." Bishr said, "You can gain His greater pleasure by paying the debts of ten debtors, removing the wants of those who are in want, giving charity to poor Muslims with large families, or distributing the sum to ten orphan boys."

Another class of rich men hoard money and worship in such a way that no expenditure is necessary; for example, they fast and stay awake at night. They live in delusion because they are miserly, which is harmful. They are those in whose clothes a serpent enters and instead of removing the serpent, they keep busy cleaning their clothes. Miserliness is so strong for others that they do not spend on good works other than *zakāh*. And even then, they give the *zakāh* only to poor people who serve them and help them in their work.

Three means of gaining fortune

The next world

In order to save oneself from the above delusions, three means should be adopted: intellect, learning and knowledge of a thing. "Intellect" means "the inborn light whereby a man knows the true nature of everything." If it does not arise in early years, it will not arise in the future. It can be increased by experience and other methods if the intellect is sharp. The Prophet (ṣ) said, "Blessed is whoever distributed intellect among His servants in different measures." Once, a man asked the Prophet (ṣ), "What is the rank of a man who is near Allah on Resurrection Day, a man who fasts all day, prays the night vigil prayer, makes the greater and lesser pilgrimages, gives charity for the sake of Allah, does jihad, serves the sick, remains present in funeral prayers and helps the weak?" The Prophet (ṣ) answered, "He will get rewards according to his intellect."

A man was once praising another man before the Prophet (ṣ), who then asked, "How is his intellect? For a fool commits more sins than sinners owing to his foolishness." Similarly, some people once mentioned a man's great devotions before the Prophet (ṣ), who then asked, "How is his intellect?" They replied, "He has none." He said, "He has not attained the rank you wish to give him." It appears that a sharp intellect is a special gift from Allah.

The second means of removing delusions is to have four types of knowledge: knowledge of oneself, knowledge of Allah, knowledge of the next world and knowledge of this world. Man is a sojourner in the world. He has been given a beastly nature as well as a spiritual nature to know Allah. When one comes to know these four matters, love for Allah arises in one's mind. When all of one's actions are to please Allah and for the next world, he will find guidance. When he prefers the present world to the next world, and prefers his passions and low desires to the pleasure of Allah, it will become impossible to save himself from delusions.

The third means of removing delusions is learning. The merits of learning have already been described in the first chapter of "Worship," so they need not be repeated here.

Index of Qur'anic verses

(1:6), 81

(2:57), 77
(2:83), 145
(2:86), 397
(2:89-90), 210
(2:109), 213
(2:156), 365
(2:180), 254
(2:204-205), 328
(2:206), 365
(2:207), 280
(2:218), 403
(2:225), 57
(2:237), 202
(2:249), 391
(2:255), 53
(2:264), 386
(2:268), 41, 264
(2:269), 36, 70
(2:271), 337
(2:284), 56
(2:286), 125

(3:14), 240
(3:39), 184
(3:119), 328
(3:120), 209, 211, 215
(3:134), 73, 192, 194
(3:139), 33
(3:159), 367
(3:178), 402
(3:180), 274
(3:185), 397, 403

(4:4), 411
(4:32), 211
(4:37), 274
(4:89), 215
(4:95), 10
(4:102), 336
(4:114), 142
(4:140), 143
(4:142-143), 329
(4:172), 363

(5:1), 153
(5:54), 367

(6:8), 364
(6:44), 402
(6:52), 364
(6:53), 212
(6:75), 24, 412
(6:76), 412
(6:110), 60
(6:125), 21
(6:153), 45

(7:12), 183, 366
(7:16-17), 42
(7:27), 336
(7:31), 74, 116, 122
(7:56), 401
(7:99), 403
(7:100), 16

(7:146), 354, 362
(7:175-176), 382
(7:176), 9
(7:179), 56
(7:182), 402
(7:199), 66, 169, 191, 192, 202
(7:200-201), 97
(7:201), 17, 44

(8:2-3), 89
(8:17), 387
(8:24), 3
(8:29), 35
(8:30), 403
(8:60), 336

(9:24), 81
(9:25), 384
(9:73), 187
(9:75-77), 295
(9:103), 294
(9:112), 88
(9:122), 409

(10:7), 26
(10:24), 312

(11:6), 264
(11:15), 250
(11:15-16), 306
(11:112), 81

(12:9), 210
(12:31), 13
(12:55), 313, 326
(12:92), 203

(13:26), 87
(13:28), 16, 61

(14:15), 354
(14:35), 255
(14:42), 402

(15:43-44), 61
(15:75), 36

(16:22), 362
(16:23), 354
(16:96), 397
(16:98), 42
(16:105), 156
(16:128), 376

(17:29), 73, 282
(17:36), 57
(17:37), 357
(17:65), 42
(17:72), 24
(17:85), 5, 308

(18:7), 244
(18:7-8), 228
(18:28), 364
(18:36), 401
(18:46), 311
(18:49), 152
(18:65), 36
(18:82), 254
(18:103), 384, 392
(18:103-104), 320
(18:110), 321

(19:54), 153
(19:69), 362
(19:71), 80
(19:77), 402
(19:78-79), 402

(20:82), 401, 405
(20:114), 49

(21:20), 383
(21:37), 49
(21:79), 36
(21:214), 391

(22:37), 59

(23:1-10), 88
(23:47), 212, 364
(23:53), 392
(23:55-56), 402
(23:60), 382

(24:2), 188
(24:21), 389
(24:22), 201, 203
(24:30), 127
(24:35), 14
(24:37), 113
(24:40), 14

(25:43), 42
(25:60), 363
(25:63), 196, 197
(25:67), 73, 282

(26:88-89), 383
(26:215), 367

(28:39), 364
(28:60), 397
(28:83), 305

(29:69), 18, 310

(30:7), 26

(31:17), 172
(31:33), 395, 397

(32:7-8), 380
(32:12), 404
(32:17), 403

(33:72), 20, 114

(34:35), 391

(35:6), 43
(35:8), 392
(35:10), 321
(35:28), 367, 407
(35:43), 214

(36:9), 95
(36:10), 61
(36:60), 43

(38:62), 364

(39:9), 382
(39:22), 21, 36
(39:53), 404
(39:72), 362

(40:1), 167
(40:35), 354
(40:60), 54, 354, 362, 363

(41:26), 365
(41:34), 198

(42:51), 28

(43:31), 364
(43:32), 364
(43:86), 210

(44:39), 242
(44:42), 242

(45:23), 9

(47:38), 276

(48:26), 183
(48:29), 14, 71, 187

(49:3), 83
(49:6), 166, 171, 172
(49:11), 151
(49:12), 51, 159, 166, 172
(49:13), 69, 390, 391
(49:15), 71

(50:18), 142

(51:49), 41
(51:56), 7, 80

(53:11), 24
(53:32), 385
(53:39-40), 404

(55:46), 405

(56:36), 151

(57:12), 33
(57:20), 87, 240
(57:21), 210

(58:11), 33, 83, 108
(58:22), 376

(59:2), 384
(59:9), 215, 274, 276, 278, 279
(59:19), 3

(62:5), 381

(63:1), 328
(63:9), 250

(64:15), 250

(65:2-3), 35, 264

(66:6), 93
(66:10), 170

(68:4), 66, 90, 279
(68:11), 169, 172
(68:13), 169

(71:12), 254

(74:31), 7

(75:20-21), 315

(76:1-2), 378
(76:9), 321

(79:24), 308, 363
(79:40), 83
(79:40-41), 9, 79, 240

(80:17-22), 377
(80:18-19), 378
(80:21-22), 378

(83:14), 16, 77

(87:16-17), 315
(87:17), 397

(89:27-28), 5, 61

(91:9), 21, 310
(91:9-10), 65

(92:5-7), 61

(96:4-5), 24
(96:6-7), 250

(99:7-8), 77

(102:1), 250

(103:1-3), 401

(104:1), 169

(107:4-6), 321

(111:4), 169

(113:3), 125

Index

'Abbās ibn Dihqān, 281
al-'Abbās ibn Mirdās, 150
'Abd al-'Azīz ibn Abī Rawwād, 372
'Abd al-Ḥamīd ibn Sa'd, 271
'Abd al-Malik ibn Marwān, 360
'Abd al-Raḥmān ibn Abī Laylā, 53
'Abd al-Raḥmān ibn 'Awf, 290, 371
'Abd al-Raḥmān ibn Ibrāhīm Duhaym, 117
'Abd al-Raḥmān ibn Samurah, 342
'Abd al-Wāḥid ibn Zayd, 107, 262
Abdāl, 96, 106, 269, 375
'Abdullāh al-Thaqafī, 137
'Abdullāh ibn Abī al-Khansā', 153
'Abdullāh ibn Abī Ya'la, 151
'Abdullāh ibn al-Mubārak, 169
'Abdullāh ibn al-Zubayr, 117
'Abdullāh ibn 'Amr, 184, 189, 206, 207
'Abdullāh ibn Ja'far, 272, 279
'Abdullāh ibn Jarād, 156
'Abdullāh ibn Mas'ūd, 45, 185
'Abdullāh ibn Salām, 141, 383
'Abdullāh ibn 'Umar, 123, 153, 305
Abū al-Dardā', 36, 67, 147, 184, 198, 227, 238, 252, 346, 367, 371, 375, 376, 407
Abū al-Haytham ibn al-Tayhān, 153, 154
Abū al-Jawzā', 117
Abū al-Ṭayyib, 312
Abū 'Alī al-Jurjānī, 361
Abū Bakr al-Ṣiddīq, 33, 37, 51, 117, 137, 147, 148, 176, 190, 200, 201, 221, 293, 342, 356, 361
Abū Bakr ibn 'Ayyāsh, 234
Abū Ḍamḍam, 196
Abū Dharr, 68, 116, 141, 194, 266, 290, 369, 370
Abū Ḥanīfah, 51
Abū Ḥāzim, 228, 264
Abū Hurayrah, 52, 105, 118, 161, 174, 193, 196, 202, 223, 260, 373
Abū Jahl, 148
Abū Jandal, 167
Abū Juḥayfah, 104
Abū Kabīr al-Hudhalī, 149
Abū Kabshah al-Anmārī, 210
Abū Khuzaymah al-Yarbū'ī, 195
Abū Mas'ūd al-Thaqafī, 364
Abū Mūsā al-Ash'arī, 214, 259
Abū Muslim al-Khawlānī, 339
Abū Sa'īd al-Khudrī, 118, 374
Abū Sufyān, 167, 338
Abū Sulaymān al-Dārānī, 39, 108, 109, 111, 229
Abū Tha'labah, 384
Abū 'Ubaydah, 226, 229, 230, 373
Abū Umāmah al-Bāhilī, 229, 293
Abū 'Uthmān al-Ḥīrī, 91

Abū Yazīd al-Bisṭāmī, 109, 360
al-Abwā', 130
Abyssinia, 112
Adam (prophet), 13, 46, 48, 55, 101, 231, 242, 356, 366, 391, 397, 400; children of, 13, 20, 43, 103, 165, 177, 184, 192, 193, 223, 244, 251, 259, 261, 297, 336, 391
al-'Aḍbā' (a she camel of the Prophet), 226
ahl al-ṣuffah, 117
Ahl al-Sunnah wa al-Jamā'ah, 246
Aḥmad ibn Ḥanbal, 51
al-Aḥnaf ibn Qays, 91, 138, 146
'Ā'ishah, 14, 37, 66, 104, 110, 118, 123, 146, 149, 152, 162, 169, 190, 193, 201, 202, 204, 205, 270, 278, 290, 326, 370, 375, 385
Aktham ibn Ṣayfī, 198
al-'Alā' ibn Ziyād, 41, 130
'Alī al-Jurjānī, 111
'Alī ibn Abī Ṭālib, 14, 23, 26, 36, 77, 85, 120, 172, 177, 190, 198, 229, 231, 232, 234, 280, 288, 302, 325, 330, 371, 373, 388, 399
'Alī ibn al-Ḥusayn, 199, 348
'Alī ibn Yazīd, 185
'Ammār ibn Yāsir, 174
'Amr ibn al-Ahtam, 198
'Amr ibn al-'Āṣ, 42, 189, 206, 207
Anas ibn Malik, 37, 68, 90, 105, 140, 160, 198, 226, 268, 371, 372
Anṣār(ī), 51, 147, 184, 207, 226, 278, 337. *See also* Madīnan Helper(s)
'aql. *See* intellect
'Arābah ibn Aws, 198
Arabia, 154, 245
'ārif, 401
al-'Āṣ ibn Wā'il, 402
al-Aṣbagh ibn Nubātah, 373
Ashaj, 197
'Aṭā' al-Sulamī, 151
'Aṭā' ibn Abī Rabāḥ, 142, 197
Āyah al-Kursī, 53
Ayyūb (prophet), 389
Ayyūb al-Sakhtiyānī, 302

badal, 38
Badr, Battle of, 146
Baghdad, 234
Bakr ibn 'Abdullāh al-Muzanī, 107
Bal'am ibn Bā'urā', 381
Banū Shaybah, 243
al-Barā' ibn 'Āzib, 67, 138, 160
Bishr al-Ḥāfī. *See* Bishr ibn al-Ḥārith
Bishr ibn al-Ḥārith, 276, 281, 303, 413
Būlas, 356
Byzantium, 112, 238, 357

Christian(s), 20, 78, 117, 148, 204, 262, 265, 349
Companions, 41, 60, 68, 69, 71, 82, 105, 116, 122, 141, 147-149, 151, 156, 160, 162, 170, 175, 176, 184, 187, 195, 196, 198, 204, 205, 207, 208, 221, 224, 225, 227, 236, 242, 246, 261, 269, 276, 278, 291, 293, 317, 322, 326, 334, 356, 358, 359, 364, 368, 372, 382, 389, 410
cursing, 147, 148. *See also la'n*

Dāwūd (prophet), 84, 184, 223, 242, 388, 407
Dāwūd al-Ṭā'ī, 82
Dāwūd ibn Hilāl, 224
Devil, the, 12, 15, 29, 40-50, 53, 164. *See also* Satan
Dhū al-Kifl, 186
Dhū al-Nūn, 110
Dhū al-Qarnayn, 204, 297, 298

al-dunyā, 7

Egypt, 85, 130, 271

fasaqa, 400
Fāṭimah (daughter of the Prophet), 105, 154, 295, 296, 391
fatwā(s), 167, 409, 411. *See also* legal ruling
Fir'awn, 148, 232, 296, 308, 363, 364, 403
Friday sermon, 37
al-Fuḍayl ibn Ghazwān, 335
al-Fuḍayl ibn 'Iyāḍ, 105, 195, 228, 305

Guarded Tablet, the, 27, 31. *See also al-Lawḥ al-Maḥfūẓ*

Ḥā' Mīm, 167
Ḥabbān ibn Hilāl, 284
ḥadīth(s), 6, 10, 12, 20, 28, 33, 36, 38, 42, 44, 50, 56, 89, 94, 102, 112, 118, 140, 141, 148, 168, 170, 183, 206, 210, 221, 231, 242, 250, 254, 260, 261, 267, 274, 285, 310, 321, 326, 331, 335, 338, 348, 354, 366, 369, 372, 408-411; *qudsī*, 12, 38, 231
al-ḥaḍrah al-rubūbiyyah, 21
Ḥafṣ al-'Ābid al-Maṣīṣī, 117
al-Ḥajjāj ibn Furāfiṣah, 117
al-Ḥajjāj ibn Yūsuf, 347
Hāmān, 364, 403
Ḥammād ibn Salamah, 173
Ḥamzah (uncle of the Prophet), 318
Haram ibn Ḥayyān, 241, 242
al-Ḥārith al-Muḥāsibī, 284, 289, 290, 335
al-Ḥārith ibn Hishām, 391
Hārūn (prophet), 232
Hārūn al-Rashīd, 112, 272, 360
al-Ḥasan al-Anṭāqī, 280
al-Ḥasan al-Baṣrī, 26, 32, 41, 44, 53, 84, 114, 142, 151, 154, 161, 162, 164, 168, 169, 172, 176, 185, 196, 198, 225, 228, 229, 231, 236, 252, 270, 302, 315, 337, 347, 371
al-Ḥasan ibn 'Alī, 269, 271, 272
Ḥassān ibn Thābit, 149
hawnan, 197
Ḥawwā', 101, 242
Helencha, 112
Hind bint 'Utbah, 167
Ḥirā', cave of, 56
Hishām ibn 'Abd al-Malik, 204
Hishām ibn al-'Āṣ, 281
Homs, 238
Hūd, Sūrah, 81
Ḥudhayfah, 82, 147, 174, 280, 368
Ḥunayn, Battle of, 154, 334, 391; booties of, 150; camels of, 150; day of, 384
al-Ḥusayn ibn 'Alī, 199, 270, 272

i'tikāf, 51
Iblīs, 46, 48, 49, 55
Ibn 'Abbās, 33, 36, 69, 125, 141, 146, 151, 152, 161, 178, 210, 229, 271, 362, 382, 385
Ibn Abī Mālik, 373
Ibn al-Mubārak, 359
Ibn al-Sammāk, 360
Ibn Jurayj, 363, 385
Ibn Mas'ūd, 45, 137, 153, 261, 264, 302, 304, 384, 407, 413
Ibn Sālim, 112
Ibn 'Umar, 119, 184
Ibn Umm Maktūm, 127
Ibn Wahb, 372
Ibrāhīm (prophet), 24, 224, 255, 412; Station of, 276
Ibrāhīm al-Khawwāṣ, 86, 96, 117

Ibrāhīm al-Taymī, 117, 335
Ibrāhīm ibn Adham, 54, 90, 113, 117, 120, 302, 318, 349, 372
Ibrāhīm ibn Maysarah, 146
al-Ikhlāṣ, Sūrah, 204
'Ikrimah, 184
ilhām, 27; *ilāhī*, 12
'ilm al-kalām, 409
'Imrān, son of, 227
'Imrān ibn Ḥuṣayn, 295
in shā' Allah, 153
India, 112
intellect, 5, 11, 188, 414
Iraq, 112, 241, 317
'Īsā (prophet), 49, 75, 83, 96, 104, 107, 117, 127, 144, 160, 161, 184, 191, 222, 225-227, 231, 233-235, 252, 258, 268, 296, 322, 325, 344, 346, 358, 359, 363, 373, 374, 412
'ishā'. *See* nightfall prayer
Ismā'īl (prophet), 153, 210
Israel, children of, 45, 127, 170, 192, 222, 223, 369
istidlāl, 27
'Iyāḍ ibn Ḥimār, 146

Ja'far al-Ṣādiq, 270
Ja'far ibn Muḥammad, 84, 184
al-Jārūd ibn al-Mundhir, 176
Jew(s), 20, 78, 148, 210, 265, 360, 381
Jibrīl, 53, 56, 159, 169, 225, 260, 267, 280, 358, 400, 413
jihad, 10, 43, 58, 83, 84, 102, 155, 257, 327, 337, 340, 346, 347, 386, 414
Jubayr ibn Muṭ'im, 275
Jubb al-Ḥuzn, 322
Judgement Day, 129, 163, 169, 192, 195, 197, 203, 205, 331
al-Junayd al-Baghdādī, 69, 109, 361

Ka'b al-Aḥbār, 14
Ka'b ibn Mālik, 359
Ka'bah, 147, 202, 203, 243, 276, 391
Kahmas, 105
kashf, 17
Khadījah, 296
al-Khaḍir, 179
Khālid ibn Ma'dān, 175, 302
al-Khalīl ibn Aḥmad, 199
khawāṭir, 40
Khawlah (wife of Uthmān ibn Maẓ'ūn), 58
Khaybar, siege of, 275
khayr, 254
Khaythamah ibn 'Abd al-Raḥmān, 50
Khinzib, 42, 55
kibr, 361. *See also* self-conceit
Kirām Kātibūn, 38
Kūfah, 241

la'n, 148. *See also* cursing
laṭīfah, 412. *See also* subtle thing
al-Lawḥ al-Maḥfūẓ, 27. See *also* Guarded Tablet, the
al-Layth ibn Sa'd, 272, 273
legal ruling, 59, 167. *See also* *fatwā(s)*
al-Likām, 86
Lote tree, 56
Luqmān al-Ḥakīm, 69, 105, 141, 144, 157, 173, 199, 228, 230
Lūṭ (prophet), 170

Madīnah, 130, 223, 270, 272, 290, 294, 304, 305, 372, 413
Madīnan Helper(s), 51, 147, 184, 207, 226, 278, 337. *See also* *Anṣār(ī)*,
Magian, 20
Mā'iz, 161
Makkah, 120, 130, 202, 203, 372, 391

Mālik ibn Anas, 51, 144, 272
Mālik ibn Aws ibn al-Ḥadathān, 191
Mālik ibn Dīnar, 105, 120, 161, 174, 190, 199, 229
Ma'n ibn Zā'idah, 271, 272
al-Manṣūr ibn al-Mu'tazz, 139
Ma'qil ibn Yasār, 342
ma'rifah, 401
Ma'rūf al-Karkhī, 123
Maryam, 296
Maslamah ibn 'Abd al-Malik, 253
Maymūn ibn Mihrān, 16, 157
Maymūnah, 127
Messenger of Allah, 41, 42, 58, 59, 66, 81, 136, 146, 147, 156, 160-162, 184, 189, 197, 200, 203, 204, 214, 369, 389, 392. *See also* Muḥammad (prophet)
Mīkā'īl, 280
Misṭaḥ, 201
mithqāls, 262
Mu'ādh ibn Jabal, 136, 137, 158, 304, 323, 324
Mu'āwiyah, 138, 152, 198, 230, 269, 270
mubāda'ah, 12
mudd(s), 116, 117
Muḥammad (prophet), 90, 95, 105, 179, 193, 207, 210, 242, 251, 255, 268, 279, 280, 293, 391. *See also* Messenger of Allah
Muḥammad ibn al-Ḥusayn ibn 'Alī, 356
Muḥammad ibn al-Munkadir, 276
Muḥammad ibn Ka'b, 172, 195, 253
Muḥammad ibn 'Umar, 117
Muḥammad ibn Wāsi', 105, 261
Mujāhid, 168, 177, 197, 321
mujtahid, 198
mukāshafah, 12
Mūsā (prophet), 46, 107, 119, 125, 154, 157, 170, 171, 179, 208, 226, 232, 242, 260, 269, 279, 358, 364, 390
Mūsā ibn al-Ashajj, 120
Muṣ'ab ibn al-Zubayr, 173
al-Muslim ibn Sa'īd, 117
Muslim ibn Yasār, 403
Muṭarrif, 158, 385

nafs, 5; *al-ammārah bi al-sū'*, 5; *al-lawwāmah*, 5; *al-muṭma'innah*, 5
Namrūd, 363, 403
night vigil prayer, 118, 330, 414
nightfall prayer, 139, 241
Nu'aymān, 148
Nūḥ (prophet), 47, 170, 225, 242, 355

Persia, 238, 357

qalb, 4
Qaran, 241
Qārūn, 403
Qatādah, 161, 364
qīrāṭs, 290
Qurayshite, 153, 280

Rabī'ah, 176; and Muḍar, 241
Rāb'iah al-'Adawiyyah, 128
Rāfi' ibn 'Umar, 342
rak'ahs, 121, 144, 202, 304
Ramaḍān, 94, 329
Resurrection Day, 10, 27, 32, 33, 51, 66, 68, 84, 102-104, 106, 114, 143, 146, 148, 155, 159, 163-165, 170, 174, 194, 198, 202, 204, 224, 225, 239, 240, 252, 260, 261, 274, 290, 292, 298, 303, 305, 317, 322, 323, 325, 332, 334, 339, 341, 342, 344, 348, 356-358, 379, 381, 391, 392, 414

revelation, 17, 27, 28, 37, 38, 49, 167, 201, 400, 401. *See also waḥy*
rūḥ, 4

Sa'd ibn Mu'ādh, 338
Sa'dā bint 'Awf, 273
Ṣafiyyah bint 'Abd al-Muṭṭalib, 391
Ṣafiyyah bint Ḥuyay, 51, 52
Ṣafwān ibn Sulaym, 137
Sahl ibn 'Abdullāh al-Tustarī, 94, 96, 106, 117, 279
Sa'īd ibn Abī Marwān, 347
Sa'īd ibn al-'Āṣ, 151
Sa'īd ibn Khālid, 273
salām, 157
Salīm ibn Jābir, 159
Salmān al-Fārisī, 82, 190, 234, 252, 379
Sam'ān (the Christian), 349
al-Sāmirī, 269
al-Sarī al-Saqaṭī, 86, 111
Satan, 5, 17, 40-44, 46-48, 50-56, 60, 61, 68, 69, 83, 84, 96, 97, 104, 106, 125-127, 130, 138, 145, 148, 156, 166, 174, 179, 183-185, 190, 192-194, 200, 205, 214, 228, 229, 239, 252, 264, 277, 301, 317, 319, 334-337, 340, 366, 369, 378, 395, 397, 398, 401, 402, 404, 409, 411. *See also* Devil, the
self-conceit, 191, 361, 362, 371. *See also kibr*
self-praise, 191, 361, 371, 385, 386. *See also 'ujb*
al-Sha'bī, 190, 262
Shaddād ibn Aws, 323, 338
al-Shāfi'ī, 51, 187, 200, 273
shahādah, 328
Shaqīq al-Balkhī, 105, 120, 348
Sharī'ah, 25, 35, 71, 75, 78, 83, 122, 136, 148, 159, 189, 199, 282, 283, 316, 406, 410
al-Shiblī, 108, 360
ṣiddīq, 115
ṣiddīqūn, 33, 85
sikbāj, 120
son of Adam. *See* Adam, children of,
subtle thing, 179, 412. *See also laṭīfah*
Sufis, 28, 35, 87, 118, 395, 411
Sufyān al-Thawrī, 50, 84, 117, 121, 136, 195, 206, 261, 264, 305, 348, 349, 372
Sufyān ibn 'Uyaynah, 177
Suhayl ibn 'Amr, 203, 391
Sulaymān (prophet), 36, 53, 184, 223, 239, 258, 354, 390
Sulaymān al-Khawwāṣ, 117
Sulaymān ibn 'Abd al-Malik, 173, 273
Sulaymān ibn Yasār, 129, 130
sunnah, 25, 119, 142, 246, 329, 392
sūrah, 179, 259
Syria, 167, 229, 347, 375, 408

tahajjud . *See* night vigil prayer
takabbur, 361
Ṭalḥah ibn 'Ubaydullah, 273
Tamīm al-Dārī, 368
al-Ṭanāfisī, 243
Ṭāwūs, 380
Thābit ibn Abī Mālik, 373
Tha'labah ibn Ḥāṭib, 293-295
Thawbān, 158
Tihāmah, hillock of, 224

Ubayy ibn Ka'b, 14, 344
Uḥud, Battle of, 90, 140, 201, 385; mountain of, 290
'ujb, 361, 371. *See also* self-praise
'Umar ibn 'Abd al-'Azīz, 85, 138, 144, 172, 185, 192, 200, 214, 231, 253, 315, 338, 372-374,

380, 383
'Umar ibn al-Khaṭṭāb, 20, 37-39, 53, 54, 68, 82, 105, 116, 119, 123, 137, 142, 145, 150, 156, 158, 167, 174-176, 178, 185, 191, 194, 195, 198, 205, 214, 229, 230, 238, 241, 242, 261, 280, 295, 304, 325, 332, 338, 339, 342, 344, 359, 361, 365, 368, 372, 375, 408
Umm Ayman, 151
Umm Kulthūm, 157
Umm Salamah, 127
'Uqbah ibn 'Āmir, 136
'Urwah ibn al-Ward, 360
'Urwah ibn Muḥammad, 194
Usāmah, 103
'Utbah al-Ghulām, 119
'Uthmān ibn 'Affān, 37, 273, 338
'Uthmān ibn Maẓ'ūn, 58
Uways al-Qaranī, 92, 240, 241

Wahb ibn Munabbih, 54, 186, 199, 232, 330, 382
waḥy, 27. *See also* revelation
al-Walhān, 42
walī, 401
al-Walīd ibn Mughīrah, 364
al-Walīd ibn 'Utbah, 152
waswās, 40
wilāyah, 401

Yaḥyā (prophet), 48, 75, 127, 184, 191, 277
Yaḥyā ibn Mu'ādh, 69, 84, 106, 118, 230, 253, 276
Yarmūk, Battle of, 280
Yasār Ibn 'Umayr, 119
Yazīd al-Ruqāshī, 85
Yazīd ibn Abī Sufyān, 119
Yazīd ibn Maysarah, 204
Yemen, 194, 241
Yūnus ibn 'Ubayd, 233
Yūsuf (prophet), 13, 85, 110, 129, 130, 154, 203, 210, 313
Yūsuf ibn Asbāṭ, 90, 151, 359

zakāh, 108, 126, 268, 272, 273, 283, 285, 289, 291, 294, 295, 327, 413
Zakariyyā (prophet), 48, 208
Zayd ibn Arqam, 221
Zayd ibn Aslam, 151, 385
Ziyād al-Namirī, 360
al-Zubayr ibn al-'Awwām, 144, 270
Zuhayr, 117
Zulaykhah, 85, 129

www.ingramcontent.com/pod-product-compliance
Lightning Source LLC
Chambersburg PA
CBHW021955160426
43197CB00007B/140